SOCIAL CRISIS AND EDUCATIONAL RESEARCH

Social Crisis & Educational Research

**Edited by Len Barton
and Stephen Walker**

CROOM HELM
London & Canberra

© 1984 L. Barton & S. Walker
Croom Helm Ltd, Provident House, Burrell Row,
Beckenham, Kent BR3 1AT
Croom Helm Australia Pty Ltd, 28 Kembla St,
Fyshwick, ACT 2609, Australia

British Library Cataloguing in Publication Data

Social crisis and educational research.
   1. Educational sociology
   I. Barton, Len   II. Walker, Stephen, 1944-
   370.19   LC191
   ISBN 0-7099-3235-9
   ISBN 0-7099-3248-0 (Pbk)

Printed and bound in Great Britain by
Biddles Ltd, Guildford and King's Lynn

CONTENTS

ACKNOWLEDGEMENTS

We are grateful for the assistance given by
Peter Sowden at Croom Helm and by Annette Winteridge
for the typing of the manuscript for publication.

Thanks also to Joan Barton and Sandra Walker for
their continued support.

LIST OF CONTRIBUTORS

Len Barton, Education Department, Westhill College,
      Weoley Park Road, Selly Oak, Birmingham, England.
Carol Buswell, Faculty of Community and Social
      Studies, Newcastle upon Tyne Polytechnic,
      Newcastle upon Tyne, England.
Martin Cole, Education Department, Newman College,
      Bartley Green, Birmingham, England.
Martyn Denscombe, School of Applied Social Sciences
      and Public Administration, Leicester Polytechnic,
      Leicester, England.
Tony Edwards, School of Education, University of
      Newcastle upon Tyne, Newcastle upon Tyne,
      England.
Mary Fulbrook, Faculty of Education, King's College,
      University of London, Strand, London, England.
Henry Giroux, School of Education and Allied
      Professions, Miami University, Oxford, Ohio 45056,
      USA.
Denis Gleeson, Department of Education, University of
      Keele, Keele, England.
Martyn Hammersley, Faculty of Educational Studies,
      Open University, Milton Keynes, England.
Andrew Pollard, Faculty of Educational Studies,
      Oxford Polytechnic, Oxford, England.
Dave Reynolds, Department of Education, University
      College, Cardiff, Wales.
Ray Rist, Institute for Program Evaluation, United
      States General Accounting Office, Washington
      DC 20548, USA.
Barry Troyna, SSRC Research Unit on Ethnic Relations,
      The University of Aston in Birmingham,
      St. Peter's College, Saltley, Birmingham,
      England.
Stephen Walker, Education Department, Newman College,
      Bartley Green, Birmingham, England.

Gordon West, OISE, 252 Bloor Street West, Toronto,
    Ontario M5S IV6, Canada.
Geoff Whitty, Faculty of Education, King's College,
    University of London, Strand, London, England.

SOCIAL CRISIS AND EDUCATIONAL RESEARCH:
AN INTRODUCTION

Len Barton and Stephen Walker

1. WHOSE CRISIS?

The papers which appear in this collection are a
selection of some of the presentations made at the
sixth Westhill Sociology of Education Conference
which took place in Birmingham in 1982. The theme
of this conference was 'Social Crisis, Educational
Research and Social Policy'. In this introduction
we should like to do two things. Firstly, to
identify the issues which influenced our decision to
bring together the three topics research, policy and
crisis as the main focus for debate. Secondly, to
indicate how we see the papers which follow in this
volume as furthering our understanding of these
issues.
     Quite clearly, a key concern in both these
discussions is the inclusion and meaning of the term
'social crisis'. This assumes that it is recognised
that research in the sociology of education is
inevitably related to social policy. Such research
might not produce policy directly or have tangible
policy-related outcomes. However, in the sense that
it is funded (directly or indirectly) by policy-
makers, has a policy saturated domain as its main
field of inquiry and, through its close association
with teacher education programmes, has policy implementors as an important audience, then it seems to
us that this research cannot avoid an involvement
with policy questions. This is not to suggest that
this involvement is a straightforward affair or that
the relevance of research for policy is easily
determined. Indeed, it was a sense of the complex
nature of such involvement which originally persuaded
us to include the notion of 'social crisis' as a
vital consideration for a conference debating educational research and social policy.

Introduction

The decision to incorporate a concern with social crisis, however, did not just spring from a perverse desire to complicate discussion. More particularly, it reflected a view that questions concerning the impact of research on policy or vice versa and of the relationship between researchers and policy-makers and policy implementors are not mere theoretical speculations but have distinctive characteristics and are problematic in quite specific ways according to the particular social settings in which they are posed and to which they refer. Such a recognition, that the uniqueness of particular periods and cultural forms in social history gives a peculiar shape and direction to sociological activity, is hardly original. However, the assertion that current debate on the relationship between educational research and social policy should be situated within a framework which incorporates a view of society in crisis needs further development - in terms of the validity of the social perspective being presented and its relevance to the issues in hand.

One of the difficulties in attempting this kind of development, however, is the imprecise nature of the concept 'social crisis'. Indeed, the fact that at the conference itself the two rather basic questions of 'What crisis?' and 'Whose crisis?' were often voiced, indicates something of the ambiguity involved. This ambiguity has several dimensions. Does the notion 'social crisis' refer to critical aspects of fiscal affairs or cultural struggles or life in cities or the world of production or ideological formations? Is the term being used to capture a sense of certain persistent features of social life, such as the crisis endemic to capitalism, or is it to be confined to certain, specific social eruptions, like urban unrest or industrial conflict? And, what is it about the social world being described that persuades one to define it as being 'in crisis'? This last point is very important. It draws attention to the peculiarly subjective dimension of the concept. The term 'crisis' is suggestive of dilemma, of a dangerous build-up of pressure, of the reaching of some turning-point. To this extent, any use of the concept involves making certain evaluations or judgements about the nature of the world it is being used to describe. Implicitly, certain events are being given the importance of being more serious than others; certain social processes are being identified as changing or finding new direction; certain activities are necessarily being depicted as at the centre of affairs and relationships; and certain occurrences are being portrayed as traumatic or abnormal for the people involved. In other words, the concept has a deeply personal component. It brings together analysis and evaluation. And, for this reason, it seems to us that an adequate development of the idea must include some articulation of the presuppositions on which it is based.

2.   EDUCATION AND THE CRISIS

It was our own experience of the world of education which initially persuaded us that it was acceptable and important to describe it as being 'in crisis'. Working in teacher education has exposed us to a series of what can only be described as critical incidents or points of tension, which have been progressively increasing in both severity and in their cumulative effect.

The most obvious of these is the massive reduction that has been made during the last few years in the number of places available in higher education for initial teacher training and the continuing series of closures of institutions involved in teacher education. For example, since the early 1970s the yearly intake of students for initial teacher training has been reduced by two-thirds and the number of institutions involved in teacher education has fallen from just over two hundred in 1971 to ninety-two (31 university departments, 17 polytechnics and 44 colleges) in 1983. In isolation, these cuts may not be viewed as particularly critical. However, what is significant is the way such reductions have been justified, the overall policy developments of which such cuts are only a part and the wider impact they have had upon those working in the surviving institutions. The reductions have almost always been justified in demographic terms through reference to falling school rolls and predictions of future birth rates. This inevitably resulted in the playing of a kind of numbers game for deciding on reductions and closures which had the practical consequence of creating and sustaining a mood of anxiety amongst many of the people involved in teacher education. Not only did one rarely know what educational criteria were being employed to decide upon particular reductions or removals of places, not only was it difficult to determine how one particular set of cuts related to some supposed long-term strategy, but also, the constant threat that one's own institution might be the next to suffer hung like the sword of Damocles over the world

3

of teacher education.   This atmosphere nurtured a
number of unpleasant and debilitating trends. Certain
institutions and departments came to see themselves
in competition for survival rather than as being
involved in a collective endeavour; energy and
effort which could have been devoted to developing
more appropriate patterns of training or to working
for curriculum and policy innovation was diverted in
the search for crude survival strategies; and, in
the prevailing climate of apprehension, the difference between a hint and a directive from central
policy-making bodies became unclear and rumour often
attained the status of fact.
     The decrease in the number of places available
for teacher education is only part of a wider attempt
to cut and contract this sector of higher education.
Most institutions, whilst living with a threat to
their continued existence, have, at the same time,
been required to respond to demands for more efficient
use of resources and for reductions in overall unit
costs and to react to a number of changes in funding
arrangements.   Not surprisingly, because wage bills
and manpower costs make up the largest part of
institutional spending, the immediate effect of these
demands has been an alarming number of redundancies,
redeployments and early retirements amongst academic
and administrative staff in most teacher education
establishments.   Notwithstanding the personal
anxieties provoked by these extreme measures, it is
the 'knock-on' effect of these staff cuts which also
causes concern.   These include some of the following
trends.   Firstly, the creation of a situation in
which there is near zero mobility in terms of promotion and, thus, the freezing of career prospects
within and between institutions.   Secondly, a
noticeable increase in competition over spending
priorities - such as struggles to develop innovative
programmes like the application of micro-electronics
in education at the possible expense of less glamorous
projects like extending the provision for the study
of the teaching of reading.   Thirdly, a trend has
developed which involves a forced and often unacceptable redefinition of what constitutes essential
administrative and technical support services; this
redefinition, which is related increasingly to finance-
led decisions and to administrative pressures rather
than to well-defined and carefully developed educational goals, threatens the well-being of teacher
education centres because it both polarises effort
and weakens the ability of individual staff to maintain
a range of academic and professional involvements.

And finally, the cuts in expenditure and resources have resulted in a creeping and insidious contraction of the curriculum of many teacher training courses. Loss of staff has usually been accompanied by quite unrealistic restrictions on replacements or reappointments and, consequently, many teacher education programmes have suffered a reduction of the number of subjects they incorporate, an erosion of the range of options on offer and serious distortions of the balance between different course components.

But, if the cuts in places and resources have been difficult to cope with, the sense of vulnerability and of uncertainty they promoted was given particular poignancy by the fact that they represented one aspect of a rapid and increasingly evident growth in central control of teacher education. What we found disturbing about this was not so much the emphasis that heavier central involvement brought in terms of issues like accountability, monitoring and the direction of government policy in teacher training - although many such projects were often imposed rather than evolved. More disconcerting was the steadily widening gap between central planners and local practitioners that accompanied the rise in the level and extent of intervention by government or state agencies. Events like the rise and fall of the Regional Advisory Councils, the introduction of the Assessment of Performance Unit, the proliferation of official documents devoted to the administration, content and direction of teacher training, the challenge to the Schools' Council and, more recently, the establishment of the National Advisory Body for local authority higher education, have all combined to make the power of central bodies more manifest and the impotence and isolation of individuals under their control more evident and more overwhelming.

The tension we have in mind here seems to be an important one. During the period in which the developments we have outlined above were growing in pace and impact, the feeling that a mood of frustration, of isolation and of despondency was enveloping more and more areas of educational life was confirmed through our contacts with students and teachers on courses and in schools. Public expenditure cuts, teacher redundancies and redeployments and teacher unemployment, curriculum contractions and curricular redefinitions, school closures and site amalgamations - all of these being pressures being experienced by teachers at the same time as they were facing demands for extensions of their roles in terms of their moral, pastoral and vocational responsibilities - seemed to produce an atmosphere in which 'inevitability theses' gained plausibility and in which the strong constraints on individuals struggling to shape their own educational destinies was emphasised. Even the reporting of these affairs was pervaded by an air of doom and gloom, to the extent that one hardly dare open the Times Educational Supplement for fear of news of more ominous occurrences.

It is worth stressing that it is the totality of pressures upon people working within education, the whole series of urgent demands and ambiguous challenges, which gives rise to the climate of confusion and anxiety we have been describing. In the case of teachers, for example, we have been reminded fairly frequently that at the same time as they are being required to cope with threats from external forces to their professional status and work roles, a debilitating experience in itself, they are also being forced to make sensitive and sometimes agonising responses to some quite critical changes in their classroom worlds. Teachers have always been required to deal with various forms of pupil disaffection, with problems related to the rate and effectiveness of pupil development and with the control or discipline difficulties which arise from having to deal with large numbers of children with differing needs and interests. However, the challenge arising from the situation in which teachers are being asked to prepare pupils for a society characterised by rapid technological change whilst, at the same time, they are having to come to terms with the realisation that many of these pupils will be unemployed school leavers, has had enormous impact. Not only have existing concerns like curriculum relevance, assessment criteria and educational objectives taken on a new seriousness, but also, the whole network of contradictions in which teachers operate, contradictions related to the difficulties of reconciling the needs of individuals with the interests of society, has been exposed in a most painful manner. Faced with a further period of widespread unemployment amongst school-leavers and the onslaught of a steady development in young people's willingness and ability to question what schools have to offer them, we wonder how teachers can be expected to cope with the challenge to the legitimacy of schooling which seems to be an inevitable consequence of such a situation.

Now, it might be argued that the circumstances and experiences we have been describing are personal problems - worthy of sympathy, maybe, but hardly

meriting the use of the term 'social crisis' for
their description.   Indeed, perhaps it is only when
one attempts to understand the conditions which
generated these personal concerns that such a description becomes appropriate.   Whilst the kinds of
critical incidents we have listed in the above account
might display certain local or idiosyncratic elements,
they also evidence a common characteristic, a shared
symptomatic, which is related to their point of
origin.   Whether or not one is considering the
effects of cuts in education, the consequences of
increased central control or the challenge of coping
with contradictions in classrooms, it is hard to
avoid coming to the conclusion that all these incidents - every one of which involves individuals in
contest with power groups or in encounter with
pressures operating from outside and above their
immediate social environment - are part of a wider
struggle, a much larger social confrontation.
Specific measures like the closure of a school, the
loss of a research grant or the redeployment of a
member of staff, undeniably cause anguish in themselves.   However, it is only when one begins to
unravel the whole chain of justifications for these
developments, the whole pattern of events and
decisions which have occasioned a particular incident,
and when one attempts to locate the basic source of
such affairs, that their more general seriousness is
revealed and their significance made particularly
acute.

3.   ANATOMY OF THE CRISIS

So, how can the cuts, contractions and changes in
the education system be explained or justified?   Of
course, we recognise that any answer to such a
question will be greatly influenced by the political
perspective of the respondent.   Putting it rather
crudely, analysis could be based either on the view
that such measures are part of a programme aimed at
social renewal, at the establishment of an efficient,
effective and economically stable society or on the
belief that such actions form part of a project
concerned with protecting privileged interests, with
preserving social differentiation.   However, notwithstanding the political stance adopted towards
the movement which gives rise to the particular events
we have previously outlined, supporters of either
school of thought would have to agree that one of
the most crucial features of this social policy is
an attempt to redefine the relationship between the

7

<u>individual and the social formation</u> - an attempt
which we believe underlies the particular tensions
and anxieties we have introduced and which justifies
the use of the term 'social crisis'.
  This claim, that both personal and public
affairs are being strongly influenced by a gradual,
yet relentless, process which involves a reconstruction of the relationship between individuals, institutions and the State, is based on an interpretation
of the fairly commonplace analysis of the movement
behind this process - modern Conservatism or, more
precisely, Thatcherism.   It has been frequently
noted that the essential vision of Thatcherism is
the priority given to the goal of creating a social
order in which market forces are allowed free play
and in which social stability is established through
the removal of barriers to the 'natural' operation
of these forces.   As Alan Walker et al (1983) have
succinctly summarised,

> This strategy is based upon 'monetarist'
> doctrines and, in particular, the
> proposition that a market economy is
> self-stabilising and that as long as the
> money supply is controlled it will tend
> to generate full employment and non-
> inflationary growth.

  Although some of the implications of the
policies based on this perspective - like the
transfer of responsibility for poverty and inequality
from societal failure to individual culpability, like
the encouragement of economic competition despite
the inevitably divisive outcomes of such encounters,
and like the reformation of those moral and familial
traditions which are seen as frustrating the larger
economic policy - although these are both horrifying
and far-reaching, they are not our main concern.
What gives Thatcherism its particularly distinctive
and radical character is neither the commitment to
a market economy nor the specific policy it constructs to establish this formation, rather, it is
the dogmatism and inflexibility with which such
endeavours are justified and pursued and the narrow-
minded centrality which is accorded to the economic
plan.   It is this basic ideology, we would argue,
that is transforming relations between individuals
and society and which is bringing the social order
into crisis.
  The transformation has many features, ranging
across redefinitions of people's educational and

welfare needs, of family and personal responsibilities and obligations, of the function of Trade Union groups, of the role of the State in the management of institutional and economic life - yet these all share the fundamental characteristic that policy in any of these areas is based upon a rationale in which the economic concern ultimately subsumes any other. Similarly, the crisis which is both precipitated and progressively deepened by this fundamental assault is complex and multi-faceted but, at the very least, has the following identifiable elements.

Firstly, the speed at which changes are being effected and the extent to which transformation permeates the whole fabric of the social network are both crucial. The almost indecent haste with which industrial, fiscal, welfare and educational policy has been radically re-shaped and re-directed means that individuals are being confronted with an extensive and bewildering array of 'reforms', with little time to ponder on their implications, their interconnections or their deeper personal significances. Even more daunting, perhaps, is the fact that the extensiveness of such reforms produces for many people the understandable impression that they are struggling to accommodate changes which are not mere local disturbances but are part of a more fundamental reorientation of the whole social system - effective reaction and resistance, therefore, becoming ever more difficult to mount.

Secondly, the policies are critical in the sense that they are essentially divisive. The brand of monetarism on which they are based, whatever is asserted in the reformist rhetoric used to defend them, is basically reactionary. This is because the eradication of inequalities between social groups cannot be achieved within this framework. The extreme functionalism of monetarism means that individuals relegated to positions at the lower end of the social hierarchy will not only have their economic and political positions steadily eroded through the operation of market forces, through the impact of public spending cuts or through the shift to privatisation but will also be required to face the ignominy of having the cause of their misfortune defined as personal, natural or inevitable.

Finally, one of the most profound consequences of the development of a political programme which is based on an ideology to which 'there is no alternative' is the effect this has on how social control is managed. What we have in mind here goes beyond issues related to changes in the amount and type of

social policing or the new moral tone and interest
which has been injected into policy debates or the
clear trend in current Conservative policy to define
and to respond to occasions of public opposition as
local problems or temporary aberrations.   We are
more concerned with the impact the ideology has on
the principles through which social control is
legitimated.   The basic insistence that there is no
alternative to the main objective of the economic
policy or to making this goal the main priority in
the policy-making process has three important influences on these legitimation principles.   Firstly,
the range of social issues in which it is acceptable
to attempt criticism or challenge is significantly
reduced.   Secondly, policy objectives or social
goals which draw on visions other than the monetarist
dream become branded as either trivial or extremist.
And thirdly, the democratic ideal by which the
control of oppositional movements and the management
of dissension is achieved through appeal to a
collectively developed rationality which is recognised as both fallible and changeable is rapidly
replaced by one which relies on recourse to a moral
evaluation which is accepted as an unshakable and
self-evident truth.
     The events we have described and the analysis
we have provided indicate that the changes in social
organisation we are calling 'crisis' are influential
at the levels of both social system and social action
and are mediated through transformation in the form,
function and operational principles of key social
institutions.   To this extent, the crisis cuts
across both private and public concerns. Of course,
analysis of the crisis requires much more extensive
and detailed development, particularly with respect
to the impact it is having on educational research
and policy.   Also, we are aware that we have
restricted our commentary to a consideration of events
which have taken place in Britain - although the
description made by participants from other countries
at the Westhill Conference, of their own experiences,
together with what is revealed in the literature
dealing with crisis in other societies, would support
the conclusion that the basic character of the crisis
is not something confined to one country.

4.   SOCIAL CRISIS AND EDUCATIONAL RESEARCH

Having revealed the presuppositions on which our
selection of the conference theme was based, it is
also necessary to make some brief indication of how

we see the papers in this collection as contributing
to the kind of development in analysis for which we
have called. Each paper has its own particular
focal concern and it would be extremely presumptuous
to attempt to summarise the specific motivations or
even the key ideas of the individual writers. In
the following notes, therefore, which are necessarily
selective, our concern is limited to charting some
of the broader themes developed and to how we see
these as relating to some of the issues raised in
the first part of this introduction.

If discussion about the relationship between
educational research and social policy is to be
developed in a framework in which the existence and
influence of the social crisis we have described is
adequately recognised, and it seems unlikely that
complete analysis could be made if such a recognition
is avoided, then two particular questions about this
relationship assume a new priority, a particular
significance. The first of these is the question of
exactly how educational establishments mediate the
wider social transformations which are evolving, in
terms of how individuals and groups experience and
respond to these changes. An examination of the
impact of social change upon educational practice
has always had a place on the agenda for sociology
of education but this becomes more pressing because
of the range, rapidity and radicalism of current
changes in policy and ideology. The second question
is to do with the basis of the privilege being claimed
for the status of sociological explanation. Again,
this is not a new concern, but the social crisis
gives urgency to the need for further reconsideration
of the adequacy of theory used in educational research
and the credibility of the methods and interpretations
employed, if only because educational research inevitably becomes a more overt political act in this
particular climate. We have used these two general
questions, therefore, as a basis for organising the
papers in this collection, although, of course, an
emphasis on one of these concerns does not exclude
an interest in the other. The book is divided into
two sections. The first of these contains papers
which discuss how particular aspects of the social
crisis are being experienced and dealt with in
specific educational contexts. The second section
brings together papers in which a major concern is
the re-examination of the theoretical and methodological foundations of educational research in a
time of crisis.

Introduction

The very range of the substantive issues to
do with the impact of the social crisis upon educational practice and policy which are discussed by
the writers of the five papers included in Part One
of this book, gives some indication of the extent
and complexity of the influence and pressures the
crisis promotes. These discussions cover such
considerations as the effect of social and economic
changes upon how teachers and pupils see school work
(Buswell), the impact of changing social conditions
on how teachers interpret and analyse their professional roles (Cole), the urgency social crisis gives
to the development and implementation of an educational policy which makes adequate recognition of
the needs and interests of racial minorities and of
how other people treat these groups (Troyna), the
redefinition of the vocational function of schooling
and the relationship between school and work which
is being forced through the results of political
change (Gleeson), and the deep ideological transformations which are exposed in an investigation of the
origins and impact of the Assisted Places Scheme
(Edwards et al). However, although there is a
diversity of interest here, there are also some
unifying themes.

An important one of these themes is the analysis
of the educational effects of a single manifestation
of the crisis, persistent and large-scale unemployment, particularly amongst school-leavers. The
enormity of this effect is well evidenced in this
analysis. We are confronted in these papers with
some stark and discomforting reminders that widespread unemployment creates a whole network of
consequences which is likely to increase personal
stress in the community, even amongst those individuals seemingly distanced from such trends. It is
not just that unemployment forces painful reappraisals
of identity and destiny for those experiencing such
a fate, but, as Buswell documents, the 'qualification
inflation' it produces and the manner in which pupils
in school respond to the possibility of unemployment
is forcing a redefinition of work and social relationships for everyone involved in schooling, and, as
Cole argues, it undermines one of the main supports
to teachers' legitimacy and authority claims. It
is not just that high unemployment throws existing
social inequalities into sharper focus, but, as
Troyna contends, it increases the real disaffection
of groups like racial minorities who suffer inequality
thereby provoking, in the search for a response to
this situation, the need for urgent reconsideration

of how our <u>overall</u> educational policies operate to
create these inequalities, to contain these inequalities or to help us combat them.   And it is not just
that unemployment is having an influence on particular
schools or on particular programmes but, as Gleeson
shows, it is that aspects of the response to the
problem - like the introduction of the Youth Training
Scheme and related emergency vocational projects -
necessarily involve a redefinition of the overall
objectives of schools and a reorganisation of the
education system.
     A second theme explored in section one is a
consideration of how the <u>legitimation crisis</u>, which
we have already suggested is a most significant
element of the more general social upheaval, is made
manifest and given a particular form through educational processes.   Both the nature of legitimation
crisis in education and how it is being confronted
is examined by Buswell, by Cole and by Troyna but
what is particularly important about each of these
contributions is the way in which the examination is
used to indicate new and serious policy questions
which arise from an appreciation of the nature of
the challenges involved.   The discussion of these
implications, which touches upon policy issues concerning control in schools, teacher training and
curriculum development, relates very closely to what
we see as the third theme explored in section one -
the question of how the crisis is provoking a fundamental reappraisal (and an actual re-structuring) of
the nature of schooling.   One of the deeper influences of current political changes is the way in
which the <u>principles</u> upon which educational provision
is related to community needs and interests are being
progressively re-defined.   The examination of the
origins and consequences of the Assisted Places
Scheme presented by Edwards et al is extremely
pertinent here because not only do they provide a
detailed documentation and analysis of the basis and
outcomes of the specific policy programme under
review, they also indicate how a consideration of
this particular project throws light upon more
general ideological shifts which strike at the very
heart of social and educational organisation.

     We have called the second part of this book
'Crisis in Research' and although this sub-title
might seem over-dramatic it catches, nevertheless,
something of the seriousness the current social crisis
gives to certain questions about how sociologists
confront and are confronted by this crisis in their

educational research and in their discussions of
educational policy.

It is not possible to attempt an exhaustive or
detailed discussion of all the various questions to
do with research and policy which are given a new
urgency and a distinctive relevance by recent critical
incidents and current social trends.   Nevertheless,
it is important to stress that the crisis can be seen
as having a profound effect at each and every point
of the sociological research process -- and especially
on considerations of three specific features of this
process, the relationship between those within and
those outside the research community, the methods
used for conducting research and the theoretical
assumptions on which investigations and interpretations of the empirical world are based.

In times of extensive social change, the relationship between researchers and their subjects and
audiences becomes critical in several ways.   However,
in the present crisis some specific issues to do with
this research relationship assume a particular and
pressing relevance.   Perhaps the most obvious of
these is the growing attack being mounted by conservative ideologues upon social science itself.   Whilst
one might anticipate that a movement which routinely
evaluates critical investigation or the challenge of
alternative visions as eccentric or dangerous will
be more than likely to regard social scientists with
a certain amount of suspicion, the growing tendency
for sociological research of education to be assessed
by key government officials as, at best, irrelevant,
and, at worst, as malicious, is alarming.   This is
not to imply that social scientists can ever take
their credibility for granted;   however, they can
expect that assessment of this credibility is conducted inside a framework in which their motives and
abilities have been judged in advance and in which
the 'proper' agenda for research and inquiry has
been pre-decided.   The dogmatism facing researchers
in this challenge, then, gives a new twist to key
ethical considerations of the basis on which researchers collaborate with policy-makers.   Not only do
issues like the possibility of research findings
being used for purposes which violate the interests
of the researcher and the researched take on a new
sensitivity but also, in deciding on the question of
the extent to which he or she will be prepared to
accept the definitions, the interpretations and the
research priorities of sponsors and controlling
bodies, the options available to researchers are
reduced.   The tension created by these dilemmas,

which are essentially to do with managing a concern
with the production of what Gray et al (1983) have
called 'good accounts' of educational processes
whilst preserving a base upon which one can both
address and influence policy-makers, is one of the
problems explored by Rist in the first paper in
Part Two of this volume.

However, the crisis does not only intensify the
pressure on sociologists to review their relations
with policy-makers. The changes which are taking
place in schools and classrooms have consequences
for relations between researcher and researched. We
have already suggested that one impact of the crisis
on education is an increase in the degree to which
individuals in schools feel isolated or oppressed
and a fragmentation of collective identification.
In such a climate, the extent to which teachers and
students will be prepared to welcome the attention
of sociologists and co-operate in the production of
'good accounts' or the degree to which they will
perceive analysis as useful and will be prepared to
act upon sociological interpretations, would both
seem dependent on how successful sociologists are in
convincing such people that researchers and researched
have a shared interest, a common, basic concern. This
is not simply a matter of ensuring that groups being
researched are not used for dubious 'academic' purposes; neither is it a question of one community
'taking' without equivocation the other's problems
as a basis for research. Rather, we would argue
that what is at stake is more fundamental. Given
the extensive and complex nature of the impact of
the crisis on education, we believe that an adequate
understanding of its dynamic and an effective challenge to those of its personal and public consequences which are deemed intolerable can only be achieved
from within a movement which refuses to accept the
essential divisiveness of the underlying ideology
which is provoking the crisis and which makes collective co-operation a priority. In such an endeavour
dialogue between different parties becomes essential.
We do not imagine that this will be easy - the communication of assumptions, deep theories and well-
established traditions of thought is difficult at
the best of times, and more so if both the academic
and the practical relevances of all concerned are to
be respected. The status, form and function of
ethnographic research in education is particularly
relevant here - if only as a medium through which
more fruitful communication and collaboration is to
be attempted - and both Pollard and Denscombe make a

consideration of these aspects of this method of
research a key concern of their papers as well as
exploring ways in which the results of such investigations can be used in teacher education.

It seems no exaggeration to claim that one of
the features of research in the sociology of education
which has made the development of the kind of collective effort envisaged above more difficult has been
the long-standing disagreements about what constitutes
an appropriate basis for sociological analysis - the
operational perspective crisis or the macro-micro
debate.   In their papers, both Hammersley and West
explore ways of confronting this crisis in the
discipline and, although they offer very different
interpretations, (and, by so doing, remind us that
it is a re-assessment of the fundamental assumptions
sociologists use to build their descriptions of the
world that is required and not a superficial synthesis
of ways of approaching research), they share an
interest in developing in the sociology of education
a coherent and internally consistent theoretical and
methodological structure which is powerful enough to
act as a basis for effective confrontation of those
educational and social problems and policies which
cause us concern.

The various crises we have tried to identify in
this introduction make it more vital that a particularly contentious theoretical issue in the sociology
of education is quickly clarified - this is the
adequacy of the descriptions and assumptions employed
to depict the basic relationship between the education
system and the social structure, especially the
economy.   A prerequisite in the development of a
structure which allows sociologists to make a convincing and influential contribution to policy debate in
a time of crisis is a reliable and empirically valid
portrayal of this relationship.   Indeed, without
such a rudimentary theoretical tool, it is difficult
to see how we can adequately appreciate or respond to
the impact on education of a crisis provoked by
specifically economic policies and ideologies.   It is
for these reasons that we consider it appropriate to
place the papers by Reynolds and by Giroux at the end
of Part Two of this collection of papers.   Both these
writers explore different aspects of this relationship,
Reynolds dealing with the question of the amount of
freedom from external forces which exists within the
education system and Giroux presenting further consideration of the ideological connections between
educational and societal processes.   However, it is
also appropriate that these two papers should appear

Introduction

in the concluding section of the book because both
contribute to a discussion of what we see as one of
the most complex and least visible aspects of the
impact of the crisis on educational affairs -- the
paradoxical manner in which certain contradictions
embedded within educational processes are exposed
by the social changes whilst others become more
obscure. The crisis has certainly given a kind of
prominence to contradictions in education between
the interests of the system's managers and the interests of the system's users, between schools' selection functions and pedagogical roles and between
policy intention and practical outcomes. But it has
also involved attempts, some of them deliberate, to
mystify the political nature of schooling, to mask
the divisiveness of certain educational practices
and to confuse the emancipatory and the restrictive
possibilities of the education system. We hope
that this book can contribute to extending debate
on this particular aspect of the crisis as well as
to discussion of those other outcomes, perhaps more
tangible but no less invidious, which are considered
in this collection.

REFERENCES

Gray, J. et al (1983) Reconstructions of Secondary
      Education, Routledge and Kegan Paul, London
Walker, A. et al 'Conservative Economic Policy: The
      Social Consequences' in D. Bull and P. Wilding
      (Eds.) (1983) Thatcherism and the Poor, Child
      Poverty Action Group, London

ACKNOWLEDGEMENT

We are grateful to several of our colleagues who
have discussed with us a number of issues raised in
this paper and particularly Martin Lawn.

PART ONE

RESEARCH IN CRISIS

QUALIFICATION INFLATION, PUPIL INVESTMENT AND A CHANGING SIXTH FORM

Carol Buswell

INTRODUCTION

A Weberian approach to education would consider
control by local authorities over school management,
school management over teachers and teachers over
pupils as increasingly characterised by the formal
application of rules of a rational nature, buttressed
by the force of legal authority, carried out in a
bureaucratic context which, in an ideal-type sense,
would lead to predictable behaviour which enables
goals to be attained.   At the same time, credentialism
has led to a concern about lack of pupil motivation
and 'instrumentalism' which has been described as
alienation in the Marxian sense.   A combination of
Weber's concept of 'rationality' and Marx's notion
of 'alienation' as they apply to schools is useful
for two reasons.   Firstly, there are common themes
and concerns within the writings of both Marx and
Weber themselves on which to build and secondly, the
'meaning' of work is related to its organisational
context which is itself part of the structural
setting and the impact of social changes on individual
and group consciousness and culture may thus be
explored.
    According to Weber (1978) rationally regulated
association within a structure of administration
finds its typical expression in bureaucracy.

> Bureaucracy is the means of transforming
> social action into rationally organised
> action.   Therefore, as an instrument of
> rationally organising authority relations,
> bureaucracy was and is a power instrument
> of the first order for one who controls
> the bureaucratic apparatus .... Increasingly,

> all order in public and private
> organisations is dependent on the system
> of files and the discipline of officialdom.

Weber considered that the progression of bureaucracy,
however, revealed a tension between technical efficiency and the human values of spontaneity and
autonomy.

> What can we set against this mechanisation
> to preserve a certain section of humanity
> from this fragmentation of the soul, this
> complete ascendancy of the bureaucratic
> ideal of life?   (Giddens 1971)

As Giddens comments, the pervasive rationalisation
which characterises modern society extends the process
of the 'expropriation of the worker from his means
of production' into most institutions in contemporary
society.
     For Marx 'alienation' consists in the fact that
something which was originally intended for use is
not produced as a useful thing to satisfy one's own
need but enters the modern market as an independent
commodity value.   Löwith (1982) points out that
Marx traced the fundamental and universal self
alienation to modern political, social and economic
structures - that is, the same rational 'orders'
that were Weber's concern.   Weber, of course, considered that capitalism had only become the most
important power in human life because it had itself
already developed within the framework of a 'rational
way of life'.   Although Marx and Weber have differing
interpretations of capitalism, Weber's 'rationalisation' and Marx's 'self alienation' both find expression
in the modern bureaucracies that pervade organised
action even outside the strictly economic sphere.
     In this study, increasing rationalisation is
expressed primarily through the systematic application
of rules - to all pupils - that had hitherto been used
occasionally.   At the same time there were increasing
demands from the local authority and school management
for teachers to 'justify' their decisions - for
example, with regard to examination entries - on
rational/technical grounds and the definition of
teachers' 'professionalism' was couched more in terms
of their obedience to the rules than in terms of their
autonomy.
     Both Marx and Weber saw the irrationality of
extended rationalisation - an inversion of means and
ends.   Weber described the multiple dependencies of

rationalism as the 'iron cage' of subordination which
subjects people to the 'apparatus'. Whilst, for
Marx, the reversal was described in terms of the
domination of things over people and the product over
the producer. Applied to education, Hextall and
Sarup (1977) describe this process by saying:

> What is being evaluated is the pupil's
> labour potential, his exchange value.
> The pupil exchanges his labour for objects -
> house points, grades, examination certifi-
> cates .... By submitting the product of his
> labour to an evaluation which deals with it
> by treating it as a unit of production to
> be ranged alongside and compared with the
> work of others, the pupil learns to see his
> work in terms of exchange value. His work
> thereby loses its individual purposiveness.
> Alienation resides in the pupil beginning
> to work with the notion of evaluation
> (exchange value) in mind.

The problem with assertions such as this is that,
without empirical evidence, they assume a universal
reaction to particular social relations whereas, in
fact, there are a variety of responses that owe
something to the fact that pupils bring their own
biographies to bear on these relations. In other
words, as well as schools 'defining pupils' - pupils
are also 'defining schools'. (King 1973.)
    Current social, economic and educational
difficulties might lead some sociologists to argue
that researchers should take the 'teachers' problems'
seriously and investigate those. In terms of
examination success this school had been increasingly
effective, in its own terms, by raising the number
and percentage of examination passes to a level
equivalent to that of local schools with more middle-
class intakes and which operated stricter streaming
policies. This school tried to balance the needs
of examination candidates against those of the
majority of pupils and had attempted not to disadvantage either group. In choosing, therefore, to
focus on A level pupils' relationship to school work
we have chosen a sociological, rather than a school,
problem. This is justified not only on academic
grounds but also because, in this way, it may be
possible to locate emerging problems and explain the
inversion of means and ends that, presumably, participants would not necessarily consciously wish to do.

THE RESEARCH

The school was a large inner-city comprehensive in
the North of England (1500 pupils and 100 teachers)
with a predominantly working-class intake.   Full-
time research had taken place in the school, on
another project, for a term in 1979.   From March
1980 to July 1982 the present research was conducted
on a one-day-a-week basis.
     In March 1980 a representative sample of pupils
who were likely to 'qualify' to stay on was picked
from the fourth, fifth and lower sixth years and the
upper sixth at that time acted as a pilot group.
When pupils left, new individuals were added to the
sample.   Fifty-seven pupils were included altogether
- fourteen were in the sample for two and a half
years (6 girls and 8 boys), twenty-six for at least
one year (16 girls and 10 boys) and seventeen for
less than a year (10 girls and 7 boys).
     Pupils were interviewed individually and
observed in at least one lesson every term, teachers
and form tutors were interviewed once or twice a
year, internal and external school reports were
collected, some pupils kept diaries and informal
participation in the sixth form common room and staff
room took place.   In this paper twenty A level
pupils are discussed:-

Lower Sixth 1979/80:   U6 in 1981/82 - 2 boys and
                                        2 girls

Fifth in 1979/80: L6 in 1980/81: U6 in 1981/82 -
                                        7 boys and
                                        3 girls

Fourth in 1979/80: 5th in 1980/81: L6 in 1981/82 -
                                        5 girls and
                                        1 boy

THE LOCAL CONTEXT

In August 1980 there were almost two and a half
thousand school leavers in the city registered as
unemployed and approximately the same number were
on government schemes.   The general unemployment
rate for the city as a whole was 11.8%, compared
with 8.1% nationally, but in parts of the catchment
area of this school the rate was 30% and above.
A careers officer said, at this time, "A colleague
went to Guildford last week and they were worried
because they had a hundred unemployed school leavers

on the books - it's a different world.   I spend
three days a week in schools trying to find out
what the kids want to do and what they're suitable
for - and then two days in the office telling them
there are no jobs at all."   Of the three hundred
and thirty 5th formers, in the summer 1980, roughly
a third obtained jobs and nearly one fifth stayed in
education.   The lack of local employment opportunities affected many pupils' decisions to stay on at
school, usually with parental encouragement.

Geoff - "I came back cos the job situation's so
          bad. Me mam said she couldn't see any
          prospects for us."

Mary - "In the fourth year me dad said I
          wasn't to stay on.   But since the job
          situation's got worse he said I'd
          better."

Karen - "My parents wanted me to come back -
          they thought I'd have a better chance
          of a job with A levels.   I knew it
          would be difficult to get a job but
          I didn't think it would be that hard -
          I didn't even get one interview."

     Some pupils who had lower grade CSEs came back
to school to 'convert' them to O levels whilst the
pupils with O levels came back to convert them to
A levels in order to attempt to enter the job market
at eighteen.   Others returned to school to pursue
non A level courses such as typing and, of course,
there were pupils who had always intended to stay on
at school to qualify for further and higher education.
Dore (1976), in discussing the appeal of education
for people in Third World countries, points out that
even modest levels of employment in the modern sector
are preferable to any level in the traditional sector
and the worse the educated unemployment rate becomes
the greater grows the desire for more and more education - "if one qualification does not get you a
job, you press on and on."   For people in areas of
high unemployment in Britain the choice is equally
stark.
     Sixteen year old school-leavers can crudely be
distinguished, by employers, in terms of O levels
and CSEs.   Staying on into the sixth form, however,
means that many pupils obtain complex combinations
of qualifications - O level, RSA, CEE, CSE, A level -
which gives them slightly different profiles in an

educational setting but which are not matched by
equally fine distinctions in the labour market.   A
Careers Officer estimated that there was only one
job 'on the books' at any one time for an A level
leaver.   Boudon (1977) maintains that the educational
and occupational systems are governed by two different
dynamics and that credential inflation is a 'perverse
effect'of individuals' investment in education which
has unintended consequences at the aggregate level -
a process that has also been described as 'credential
capitalism' (Collins 1979).   Boudon's analysis,
however, rests only on consumer action and does not
explore the role of institutions and public policy in
meeting, denying or exacerbating these demands
(Swartz 1981).   It has also been suggested (King
1982) that schools, by adhering to the ideology of
educational meritocracy, have determined and fed
credentialism.   But it is clear that local employment
opportunities and qualification inflation contribute
in no small measure to teachers' responses in encouraging pupils to gain more qualifications and to break
the pattern of early leaving called, by these teachers,
the 'North East blight'.

The fact that extra schooling and qualifications
do not necessarily relate to job success is obscured
because of the complexity of a large sixth form, the
combinations of qualifications on offer and the fact
that most pupils taking A levels decided - in the
end - to apply for higher education with the realisation that there were no more jobs two years later
than there had been previously.   Several sixth
formers who gained, from a CSE base, some O levels
went on to courses in further education that they
could have entered at sixteen - a second-chance route.
Overall, though, it seemed to be the case that the
qualifications obtained in the sixth form were more
likely to qualify pupils for more education rather
than for jobs.   A Careers Officer said that, in any
case, employers preferred people who had been on
YOPs courses rather than from school because they
thought the youngsters had 'matured' and knew 'how to
work'.

With his concept of 'habitas' Bourdieu (Swartz
1981) maintains not only that there is an unconscious
calculation of chances for success or failure in
situations of conflict but that there is a structural
lag between changing opportunities and aspirations.
He was writing in the context of increased opportunities and the more slowly increasing aspirations of
the working-class.   At present the structural lag
seems to be between declining opportunities and

aspirations that are still increasing. None of the
pupils in the sample had a parent or sibling who had
gone to University and it seemed that many parents
regarded A level and sixth form study as holding the
same 'worth' that it did when they were young. One
girl, for example, who had left school to work in a
shop and subsequently returned to the sixth form to
take some O levels said "When I was in the shop me
mam didn't like people asking her what I was doing -
cos she's a bit of a snob. Now she boasts to everyone that I'm a sixth former." One of the House
tutors also remarked "We've found most parents are
keen to support their children. I think a lot of
parents feel - it still being very much a working-
class area, I hate to use that term but you know
what I mean - some parents still have that feeling
of 'pride' that their child is in the sixth form.
I find that rather endearing."

THE SCHOOL CONTEXT

Whilst pupils' individual futures might have been the
main day-to-day concern of the teachers, there were
additional pressures with which to contend. There
was some concern in the summer of 1980 that 'cuts'
might fall more harshly on schools without large
sixth forms and in December 1980 the LEA decided that
the school would merge with a neighbouring one, as
part of the 'falling rolls' exercise. The school
and parents decided to fight the decision by lodging
an appeal with the DES and, obviously, a growing and
viable sixth form was one of the planks of their case.
The DES did not finally decide to reject the appeal
until February 1982 so this issue was part of the
background throughout the study. Also, in the
middle of the research period three teachers were
compulsorily redeployed which added to concern,
although the LEA had a 'no-redundancy' policy for
teachers.
     The school, like many others, had Academic,
Pastoral, Management and Heads of Departments
committees which discussed policy and passed it down
the line. Increasing amounts of data were demanded
by the LEA including information on decisions regarding examination entries with justifications for
double-entries which, in the context of cuts, was
meant to enable the authority to monitor and plan.
'Accountability' was the catchword.
     Some of the control mechanisms that teachers
applied to pupils also applied to themselves. The
weekly news-sheet issued to all staff contained

information about school events, meetings and deadline
dates for the completion of various forms and reports.
In addition, it nearly always contained instructions
to teachers regarding rules that pupils were infring-
ing that teachers should be enforcing, e.g.:

> "Will tutors remind their groups not to sit
> on the wall at the front of the school, not
> to go through the staff car park and not to
> cross over the grass in front of the school."

The news-sheet also gave teachers instructions about
their own behaviour, e.g.:

> "Please note that the school clock does not
> have the same accuracy as some of your
> time pieces.   Nevertheless this is the
> time by which we operate.   Your co-operation
> in registering on time is appreciated, as
> would be your retention of classes until
> the bleeps have sounded."

A notice on the staff board headed 'Professionalism'
gives an indication of the way the term was defined
by senior staff:-

> "It is not good enough for one to have to
> remind staff two or three times about
> requests for information or the completion
> of pupil profiles."

Teachers' time was circumscribed in ways similar to
that of pupils.   Senior staff usually appeared in
the staff room at the end of breaks to inform people
that they should be going to their lessons and tannoy
announcements during the lunch-hour calling people to
meetings, at which they were expected to be present,
were common.   Another notice that appeared on the
staff board stated "Non contact periods are intended
for marking and preparation and not for reading news-
papers in the staff room."   Collins (1975) would no
doubt describe the school as a 'double control
hierarchy'.

THE SIXTH FORM

Between 1979 and 1982 the sixth form almost doubled
in size from fifty-eight to one hundred and seven
pupils, although the balance between pupils doing
two or more A levels and those doing one or no A
levels remained roughly the same.   In 1981, for

example, fifty-nine pupils were doing two or more
A levels compared with thirty-eight who were doing
one or none.   So pupils were being encouraged, or
deciding themselves, to do A levels to the same
degree that pupils were opting for non A level courses.
Of the twenty A level pupils discussed in this paper
six would probably have left at the end of the fifth
year had they been able to find a job.   The twenty
are drawn from three different year cohorts, they
represent the range of subjects offered and comprise
ten girls and ten boys.
    Once the pupils had entered the sixth form the
ostensible reasons for staying on seemed to be of
little consequence in determining the relationships
to school work that developed, nor did particular
subjects or teachers relate more to one response than
another.   An analysis of internal and external
reports, pupil interviews, pupil diaries, teacher
interviews and observations revealed patterns of
orientation to school work that appeared early in the
lower sixth year and, apart from odd occasions, changed
little over the two year period.
    When in the fourth and fifth years, in early 1980,
the pupils had ideas about what the sixth form would
be like - mainly couched in terms of increased status
and time.

Peter   -   "The teachers will be different because
              we'll be the top ones in the school
              and expected to set an example."

Alex   -   "It'll be different cos you won't have
              all the boring lessons that you don't
              really like and you'll have quite a
              bit of free time.   The teachers will
              be different cos the disruptive ones
              will have left."

Lorna   -   "I think the teachers will treat you
              more equal cos you've supposed to be
              grown up and have more sense."

Harriet   -   "I think you'll have to try and work
              harder yourself instead of being pushed
              by teachers."

Apart from one of the pupils, who had a sister in the
sixth form, the rest did not really have much idea
of what went on and their views were based on what
appeared to be the case.   At this time there were
some very visible and noisy non A level sixth formers

who were to be heard and seen at most times of the day - and their relationship with some teachers was jokey, personal and often verging on the cheeky. Some of the A level pupils at this time, including the girl defined as the 'cleverest' in the sixth, were friendly with the visible group both inside and outside the school. There was an impression of a cohesive, friendly and noisy collectivity. The fifth formers were allowed into the common room in the summer term and the more extrovert ones settled into this group immediately.

RULE ENFORCEMENT

Excerpt from field notes September 1980:-

> 11.30 a.m. - quite a noise issuing from the common room as I go in. Judy, Kim, Trudy and Dorothy (non A levellers) are there, Richard (A leveller) is playing his guitar quietly and another A level boy is sitting in the corner reading. I comment on the increased number of plants on the window-sill and Kim says that she's brought some of them from home and Judy has obtained cuttings from the Biology lab. They offer me coffee and Kim says that reminds her that she must 'get on to the others' as she's been the only one taking home the tea-towels to wash. Trudy takes Richard's guitar and demonstrates a simple tune that he's taught her to play. Marianne (A leveller) comes in and there's some debate about who is going to the corner shop to purchase items for lunch. I ask them if they're allowed to go to the shop before lunch-time - they laugh and say they're not supposed to, but they always do and no-one 'bothers'. As I go out I read some witty notices they've put on the board asking for volunteers for the play and items for props. I go down to the work-room - a bit of shuffling as I open the door, then a sigh of relief as upside-down books are once again abandoned and the cards and darts re-appear. At lunch-time I can't get a seat in either room - the darts players have taken over the work-room and in the common room it is a crush and a radio plays beneath the incredible noise.

As can be inferred from these notes, there was
a rule about not leaving the premises - which was
ignored - and a rule about working in the work-room,
which was clearly enforced from time to time depending upon the amount of noise and the particular
teachers that might happen to pass.   It is a parallel
of the 'leniency pattern' of bureaucracy described by
Gouldner (1954).   Soon after those notes were written
the dormant rules became enforced and new rules were
added.   The pupils were no longer allowed to leave
the premises without permission, the common room was
checked at the beginning of each lesson and pupils
sent to the work-room or library, the coffee was
locked away to be collected at break times, and the
work-room became supervised during lesson time by a
rota of teachers with non-contact periods.   As far
as work was concerned the chasing-up of recalcitrant
homework-doers began in earnest, with parents being
contacted in some cases.   A year later the field
notes read:-

> 11.30 a.m. - no-one in the common room, a
> teacher has just sent two pupils off to the
> library.   The only notices on the board
> are 'official' ones and no plants inhabit
> the window-sill.   Go to the work-room -
> pupils are sitting round tables working and
> a teacher sits at the end of one of these.
> There isn't dead silence - this particular
> teacher is not as strict as some.   At lunch-
> time a few pupils are still in the work-room,
> there are a few in the common room and the
> rest have officially gone 'home'.

The reasons for the increasing control over the
pupils owed something to the discrepancy between what
some teachers thought the sixth form should be like
and what it appeared to have become.   For example,

Mr. Z   -   "Most of them are only interested in
            pop groups.   There are so many of
            them with long hair.   I don't know
            them - I just pass them in the
            corridor."

Mrs. X   -   "I've got doubts about a lot of these
            pupils staying on - they perhaps
            should be doing what they're doing
            here in a Community Centre or some-
            thing.   I don't want to sound awful
            but it's an expensive method of keeping

them off the streets. I suppose
I'm old-fashioned, but I think in
terms of the sixth form being
'academic' and I think that the
pupils that are capable of doing
A level work - well, the ethos of
work isn't so strong with all these
others staying on."

Miss H   - "In the first term I was worried about
their whole attitude - I brought it
up at a meeting. There was a phase
when I was met with either rudeness
or silence. We have very little
contact with them really. Dress is
a problem - I think they're indulged.
I'm old-fashioned enough to think
they should be setting an example.
There's more of an even keel now -
I think it's better since people
complained. When you've got a
mixed sixth form there's always the
worry that some may be seen to be
having a 'fun time' and that may
distract the academic children from
their study."

Miss D   - "Nobody could call it an academic
sixth form. I think it's got to be
structured so that they don't get
the idea they're going to play for
two years ... If some of these people
went out and talked to bosses like
they talk to teachers they'd be out
on their ear. You expect them to
be mature, but it doesn't come
naturally ... They've got this
faulty attitude ... I think some of
our kids get too much leeway."

These comments, and others like them, were made by
staff who did not teach the sixth form and there was,
it seems, an element of fear present:-

Mrs. N   - "I've never been in the sixth form
common room. When I pass by all the
sixth formers seem to look at you as
if to say 'It's only a teacher'. I
was in the library on duty the other
week and they were making an awful
noise. I didn't do anything - and

> after a while I thought 'what are
> you afraid of? They're only
> pupils'. So I went and told them
> to be quiet."

Some teachers who taught the sixth form were concerned
about the pupils' attitude to work:-

Miss O   - "There's an element in the sixth form
          I'd call 'dubious'. They always seem
          to be hanging around ... I teach them -
          and some of them are smashing kids -
          but they're so chatty. The type of
          kid we get needs to be guided, they
          can't be left to their own devices
          all the time or they'll fritter it
          away and do nothing."

Most of the sixth form teachers, however, did not
generalise about the pupils, but differentiated
between them and expended much effort and time on the
non-workers attempting to persuade them to 'change
their ways'. These concerns gave rise to the
school's attempt to 'claim' the pupils' non-lesson
time. Staff insisted, practically every day, that
there were no 'free' periods they were 'private study'
periods. The latter term never gained currency
among the pupils who, two years later, still referred
to free periods.
    The concern about the pupils' work received an
added impetus after the exams at the end of 1980
where, it was maintained, there was a great deal of
'underachievement'. This was an interesting conclusion as, a term previously, nine of these twenty
pupils had obtained fewer than five O levels and were
now doing two or three A levels - often in addition
to an extra O level or two. That this required
considerable effort was realised.

Mr. F   - "A lot of our pupils need an awful
          lot of help. A lot of the A level
          kids aren't obvious A level candi-
          dates - they're not obvious As and
          Bs.

Mr. P   - "There are pupils who go into the
          sixth form not ever having worked
          before and who don't know what
          homework is because they didn't
          need to do it for CSE - even if they
          got a Grade 1."

Most teachers agreed with the idea of a 'comprehensive' sixth form and in the growth of non A level subjects.   In practice, however, unemployment and qualification inflation served to increase the A level contingent and present the teachers with more 'mixed ability' groups than hitherto.

Strauss (1973), in his study of a psychiatric hospital, concluded that personnel only showed a single vaguely ambitious goal - to return patients to the outside world in better shape - and beneath this 'symbolic cement' were considerable disagreements and discrepancies.   In this school the shared goal might be seen as sending children out of the organisation better equipped or qualified to deal with the future - but there was clearly disagreement about how this was best achieved.   Some teachers regard a training in 'good behaviour', the 'right attitude' and conformity in dress as essential whilst others - mainly A level teachers - consider a large amount of work and self-sacrifice as necessary for achieving qualifications.   This leads, not only to different kinds of control being exercised over pupils, but also to some division among the teachers. For example, the Drama department was very successful in motivating and involving many pupils in a way that met one of its goals - namely, the self-development of pupils as individuals who could express themselves with confidence.   As the pupils became more involved, however, other teachers saw the activities differently.

Miss O   - "I'm a bit dischuffed the way drama and music interests have completely taken over some of the kids ... I'm concerned about the amount of time they're spending on it.   It causes a bit of resentment cos you're trying to get results and the kids qualifications.   There is room for making these kids face up to reality - and reality is often quite cruel."

Miss D   - "Our kids seem to be star-struck now. They all want to be actors or musicians or whatever.   It's good for them to do it - but how many of them are going to be actors?"

An organisation, according to Blau (1971), can be ruled by recruiting anybody and then controlling them with a chain of command or by picking suitable people and relying on normative identification. In comprehensive sixth forms both of these types of recruits exist - but the chain of command developed primarily for the 'anybodies' feels more repressive to the 'suitables' who expect something different.

PUPILS' RESPONSES

The increasing control over their activities was felt acutely by the A levellers for whom the sixth form differed from expectations. The resentment revolved around the school attempting to claim their 'free time' whilst also attempting to claim their 'home time'.

Peter - "I want to do A levels but I don't see any end to it. I thought you'd have social life and friends as well as work. You have to practically fill up your timetable - that was a shock. I think it's because this school is working-class and they don't trust us. At other schools they've got cookers and things and can play records in their free time."

Roger - "The sixth form's a lot different from what you expect. You have the idea it will be easy - a bit of work and sitting in the comfy chairs drinking coffee. But it's not like that at all. It's a bit of a con that they treat you different - there's not a lot of change. I thought they'd have more respect for you in classes, but they don't. You're still a pupil and the teachers have this dominance over you. The atmosphere is pathetic."

Don - "The free lessons are disappointing. I thought you'd be able to play cards and that. I think you should be able to, after you've been to lessons."

Lesley - "I resent the way you're treated some-times - I don't think you're given enough freedom. During free periods if you want to sit in the common room it's up to you - you've got to do the work some time."

Qualification Inflation

Gordon, who took his A levels in 1981 and failed,
returned to the school for a further year and reviewed
the changes:-

"All the pupils just work now and then go
home - it's all pushin' and pushin'. Free
periods should be _free_. Two years ago it
was great - the Annes and the Marys passed
their exams and had a good time as well.
I think the sixth form has died - they're
placing too much emphasis on work - but
people aren't working any more than they
used to. Teachers are chasing you up all
the time, so people just flit about to
avoid them. They should let you sit in
the common room, it didn't do anybody any
harm - I'm the exception! It _was_ great -
you got things done and had a good laugh.
There were things on at night too, there
doesn't seem to be anything now. The
Head doesn't like people sitting about and
talking to one another, he can't see the
whole aspect of the sixth form - all he
considers is the work. He likes to see the
plays but he doesn't know you have to sit
about reading the script, sneaking off to
the drama theatre to practise with the
lights and that. He can't see that part.
It's not a proper sixth form now, it's all
work orientated. Judy and Kim wouldn't
fit in now. The clever ones keep themselves apart whereas last year Marianne
was clever but she mixed in - they all did.
I couldn't bring me guitar in now, it's
lost its atmosphere completely. Some
teachers try to organise things after school
but not many pupils take advantage of it -
they do their work and go home."

The dichotomy between work and non work described here
and the reluctance to participate in activities centred
round the workplace are distinguishing features of the
ideal-type of instrumental orientation (Goldthorpe
1968) usually discussed in relation to waged workers -
but the parallel is striking.
    Some of the pupils responded to these changes
with varying degrees of resistance to the claims of
the school over their time. Four boys adopted a _no
work_ pattern.

Peter - "It's a shock to get so much work - it's

> depressin'. There's work every night -
> but there's things like sport I'd like
> to do - and girls and that ... I put
> social life first, it's impossible to
> combine the two - we get that much work
> you'd have to stay in all night to do
> it. I believe I have the ability but
> I don't feel interested. Once you've
> been told off once you might as well be
> told off again ... I can't be bothered
> with homework and Roger is bugging me
> because he's always talking about how I
> should stay in and do the work and not
> go out - the teachers are bugging me too."

The House and form tutors had talks with Peter and
suggested that he should give up some of his sport.
But in the upper sixth he continued to do no work,
whilst playing a great deal of sport, and was continually chased up by teachers. In the January
before his A levels he, with three other boys, was
threatened with expulsion unless a certain number of
essays were completed by half term. He managed to
do enough of them to avoid expulsion but only passed
one of his A levels in the summer and returned to
school for an extra year. Gordon, who was a year
ahead of Peter, had an almost identical case history
and in his third year passed two A levels in November
and January and was expelled for lack of work before
he had taken the third one in the summer. The other
two boys in this group also failed their A levels and
their histories follow a similar pattern.

These boys 'chose' social life partly because they
had a readily available alternative in sport - at which
three of them excelled. They had joined teams and
clubs outside the school which involved practices as
well as matches and all the socialising that goes with
both. This sort of social life is not so readily
available to girls in such a time consuming way. The
only A level girl in the sample who went out regularly
three times a week belonged to a Church that had activities in which she participated. The other girls,
if they went out, went to a pub on Friday or Saturday
evenings with a group. Although these four boys
wanted the qualifications and three of them said, in
the fifth year, they intended to go into higher education, they all said that they had no regrets about
choosing the 'social life'. When, in Gouldner's
(1954) study, the organisation moved from the 'leniency'
to the 'punishment-centred' bureaucracy he describes
how the workers did as little as possible and the forms

of reaction available to them only confirmed the
management's view, which resulted in more control and
a consequent vicious circle.   Industrial sociologists
have, of course, long recognised that orientations to
work are partly shaped by the experiences of work
(Brown 1973 and 1974).

Another response to work was that of <u>resentful
compliance</u> - one girl and three boys came into this
category.

Helen - "I'm getting fed up with working.   The
          lessons are all right, it's all the rest.
          I don't know if I'll go to University
          now after all this.   I think you have
          to choose between work and social life
          ... I don't like school now - a lot of
          people are getting lazy and not doing
          homework and staying off.   It makes me
          want to do the same.   It's all school
          and homework - I hate it."

Mike   - "I want to go straight into a job after
          A levels - I couldn't stand any more
          of this.   I do me homework every night
          as soon as I get in - I don't put it
          off.   I force myself to do it ......
          The work is the worst thing, having to
          go home and do more."

In the event, Mike applied to University as a 'safeguard' and obtained the required grades - but at the
last minute could not face the prospect and postponed
the place for a year.   He tried, unsuccessfully, to
get a job and after a year on the dole entered
University.

Jim had said similar things about not wanting to
do any more work after A levels because he was fed up
with it all but, in the end, also applied for University:-

          "Physics seemed the best of a bad bunch.
          I don't really like it - I don't look
          forward to any of the lessons.   It'll
          be a waste of time if I don't go to
          College, it's best to keep going as far
          as you can.   I've put Physics down cos
          there's loads of chances with that.   I'm
          doing it for the qualification - I'm not
          looking forward to it at all."

All these pupils acquired the necessary grades

and went off to higher education without any joy at
the prospect. They were a despondent group who were
not, however, a worry to the teachers who had not
much to say about them except that they were quite
good workers.

Another group of pupils had a <u>restrictive</u>
attitude to work in the sense that they decided how
much they were prepared to do - which was a fair
amount in the case of these particular people - but
they would not be pushed into doing more to the
exclusion of social life. The four pupils that
came into this category were girls who were defined
as 'very able' and the push that was being exerted
was to enable them either to take Oxbridge entry or
to achieve the highest grades at A level.

Lesley - "I'm supposed to be thinking about
Oxford, but I don't know if I'm
prepared to do the work. I enjoy
the teaching situation - the actual
lessons - but I don't do enough by
myself really. I like going out and
I'd be just as happy at another
University."

One of the teachers recognised this:-

Mr. B - "Lesley is able and highly intelligent -
she ought to get an A. If she's
willing to dedicate herself wholly
then she's Oxbridge material. I think
there's a limit, in terms of effort,
beyond which she's not prepared to go.
That's a very high limit in terms of
preparation for A level and I've got
no complaints on that score."

Sarah - "Four A levels is a lot - although if
I stayed in and worked all the time it
wouldn't be. I don't want to go to
Oxford - it's too hard to get in and
there's too much pressure. I go out
twice a week. I try and maintain a
balance between work and social life
but sometimes my social life becomes
more dominant. Last year I wouldn't
have neglected the school work for
anything but this year I do. The
social side of the sixth form is non-
existent, to me school is nothing but
work."

Qualification Inflation

Mandy   - "I'm not prepared to work all the time.
          Mr. B suggested I should apply to Oxford,
          but I'm not prepared to do the work -
          I've got to go out sometime.   At the
          beginning of this week I was really
          cheesed off with the fact that there's
          a few of us that go to extra lessons
          before school (S level) and Mr. F.
          expects us to go - always the same ones.
          This week I just said I wasn't going."

This restrictive attitude is the least striking
response, but may be important since it has been said
to be the strategy used most often by workers for
making their future behaviour more unpredictable and
enlarging their area of discretion (Silverman 1970).
    Thus, more than half the pupils in this sample -
and observation suggests in the sixth form as a whole
- developed attitudes to work that could be described
as varying degrees of alienation.   The dichotomy
between work and non work areas of life is pronounced
and 'social life' is defined as an activity outside
the home with peers.   This is a distinguishing
feature between these pupils and three hard-working
girls, in the sample, who were highly involved in
family life and one of whom had heavy responsibilities
at home.   One girl just ' liked working' and the
other said:-

Lorna   - "I only go out once or twice a month -
          partly because of all the work and
          partly because there's nowhere to go
          if you don't have money.   What would
          I do if I didn't work?"

    There was one hard working boy who had a
definite career goal in mind and abandoned his social
and sporting activities in order to concentrate on
'getting the grades'.   Most of his discussions
revolved around marks he had obtained and how he
could improve them and he most nearly matches the
common idea of an 'instrumentalis'.

Roger   - "I'm taking A level Accounts in a year -
          it's mainly to use it as a safety net
          underneath me Maths - cos I think I'm
          going to fail that.   I want to come
          out with three A levels and if I pass
          Accounts that'll be one.   Loads of
          people aren't doing any work - but I
          know what me standard is now we've had

40

> the exams and I want to improve on
> that."

After he had passed Accounts at the end of the lower
sixth he took up Sociology A level for the remaining
year and said:-

> "It's better than just another O level.
> I'd rather put me time into doing
> another A level which will be better
> for me."

There were four pupils - two boys and two girls -
who seemed to cope. They did enough work to get by,
although not as much as the teachers would have liked,
and had some social life outside the home. What
distinguished these four was the fact that they were
all in the middle of the A level 'ability' range -
not exceptional enough to be pushed and not marginal
enough for work to be a concern.

The majority of pupils, therefore, exhibited
privatised responses in as much as their attachments
to, and involvement in, work and the social relations
of work were slight. (Giddens 1982). But pupils'
resentment was directed towards the perceived imposition of work by the teachers and whilst being aware,
at one level, of the social context they were momen-
tarily escaping - they did not explain the demands
that affected them in these broader terms. Where
they did recognise the social context as leading to
increased demands by teachers they tended to explain
it in terms of teachers' self-interest.

Pat   - "They want everyone to stay on because
          of the merger. They want to show
          what a wonderful sixth form they've
          got."

Mandy   - "They want the extra money you get if
          you've got more sixth formers."

Malcolm- "All they want is results."

Jim   - "If you do the work they just want
          more - they want as much as you can
          do."

Goldthorpe's (1968) ideal type of instrumental
orientation by privatised workers includes the
feature of expenditure of effort being made for
extrinsic rewards with a concern to maximise returns

for that effort. The pupils who did no work always explained their failures in terms of a laziness that was their 'choice' but, by the same token, pupils that did work hard expected their results to match the effort they had put in compared with other pupils. After Pat, one of the hard workers, had failed an O level she said:-

> "I don't know how I failed, I couldn't get over it - I was shattered. I was always reading books on that subject. I don't know how Peter passed, he never did anything, he didn't deserve to pass. I was very upset."

Teachers, however, differentiated between 'ability' and 'hard work'.

Mr. B - ".... if I can make a crude distinction here - there are some pupils who, through hard work and careful teaching, will get through A level with a lower grade. They are, in a sense, not intelligent - they're conscientious. There's a qualitative difference between the two."

Mr. J - "There are branches of the work which need real flair and she hasn't got that sort of gift in the subject."

Mr. K - "When he's doing experimental work he's got a feel for it. This is where, apart from the work, you get a feel for the bright kids in the sixth."

This 'flair' is something that might, in part, manifest itself as a result of non-instrumental attitudes to work - that is, an interest in the subject over and above the requirements of the work to be handed in. The number of pupils that expressed this sort of interest was small, as teachers often recognised.

Mr. B - "Sue is different because I think she's genuinely interested in being educated for its own sake ... I think she's the only pupil in the sixth that I'd be inclined to make that comment about."

CONCLUSION AND POLICY IMPLICATIONS

Weber (1968) maintained that every system attempts to gain legitimacy and the type of legitimacy claimed will affect the type of obedience and mode of exercising authority and will, therefore, have variations in effect. But, as Albrow (1970) points out, the application of rules is realised not only through techniques but also norms. Collins (1975), in reviewing the sociological findings with regard to organisations, concludes that these findings suggest that control by coercion leads to alienation and attempts to escape or counterattack - and control by normative ideals requires ceremonial membership in a status community which results in identification with organisational purposes. This school, in emphasising and applying rules more stringently came to use the former system of control and, at the same time, removed the pupils' claim to status - by limiting their movements and supervising their time - which is the basis on which normative compliance to institutional demands might have been built.

Factors outside the school, leading to a change in the composition and size of the sixth form, were the impetus for a shift in control techniques which affected the pupils in terms of the teachers' demands on them - to which they responded at an individual level. Thus, the external world was mediated through the teachers' action in the organisational context and entered the culture and consciousness of the pupils in a different form. Rather than the development of social consciousness which enabled them to view their position in the structural context, they developed alienated and privatised orientations dominated by the central concern of the interpersonal demands made upon them. These orientations, for some, resulted in lower 'achievements' than might otherwise have been the case - they thus 'locate' themselves individually, and by 'choice', in a more disadvantageous position. A similar process, in fact, to that described by Willis (1977) with regard to pupils at the other end of the school 'spectrum'.

The inversion of means and ends, with which both Marx and Weber were concerned, can be attributed partly to the different meanings that teachers and pupils attach to the mechanisms of control. For teachers control revolved around their attempts to ensure 'achievement' in a changing environment. For the pupils, however, this was seen as domination by a group whose sole purpose seemed to be to make their life miserable. The structure, of course, can to some extent, control behaviour - but not the meanings that people place on their behaviour (King 1973).

The forms of control used towards pupils are similar to those increasingly applied to teachers, as has been mentioned, and it has been maintained (Buswell 1980) that some individual teachers are increasingly becoming deskilled with, for example, extra-classroom control of the curriculum and assessment. Rationalisation is therefore likely to produce varieties of similar responses among teachers towards work and the organisation as that exhibited by pupils - depending on teachers' own biographies, their place in the hierarchy and their opportunities for reskilling. There is thus likely to be an interplay of alienated responses between some teachers and some pupils.

That there is an element of 'class control' in the system described, as Peter maintained, seems probable when contrasted with the controls operated towards sixth formers in the independent schools, and at least one middle-class comprehensive, in the area. In these schools it is usual for sixth formers to be allowed to leave the premises, after stating where they intend to go, during non-contact time and the social atmosphere of these sixth forms is more obvious. These middle-class pupils are regarded as 'trustworthy' enough also to complete the work requirements. At lower levels in these schools it might be argued that, especially in the independent sector, they have the final control of expelling pupils who are not normatively compliant, but at sixth form level the school in this study did expel, and threaten to expel, pupils who did not work.

Although Carnoy (1976) sees exact parallels between the factory assembly line and the educational assembly line schools are not, in fact, factories in spite of attempts to organise them along similar lines. Some tasks in education can be circumscribed, accounted for and measured - but can only be qualitatively maintained or improved by the desire of participants to give something of 'themselves' to the work. It is this aspect of the personal relationship to the task that is affected when rational organisation is such that forms of alienation result. Could it be otherwise? The strength of rational organisation is that, in theory, it allows goals efficiently to be achieved. The weakness of such organisations is that as power accrues to the top of the hierarchies alienation and privatisation result in the displacement of some of the goals. Schools that incorporated teachers and pupils into decision-making, with some genuine power sharing, might make themselves more 'inefficient' in some respects and infinitely more 'efficient' and less alienating in others.

With regard to the privatisation aspect of the orientations writers such as Habermas (1976) see this as crucial at the societal level. He, for example, maintains that advanced capitalism has reduced the need for legitimacy to two requirements. Firstly, structural depoliticisation justified by democratic or technocratic systems theories and, secondly, civic privatism which is a political abstinence combined with orientations to career, leisure and consumption and incorporates elements of an achievement ideology transferred to the educational system. He considers that rising expectations of success - proportional to the need for legitimacy - could lead to a 'legitimation crisis' when demands are not met but such a crisis may not occur whilst a sufficient degree of civic privatism is maintained.

In discussing various 'crisis tendencies' in modern capitalist societies one of which is a 'rationality crisis' at the level of the political system, he points out that the spread of organised rationality undermines the cultural traditions that are important for legitimacy and which cannot be regenerated administratively. Another tendency is the 'motivational crisis' at the level of the indi- vidual and emanating from changes in the socio- cultural system, partly because of 'overloading' with respect to new demands which cannot be met - and the most important motivation contributed by the socio- cultural system is that of privatism which legitimates the whole structure. Habermas considers that the socio-cultural system will not be able, in the long run, to reproduce the privatistic syndrome necessary for the continuance of the system. This is for several reasons, one of which is that the components of bourgeois ideology - possessive individualism and achievement orientation - are being undermined by changes in the social structure. The expansion of the educational system, he suggests, is increasingly independent of changes in the occupational system and the connection between formal schooling and occupational success will become looser in the future. Added to this is the penetration of monotonous labour processes to previously autonomous occupational role positions and increasing instrumental attitudes in traditional middle-class occupations.

The privatism that this data reveal would, in this view, be one of the crucial factors for the legitimation and continuation of the present social system. But the tendencies that Habermas considers would weaken these orientations are also present without any evidence, in this study, that they are doing so.

Further examination of the educational system in terms of rationality and the orientations that emanate from it would contribute to that which Giddens (1977) considers as one of the academic problems of major significance:-

> ..... the question of how far the alienative characteristics which Marx attributed to capitalism as a specific form of class society, in fact derive from a bureaucratic rationality which is a necessary concomitant of industrial society, whether it be 'capitalist' or 'socialist'.

ACKNOWLEDGEMENTS

I am grateful to my colleague John Donnelly for his generosity in discussing ideas and to the staff and pupils of the school for their help and tolerance.

REFERENCES

Albrow, M. (1970) Bureaucracy, Pall Mall Press, London

Blau, P.M. and Schoenherr, R.A. (1971) The Structure of Organisations, Basic Books, New York

Boudon, R. (1977) 'Effets pervers et ordre social', Presses Universitaires de France, Paris Discussed in D. Swartz (1981) 'Classes, educational systems and Labor Markets', Archives Europeennes De Sociologie, 22, 2

Brown, R.K. (1973) 'Sources of Objectives in Work and Employment', in J. Child (ed.) Man and Organisation, Allen and Unwin, London

Brown, R.K. (1974) 'The Attitudes to Work Expectations and Social Perspectives of Shipbuilding Apprentices', in T. Leggatt (ed.), Sociological Theory and Survey Research, Sage, London

Buswell, C. (1980) 'Pedagogic Change and Social Change', British Journal of Sociology of Education, 1, 3

Carnoy, M. and Levin, H. (1976) The Limits of Educational Reform, Longman, London

Collins, R. (1975) Conflict Sociology, Academic Press, London

Collins, R. (1979) The Credential Society, Academic

Press, London

Dore, R. (1976) The Diploma Disease, Allen and Unwin, London

Giddens, A. (1971) Capitalism and Modern Social Theory, Cambridge University Press

Giddens, A. (1977) Studies in Social and Political Theory, Hutchinson, London

Giddens, A. and Held, D. (1982) Classes, Power and Conflict, Macmillan

Goldthorpe, J.H. et al. (1968) The Affluent Worker, Industrial Attitudes and Behaviour, Cambridge University Press

Gouldner, A. (1954) Patterns of Industrial Bureaucracy, Collier-Macmillan, U.S.A.

Habermas, J. (1976) Legitimation Crisis, Heinemann Educational Books

Hextall, I. and Sarup, M. (1977) 'School Knowledge, Evaluation and Alienation', in M. Young and G. Whitty, Society, State and Schooling, Falmer Press

King, R. (1973) School Organisation and Pupil Involvement, Routledge and Kegan Paul, London

King, R. (1982) 'Organisational Change in Secondary Schools: An Action Approach', British Journal of Sociology of Education, 3, 1

Löwith, K. (1982) Max Weber and Karl Marx, Allen and Unwin, London

Salaman, G. (1979) Work Organisations, Longman, London

Silverman, D. (1970) The Theory of Organisations, Heinemann, London

Strauss, A. et al. (1973) 'The Hospital and its Negotiated Order', in G. Salaman and K. Thompson (eds.) People and Organisations, Longman, London

Weber, M. (1978) Economy and Society, G. Roth and C. Wittich (eds.), University of California Press, London

Willis, P. (1977) Learning to Labour, Saxon House, England

TEACHING TILL TWO THOUSAND : TEACHERS' CONSCIOUSNESS IN TIMES OF CRISIS

Martin Cole

"Thank God : it's Friday", the familiar teachers' motto, serves to remind us that teachers frequently see their work in terms of crisis. This paper will argue, though, that teachers are entering an era which will be characterised by crisis of a kind and degree they have not previously known.

In adopting such a prophetic stance this paper takes on the risk that future events will expose all too clearly the limitations of its analysis. But risky though the enterprise may be, asking how the future is going to work can usefully stimulate us to formulate the questions we ought to be asking about how the present works.

If, with Habermas, we believe that advanced capitalist societies are entering a legitimation crisis we should not expect that schooling will be unaffected by that development. This paper will begin by defining briefly the ways in which teachers are beginning to experience the legitimation crisis in their classrooms. But there are additional developments, relating specifically to schools, many of them deriving ultimately from birth-rate fluctuations, which add an extra dimension to the crisis experienced by teachers; the paper will therefore proceed to define what may be called the teacher motivation crisis.

It will be further argued that both of these crises, the legitimation crisis and the teacher motivation crisis, are closely inter-related: that one can be expected to exacerbate the other, while a resolution of either will require at least an amelioration of the other.

The latter part of the paper will propose an analysis of the ways in which teachers may subjectively experience those crises and the possible consequences of that experience for the role of teachers in the production and reproduction of the structures of schooling and in the performance of the social control function of schooling.

Firstly, then, we turn to a consideration of the classroom legitimation crisis. Already teachers report instances of pupils resigned as early as age twelve to a prospect of unemployment on leaving school. For teachers who for years legitimated their power, the curriculum and much else about schooling by reference to the preparation of pupils for employment, the implications are daunting. Ethnographic studies of pupils' orientations to school have stressed the sizeable proportion of pupils whose orientation is a largely instrumental one, with certification their chief goal. For such pupils a realisation that exam qualifications cut no ice in the dole queue becomes a failure to see any point in school: teachers, their knowledge, their pedagogic skills, are devalued. The teacher who, in these circumstances, cannot fall back on a talent to entertain, to help pupils 'have a laugh', has nothing to offer such pupils. In this situation the conflict in the classroom which genera-tions of teachers have mainly succeeded in suppress-ing will surely be sharpened. (1)

But it is not just that more pupils will come unwillingly to schools which do not serve their purposes; it is also that the strategies teachers conventionally employ in the management of classroom conflict are attenuated. The continuous testing and grading which secondary teachers often employ to remind pupils of the ultimate qualification 'carrot' will lose its impact; the threat of unfavourable references to support future job-applications will be an empty threat; the sanction of not entering for the exam pupils who do not work in class will no longer impress. In a number of ways teachers have often tried to give the impression that they can control pupils' future employment destinies: such control was probably to some extent mythical; we may now expect the myth to be exposed.

If a high level of school-leaver unemployment persists, and if attempts to disguise the phenomenon by means of YOP or MSC training schemes fail, we can expect the legitimacy of teachers' authority, their curricular knowledge and their pedagogic skills to be questioned by an increasing proportion of pupils, and we can expect the corresponding sanctions teachers use to manage classroom conflict to be progressively weakened. Moreover, at the same time, assuming continued pressure on public spending, the physical and manpower resources for teaching will continue to be in short supply.

Such an analysis of future teacher-pupil relations would seem bad enough news for teachers. But
I believe it is only half the story, and I shall now
turn to the second element of the crisis facing
teachers: their personal motivation crisis. Initially
the analysis of the teacher motivation crisis will be
facilitated by drawing a distinction between the
intrinsic and extrinsic rewards teachers may find in
their work. The intrinsic rewards have probably
been most clearly defined by Lortie in his American
(1975) study in which he refers particularly to the
psychic rewards which may flow from favourable relationships with both pupils and fellow-teachers, from
a fulfilment of the desire to perform a service on
children's behalf and from craft pride generated by
evidence of successful teaching and the esteem of
colleagues.

All of these aspects of the intrinsic rewards
of teaching are threatened by the classroom legitimation crisis as relations with pupils become more
strained and as teachers find it more difficult to
convince themselves (let alone pupils) that they are
performing a service for children; craft pride
becomes more difficult to achieve - or, at least,
the criteria on which a sense of success is based
have to change, moving further away from criteria
related to learning toward those related to control.
How many teachers will take pride in the degree to
which they have merely contained the crisis?

But the threat to the intrinsic rewards of
teaching is, again, only part of the prospective
story of teachers' personal motivation. The extrinsic rewards of teaching - salary, status and security
- are also coming under threat. Threats of redeployment and the closure of some schools as a result of
falling rolls are obvious to most teachers. My
discussions with teachers, however, suggest that there
is less appreciation of the long-term consequences
for teachers of birth-rate trends and the associated
effects on the teacher labour-market. The massive
intake of teachers into the occupation in the '60s
and early '70s (a response to the '60s baby-boom)
has produced an age-structure of the occupation which
reveals a predominance today of middle-aged, mid-
career teachers, Those approaching retirement are
relatively, therefore, a smaller proportion of teachers
than might be expected. And even when these people
retire the effect of falling rolls may be that the
posts they occupied disappear rather than become
available for promotion.

In short, teachers' promotion prospects are diminishing and will continue, I believe, to diminish for some time to come. Teachers will have, in Roth's (1963) terms, to establish new 'career timetable norms' and individuals''time perspectives' on their personal careers will have to shift. No longer will it be appropriate to assume, as teachers have during the last two decades, that progression to Scale 2 after three to four years is probable, that ambitious secondary teachers can reasonably expect to head departments or primary colleagues to be deputies or even heads by age 35. The changes in the teacher labour-market which produce this decline in the rate of upward career mobility also result in diminished opportunities for sideways movements from school to school on the same salary scale. Teachers who fit uneasily into their particular schools will feel increasingly trapped.

The overall level of salaries, too, we might expect to diminish in real terms. Given continued pressure on public spending and given that the insecurity engendered by the threat of redeployment and reduced promotion prospects will inhibit teachers from aggressive collective bargaining, we can expect salaries to suffer.

So far I have considered the intrinsic and extrinsic rewards of teaching separately. It may be, however, that they are importantly linked in many teachers' minds. My own research on teachers suggests that a lack of either kind of reward is frequently compensated if the other kind is experienced. If, weighing day against day, year against year, teaching is found to be intrinsically rewarding many teachers appear relatively unconcerned about the extrinsic rewards (some indeed deliberately sacrifice the salary and status attached to positions of responsibility in order to hang on to intrinsic rewards experienced in classroom teaching). Conversely, where the intrinsic rewards are felt to be at a low level, promotion prospects and holidays are commonly used to arrive at a personal accommodation of dissatisfaction. Or, at least, dissatisfied teachers cling to the belief that a change of school will resolve their discontents - a kind of 'grass is greener' syndrome.

I think it will be clear that all of these kinds of compensation where one kind of dissatisfaction is traded with a different kind of satisfaction are likely to be less available to teachers in the future. In a situation where the intrinsic and extrinsic rewards of teaching are <u>both</u> diminishing it is less easy for one to compensate a lack of the other; instead continuance in teaching will more likely reflect the purely negative phenomenon that there is nothing else the teacher can do: again, teachers will feel trapped.

I think it can be argued, then, that at least for the next two decades (that is, roughly, until the great phalanx of middle-aged, mid-career teachers retires) teachers will face two major and inter-related crises - the legitimation crisis of the class-room, and teachers' personal motivation crisis.

The immediate consequences of these crises are not difficult to imagine. Clearly, we may fear for teachers' mental health. If David Hargreaves could write a few years ago (1978) in a brief paper called "What Teaching Does to Teachers" about the "debili-tating occupational disease" of teaching, with its "progressive emotional exhaustion", the "cynical apathy" of the "worn-out teacher", the "alienation" and "personal withdrawal into defensive strategies", how much more quickly and painfully will teachers fall prey to the disease in years to come?

These are perhaps consequence enough for those of us who are teachers, or who work with teachers, or who care about teachers. But we must also con-sider possible consequences on a broader front. If the functions of schooling include the facilitation of social control and the legitimation of the exist-ing social order, can these continue to be achieved if the teachers, the front-line troops, are not fighting fit? Of course, teachers are not society's only agents of social control, but are any other agents asked to perform in a face-to-face confronta-tion hours daily, heavily outnumbered and armed with such limited weapons as the incentive of doubtful employment prospects, the conventional school curri-culum, the drab school environment and the pedagogi-cal practices imposed on teachers by the constraining conditions of schooling?

Administrators and academics alike have been inclined to take rather for granted teachers' complicity in the control and legitimation functions of schooling. Perhaps future events will serve to expose more clearly what Bernstein (1977) has called the "ambiguous" position of teachers who, while mostly subscribing to such ideological messages of the education system as "autonomy of self or mind" nevertheless function daily as "agents of symbolic control"?

In 1975 Sharp and Green concluded their study of avowedly progressive primary school teachers whose

practices seemed often to deny their claimed intentions with the remark that

> Unless and until educators are able to
> comprehend their own structural location
> ... they will continue to be unwilling
> victims of a structure that undermines
> the moral concerns they profess ...

Could the effect of the coming classroom legitimation
crisis be to reveal to more teachers more clearly
their structural location?   And, if we add in the
effects of the teacher motivation crisis does it
suggest a greater resistance by teachers to performing their ill-rewarded roles as victims?

Will those who manage teachers (heads, LEAs and
so on) find strategies for resolving teachers'
personal motivation crises so that they can continue
to recruit them to control and legitimation functions?

In order to begin to examine such questions we
must not take teachers for granted but try to understand how the crises defined above may be subjectively
experienced by teachers themselves;   only then can we
assess some of the possible consequences suggested.

To date, though, teachers have not only been
somewhat taken for granted in the sociology of education, they have also been the victims of rather
crude theory, or no theory at all, or of very insular
sociological approaches.   As a result writing about
teachers has tended to be polarised into two competing schools of thought.

The first of these and, though with some recent
variations, still the dominant theme, has teachers
as objects manipulated by their socialisation and
the structural constraints on their activities to
comply with a well-defined set of values and code of
practices.   This approach is clearest in these post-
war studies of the role of the teacher which derive
from structural functionalism;   Hoyle's 1969 work is
a relatively recent and well-known British example.

A subtle variation of this theme of the highly
socialised teacher seems to me evident in some
passages in Waller's historic (1932) study, in
Lortie's (1975) American study and in Mardle and
Walker's (1980) paper where the apparent conservatism
and docility of teachers is explained by the assertion
that the structures of education ensure that only the
conservatively oriented or critically unreflexive
choose to enter teaching.

Sociologists have often castigated teachers for
explaining away children's underachievement through

reference to alleged deficiencies in those children;
they have not, however, been averse to rationalising
their own inability to produce reflexive and innovative teachers in terms of inherent deficiencies in
students and teachers: a "teacher-deficit" model of
schooling!

The alternative school of thought, and probably
the less popular one, is less easily illustrated for
its expression is more often implicit than explicit.
It sees teachers as fully conscious, reflexive actors
who have choices: they are not made by the structures
of schooling, indeed, they are the makers. This
view is implied, rather than directly stated, in some
of the writings of the deschoolers like Illich, Reimer
and Holt, and has perhaps been inferred by some from
the symbolic interactionism of Becker et al., from
the phenomenological new directions of Young et al.,
and from some of the neo-Marxism of the late 70s
in which teachers sometimes seem to be regarded as
witting conspirators in the reproduction of inequality. However, it is probably true to say that these
inferences have been drawn more from a simplistic
appreciation of the spirit of these writings than
from the letter.

(Indeed Becker (1964) does conceive of "situational
adjustment" - the process by which "the individual
turns himself into the kind of person the situation
demands" while, classically, Marxism would view any
"false consciousness" on teachers' parts as product
rather than cause of social structure. The
deschoolers, however, lacking any coherent sociological theory, simply do not address the debate.)

The polarisation in thinking about teachers
(at the level of assumption if not of fully developed
theory) is of course only one symptom of the classic
and fundamental tension in social theory between
those explanations which stress structure and those
stressing action, between deterministic and voluntaristic views of behaviour, between a concern with
statics and one with dynamics, between man viewed as
subject and man viewed as object.

This polarisation is particularly inappropriate
to the study of teachers who can be regarded as
located at the interface of 'structure' and 'action'
in paradigmatic terms. In other words, to the
structuralist the teacher is significant as the person
who vitally mediates whatever 'goals' or 'functions'
may be attributed to the education system in the
confrontation with the clients (i.e. pupils), who at
the same time represent other aspects of the social
structure (class or status, race, sex, etc.). This

mediation is subject, however, to all those interactional processes within schools and classrooms
which interactionists, phenomenologists and ethno-
methodologists have described.   It is unlikely today
that even the most ardent structuralist would deny
the evidence that at the micro-level of the school,
and (even more so) of the classroom, teachers and
children are engaged in significant degrees of
negotiation and reality-construction.

For the interactionist, however, awareness of
these interactional processes in which teachers
engage (with both pupils and other teachers) must be
tempered by a recognition that teachers are not
autonomous, whatever physical isolation from other
adults the classroom appears to provide.   Teachers
have to coexist with other teachers, superiors and
parents, and cope with manifestations of the wider
social structure in the form of the law, resource-
provision, examination systems, the distribution of
occupational opportunities, etc.

If this analysis of the teacher's location at the
paradigm interface is accepted it becomes clear that
teachers cannot be fully understood other than through
an attempt to view them at one and the same time from
a plurality of sociological perspectives.

At the first Westhill conference in 1978 almost
every paper began with a survey of the way in which
the pendulum had been swinging between these theoretical poles in the sociology of education: Andy
Hargreaves called it a "wild oscillation between two
poles of sociological explanation".   There were
numerous calls for attempts to resolve these tensions
between perspectives: Olive Banks pleaded for a
'building of bridges';   Sara Delamont wanted a
'rapprochement', Ivan Reid talked of a 'synthesis'.
(All quoted in Barton and Meighan 1978)

Perhaps this is an appropriate time to take
stock and consider how far we have gone in answering
these demands;   my own answer would be 'not far'.
But there was another plea at that first conference
which has been quite extensively answered – the plea
for more ethnography.   We now have a certain amount
of ethnographic material concerning teachers.   The
manner in which some ethnographic studies of teachers
have been conducted seems, however, sometimes to have
compounded the sin of the over-socialised conception
of the teacher of which the structural functionalists
are generally accused.   I am thinking here of Andy
Hargreaves' (1981) discussion of a middle school's
staff meetings and the resulting suggestion that
teachers exhibit a form of 'hegemony', and I am

thinking of Peter Woods' (1979) remark that committed teachers have an 'institutionalised consciousness'.

Both Andy Hargreaves and Peter Woods perform a valuable service in exposing and analysing the sub-cultures of school staff-rooms but there are limits to the extent and accuracy with which such studies can reveal the consciousness of teachers. The problem is crucially revealed when Woods (1979, p.238) refers to teachers' personal orientation as being "most clearly evident in the staffroom at times when it served as a private area or 'back region'". In the staff-room, he continues, "the teacher might be released from the exigencies of role, either as survivor or as professional and might view school activities through a private framework". This seems questionable. While it is true that in the staff-room teachers may be released from their class-room and professional-in-the-public-eye roles, surely that does not mean that they are role-less? While the staff-room may be a venue for the private thoughts of teachers, it is only private to them as a group; from the individual teacher's perspective the staff-room is a highly public place. On this analysis the staff-room may rarely be a 'back region' but is mostly another 'front region' where teachers feel constrained to contrive a particular presentation of self.

Woods himself portrays the staff-room as a fairly emotionally-charged interactional setting, where ritual and solidarity are important, which suggests that the informal constraints on the actor will be considerable. Talk to teachers away from their staff-rooms and one discovers the extent to which the staff-room, as well as the classroom, is a locus of tensions and conflicts where it can be a struggle to survive.

Similarly Andy Hargreaves' analyses of staff meetings appear to expose a hegemonic consensus. But would the consensus represent hegemony if it were shown to be only skin-deep: a conscious construction by the participants each of whom is offering a strategic presentation of self in this very public (some would consider threatening) setting?

The very fact that, as Hargreaves observes, it is those in powerful positions (heads and deputies) who most employ the strategy of contrastive rhetoric for steering discussion toward a desired consensus suggests a tacit recognition by these parties that there are alternative and dissenting sentiments and that some teachers, if not subtly dissuaded, would wish to express them. A genuine hegemony amongst teachers would make it unnecessary and indeed unthinkable for heads to steer staff discussion as it is suggested they do.

Ethnographies of staff-rooms may very usefully tell us about the kind of culture expressed there and about the interactional strategies employed in that setting, but it may be dangerous to try to infer from such data the nature of the individual teacher's consciousness. It would be a serious error to think of the culture of the school staff as representing the aggregate of the teachers' consciousness.

In-school ethnography has thus merely produced, albeit by novel means, a variation on the old theme of the highly socialised teacher. As a response to these methodological problems, and as a fresh attempt to resolve the still-prevalent dualism, my own research on teachers' consciousness and on their subjective experience of schooling has depended on interviewing teachers away from the school setting (in fact, in their own homes) and in circumstances as confidential as could be contrived. This is not to suggest that interviews are not also interactional settings in which the participants may present themselves in certain strategic ways so that the interview is a joint social construction or, in Silverman's (1973) words, a "managed accomplishment". Interview data must always be viewed in the light of this possibility and means sought to try to reduce the problem.

One such means in my own research has been to ensure that interviews were, and were seen to be, entirely confidential and voluntary. It was, for example, made clear to respondents that I would not know (or wish to know) the identity of the schools in which they taught. Interviews were also largely unstructured and to avoid the imposition of the interviewer's prior conceptual framework, an attempt was made to conduct interviews in the language and using the categories which the respondents themselves introduced.

The analysis of some 50,000 words of transcript derived from these tape-recorded interviews has focused mainly on an attempt to generate a model of teacher consciousness. The theoretical inspiration for this attempt came from the work of Giddens (1976, 1979). He more than anyone has exposed the dualism in social theory which has led to sometimes bitter debate between advocates of structuralist and interactionist sociologies, the dualism which has afflicted the sociology of teachers and teaching.

More than this, Giddens has pointed to a possible

resolution of dualism by means of his theory of structuration. Here the oppositions of society and individual, determinism and voluntarism, structure and action, and so on, are dealt with by denying that they are oppositions. Giddens maintains that neither element in any of these dualisms can be understood without reference to the other, so that (in his words) (1976, p. 120) "social structures are both constituted by human agency, and yet at the same time are the very medium of this constitution." Giddens arrives at his theory of structuration via, among other routes, the philosophy of language and linguistics, and he explains the theory quite often by drawing analogies between social structure and language.

Language is often described as a living thing: it is the usage of the rules and resources of communication which keeps language alive. Writers of textbooks of grammar and usage in effect kill language by reifying usage at some presumed point in time and by some presumed elite of speakers and writers. Speech, in realising language rules in action, serves mainly to reproduce those rules - indeed if it did not we might lack the consistency and continuity on which communication depends. However, in every utterance there is the scope for the speaker to participate, however subtly and minimally, in the production of new language rules and resources through the redefinition of words or adjustment of syntax. This point may be illustrated by consideration of the sentence: 'The weather has been miserable this morning but hopefully the sun will shine this afternoon.' This sentence would be widely understood, and similar ones employed, by contemporary English speakers. It would have been similarly understood ten years ago, and yet it is most unlikely that it could have been heard then. The use of the word 'hopefully' in this way, though decried by those who reify language in textbooks as syntactically anomalous (- the sun cannot 'hope'), seems to have been established in Britain within a matter of months during the late seventies, not as a result of some authority, earthly or supernatural, amending the rules of language to allow us to use the word in this way, but simply as the result of the production and reproduction of the new 'rule' by ordinary speakers.

Similarly, in societal terms, actors, since they 'know how to behave' contribute through their actions to the continuous production and reproduction of the social structure of rules which actors know, which order much of their action, and without which social

life would be impossible.   Yet in every action there
is the potential for actors to participate in changing the 'rules' or structure which in turn they may
know and realise in further action.   In this way
Giddens is able to deal with a recurrent difficulty
in sociological theory: accounting for both continuity and change;   as he puts it: "change or its
potentiality is thus inherent in all moments of
social reproduction".

Integral to Giddens' theory of structuration is
a discussion of consciousness in which he distinguishes the unconscious from two modes of consciousness: practical consciousness and discursive consciousness.   Practical consciousness is defined in
terms of "tacit stocks of knowledge which actors
draw upon in the constitution of social activity":
there is a clear similarity here to Schutz's "cookery-
book knowledge".   Discursive consciousness, on the
other hand, involves "knowledge which actors are
able to express on the level of discourse".   Again
Giddens employs the analogy with language to explain
the different modes of consciousness: "There is,"
he writes, "a vital sense in which all of us do
chronically apply phonological and grammatical laws
in speech - as well as all sorts of other practical
principles of conduct - even though we could not
formulate those laws discursively ..."   In other
words, if we were to ask a speaker of an English
sentence to explain why he ordered the words in
that sentence as he did, and not in some other way,
he would most likely reply with some such response
as 'that's the way it's done';   such an answer is at
the level of practical consciousness.   Speakers with
some discursive penetration of the rules of language
would attempt to articulate the grammatical laws
instantiated in their sentence, the precision and
fullness of their answer reflecting the degree of
their discursive consciousness.

Similarly we may know how to act without prior
mental planning which relates the proposed act to
clear 'rules', and challenged to explain our behaviour
we would in these instances be likely to refer to
notions of 'common sense', the 'obvious', the 'taken
for granted'.   Some may be able to articulate 'rules'
of social behaviour relating to their action but often
action conceived at the level of practical consciousness is only understood discursively by the actor
after the event when he is called upon to account
for that action.

Practical consciousness is particularly significant for the continuity of social reproduction since

it is the mode in which "routinization" or the "continual regrooving of established attitudes and cognitive outlooks" is most likely to occur. On the other hand it appears that production of new structure is more likely to follow from discursive consciousness in actors since it is only in this mode that routinization can be questioned or challenged.

Such an analysis of consciousness provides a subtler framework for thinking about teachers than, say, the concept of socialisation which has been much used in the sociology of teachers but which seems inherently deterministic. In Giddens' terms, the over-socialised conception of teachers referred to above would be represented by a very low degree of discursive consciousness amongst teachers. Similarly, the data on teachers that may be collected by sitting-in on staff-room talk (as in the Hargreaves and Woods researches discussed above) can largely be seen as the "regrooving of established attitudes" which actors achieve by operating at the level of practical consciousness.

The purpose of the programme of interviews with teachers has not been to produce generalisations about teachers so much as to suggest some possible key features of a model of teacher consciousness. However, even the picture provided by some two dozen interviews is rather broader and more complex than that painted in most of the sociology of teachers. Some teachers' thinking did seem firmly rooted in the common sense, 'that's the way it's done', taken-for-grantedness of practical consciousness. But it was also possible to find examples of teachers who exhibited a considerable degree of what seemed to be discursive consciousness.

Of course, it must be emphasised here that the attempt to relate Giddens' theory to the empirical data is fraught with problems. The very subtlety of his analysis defies easy operationalisation for empirical purposes. Is it a strength or a weakness of a sociological theory that it cannot be translated into readily observable categories? Whatever the answer, the problems for the researcher are clear, and they are almost sufficient to send him rushing back to the comfortingly concrete categories of mid-century positivism and to the neat 'tick-the-box' methodologies it encouraged.

An attempt was, however, made to break down the concept of discursive consciousness into a number of component dimensions that might be recognisable in transcript data. Thus it was regarded as evidence of discursive consciousness when respondents (a) tried to be analytic in their discussion rather than simply descriptive or narrative, (b) offered some sort of extended explanation for their observations rather than a normative evaluation, (c) introduced abstract concepts instead of focusing just on particular concrete events, (d) revealed scepticism and a willingness to tolerate ambiguity rather than the dogmatic certainty that tends to accompany normative evaluation.

Such a framework does not of course resolve the problem and the risk remains that the researcher will recognise as discursive consciousness what is merely a case of the respondent sharing the researcher's taken-for-grantedness!   Ideally the research data should be available for every interested party to make their own analysis: a comparison of different analyses would be most revealing (of the analysts' subjectivity, if nothing else).   Such openness would at least facilitate what Popper suggested is the only kind of 'objectivity' achievable in the circumstances: the validation of the academic community.

Some of the more discursively aware teachers interviewed revealed, in remarks about curriculum exams, pedagogy and school regime, a personal sense of contradiction or ambiguity.   Mr. Snaith was a particularly striking example:

   *   T.   Erm.   Er, well, yes in that I feel ineffectual really, I can't seem to do much about it ... you know ...

      I.   Yes, why, why do you feel ineffectual?

      T.   From the point of view of children not, erm, accepting erm ... accepting the values which I don't want to accept or at least I don't want them to accept, you know that they are part of a hierarchy and that there are elites that they can't hope to, to come anywhere near, that they shouldn't erm ... they... perhaps it's the children round here, I don't know, I feel it's the same with any children, they seem to recognise through school the erm, the slot in society which they should occupy, and because of what we do in school, we kind of perpetuate that

* Throughout excerpts from transcript 'T' refers to teacher and 'I' to interviewer.

> feeling, or at least I feel I do;
> there are times when I want to get
> out of teaching because I don't want
> to be part of perpetuating that, I
> want children to have wider horizons
> and think that they can be whatever
> they want to be rather than that they,
> they ... you know ...

Mrs. Johnson was also conscious of a tension between her personal aims and the practices she felt constrained to implement:

> I.   Well, in what way would you want to
>   alter the training?

> T.   Er, ... Oh I'd want it to be more
>   practical er ... a lot ... more
>   practical ... with less emphasis on
>   academic success ... and less emphasis
>   on pouring, er, stuff, into and stuff,
>   well I call it stuff, down children's
>   throats using a funnel.

> T.   This is what it is, half the time ...
>   the children don't want to know and
>   will never use a lot of the stuff that
>   is put into them, and forced into them.

> I.   You think it is training that brings
>   about that sort of attitude to
>   teaching, is it?

> T.   I think it's training ... ah! no I
>   wouldn't say that ... I think it's
>   training that has brought about the
>   present attitude, how we would counter-
>   act that and get rid of it I'm not
>   really sure.   But I think if we erm
>   .... I think people are forced into a
>   groove where they feel they've got to
>   push all this stuff into the children
>   and there's no way they can stop
>   themselves.   And I find myself doing
>   it sometimes myself ... I keep on and
>   on until the poor child gets it right
>   ... and I really wonder why I bother.

You could spend a very long time sitting in school staff-rooms and not hear teachers talking in this way.   These teachers were well aware, more

aware than some ethnographers seem to have been, why
their discursive penetration of schooling would not
be evident in the staff-room setting: Mr. Snaith,
for example, could hardly have put the matter more
clearly than when he said during his critical comments
on the interview method which I invited at the end of
the interview:

> T.   ..... I think one thing I want to say
> straight away to you is that erm, I
> think you're on to a loser as far as
> most people, most teachers that I know,
> and myself included, in that I think
> there's a danger that you could prejudge,
> I think I've said this before really,
> the depth of thought really of er,
> teachers. You know, in other words, ..
> ... there is in a lot of teachers this,
> this conflict, this contra... this sense
> of contradiction between what they really
> feel and what they're doing, yeah, as
> far as the sort of sociological, role-
> playing of a teacher, what the role is
> of a teacher, but, you see, I think
> that unless you actually come into a
> situation as you've done with me and
> raise these issues and these questions
> I think from day to day teachers just
> don't think of a, of a contradiction;
> I mean but, but, by saying that I,
> they're not aware really of, of their,
> an ideal state in themselves; you're
> so wrapped up in the erm, the pragmatic
> issues of teaching, you know and find
> ... to be quite honest it can become
> and does become an exercise in finding
> the most expedient way of dealing with
> situations through the day, so therefore
> you're kind of geared to practical
> decisions rather than theoretical
> decisions.

The school setting is thus shown to be one that
both discourages the exercise of teachers' discursive
consciousness and inhibits its expression when it is
exercised. Why exactly should this be? In Giddens'
analysis of consciousness "routinization" and "continual regrooving of established attitudes" serve to
hold down potential sources of anxiety: "the familiar"
Giddens says, "is reassuring, and the familiar in
social settings is created and recreated through

human agency itself ..." Perhaps we should understand the staff-room as the location of a fairly intensive collective regrooving of established attitudes which is made necessary by the anxieties peculiar to teaching. Such an analysis would embrace Lortie's (1975) discussion of the endemic undertainties of teaching, Macpherson's (1972) vivid portrayal of 'ritual griping' about head or problem pupils; it would embrace Woods' (1979) analysis of the functions of staff-room laughter.

The anxiety that necessitates the continual reassertion of a familiar consensus in the staff-room might most obviously be attributed to the conflict of the classroom confrontation with pupils. However, interviewees said surprisingly little about the classroom as a source of dissatisfactions experienced in their work. It may be, of course, that they were inhibited from talking about classroom difficulties by the fear that these would be interpreted as lack of professional competence. But there is another possibility: that teachers are able to make some sense of such difficulties and may stoically accept them as part of the job. What they talked much more about, perhaps because it is less easy to come to terms with and in the long run, therefore, more corrosive, is the tension felt in relations with fellow teachers and often heads. (2) For some, the classroom, far from being the battlefield, was the haven where they could retreat from the tension experienced in dealings with colleagues and superiors. It is no coincidence, surely, that it was those teachers who exhibited the higher degrees of discursive consciousness who were most aware of tensions amongst school staffs? Their more analytical and reflexive perspective on their colleagues made them aware that beneath the apparent consensus which they jointly contrived in their staff-room interaction lay some serious ideological tensions.

But how do we explain the variation in the degrees of discursive consciousness which my interviewees revealed? The number of respondents does not permit large-scale generalisation, but in the particular cases of the more discursively conscious teachers I interviewed in almost every instance participation in part-time studies for a degree (either B.Ed. or an OU degree which included the School and Society course) seemed to have been a major factor. This was not just my assessment, it was the respondents' too. Thus Mr. Snaith:

T.   Erm, yeah, I think the fact that I erm I did E202 certainly has influenced my way of thinking in that, if anything at all, the course itself was a kind of er awakening thing, it sort of motivated you to think twice about what was happening ... and the erm, I'm thinking of one or two of the more extreme erm teaching ideas erm, of Paulo Freire is it, if that's what his name is, well that for instance, I never considered teaching or education from that perspective, and er having read that, erm 'Pedagogy of the Oppressed', that had, had a really, sort of hit me on the chin in a way, you start to criticise, I started to criticise everything I was doing, all the sort of values I'd accepted of education - not just what I was doing but what happened to me through my schooling, when I was a boy.

.... and Mrs. Johnson:

T.   I feel that ... I found the course at --------- extremely enlightening ... erm, I think probably learnt more from the course at ------ than I did from all four years in my, in college .... because you kind of, it was like throwing back the veil on it all, you know.

.... and Mrs. Williams:

I.   And you're saying that it's specifically this Open University course that's made you have these second thoughts about the curriculum?

T.   Yes, that's what really started me ... it started me thinking first of all about Maths because that's what this OU course is about .... now I started with Maths but since then I've honestly looked round, why do I teach them 'Coffee in Brazil', what use is that? And it's made me far more critical, to such an extent that my scheme for this term in Environmental Studies was again something like 'South America' and I couldn't honestly justify

> to myself the time that I would spend
> researching it, the time the children
> would take making notes and writing
> and colouring in pictures, I couldn't
> justify that waste of time, so I had
> a word with the Head, explained my
> feelings ...

It is significant that in these cases the spur
to a greater discursive penetration of schooling had
come from activity <u>outside</u> their schools.   It is
also significant that the effect of this greater
discursive penetration was almost always limited to
the private reflections of the individuals concerned -
this generally took the form of a greater sense of
dissatisfaction with certain aspects of their work,
in one or two cases to the extent of causing a serious
reappraisal of the desire to remain in teaching.   Only
one teacher had felt able to talk in any detail to
staff-room colleagues about the thoughts her degree
studies had provoked.   Otherwise the schools in which
these teachers worked, and the contrived consensus of
their staff-rooms, remained undisturbed.

Moreover, it seemed that the raising of the
level of these teachers' level of discursive consciousness might be a temporary phenomenon.   Mr. Snaith
describing the effect of his OU School and Society
course put it most clearly:

> I.   You say that Freire's book had great
> impact on you when you read it, I
> mean do you think, erm ... how long is
> it since you finished the course, just
> over two years ...?

> T.   Yeah.   That's right.

> I.   .... I mean do you think there is still
> some influence on your thinking about
> teaching?

> T.   (Pause)   If I'm honest I think less and
> less.   You know the longer the time
> goes from reading that the less I recall
> of it, being honest, and the less sort
> of influence it does have on me, partly
> because, erm, ... I'm trying to think
> of a metaphor to illustrate it ...
> you know, it's rather like rowing up a
> river on a raft or something and somebody
> from the bank throws something at you

and knocks you off course for a
while, but you come back on to the
course and you've only got a memory
of what happened, the incident that
threw you off course; you still go
down that river, you know ... and
that's how I feel about it, I feel
that's the most accurate metaphor I
can think of.

It seems that, having completed his degree
studies, Mr. Snaith's thinking was gradually re-
routinized with the encouragement and aid of school
and staff-room.

Perhaps, therefore, in thinking about teachers'
consciousness, we should place the practical and
discursive modes of consciousness in a hierarchical
relationship one to another. We might think of
practical consciousness as representing the upper of
the two strata; it is the stratum wherein the teacher
finds familiar recipes for coping in the classroom;
the recipes include familiar categorisations of
knowledge, of pupils' ability and behaviour; it is
also where the teacher finds those sentiments and
kinds of humour which are the currency of staffroom
solidarity and with which may be bought a sense of
security and the esteem of colleagues. It seems
likely also that it is at this upper stratum of
practical consciousness that teachers experience most
of the intrinsic and extrinsic rewards of teaching
that sustain them from day to day, year to year. In
relation to intrinsic rewards teachers in effect ask
themselves: "Do I enjoy teaching?"; in relation to
extrinsic rewards they ask "Is it worth it?" Provided
a teacher can answer at least one of these questions
with a reasonably unequivocal "yes", it seems that
there is little need or encouragement for a teacher
to ask any more searching questions.

It is for this reason that the discursive mode
of consciousness seems to represent a lower stratum
and one to which some teachers appear rarely to have
recourse. It is at this discursive level that
teachers might ask themselves the question "Do I
believe in what I'm doing as a teacher?" It is at
this level that teachers might compare the practices
in which they are daily constrained to indulge with
their personal belief-systems; it is at this discursive level of consciousness that teachers might
personally experience the contradictions or ambiguities of their structural location. But schools
and staff-rooms are the setting for a great deal of

routinization so that teachers are actively (though not necessarily purposefully) discouraged from exercising the discursive mode of consciousness. Teachers can, as some of my examples suggest, display considerable discursive consciousness of their work but it seems that this is most likely to be a response to particular stimuli such as taking degree courses in education outside school.

By viewing teachers in terms of this hierarchy of consciousness we may avoid the temptation to which the sociology of education has tended to succumb of reducing teachers to mere "cultural dopes", passive products of their socialisation, unreflective and incapable of comprehending their actions other than in purely pragmatic terms. Instead we are able to see them operating mostly in the context of that practical consciousness (within which all of us conceive most of our social behaviour) as a response to the day-to-day anxieties endemic to teaching. These anxieties in part derive from the structures of schooling which are able to be reproduced from year to year <u>because</u> teachers operate in the practical mode of consciousness. Thus teachers are able to sustain <u>themselves</u> by their operation at the practical level of consciousness, while the system of education is able to sustain <u>itself</u> because teachers think in that way. Or, to repeat Giddens' tenet: "social structures are both constituted by human agency, and yet at the same time are the very medium of this constitution".

Some of the teachers I interviewed had asked themselves the question "Do I believe in what I'm doing as a teacher?" and answered it "not very much". However, they had all persisted in their occupation and not, in their own estimation, just because there were no suitable alternatives. Rather their continued commitment reflected the fact that the doubts and frustrations they experienced at the discursive level of consciousness were sufficiently compensated by rewards, intrinsic and extrinsic, experienced at the practical level of consciousness. Of all the teachers interviewed, Mr. Snaith appeared to have had his level of discursive consciousness raised most significantly and as a result his commitment to teaching has been severely tested - there have been times when he has wanted to leave teaching. Here he explains some of his frustrations and the means by which he daily accommodates them:

     T.   ... this is part of the thing that
             I don't like about the system, perhaps

it's capitalism, in that it seems
to give erm, children, education and
the children, seems to give them just
enough reward to keep them content ...
to make sure that they don't have too
high horizons shall we say, and they
don't come back too far and look at
what's happening to them from a
distance, er, that kind of thing, erm
and I feel it's happening to me and
has happened to me, I've had rewards
from teaching, financial rewards that
is, I've had promotion and from the
day to day thing I mean a lot of it
is fun, you know perhaps I've over-
criticised it and I sound over-
frustrated - I'm not, you know, some
days it's great, a lot of aspects I
enjoy about it.

I.   On those days when it's great, what is
it that makes it great?

T.   I don't know, erm, all sorts of things
....

T.   .... but all sorts of little things,
you know, sharing a joke with children
or with other members of staff you know,
erm, I'm a games teacher as well, we've
won football tournaments before, erm
that's, that's good.

I.   Mmm, mm.   Do you think that if there
were more of those sort of little
rewards that erm, you might be less
conscious of the other kinds of
frustrations and dissatisfactions that
you feel?

T.   Mmm.   Well, erm, yes, erm, the, the
little rewards tend to deflect you from
being aware of the larger, more ... erm
... the inertia of the whole thing.

Several teachers described in similar terms the
way in which the little minute-to-minute, day-to-day
rewards of teaching, intrinsic or extrinsic, were
able to deflect them from intellectual worries about
what they did as teachers.

> T. No, it's the sort of person who's
>   going to be a teacher who's got to pay
>   attention to detail who does tend to
>   become petty minded I think ....
>   Erm, I don't know, I think one tries
>   to avoid thinking in these terms in
>   everyday teaching; that's part of the
>   problem, you learn to live with the
>   problems that exist, if you ignore them
>   hard enough they go away.

In other words, rewards at the level of practical consciousness serve to conceal, from teachers themselves as well as from those who observe them, the contradictions of teaching which would be experienced at the discursive level of consciousness.

But what happens if, as described above, the intrinsic rewards of teaching become much more scarce? Teachers, surely, will find it less easy in the next twenty years to coast along buoyed up by such rewards? Lacking job-satisfaction at the level of practical consciousness will they not be more inclined to ask themselves the discursive question "Do I believe in what I am doing?" If so, the effect is a restructuring of teachers' consciousness so that among teachers generally there will be a greater discursive penetration of schooling and its functions. This suggests the prospect of rather more teachers comprehending their "ambiguous position" in Bernstein's terms, or their "structural location" in Sharp and Green's.

The penetration described here would seem to threaten the continuity of the social control, reproductive and legitimating functions of schooling. Where teachers' dissatisfaction at the level of practical consciousness leads to a discovery of dissatisfactions at the discursive level, too, there would appear to be a serious challenge to the routinization of schooling. The consequence is an enhanced potentiality for change, though it is difficult to predict to what degree this discursive consciousness might be shared amongst teachers and might therefore lead to collective action intended to change their predicament. The latter is the kind of analytical problem staffroom ethnography may be best able to address.

The prognosis presented here will surprise many; it certainly opposes the intuitive consensus (frequently voiced over sociologists' coffee cups but rarely articulated in detail) which assumes that increased anxiety and conflict in a society, system

or institution produce a regression to the espousal
of 'safe' consensual attitudes and assumptions, and
an inhibition of innovation.

The contemporary observation that is often
employed to support this familiar hypothesis is that
relative economic decline and growing unemployment
have been accompanied by a greater support for conservative politics and moderation in collective
bargaining. The problem with such historical evidence is that it is usually selective and can be
countered with alternative selections.

The case of unemployment may be answered with a
reminder that unemployment is still the lived experience of only a small minority and that it is only
such experience, not the mere thought of it, that
could be expected to have a radical impact on attitudes. On this analysis unemployment is not -
experientially - a 'problem' for the great majority
of people, but the <u>fear</u> of unemployment is sufficient
to encourage many to adopt strategies in competition
with other employees, in relations with employers,
and even in casting votes, which focus on safety and
avoiding risk: "Don't rock the boat when it's in
danger of sinking anyway - especially if <u>you</u> are
standing on a particularly slippery part of the deck!"

We may understand the present situation of
teachers in similar terms. Few teachers experience
redeployment or unemployment personally but the many
make the entirely rational calculation that when
your post is not entirely secure and the promotion
market is exceptionally competitive it is not the
right time to risk offending the head teacher or
losing the esteem of colleagues by challenging the
staff-room or staff meeting consensus.

Again we see the importance of not taking the
<u>apparent</u> consensus some researchers find prevailing
amongst school staffs as indicative of the consciousness of individual teachers. There are particular
reasons at the present time why staff-rooms should
exhibit a good deal of what Lacey (1977) has called
"strategic compliance".

But what of the future if the twin crises in
legitimation and teacher motivation become the
common experience of a <u>majority</u> of teachers? Such
a situation is simply not analogous to that of
society at large in which only a small minority
directly experience the rigours of unemployment.
What is postulated here is a future situation in
which the common-sense recipes teachers use cease
to work so well and increasing classroom conflict
accompanied by a loss of the intrinsic and extrinsic

rewards of teaching is the <u>common</u> <u>lived</u> experience of teachers. Such a situation would appear to fit Giddens' description of one of the circumstances in which 'deroutinization', and consequently change, may take place:

> Any influences which corrode or place in question traditional practices carry with them the likelihood of accelerating change. (P. 220)

In pre-industrial societies traditional practices found to be ineffective may simply be replaced by other traditional taken-for-granted practices. However, in a society like ours in which, Giddens suggests, there is a "disavowal of tradition as such as a form of legitimation", and where there are organisational structures attuned to "conscious social innovation", the more likely response is a more discursive questioning of the taken-for-granted.

There are important implications here for those who work with teachers, and especially for those who teach practising teachers. Many of us involved in in-service teacher education are inclined to define our goals in terms of "consciousness-raising". In the language of this paper what is meant is the encouragement of a greater exercise of the discursive, rather than the practical, mode of consciousness. Those who attempt this task will be familiar with the reluctance of many teachers to distance them-selves from the consensual cook-book knowledge of staff-rooms and to adopt more reflexive and critical stances in relation to classroom practices. Faced with this frustration many of us have resorted to that 'teacher-deficit' model of schooling which sees teachers as "cultural dopes", though we have disagreed amongst ourselves as to the extent to which this potent socialisation is achieved before, during or after the experience of training and of teaching itself.

This paper proposes a rather different analysis in which teachers' adherence to the assumptions and prescriptions of their shared cook-book knowledge, sustained through practical rather than discursive consciousness, arises from a want and need for the confirmation of that knowledge necessary to allay anxiety and secure craft pride. Practising teachers view in-service courses from the standpoint of that need: hence the recent remark from a teacher to a colleague after a discussion in which the latter thought he had coolly and tactfully analysed some of the questionable educational consequences of conventional patterns of classroom communication: "You really despise teachers, don't you?"

Teachers' need for confirmation of their routinized recipes for survival is a need, in Giddens' terms (1979, p. 128), for a "continual regrooving of established attitudes" which is "reassuring" and through which "potentially corrosive effects of anxiety are contained". The need arises, then, from the daily lived experience of schooling.

However, if the prognosis of this paper is correct, a growing inability to come to terms with the daily lived experience at the level of practical consciousness will lead in future to a more discursive consciousness in teachers of the contradictions inherent in contemporary schooling and of the tensions that exist between educational ideologies, practice in schools and social structures. Teachers may yet, therefore, provide a receptive audience for the efforts of the raisers of consciousness.

Of course, any serious challenge to the routinization of schooling which might result from higher levels of discursive consciousness amongst teachers would bring schools and teachers into more open conflict with other elements in the social structure. The discursive consciousness of politicians, ratepayers, parents, pupils and employers in relation to schooling may also be susceptible to stimulation! Already, attempts by government to win greater control over curriculum, examinations, the content of teacher training and the recruitment and dismissal of teachers may be seen as early shots in such a conflict.

NOTES

(1) There may be some consolation for teachers in the notion that able pupils who feel assured of school success and subsequent employment will, in the climate of increased competition, be even more earnest in their conformity with teachers' expectations which may, in these pupils' eyes, have an enhanced legitimacy.

(2) Moreover, whereas teachers generally have the power to coerce pupils who challenge their ideas, no such simple solution is available to them in the face of challenges from their equals in the staffroom.

REFERENCES

Barton, L. and Meighan, R. (Eds.) (1978) <u>Sociological</u>
    <u>Interpretations of Schooling and Classrooms: A</u>
    <u>Reappraisal</u>, Nafferton, Driffield
Becker, H. (1964) 'Personal Change in Adult Life',
    <u>Sociometry</u>, <u>27</u>, 1
Bernstein, B. (1977) <u>Class, Codes and Control</u>,
    <u>Vol. III</u>, Routledge and Kegan Paul, London
Giddens, A. (1976) <u>New Rules of Sociological Method</u>,
    Hutchinson, London
Giddens, A. (1979) <u>Central Problems in Social Theory</u>,
    Macmillan, London
Habermas, J. (1976) <u>Legitimation Crisis</u>, Heinemann,
    London
Hargreaves, A. (1981) 'Contrastive Rhetoric and
    Extremist Talk', in L. Barton and S. Walker
    (Eds.) <u>Schools, Teachers and Teaching</u>, Falmer,
    Lewes
Hargreaves, D. (1978) 'What Teaching Does to Teachers'
    <u>New Society</u>, 9 March 1978
Hoyle, E. (1969) <u>The Role of the Teacher</u>, Routledge
    and Kegan Paul, London
Lacey, C. (1977) <u>The Socialisation of Teachers</u>,
    Methuen, London
Lortie, D. (1975) <u>Schoolteacher: A Sociological Study</u>,
    Chicago University Press
Macpherson, G. (1972) <u>Small Town Teacher</u>, Harvard
    University Press
Mardle, G. and Walker, M. (1980) 'Strategies and
    Structure: Some Critical Notes on Teacher
    Socialization' in P. Woods (Ed.) <u>Teacher</u>
    <u>Strategies</u>, Croom Helm, London
Popper, K.R. (1945) <u>The Open Society and its Enemies</u>
    <u>(Vol. II)</u>, Routledge and Kegan Paul, London
Roth, J.A. (1963) <u>Timetables</u>, Bobbs Merrill,
    Indianapolis
Schutz, A. (1972) <u>The Phenomenology of the Social</u>
    <u>World</u>, Heinemann, London
Sharp, R. and Green, A. (1975) <u>Education and Social</u>
    <u>Control</u>, Routledge and Kegan Paul, London
Silverman, D. (1973) 'Interview Talk: Bringing Off
    a Research Instrument', <u>Sociology</u>, <u>7</u>, 1
Waller, W. (1932) <u>The Sociology of Teaching</u>, Wiley,
    New York
Woods, P. (1979) <u>The Divided School</u>, Routledge and
    Kegan Paul, London

MULTICULTURAL EDUCATION: EMANCIPATION OR CONTAINMENT?

Barry Troyna

> The employability of a school leaver is
> determined largely by the academic quali-
> fications which he or she has obtained at
> school and since West Indians ... are
> underachieving at school they will clearly
> be at a disadvantage in the jobs market.
>
> (Committee of Inquiry into the Education of
> Children from Ethnic Minority Groups
> (Rampton Committee), 1981, p. 52)

> Education.   What good is that to the
> black man?   Qualifications? Them mean
> nothing so long as you're black.
>
> (Black youth quoted in Cashmore and Troyna,
> 1982, p. 16)

'THE SEEDS OF RACIAL DISCORD'

"... there is no theory of multicultural education,
in the sense of an articulated body of theoretically
valid knowledge with scientific characteristics and
predictive capacity" wrote James Lynch in the intro-
ductory chapter to his book, Teaching in the Multicultural School (1981, p. 5).   Few would dissent from
this view.   Yet, despite the inchoate nature of
multicultural education, policies and practices which
are subsumed under this generic concept continue to
proliferate in the UK, and elsewhere.   Even as the
economic crisis develops and its impact on the education system becomes progressively more severe,
multicultural education continues to flourish.   Its
anomalous position in this respect has been demonstrated most vividly during the past eighteen months
when an increasing number of Local Education Author-

ities (LEAs) have deployed a relatively large amount
of their limited resources to facilitate the implementation of multicultural education initiatives.
In June 1982, for example, the Education Officer of
the Inner London Education Authority (ILEA) requested
around £60,000 from his Schools Sub-Committee to
support his latest proposals for multicultural education reforms.   Other LEAs, up and down the country,
have embarked on similar, though less ambitious programmes of expansion, all of which have entailed the
allocation of a not inconsiderable amount of funding:
the setting up of multicultural education units;   the
appointment of specialist advisers and inspectors;
expansion of English as a Second Language (ESL) and
mother tongue teaching provision;   establishment of
initial and in-service teacher training courses, and
so on.   In short, multicultural education has become
the new orthodoxy in the 'progressive' education
movement;   as one teacher in a Midlands school put it:
"We've had mixed ability; we've gone community, and
now its bloody multiculturalism" (quoted in Birley
High School, 1980).
    It is no coincidence that this flurry of activity
has taken place in the period since the civil disturbances rocked virtually every major English city in
the summer of 1981.   Until then, only ILEA and
Manchester Education Committee had formally declared
their commitment to multicultural education in
Authority-wide policy statements.   By late 1982,
another sixteen LEAs, in a variety of circumstances,
had followed this path;   along with the ILEA and
Manchester LEA they are now publicly affirming the
notion of multicultural education and setting up a
coherent and unified package of innovations along
this line.   Broadly speaking, this educational
response parallels what took place in the USA after
the 1965 'race riots'.   Then, as James Banks informs
us, a number of reformist measures were introduced
which were designed to counteract the 'white bias' in
the education system (particularly in curriculum
content) and, consequentially, to improve the academic
performance of minority group students (1981, p.20).
These strategies have been characterised elsewhere
as the 'benevolent multiculturalism' approach and
are predicated on two of the assumptions which Brian
Bullivant has identified as "part of the rhetoric
and conventional wisdom of multicultural education";
namely:

> (a)   that by learning about his (sic) cultural
>   and ethnic 'roots' an ethnic child will

improve his educational achievement;

(b)   the closely related claim that learning
        about his culture, its traditions and
        so on will improve equality of opportun-
        ity.   (Bullivant, 1981, p. 236)

Similarly, in the UK, concern about the relatively poor performance of black youth (i.e. those of
Afro-Caribbean origin) and the almost uncritical
acceptance of these two ground assumptions have provided the rationale for educational initiatives which
in their broadest sense, claim to take account of the
"racially-mixed and culturally-varied" nature of
British society (Cohen and Manion, 1983, p. 11). But,
it is important to point out that concern about poor
performance is not a recent phenomenon; it has a
history which can be traced back to the 1960s. Yet,
despite repeated demands for the reappraisal of
curricular, organisational and pedagogic procedures
along multicultural lines and the decision by a growing number of black parents and community groups to
establish their own 'supplementary schools' to provide their children with the skills presumed to be
lacking in formal educational institutions, the DES,
LEAs and their individual schools stubbornly resisted
any changes, at least until very recently. As
Sally Tomlinson has noted, a number of interested
parties had submitted a total of 228 recommendations
for clear, unequivocal policies on this issue between
1973 - 1981, most of which fell on deaf ears: "Those
working in multi-ethnic education", wrote Tomlinson,
"could be forgiven for feeling, to paraphrase
Churchill, that never in the field of policy-making
have so many recommendations been made to so little
effect" (1981, p. 150). With one or two notable
exceptions, then, the UK education system retained
its unswerving commitment to assimilationist approaches to the education of minority group pupils - an
approach which demanded the suppression of ethnic
and cultural differences in the classroom, characteristics assumed to have the potential to inhibit
assimilation (Troyna, 1982).

Why, then, did it take the outbreak of unrest in
the summer of 1981 to precipitate a reappraisal of
the educational response to this issue? Two closely
related factors may be offered. First, although the
relatively low academic performance of black pupils
had been identified as far back as the late 1960s,
educational researchers tended to 'explain' the
'phenomenon' in relation to theories of cultural

deprivation and disadvantage or, in the case of
Alan Little's research in the ILEA, in terms of the
immigrant child's unfamiliarity with the UK education
system (Little, 1975). In other words, factors
which had been habitually invoked to explain working
class failure in schools were now readily applied to
black pupils: language deficiency, inadequate pre-
school socialisation, single parent families, lack
of parental interest in education, and so on. Against
this background, questions about the legitimacy of the
state education system's ideological and policy response to the presence of black pupils were routinely
avoided. Instead, the claim that the "successful
assimilation of immigrant children" was dependent on
"a realistic understanding of the adjustments they
have to make" was tacitly agreed by most concerned
with this issue. (DES, 1965, emphasis added.)
By the late 1970s, however, it became clear
that this diagnosis was entirely erroneous. For one
thing, the optimistic prognosis that underachievement
would diminish with the passage of time could no
longer be sustained. Research carried out by
Christine Mabey showed that the relatively poor performance of black youth deteriorated, rather than
improved, as they progressed through their school
career (1981). 'Underachievement' was a persistent
rather than ephemeral trend; as Monica Taylor concluded from her review of studies in this area:
"The research shows a strong trend to underachievement
of pupils of West Indian origin on the main indicators
of academic performance" (1981, p. 216). At the
same time, the development of black supplementary
schools in the UK symbolised the black communities'
growing disillusionment with the failure of the state
system to reappraise its routine practices in relation
to the changing ethnic composition of its pupil population. As Nel Clark, founder of the Dachwyng
Saturday School in London emphasised: "It is an
important step to realise that the supplementary
school exists to help children not because they failed
to achieve through the system, but because the system
is racialist, and has failed them" (1982, p. 126).
Such considerations had simply not been scrutinized
systematically by educationists and researchers before;
instead, they had preferred to construct their explanations of underachievement in well-established paradigms and had adduced reasons for failure which complemented rather than dissented from existing policy
and practice.
A reappraisal of the relationship between schooling and black youth had also been impelled by more

overt and far-reaching political considerations. Put simply, the emergence of a 'moral panic' over black youth in the 1960s and 1970s was, in some senses, seen to be closely related to the failure of young blacks to secure academic qualifications and hence, a job (Fisher and Joshua, 1982; Hall et al., 1978).

As early as 1969, the Select Committee on Race Relations and Immigration in its report, The Problem of Coloured School Leavers, had typified the youths as a "social time bomb" which could be detonated by the onset of prolonged and widespread unemployment. The Committee asserted that these youths "may be less patient in surmounting the difficulties that confront them than their parents have been" and warned that in the continued absence of "equal treatment", "the seeds of racial discord may be sewn" (1969, pp. 6-7). In this scenario, the role of education was heavily stressed: in 1974, for instance, the Community Relations Commission pointed out in its report to the Home Secretary that the educational system was not providing a substantial number of "young black people with qualifications adequate to meet either their own expectations or the actual demands of adult life" (1974, p. 27) and that, "many schools have not adjusted to the needs of West Indian pupils, but were carrying on as if nothing had changed from when all pupils were indigenous and white" (p. 7). In all, the CRC highlighted the vital role assumed by education in contributing to the high incidence of unemployment, homelessness and disaffection among black youth. Nor was the CRC a lone voice; six years later, in its submission to the government report, Racial Disadvantage, the DES argued substantially the same point, suggesting that ameliorative action in the form of curriculum amendment was necessary to avert an impending crisis: "A curriculum which draws positive advantage from different cultures may help to prevent the alienation from school and society in general of some minority group pupils ..." (1980, p. 240). (1)

What happened at Brixton, Toxteth, Moss Side and elsewhere in 1981 demonstrated, in the most vivid manner, the pertinence and veracity of these earlier warnings: 'the seeds of racial discord' had come to bloom. Few informed commentators agreed with Mrs. Thatcher's assertion that the disturbances had "nothing whatever to do with the dole queues" and while the specific precipitating factor(s) may have varied from place to place, Lord Scarman's claim that the problem which black youth habitually encounter in the search for work provided "a major factor in the complex conditions which lies at the root of the disorders" seemed an accurate appraisal (1981, p. 107).

Against this background, demands for action gained new urgency and a fresh vitality. As we have seen, report after report in the late 1960s and throughout the '70s had pointed to the strong trend towards black educational 'underachievement'. Now, if we accept the proposition that failure at school contributes directly to the disproportionately high levels of un-employment amongst black youth, which in turn contri-buted to the disturbances, then the target site for state intervention must clearly be the school. The current willingness of educationists, both at the policy-making level and on the chalk face to eschew traditional assimilation approaches in favour of a cultural pluralist model testifies to the extent to which this proposition has been accepted. Put simply, the fear has been another 'explosion', the solution: enhance the academic performance of black youth, the means: multicultural education.

Put this way, it is clear, as Andy Green has argued, that "multiculturalism lies in the long tradition of social democratic education" (1982, p.24). In the same way as, say, compensatory education ini-tiatives in the 1960s were designed to repair the meritocratic credibility of schools by providing equality of opportunity to pupils of working class origin, so multicultural education, by using similar rhetoric and symbolic political language, aims to ensure that black youth are not short-changed in their schooling. Both rest on the same premise: the liberal-democratic notion of schooling as a means of occupational and social mobility. As the Home Affairs Committee pointed out in their report on Racial Disadvantage:

> Disadvantage in education and employment
> are the two most important facets of
> racial disadvantage. They are closely
> connected. Without a decent education
> and the qualifications which such edu-
> cation alone can provide, a school leaver
> is unlikely to find the sort of job to
> which he aspires, or indeed any job.

> (1981, para. 126)

In a period when jobs are becoming increasingly scarce, the credential bias of the labour market seems to have been thrown into even sharper relief, and educational qualifications are conventionally ascribed with a determinative role in facilitating access to first and subsequent jobs: "the lack of credentials, or the possession of a devalued credential tends to bar an individual from any hope of social mobility or promotion" insisted no less an authority than the OECD (1977, p. 79). It is this commonsense view of the relationship between success in education and employment spheres which provides the ideological framework within which multicultural education is espoused. Not only is it conceived as "the catalyst that would reverse the 'underachievement' of black school children", as Hazel Carby puts it (1982, p. 197), it is endowed with far greater emancipatory powers. As the Rampton Committee asserted:

> The evidence summarised in this section shows that many West Indians are underachieving in relation to their peers, not least in obtaining the examination qualifications needed to give them equality of opportunity in the employment market (1981, p. 10, emphasis added)

And James Rushton's appraisal of multicultural education concurred with this:

> ... the curriculum in the multicultural school should encourage each pupil to succeed wherever he or she can and strive for competence in what he or she tries. Cultural taboos should be lessened by mutual experience and understandings. The curriculum in the multicultural school should allow these experiences to happen. If it does, it need have no fear about the future careers of its pupils (1981, p. 169, emphasis added)

On the face of it, multicultural education would seem to have much to offer. After all, the available evidence points to black educational 'underachievement' (Mortimore and Mortimore, 1981; Taylor, 1980; Tomlinson, 1980); and even if we accept that many of the relevant studies are flawed, both conceptually and methodologically - the overwhelming emphasis on differences (or otherwise) along ethnic lines, for example, has led to a recurrent neglect of the profound influence of social class on educational performance - at least two researchers have ensured that their ethnically mixed sample of students were matched for social class. The result? The performance of black

pupils in public examinations was lower than for all
other groups (Craft and Craft, 1981).   On the other
side of the coin, we find that while the chances of
any school leaver finding a job are uniformly bleak -
irrespective of background - the chances for young
black people are even more remote.   In some parts of
London and Birmingham, for example, black youth unemployment constitutes around fifty per cent and above
of those registered unemployed at the local careers
office (see Cashmore and Troyna 1983, chapter 4 for
details).   In addition, the rate of increase of black
youth unemployment is significantly higher than for
white youths, according to the data presented by the
Runnymede Trust (1981, p. 3).
      The credibility of the multicultural philosophy
hinges on the view that these two sets of data are
directly and causally related;   that is, black underachievement in the labour market is attributable primarily to their lack of success in the academic paper
chase.   From this perspective, the Rampton Committee's
claim that enhancing blacks' school performance will
ensure that they enjoy "equality of opportunity in the
employment market" seems entirely feasible and an
acceptable rationale for intervention.   In short, it
lends empirical weight to the conception of multicultural education as an emancipatory tool for black
youth.   Nevertheless, in order to sustain this
admittedly attractive argument it is necessary to
scrutinize the commonsense notions on which it is
based.   Firstly, the assumption that school leavers
obtain jobs which are commensurate with their levels
of ability, as measured by their educational qualifications.   And secondly, that school leavers of equal
merit have equal chances of success in their search
for a job, irrespective of ascribed characteristics
such as ethnic background.   As we shall see, although
there is a relationship between success in education
and employment spheres the picture is more complex
than the Rampton Committee and others would have us
believe. (2)

'A SERIES OF DISPARATE LINKS'

Since the onset of the present recession in the mid-
1970s, young people have been especially vulnerable
to unemployment;   the causes of this disproportionate
rise in youth unemployment need not detain us here
(but see Makeham, 1980).   What is more important in
this context is that worsening unemployment has led
to an increasingly widespread acceptance of the
'implicit contract or tightening bond' thesis.   This

thesis holds that the possession of educational credentials affords some protection against unemployment,
that a good education leads to a good job and the
better the education, the better the job.   The corollary, then, according to the OECD is that "the position of those who are left aside in the scramble for
some sort of credential or label is becoming desperate"(1977, p. 79).

Broadly speaking, the possession of educational
qualifications may be said to represent formally the
competence and ability of the holder to perform
successfully a given task, or a series of tasks. In
short, it may be presumed to relate to the concept
of skill: as Madan Sarup suggests, "'schooling' is
often connected with 'training', the performance of
certain 'technical' functions" (1982, p. 26).

In 1966, Michael Carter was claiming that many
school leavers were involved in jobs that "mentally
retarded children could do adequately and perhaps
better" (1966, p. 167).   The tightening bond theory
would suggest that this is no longer the case;   the
fact of the matter is, however, that there remains
a wide range of jobs for the school leaver which
require, at best, a minimum level of skill and which,
therefore, are only tenuously related to educational
qualifications.   For instance, in their study of
male manual workers in Peterborough in the 1970s,
Bob Blackburn and Michael Mann found that 95 per cent
of their sample had no formal educational qualifications and that almost all workers use less skill at
work than they do, for example, "in driving a car".
They estimated.that: "in Peterborough about 85 per
cent of the workers possess the necessary ability to
undertake 95 per cent of these jobs and though these
figures might vary in other 'unqualified' labour
markets we do not consider them atypical" (1979, p.12).
Indeed they are not;   as recently as 1976-7 sixty per
cent of school leavers in England and Wales entered
the labour market with either very low academic
qualifications or none at all, according to the Department of Employment (quoted in Hawkins, 1979, p.49).

A number of recent studies have also indicated
a lack of uniformity in the way employers respond to
formal educational qualifications in their selection
processes.   Eileen Reid's interviews with recruitment
officers in 300 employing establishments in England
and Wales, for instance, showed that fewer than half
had said that "they specified formal qualifications
and that in all types of jobs except one ... over
half of the respondents who reported that educational
qualifications were specified said that they would

nevertheless consider applicants without the specified qualifications" (1980, p. 54). Reid's research, along with a recently completed report on the same issue in Scotland (Hunt and Small, 1981) corroborates David Ashton and Malcolm Maguire's argument that: "Rather than considering the relationship between education and the labour market as a single tightening bond ... it may be better to conceptualize it as a series of disparate links" (1981, p. 5). It would seem, therefore, that educational credentials do not constitute the <u>sine qua non</u> of entry into the labour market; what is more, the experience of black school leavers in their search for work undercuts the tightening bond thesis even further.

In general, the black unemployed, of all ages and both sexes, tend to be better qualified than their white counterparts and this is a pattern which seems to hold true for young black school leavers. Ken Roberts and his colleagues found that amongst the non-registered young unemployed in different parts of the country, black youth tended not only to be better qualified but were also more likely to enrol in further education (1981). And a recent study carried out by Muhammad Anwar confirmed at least part of this picture by showing that 46 per cent of white unemployed youth had no formal education qualifications, compared to 33 per cent of their black equivalents (1982, p. 17). On this evidence alone, then, it seems clear that reformist strategies designed to improve the academic performance of black youth will do little to remove the obstacles which confront them in their search for work. Indeed, such measures could exacerbate their problems if Malcolm Cross' interpretation of recent data is to be taken seriously, he suggests that:

> ... the <u>relatively</u> poor position of the young black unemployed is not confined to the lower echelons of the employment structure. In fact, if the <u>National Dwelling and Housing Survey</u> data are any guide, the opposite is true: the ratio of non-white to white unemployment is highest for young people with non-manual and skilled manual occupations even though the unskilled, from whatever race, suffer higher levels of unemployment (1982, pp. 47-8). (3)

It would seem, then, that the educational experiences of young people are only partially related to either the likelihood, or level of entry into the labour market. For black school leavers this is particularly the case, and the discrepancy between their experiences in the frantic search for a job and those of their white counterparts cannot be attributed in any significant measure to their performance in the academic paper chase. How could it be when, in many cases, those black youth who are currently without a job have overtaken white youth in this chase. Clearly, we have to look elsewhere to account for their high presence amongst the ranks of the unemployed.

'BUSINESS AS USUAL'

I have argued elsewhere that racism and discrimination against people perceived of as racial minorities constitute one of the most divisive social facts in the UK (Troyna, 1983). Despite the introduction of anti-discrimination legislation in 1965, 1968 and 1976, racialist practices operating in the selection and recruitment of labour continue to play a powerful part in the determination of the life chances of black and brown school leavers. Now, it is likely that both this observation and the evidence I shall adduce to substantiate it are already familiar. Even so, I regard their inclusion as more than perfunctory. In the first place, they should be sufficient to undermine what are frequently referred to as 'pathological' conceptions of black youth: the noxious theory that the differentially worse experiences of black youth in the transition from school to work derive either from the fact that their aspirations are unrealistic in terms of their qualifications and that they seek jobs which they have little hope of obtaining or, that they have no wish to participate in conventional employment spheres. (4)
    More specifically, the irrefutable evidence of racialism in this context will help to sustain my argument about the limited role which multicultural education can play in alleviating inequalities. In other words, to assume, as multicultural proponents often do, that the determinants of inequality are within the terrain of education is misconceived.
    Soon after the introduction of the first in a series of protective laws to combat racial discrimination, W.W. Daniel in his summary report of the PEP survey into this practice wrote that: "In employment, housing and the provision of services there is racial discrimination varying in extent from the massive to the substantial" (1968, p. 209). Since then, the 1968 and 1976 Race Relations Acts have successively extended the range of anti-discrimination laws although

their success in eliminating racialism in the labour
market remains limited. For instance, recent studies
carried out by the Commission for Racial Equality in
South London and Nottingham demonstrated unequivocally
the extent to which employers discriminate against
black and brown school leavers in their selection
process (CRE, 1978; Hubbuck and Carter, 1980). In
the South London study, the CRE found that unemployment among black school leavers was three times
higher than among white school leavers, a discrepancy
which could not be accounted for either by difference
in qualifications or differential attempts to find a
job. Clearly, the refusal to offer black candidates
an interview, purely and simply because of skin colour,
constitutes the most obvious form of direct, self-
conscious discrimination. Slightly more subtle,
though certainly no less invidious, is employers'
predilection towards stereotyping based on the ascribed characteristics of interviewees; "this represents
one of the most intractable problems", write
Ed Rhodes and Peter Braham, "because the influence of
ascriptive criteria is often hard to identify" (1981,
p. 376). These factors, alone, are often sufficient
to disadvantage black candidates in the selection
process but it is also important to point out that
racism, embedded in the group network at the workplace,
is also often invoked by employers as a rationale for
the non-appointment of blacks, and the CRE's investigation into the recruitment practices of British Ley-
land in Birmingham revealed the persistent use of this
rationale for discrimination (1982).
The significance of these practices is highlighted
when considered alongside my earlier contention that
in their selection procedures, employers often subordinate the importance of formal educational qualifications to more subjective, non-academic criteria such
as suitability and reliability. As Richard Jenkins
concluded from his study of recruitment procedures in
the West Midlands: "In as much as the procedure is
completely - or nearly completely - informal, it
allows discrimination room to operate with a certain
amount of impunity" (1982, p. 18).
The 1976 Race Relations Act differentiated
between direct and indirect discrimination; the
former refers to those self-conscious and volitional
practices such as those just described. In contrast,
indirect discrimination refers to treatment of racial
groups which in a formal sense may be equal but which
is discriminatory in effect. In other words, indirect
discrimination can occur without any direct references
to attitudinal factors or individual prejudices. In

the UK, such practices and procedures may be said to constitute institutional racism, as defined by A.K. Spears:

> Since it is institutionalised, all cases of racism do not result from the wilful acts of ill-intentioned individuals. It is in its most profound instances, covert, resulting from acts of indifference, omission and refusal to challenge the status quo. Thus, an individual need never have wilfully done anything that directly and clearly oppresses minorities, she/he need only have gone about business as usual without attempting to change procedures and structures in order to be an accomplice in racism, since business as usual has been systematized to maintain blacks and other minorities in an oppressed state (1978, pp 129-30).

In short, by conforming to the operating norms of the organisation and by going about their business as usual, employers allow the institution to perpetuate inequality. In this context, the tendency for employers to rely on informal channels, or 'word of mouth' networks of recruitment represents one of the main ways in which the potential of blacks to enter the labour market is systematically inhibited. Let me develop this briefly.

Quite clearly, the use of particular recruitment channels has important implications for the degree of openness of the labour market. Although the extent to which 'word of mouth' recruitment operates may vary between organisations, even from manager to manager within the same organisation, it would seem that in the current situation of increased competition for vacancies, and the scarcity of financial resources, it is becoming an increasingly popular mode of practice (Manwaring and Wood, 1982). Its advantages over formal recruitment procedures via, say, Job Centres, Careers Offices and newspaper advertisements are difficult to deny. First, it minimises the uncertainty associated with the recruitment process; second, it keeps the cost of recruitment to a minimum; finally, according to at least one study, it complies with the demands of the trade unionists that employees' families get preferential treatment (Lee and Wrench, 1983). All in all, then, Manwaring and Wood's claim on the basis of their research into recruitment practices would seem a fair appraisal of the situation:

Multicultural Education: Emancipation or Containment?

"Currently in many firms the chances of a complete 'outsider' getting a job in the near future, even given vacancies, seems to many of our personnel managers very remote" (1982, p. 20). (5)
     At first glance, it is not immediately clear why the development of an extended internal labour market through increased reliance on informal recruitment channels should work to the detriment of black school leavers; but it does.   Partly this is due to the relatively greater reliance of young blacks (and other ethnic minorities) on the statutory services.   This differential use of job search methods effectively excludes black youths from the range of job opportunities available to white youngsters.   As Shirley Dex points out; in contrast to young blacks, "whites appear to draw on the contacts and information of family and friends to secure jobs" (1982, p.20).   The continuation of this process, the adherence to a 'business as usual' approach, in other words, will also ensure that there is a status quo in the ethnic composition of an organisation as well as the reproduction of a black labour force in the lower levels of the employment market.   The evidence, then, is irrefutable: disadvantage in trying to get work is being reproduced among the offspring of black migrants born and educated in the UK.

THE ROMANTIC VISION OF SOCIETY

Banks has defined multicultural education as "a generic concept that implies systematic school reform" (1981, p. 55).   Because of its diffuse nature, multicultural education permits a range of interpretations and practices.   Nevertheless, in its most popular form the imperative is clear: improve the academic performance of black youths to ensure that they will not confront any barriers, over and above those faced by white youths, in the realisation of their life chances.   Proponents of multicultural education conventionally take as their starting point the unassailable view that the norms and values of UK society are racist and that these permeate the education system in the form of an Anglo-centric curriculum and via the disparaging and offensive representation of other cultures in teaching materials.   It is contended that these disable the group- and self-identity of minority group pupils, reduce their interest in classroom matters and negatively affect their performance in public examinations.   Armed with few, if any, academic qualifications their chances of gaining

entry into the labour market are deeply impaired.
Equality of opportunity, the moral buzz word of multi-
culturalists, can only be attained if academic results
are improved; the reappraisal of curricular and
teaching materials so that they reflect minority
groups more positively will, they contend, restore
black pupils' interest and motivation, provide them
with the confidence to pass examinations and place
them on equal footing with white school leavers in
their search for work.

The proponents of this new orthodoxy suggest,
either implicitly or explicitly, in their formulation
of policies and practices, that the disadvantages of
black youth derive largely, if not entirely, from
cultural and/or identity deficiencies. In so doing,
these proponents have lost sight of the original
premise on which their proposals rest: namely, that
the UK is a society which is suffused with racism.
It is this unassailable fact and not differential
academic performance which inhibits the life chances
of young blacks. As Brian Bullivant has argued, the
emphasis on the promotion of minority life styles in
the classroom, a key feature of multicultural education, will do little to remove the barriers which
block black youths' chances of upward social mobility:

> Naive, romantic pluralists contribute to
> the problem when they stress educational
> programmes and curricula that emphasise
> only life style concerns. This is easy
> to do, as they appeal to the vision of
> society that stresses its 'niceness' and
> one-big-happy-family 'holism', rather
> than the competitive nastiness of the
> real world. This is far less romantic,
> but much more pertinent for education
> (1981, p. 233).

The refusal by the Schools Council to publish
Dawn Gill's report, Assessment in a Multicultural
Society: Geography (1982) precisely because it
focussed on racism and the "competitive nastiness of
the real world" is merely the latest example in the
routine attempt to confine the multicultural education
debate to 'romantic' and innocuous issues (Dorn and
Troyna, 1982).

It is not difficult to see why; to admit to the
debilitating effect of racism on life chances would
undermine the ideological notion of schooling as a
good thing. Instead, by structuring blacks' perceptions of their disadvantage in terms of cultural and

identity deficits and by formulating educational programmes designed to reduce those deficits, multi-culturalists contain and defuse the potential for resistance.

Whether this coercive strategy is succeeding, however, is another matter. Sarup has argued that youth unemployment, in general, poses serious problems for the state because: "If after 'fifteen thousand hours' at school there is no job, the usefulness of schooling, and the nature of society, will be increasingly questioned" (1982, p. 31). One headteacher recently admitted such doubts are already beginning to surface among "thinking fourth and fifth formers" (quoted in O'Connor, 1982). And, for some time now, a handful of contributors to the debate about black educational underachievement have suggested that the employment difficulties which these youths are likely to face when they leave school have an influence backwards on their motivation to succeed at school and, consequently, on their levels of academic performance. As Green puts it: poor performance is likely to have derived from "the alienation and demotivation that results from the knowledge that schooling and educational qualifications have little pay-off for those whose future at work will most likely be decided on the colour of their skin, regardless of merit" (1982, p. 33). The research of Anwar (1982) and George Gaskell and Patten Smith (1981) provides empirical support for this argument by showing that a large number of black youths, though retaining a commitment to the work ethic, accept that racism is likely to impede seriously any chance of realising their aspirations. (6) As one black schoolgirl put it to the researcher, Kathryn Riley: "if a white person and a black person went to the same school and got the same degrees, the white person is entitled to get (the job) more than the black; I mean, we're all classed as stupid" (1982, p. 12). Her observation succeeds in placing multicultural education in its proper perspective. Education does not take place in a social vacuum and any benefits which may derive from initiatives designed to improve the academic performance of black pupils are likely to be nullified by the ubiquitous fact of racial discrimination in the transition from school to work.

CONCLUSION

Recent criticisms of multicultural education have, in general, either followed Chris Mullard's contention that it sanctions divisions along ethnic lines (1981) or, focused on Maureen Stone's provocative claim that the new orthodoxy is likely to exacerbate rather than alleviate black inequality. Stone argues that educationists should not be concerned with attaining "mental health" goals but should concentrate on "teaching methods associated with skills and knowledge and the development of abilities" (1981, p. 254). In this paper I have not engaged in either of these debates; instead, my intervention has developed along a different trajectory which has established first, the differential experiences of black and white youth in the transition from school to work and second, the importance of labour market processes as a determinant of life opportunities. It is in this context that the efficacy of ascribing multicultural education with emancipatory powers can most realistically be considered. Unfortunately, the crucial link between multicultural education and the labour market has consistently been overlooked and this has led, therefore, to an impoverished appraisal and analysis of this issue.

From this vantage point, it seems that multicultural education may enjoy some success as a strategy of containment by persuading pupils and parents (as well as teachers) that education remains the main distributor of life chances and that by tinkering with educational methods and techniques black youth will obtain better results and attain equality of opportunity. The reality of the labour market suggests otherwise: and as an emancipatory tool for black youth, multicultural education is doomed to fail.

Perhaps a more optimistic appraisal can be made of the programmes and policies initiated from an anti-racist perspective. Currently, these programmes are at an elementary stage of development and 'anti-racist education' tends to be more of a political slogan - symbolising a detachment from the multicultural education philosophy and its emphasis on cultural pluralism - rather than a coherent and consensual mode of operation. It proceeds along a different trajectory to conventional multicultural education programmes in so far as it explicitly recognises racism as the crucial determinant of the life chances of black youth (St. John-Brooks, 1983). In itself, this represents a significant development although how prevalent this perspective becomes in the UK education system remains to be seen. There are, after all, a significant number of schools up and down the country which have yet to reach the stage of multicultural, never mind anti-racist, education.

Similarly, pedagogic practices based on anti-racist approaches may be less successful than many of its exponents acknowledge. The research of Lawrence Stenhouse and his colleagues, for example, warns us of the potentially counter-productive results of explicit attempts to teach against racism (1982). Assessments of the efficacy of anti-racist education, then, must be held in abeyance at least until a coherent strategy along these lines is developed and, most importantly,'put into practice. Despite these caveats, the fact that discussions about systematic racial inequality within and beyond the school gates are now firmly on the agenda of some LEAs and their schools must, however, augur well in the struggle against racism.

FOOTNOTES

David Ashton, Roger Dickinson and Richard Jenkins all made helpful comments on an earlier draft of this paper. Responsibility for the final version is entirely my own, however, and the views expressed are not necessarily those of the SSRC or my colleagues at the Research Unit on Ethnic Relations.

(1) Andy Green has made a similar point in suggesting that these and related issues provided the *leitmotif* of official reports during the 1960s and 1970s. He writes that: "Concern over class-room disruption by black pupils, violence, rejection of school mores, lack of work motivation and so on has always been more or less explicit in DES and Select Committee reports on race and education" (1982, p. 23).

(2) Naturally, education qualifications are important as a pre-requisite for some jobs, especially those in the higher echelons of the labour market. Without qualifications, school leavers are unable to enter the race for these jobs. Even so the possession of qualifications does not ensure success in this race and, as I shall demonstrate, this is particularly so for black youth.

(3) Similarly, Gloria Lee and John Wrench have shown that by staying on an extra year at school to take further examinations (which, it is hoped, will enhance chances of obtaining apprentice-ships) actually disqualifies youths from considera-tion for these schemes. By the time s/he has left school in the sixth form, the youngster will be too

old for an apprenticeship (1983).

(4)   The articles which Douglas Smith and I have compiled for our reader for the National Youth Bureau, Racism, School and the Labour Market, undermine this 'pathological' explanation of black youth unemployment even further.

(5)   The CRE's recently completed investigation into the under-representation of black workers at the Company's Banner Lane plant in Coventry (ten out of 6,800 employees in 1975) showed that this was primarily due not to direct discrimination but to "the company's method of recruitment for hourly-paid jobs.   They did not advertise or use Job Centres" (1982, p. 1).   The CRE also found that all jobs covered by union agreement "were advertised internally throughout the plant, and over half of all vacancies were filled in this way, especially clerical and engineering posts" (p. 18).

(6)   In the USA, Sethard Fisher found that the idea of 'blocked opportunities' was a contributing factor towards the high incidence of 'anomie' amongst black high school students (1981).

REFERENCES

Anwar, M. (1982) Young People and the Job Market – A Survey, CRE, London

Ashton, D. and Maguire, M. (1981) 'Employers' perceptions and use of educational qualifications', Educational Analysis, 8, 2, pp. 25-37

Banks, J. (1981) Multiethnic Education: Theory and Practice, Allyn and Bacon, Boston

Birley High School (1980) Multicultural Education in the 1980s, Manchester Education Authority

Blackburn, R.M. and Mann, M. (1979) The Working Class in the Labour Market, Macmillan, London

Brooks, D. (1975) Race and Labour in London Transport, OUP for the Institute of Race Relations and the Action Society Trust, London

Bullivant, B. (1981) The Pluralist Dilemma in Education, Allen and Unwin, Sydney

Carby, H.V. (1982) 'Schooling in Babylon', in Centre for Contemporary Cultural Studies, The Empire Strikes Back, Hutchinson, London, pp. 182-211

Carter, M. (1966) Into Work, Penguin, Harmondsworth

Cashmore, E. and Troyna, B. (1982) 'Black Youth in Crisis', in E. Cashmore and B. Troyna (Eds.), Black Youth in Crisis, Allen and Unwin, London, pp. 15-34

Cashmore, E. and Troyna, B. (1983) Introduction to Race Relations, Routledge and Kegan Paul, London

Clarke, N. (1982) 'Dachwyng Saturday School', in
    A. Ohri, B. Manning and P. Curno (Eds.)
    Community Work and Racism, Routledge and Kegan
    Paul, London, pp. 121-127
Commission for Racial Equality (1978) Looking for
    Work: Black and White School Leavers in
    Lewisham, CRE, London
Commission for Racial Equality (1981) BL Cars Ltd:
    Report of a Formal Investigation, CRE, London
Commission for Racial Equality (1982) Massey Ferguson
    Perkins Ltd: Report of a Formal Investigation,
    CRE, London
Committee of Inquiry into the Education of Children
    from Ethnic Minority Groups (1981) West Indian
    Children in Our Schools, (Interim Report),
    HMSO, Cmnd. 8273, London
Community Relations Commission (1974) Unemployment
    and Homelessness: A Report, CRC, London
Craft, M. and Craft, A.Z. (1981) The Participation
    of Ethnic Minorities in Further and Higher
    Education, Summary and Conclusions of a Report,
    Nuffield Foundation, London
Cross, M. (1982) 'The manufacture of marginality',
    in E. Cashmore and B. Troyna (Eds.), Black
    Youth in Crisis, Allen and Unwin, London·
    pp. 35-52
Daniel, W.W. (1968) Racial Discrimination in England,
    Penguin, Harmondsworth
Department of Education and Science (1965) The
    Education of Immigrants, (Circular 7/65),
    14 June, HMSO, London
Dex, S. (1982) 'Black and white school leavers:
    the first five years of work', Department of
    Employment Research Paper 33, DOE, London
Dorn, A. and Troyna, B. (1982) 'Multiracial education
    and the politics of decision-making', Oxford
    Review of Education, 8, 2, pp. 175-185
Fisher, G. and Joshua, H. (1982) 'Social policy and
    black youth', in E. Cashmore and B. Troyna
    (Eds.) Black Youth in Crisis, Allen and Unwin,
    London, pp. 129-142
Fisher, S. (1981) 'Race, class anomie and academic
    achievement: a study at the High School level',
    Urban Education, 16, part 2, pp. 149-173
Gaskell, G. and Smith, P. (1981) 'Are young blacks
    really alienated?', New Society, 14 May,
    pp. 260-261
Gill, D. (1982) Assessment in a Multicultural
    Society: Schools Council Report: Geography,
    unpublished

Green, A. (1982) 'In defence of anti-racist teaching', Multiracial Education, 10, 2, pp. 19-35

Hall, S., Critcher, C., Jefferson, T., Clarke, J., and Roberts, B. (1978) Policing the Crisis: Mugging, the State and Law and Order, Macmillan, London

Hawkins, K. (1979) Unemployment, Penguin, Harmondsworth

House of Commons (1981) Fifth Report from the Home Affairs Committee Session 1980-1981: Racial Disadvantage (1), HMSO, London

Hubbuck, J. and Carter, S. (1980) Half a Chance: A Report on Job Discrimination Against Young Blacks in Nottingham, CRE, London

Hunt, J. and Small, P. (1981) Employing Young People: A study of Employers' Attitudes, Policies and Practices, Scottish Council for Research in Education, Edinburgh

Jenkins, R. (1982) Acceptability, Suitability and the Search for the Habituated Worker: How Ethnic Minorities and Women Lose Out, paper presented to the conference, 'Management and mismanagement of labour', University of Loughborough, 29 September

Lee, G. and Wrench, J. (1983) Skill Seekers: Black Youth, Apprenticeships and Disadvantage, National Youth Bureau, Leicester

Little, A. (1975) 'Performance of children from ethnic minority backgrounds in primary schools', Oxford Review of Education, 1, 2, pp. 117-135

Lynch, J. (1981) 'Educational Theory and practice of multi-cultural education' in J. Lynch (Ed.) Teaching in the Multi-cultural School, Ward Lock, London, pp. 5-10

Mabey, C. (1981) 'Black British literacy', Educational Research, 23, 2, pp. 83-95

Makeham, P. (1980) 'Youth unemployment', Department of Employment Research Paper, 10, Department of Employment, London

Manwaring, A. and Wood, S. (1982) Recruitment and Recession, paper presented to the conference 'The management and mismanagement of labour', University of Loughborough, 29 September

Mortimore, P. and Mortimore, J. (1981) 'Achievement in schools III: ethnic minorities', ILEA Research and Statistics Report, ILEA, London

Mullard, C. (1981) 'The social context and meaning of multicultural education', Educational Analysis, 3, 1, pp. 97-120

O'Connor, M. (1982) 'Work is no longer even mentioned as an option', The Guardian, 19 October, p. 11

OECD (1977) Selection and Certification in Education
    and Employment, OECD, Paris
Reid, E. (1980) 'Young people and employment (i):
    employers' use of educational qualifications',
    Educational Policy Bulletin, 8, 2, pp. 49-64
Riley, K. (1982) 'Black girls speak for themselves',
    Multiracial Education, 10, 3, pp. 3-12
Rhodes, E. and Braham, P. (1981) 'Black workers in
    Britain: from full employment to recession',
    in P. Braham, E. Rhodes and M. Pearn (eds.),
    Discrimination and Disadvantage in Employment,
    Harper and Row/The Open University, London,
    pp. 365-395
Roberts, K., Duggan, J. and Noble, M. (1981)
    'Unregistered youth unemployment and outreach
    careers work', Department of Employment Research
    Paper 31, DOE, London
Runnymede Trust, (1981) Employment, Unemployment and
    the Black Community, Runnymede Trust, London
Ruston, J. (1981) 'Careers and the multi-cultural
    curriculum' in J. Lynch (ed.), Teaching in the
    Multicultural School, Ward Lock, London,
    pp. 163-170
Sarup, M. (1982) Education, State and Crisis: A
    Marxist Perspective, Routledge and Kegan Paul,
    London
Scarman, Lord (1981) The Brixton Disorders 10-12
    April 1981, HMSO, Cmnd 8427, London
Select Committee on Race Relations and Immigration
    (1969) The Problems of Coloured School Leavers,
    HMSO, London
Spears, A.K. (1978) 'Institutional racism and the
    education of blacks', Anthropology and Education
    Quarterly, 9, 2, pp. 127-136
St. John-Brooks, C. (1983) 'New efforts to combat
    racism at school', New Society, 3 February,
    pp. 180-181
Stenhouse, L., Verma, G., Wild, R. and Nixon, J. (1982)
    Teaching About Race Relations, Routledge and Kegan
    Paul, London
Stone, M. (1981) The Education of the Black Child in
    Britain, Fontana Books, London
Taylor, M. (1981) Caught Between: A Review of Research
    into the Education of Pupils of West Indian
    Origin, NFER-Nelson, Windsor
Tomlinson, S. (1980) 'The educational performance of
    ethnic minority children', New Community, 8, 3,
    pp. 213-235
Tomlinson, S. (1981) 'Inexplicit policies in race
    and education', Educational Policy Bulletin, 9,
    2, pp. 149-166

Troyna, B. (1982) 'The ideological and policy response to black pupils in British schools', in A. Hartnett (ed.), The Social Sciences in Educational Studies, Heinemann Educational Books, London, pp. 127-143
Troyna, B. (1983) 'Multiracial education: just another brick in the wall?', New Community, 10, 3, pp. 424-428
Troyna, B. and Smith, D. (1983)(eds), Racism, School and the Labour Market, National Youth Bureau, Leicester

SOMEONE ELSE'S CHILDREN: THE NEW VOCATIONALISM IN FURTHER EDUCATION AND TRAINING

Denis Gleeson

If the Conservative party's assessment of the State of the British economy was expressed in the slogan, "Labour isn't working" (Saatchi and Saatchi, London, 1979), the reality of the mid 1980s is that there is no work left to do.   Yet somewhat paradoxically, rising unemployment has, in recent years, resulted in a call to extend vocational training, particularly in relation to the 16-19 age group.   Indeed, a stated intention of Conservative (DoE 1981) and Labour Party (1982) policy on training is both to increase student participation in Further Education and Training, beyond its existing low levels, and to broaden the skill base of workers likely to be made available to employers once economic recovery gets under way. However, the view that youth training possesses any strong degree of purchase on the job market, or that it is likely to improve the 'life chances' of individuals, is open to question: not least because it assumes a causal connection to exist between the content of training and the form of the occupational structure which it "serves" (Gleeson and Mardle 1980).
This paper examines one aspect of this issue, namely the effect a fall in the demand for youth labour has had in establishing the Youth Training Scheme (YTS) and the likely effect this scheme will have in creating a new vocational public.   The main argument suggests that the emergence of youth training has little to do with technical changes in production, or with making capital and labour more efficient.   Rather, it is seen here to be more concerned with regulating youth labour markets and with establishing training as a substitute for employment (Gleeson 1983).   In so doing, the new training initiatives are seen to represent a political force which both alters the traditional relationship between school and (non) work, and hands school leavers over

98

to employers, and other agencies, for more positive
vetting (Lenhardt 1975). Despite the apparent
vocational realism built into recent training programmes, it will be argued that their effect widens
rather than reduces the fit between training and work.
Briefly, four main factors are seen to account for
this:

> Training policy increasingly erodes job
> opportunities by subsidising employers
> to train rather than employ school leavers.

> Training is increasingly disconnected from
> productive labour and separated off from
> direct contact with the conditions of
> production.

> Training is increasingly associated with
> regulating the displacement of groups out
> of the job market (and society) rather
> than into it.

> The content of training is increasingly
> non-technical in orientation: the pre-
> dominant emphasis being on "life" and
> "management" skills rather than the
> acquisition of technical or functional
> skills.

In the sections which follow I shall seek to qualify
such assertions, but for the moment it would first
seem important to say something about the background
to the issues involved.

BACKGROUND

The background to this paper concerns the recent
establishment of State training in Britain which, in
the absence of alternative employment opportunities,
has become one of the largest 'employers' of labour.
Yet despite the rapid growth of vocational courses
in recent years, Further Education and Training has
remained a neglected area of sociological enquiry;
its peripheral and entrepreneurial character perhaps
reflecting the low esteem in which technical knowledge
is viewed. With a few notable exceptions research
in the sociology of education, in the 1960s and 1970s,
focused mainly on issues relating to schooling, with
little or no reference to the activities of industrial
trainers or the educational interests of young people
at work. Compared with the influence of research on

issues relating to the school, sociological investigation of FE and training has remained largely undeveloped. Even at the school level it is possible to detect a certain intellectual squeamishness about vocational training and craft knowledge: few empirical studies, for example, have dwelt long on the social relations associated with the technical classroom or workshop practice. Similarly, the links between school, FE and Industry, and the more specific connection between technical qualifications and employment have, until the recent establishment of YTS, attracted little critical attention or research interest.

Perhaps one of the least examined aspects of contemporary sociology of education is the way in which training actually affects society (Meyer 1977). Surprising as this may sound the question about how training structures and stratifies populations, has been largely ignored by recent sociological perspectives. While great emphasis has been placed on understanding the ethnographic and interactional context of schooling, at one level, and the ideological and reproductive relationship between schools and economic crisis at another, the institutional effects of education on society have been viewed at times in an over-simplified fashion. At both levels it is as if education simply constitutes an agent or derivative of something else, which finds its expression within the deeper relations of capitalism, the State, 'the hidden curriculum' or whatever. The end result is that the process of education has become divorced from its political consequences, and the question regarding the ways in which further education and training influences, or acts on, the arrangements of society, has been largely ignored. Here, I am referring to the institutional modes by which training has become a substitute for productive labour, a means of allocating young people to the job market, a mechanism for regulating previously unregulated social behaviour, and so forth. What remains less than clear at the present time is the likely effect obligatory training will have on the emerging political identities of young people, and it is to this issue that I now wish to turn.

ON THE QUALITY AND QUANTITY OF TRAINING

Despite the expressed intention of both the Government and the Manpower Services Commission to extend the quality and quantity of training to all young people (MSC 1982a) there is little doubt that the Youth

Training Scheme is principally directed toward the forty per cent of the school-leaving population who leave school with only the minimal level of formal qualifications. Effectively YTS is designed to remove large sections of 16 and 17 year olds from the labour market by 1985, thereby reducing the registered level of youth unemployment. Moreover, the White Paper which precipitated the establishment of YTS confidently predicts that its proposals for youth training will enable trade unions, employers, educationists and government "to more clearly see what they need to do for the system to work". Elsewhere other observers have noted that the White Paper's recommendations mark a significant break between the 'old' (voluntaristic) and the 'new' (corporate managed) FE system, and thus constitute "... the most far reaching proposals for industrial training ever put before parliament" (Guardian, 16 December 1981). Essentially the proposals of the Youth Task Group Report (MSC 1982a) both confirm and extend the kind of training schemes already initiated by the MSC since the mid 1970s, but on a larger and more systematic scale.

However, notwithstanding the claim of this report to provide a permanent bridge between school and work, its proposals for improving both the quality and quantity of training remain, to say the least, limited in scope and design. Already, the indications are that the level of vocational training for YTS trainees falls significantly below that of existing training arrangements and that, under the new scheme, an 18 year old will have had even less work experience than apprentices, or other young people, working in a full or part-time capacity (Jones 1982). Whether or not this factor will aggravate, rather than alleviate, the existing difficulties experienced by school leavers in finding permanent work, remains to be seen. But if the experience of YOP is anything to go by, there is every indication that repeated involvement in short-term training schemes may actually disqualify young workers from entering full-time employment, skilled or otherwise (Raffe 1983). Moreover, it remains less than clear how the envisaged type of training "involving basic literacy and numeracy, practical competence in the use of tools, machinery and office operations" (White Paper 1981) will enable young people "to make their way in the increasingly competitive world of the 1980s" (Youth Task Group Report 1982). So far the MSC has offered no evidence which suggests that these are skills that employers want. Indeed, there is little question that within this prevailing climate of doubt 'basic skills' have become closely associated with the perceived inadequacies of the 'less able', unemployed young person. Perhaps nowhere is this better illustrated than in some of the curricular assumptions which underlie 'social and life skills' objectives.

> We would like to see life skills as the all embracing term. Life Skills could then be subdivided into 'Social Skills' and 'Coping (or Life Management) Skills'. 'Social Skills' would include more than face to face contact, since people may relate to others via letters, the telephone, and on a group or individual basis. 'Coping Skills' would include dealing with everyday apparatus and procedures, such as using a public telephone, filling forms, reading maps, finding accommodation and so forth.

> (FEU, 1980, Developing Social and Life Skills)

Not only does this kind of prescriptive approach reflect a limited view of the trainees' intelligence, but it also conveys an implicit statement with regard to his/her position in society. Society as such is not thrown open to question by such guidelines; rather it is the individual who must adapt and respond to society if he/she is to survive. As a result there is no reference to the individual acting on society, or of him criticising or struggling with the forces that ensure his entrapment (FEU 1980, FEU 1982). Essentially, 'life management' in this context does little more than evoke the traditional rubric of 'liberal studies', which conflates the wider network of social relations in industry with such technical activities as report writing, filling in job applications and learning a little bit about "Kulture". Elsewhere, the numerical horizons of young trainees is found to be no less great; as a recent MSC document (Freshwater, 1981) on the "additional skills" thought necessary for further training indicates,

> Reading numbers
> counting,
> measuring length or distance,
> reading words,
> listening to get information

are all considered of vital importance. Here, the

reference to such skills as <u>additional</u> is revealing,
since it assumes that the majority of school leavers
leave school without even the most rudimentary skills.
Not only does this unqualified assumption reflect the
kind of criticism made of schools in the Great Debate
but, perhaps more importantly, it also fails to recognise what is happening at college and work practice,
where increasing numbers of recruits are overqualified
for what is presently on offer.

In view of these remarks there would seem little
evidence to substantiate the Government's confident
assertion that "we know enough about the system to
make it work". Indeed, contrary to popular belief,
employers have kept silent regarding the direction
which the new training initiatives might take. They,
more so than government, recognise that the present
range of available jobs in the economy, are generally
routine and undemanding and that, both now and in the
future, these jobs (where they exist at all) will not
require a very sophisticated level of further education and training (Rees and Atkinson, 1982). Consequently, it might be argued that, in its present form,
the debate about training is meaningless; it simply
obscures the real issue of unemployment and the way
in which training schemes have, themselves, become
substitutes for employment. Thus despite the government's professed intention of more closely integrating
education and work, the general indications are that
the gap between the two is widening, both as a direct
result of the new training policy and the unwilling-
ness of employers to recruit full time workers from
non traditional sources (Wickham, 1982).

That the Employment Secretary should, therefore,
preface publication of the White Paper as a "great
event" should not obscure from view widespread dis-
quiet about the divisiveness of MSC schemes which are
seen to support a dual system of training: one that
generates a form of apartheid between those who
receive real training for real jobs and those who
receive life support skills for the dole (Cohen, 1982).
As such the new vocationalism of YTS does little to
challenge entrenched assumptions regarding high status
knowledge in the curriculum, and its close connection
with the labour market hierarchy. The dominant
emphasis here, for example, on theoretical, scientific and abstract knowledge, has gone largely unquestioned within MSC programmes. For the so called
'disadvantaged', however, the dominant pedagogic
experience has been extended and remains firmly
anchored within practical, relevant and vocational
knowledge: a form of control traditionally associa-

ted with ensuring the lower orders' obligation to the
system and their awareness of its dominant moral
codes (Meyer 1977, Atkinson et al 1983). In this
respect investment in 'voc prep' fulfils a hitherto
ignored function, that is of safeguarding traditional
academic knowledge by preventing its proliferation
to the masses whose participation in extended education (staying on) might otherwise dilute the vocational relevance of academic qualifications to the
middle class (Johnson 1982).

Thus, it is within this broader context that
training not only separates off various categories
of young people as distinct social and intellectual
types and on criteria which has only marginal relevance to the kinds of jobs they are likely to perform,
but it also becomes indistinguishable from the labour
market that it once 'served'. The question I wish
to address now is, what are the likely political
effects of this on young people?

POLITICAL EFFECTS OF TRAINING

In seeking to answer this question it would first
seem important to recognise that training for unemployment does not facilitate the socialisation of
youth into society, but out of it (Lenhardt 1975).
As Thurow (1975) has noted, educational qualifications
are not so much indicators of skills required by
occupations (or not as the case may be), but general
indicators of the ability to acquire appropriate
skills through experience. Perhaps not surprisingly,
the qualifications and experiences connected with
training for unemployment (work experience, life
skills and so forth) do not embody the general indicators of competence seen necessary by employers to
gain access to the job market. If anything, they
actually disqualify youth from the labour market, by
separating them off as the inveterate unemployed
(Loney 1983). As a consequence training for the
disadvantaged has no specific vocational end in view
other than being a form of protective custody, which
removes the possibility of the young unemployed from
having unregulated social and leisure experiences
(Lenhardt 1978).

From this viewpoint the call to extend vocational training has, in reality, very little to do
with technical changes in production or with the
desire, expressed in official jargon, to produce a
"better equipped, better educated and better motivated labour force" (Youth Task Group Report 1982).
Moreover, the swelling numbers entering vocational

courses at the present time should not be confused with any perceived shortage of workers in the economy with particular skills. The problem if one can refer to it as such, is the excess supply of young adult labour, and the kind of moral panic (or "structural legitimacy problems" (Offe 1973)) this presents, real or imagined, to the wider principles of authority and control in society. In this respect the State's managing interest in training is not primarily concerned, despite appearances, with making capital and labour more productive. Instead, it is more administratively involved with establishing <u>new criteria</u> for allocating 17 and 18 year olds to a declining job market, at a time when conventional controls have largely broken down (Moos 1982).

However, the part played by the New Training Initiative in this process is not solely one of allocating young people to the job market; it does more than that. The weakness with the job allocation perspective (Thurow 1975, Collins 1979) is that it is too static: it ignores the ways in which emerging formal patterns of education and training actually embody theories of socialisation, power and so forth, which themselves become, in Meyer's (1977) terms, "Institutionalised as rules at the collective level". In other words the administrative structure of youth training should not be viewed as separate from the kind of political philosophy that spawned it, since they are both one and the same thing. As the following remarks from a recent MSC document only too clearly indicate, the imperatives of training cannot be separated off from the imperatives of nationalism.

> As a country, we must now set ourselves the aim of achieving urgent and radical changes to our training arrangements if our industry and our commerce and our work force - both young and adult - are to be adequately equipped to face the future ... The compelling need therefore is for a training system which enables all workers to acquire a basic range of skills and to develop and adapt them throughout their working lives (MSC 1981)

What is interesting about such familiar remarks is not so much the way in which they equate the interests of labour and capital, but the way in which they express a particular view regarding the existence of a common class, culture and citizenry. Perhaps for

this reason alone recognition of the political effects
of training needs to go beyond simplistic theories of
socialisation, which emphasise the conditioning influence of the curriculum on young people's attitudes.
Despite the recent interest shown by sociologists of
education in how students learn to internalise capitalist values via their interaction with education,
there exists little evidence that the institutional
effect of education is experienced by young people in
this way. Important as this question may be, training represents something stronger than 'social control': it also represents a political force which
structures, rather than simply reflects, the wider
relations of labour and class and, in so doing, promotes a new generation, a vocational public, ordered
by measured expertise (Lenhardt 1982). It is not
just that the rules governing the new vocationalism
permit only a limited expression of intelligence and
restrict young people's autonomy (Edgeley 1978), it
also regulates the kind of behaviour that is expected
of them in terms of their social orientation and
readiness to work (Moore 1983). A particularly
pernicious feature of the governing criteria of the
new training initiative is that it is rooted in the
personality structure of the unemployed themselves,
in their assumed personal inadequacies, deficiencies
and so forth (Stafford 1981). The young person's
inability to find work is thus situated for him or
her via vocational training: it represents an
objective appraisal, if not confirmation, of the
individual's lack of ability and skill to compete
successfully in the job market. It is in this way
that the collective fate of the young unemployed
becomes ideologically represented, via the curriculum,
as a skills problem, at the individual level. Elsewhere, Lempert (1981) has noted how such organising
principles of vocational training, already an
established feature of the educational system in
West Germany, reify individual differences.

> Corresponding to the profit interests
> of private firms, vocational education
> contributes to a very high specialisation
> (either theoretical or abstract), an
> abstract achievement orientation (instead
> of interest in concrete work tasks),
> hierarchical conformity, low sense of
> responsibility for other people and for
> future generations, selfish competition
> (at the expense of solidarity and co-
> operation) and the beliefs of self-worth

of the 'winners' and a lack of self-worth among the 'losers'.

As a consequence, the process by which young people come to interact with and anticipate the new training structures involves them, at least to a degree, in coming to terms with the stigma attached to their own failure. Once established, such structures ensure the kind of framework within which trainees themselves will contribute to the maintenance of reified social relations, through their interaction with curricular arrangements which mirror their alienation. This mechanism whereby young people actively contribute to their own alienation from society is interpreted by Lenhardt (1981) as a form of expropriation, whereby individuals are deprived of control of the conditions of their own existence: instead of providing them with a range of technical skills and competencies (that might be applied in a productive setting) training is seen to represent an expression of particular authority relations in industry. Here the political effect of training reduces the social relations of production to a narrow set of technical propositions or constraints wherein learning about such topics as 'understanding British Industry' or 'entering the world of work', simply become euphemisms for learning about one's place. Thus questions regarding how industry is organised and managed, how wealth is accumulated, or how skills, wages and jobs are legitimated and sustained (all factors which place the individual), become objectified within the framework of the vocational curriculum. As a recent communiqué from the MSC (1982b) to local colleges has sought to confirm, teaching 'politics' has little to do with learning about industry.

> ... material with a political or generally controversial content should not be included ... Inclusion in the course of political and related activities could be regarded as a breach of your agreement with the MSC and could result in the immediate closure of the course. (See Appendix 1)

Notwithstanding the rather obvious problem of how to teach students about work in industrial society without raising political issues, such a directive itself also conveys an obvious political message concerning the MSC's intentions: it reflects the MSC's attempt to distance the 'crisis' of unemployment

from the curricular programmes that it has since
initiated (Moss 1983). It is within this overall
structure that students' political horizons are
controlled and their broader vision of the issues and
possibilities which surround them severely restricted.
Thus, despite the vocational realism employed in youth
training schemes the major impact of FE and training
is not one of inculcating skills, that is, of inter-
nalising in students appropriate technical or affec-
tual qualities required by occupations. Neither is
it simply a matter of training becoming a substitute
for employment. Such interpretations not only over-
estimate the socialising and custodial effects of
training, but they also underestimate the political
consequences which training has on the overall structure and political position of youth in society.
Perhaps the kind of question recently asked by sociologists of education, regarding what kind of knowledge
"gets into" the curriculum (Apple 1979) should be
replaced by another: what kind of knowledge "gets
left out" of the curriculum, even expropriated,
within the arrangements of training practice. The
question is put in this way because I believe the
major impact of FE and training upon individual
behaviour is not mediated by socialisation alone,
whatever its content may be. Rather it is structured by institutional processes which block out
(Moore 1983, Gleeson 1983) or obscure from view
knowledge of the wider political and economic factors
that most affect young people (Johnson 1982). Here
I am referring to the ways in which the social structure and aspects of the relationship between individual and society,'accepted' features of the liberal-
democratic curriculum of the 1960s and 1970s, are
not discussed within MSC training programmes. The
procedures taught in the new vocationalism are neces-
sitated by natural constraints (e.g. the inevitability
of unemployment) which are not mediated by social
relations. Whether intended or not curricular initiatives which prepare trainees for earning a living
or making out in non work situations, such as 'starting your own business', preparing for 'self-employ-
ment', 'making benefits work for you', pre-set young
people to think of their role <u>outside</u> the conventional
job market. One consequence of this is that trainees
and apprentices are made more aware of what mainstream
society expects of them but which is, as 'outsiders',
nevertheless beyond their reach. Moreover, it is
unlikely that the recent provision of 'generic' or
transferable skills will challenge such 'work'-'non-
work' divisions. The reason for this is that the

so-called 'new' approach to flexible training (incor-
porating "occupational training families" OTFs) shares
much in common with the traditional pattern of training and apprenticeship which it seeks to replace. In
recent government documents and reports, for example,
the line of causation in curriculum development is
seen to run from occupations to education (Hayes 1983,
FEU 1983): the challenge to education being seen as
one of responding more coherently to the needs of
industry. The dominant assumption is that it is the
type of training, its technical content and so forth,
which determines the structure of occupations, and
the way in which new patterns of technological work
will be performed. While this approach may subordinate training to industrial control, it has very
little to do with making either industry or workers
more efficient.

Having said this, however, it would be misleading to assume that all forms of curricular intervention are doomed to failure. In view of the above
remarks it could be argued that the kind of relationship between training and capitalism so far described
is inevitable; its purpose being to prevent the
formulation of a political consciousness among the
young: no more, no less. The problem with this
perspective is that it not only posits a neat causal
connection between training and capitalism, but it
would also seem to accept the existing order of things,
as given. It is, in other words, highly conservative
in orientation: it ignores, for example, the ways in
which work-place experience (as opposed to work
experience) can provide another important means to
empower a collectivity to change society, rather than
helping individuals to adjust to social and industrial
change (Freeland 1980). According to Freeland, work-
place experience should not be viewed as a passive
exercise, wherein students simply "taste" work, or
learn to fulfil employers' expectations. Rather, it
is seen here to fulfil a more critical and meaningful
function, not least when it is linked with a productive view of work.

> ... work-place experience should be used
> as a means through which students can
> develop an understanding of the nature
> of the work process, the social relations
> of production (ownership, control, profits
> and wages, the role of trade unions, etc.),
> and the pattern of industry in the commun-
> ity. This can be achieved through the
> development of company studies (historical

and structural), industry studies
and combining them with community
studies. The industry studies should
not be restricted to work-place experience sites but should include studies
of service and control industries such
as education, health, welfare, the
media and the legal system.

The community studies should be critically
oriented in the sense of locating the
community's problems and needs, local
employment trends (which would include
the impact of technological change),
community services and organisations
(including political party branches),
and planning and its consequences ...

(Freeland 1980)

Thus, in raising the question about what gets
left out of the curriculum in this paper, the issue
about what to _include_ in the curriculum is also of
crucial importance – even though this may not directly
address the broader structural question of the relationship between capital and labour. To date this
issue has remained taboo in the sociology of education
and among the left, not least because all curricular
knowledge has been viewed as ideologically suspect or
irrelevant. One consequence of this has been that
issues regarding the content and control of education
have been separated off reflecting one critic's
observation that "... it is easier to critique developments in theoretical terms than to contribute more
positively to political struggles over the curriculum
(Whitty 1982). Clearly, unless one adopts a strongly
determined view of the relationship between training
and capitalism (Anderson et al 1982) there can be
little way of knowing where the opposition points to
the new vocationalism might rest. While the framework of training is at present determined by State
policy, it should be recognised, however, that it is
largely the institutional process of education itself
which is currently legitimating the new training
enterprise. Yet to date there has been little
attempt to challenge recent training initiatives from
within education and, as a consequence, the MSC's
managing interest has gone largely unopposed. While
this partly reflects the weakness of the teaching
profession, the unions and the labour movement at the
present time, it also represents a deeper cultural

ambivalence about the educational requirements of so-called 'less able' young people - referred to here as someone else's children. To say that their predicament is simply a feature of capitalism provides little solace to them. Perhaps not surprisingly it has been left to this group to indicate their own opposition to the new schemes, and what it is that they want from training and work. In this respect it is principally the failure of youth training schemes to become more closely linked with productive labour that is leading trainees and their parents to oppose the new vocationalism. At one level such opposition is expressed in apathetic ways, to the numbingly unimaginative content of the curriculum, which follows well established lines, such as woodwork, metalwork, painting, decorating, sewing, and so forth (Atkinson et al 1983), while, at another, some trainees are organising against YTS schemes, joining unions, 'truanting' and even going on strike. In recent 'right to work' marches one of the more interesting slogans has been "Jobs not YOPs" (Moos 1983). Consequently, such opposition is not principally directed against training as such, but its lack of connection with productive labour, and all that that entails (Newell 1982). It is to this issue that I now wish to turn.

CONCLUSION

Despite the current crisis generated by youth unemployment the promise of a better future via training remains a powerful, if not convenient, ideological form of expression. Yet, as I have sought to argue, when young people are denied entry to the labour market by being made 'trainees', that does not necessarily mean that they have achieved a greater degree of control over their lives. Increased levels of participation in Further Education and training, in other words, cannot simply be equated with expanded opportunity. A principal argument of this paper has been that mass 'training', in its present form, does little more than institutionalise youth unemployment as an inevitable consequence of the 'market mechanism', and to reinforce the generally accepted view that youth employment is a thing of the past. Current training policy, for example, is modelled on the structural inevitability of youth unemployment and this has become a powerful mechanism for stifling social criticism, the consequences of which have not yet been fully realised in conventional educational circles. Yet within existing youth training schemes young people are being 'employed' on low wages (adult's

work on youth's allowances) without minimal legal or
trade union protection.   If this process is to be
challenged then an effective <u>employment and training
policy</u> needs to be pursued: one that, for example,
establishes work and training as a right for all, in
the same manner that legal rights and rights to education, health care, welfare and so forth, have
become an integral part of the liberal democratic
state (Rustin 1983).   Thus, to view training policy
in a vacuum, without reference to the ways in which
it actually generates unemployment, depresses adult
and youth wage levels and limits trade union effectiveness, ignores the political 'function' of training at the present time.

While any proposal to extend employment opportunities may prove unpopular with Thatcherite politicians and monetarists, mainly because it acknowledges
the failure of the market to redistribute resources,
historical circumstances (notably in the post-war
period) suggest that full employment is by no means
an impossible dream, even in times of world recession.
Moreover, the high cost of unemployment, including
the cost of training and employment subsidies, benefits, tax and national insurance loss, and loss of
rent and rate income, suggests there is little economic
reason to doubt why a policy of full employment should
not be actively pursued at the present time.   Furthermore, there is no reason why training provision, linked
to a policy of full employment should follow existing
institutional arrangements, or be completed in some
predefined way by the age of eighteen or twenty.
Greater flexibility and choice by workers about where
and when they undertake training, and at what level
and at what point in their lives, would certainly
focus more critical attention on the least examined
aspect of the present debate about training, namely
the use and relevance of training to the workers
themselves.

It might, of course, be argued that the pursuit
of such an alternative viewpoint in Britain at the
moment is unrealistic: that Tory conceptions of
'educational choice' do not allow for workers to make
decisions about their own working lives.   But as I
have sought to argue in this paper existing training
initiatives are equally unrealistic: "training for
the dole" (Cohen 1982) being perhaps the most naive
form of <u>idealism</u> yet invented.   It is only by starting to debate such matters that the present arrangements of training may be challenged.   However, any
programme for change cannot consist of a purely
"conceptual alternative" (Hoare 1967);   it also

involves integrating theoretical and practical issues
which take account of the young workers <u>active parti-
cipation</u> in the work and training process. In this
respect a number of important policy recommendations
have been recently advocated, including:

> The establishment of rights for trainees
> and students to negotiate their own
> education and training and to enjoy
> equality of choice.

> Legislation to require employers to
> release employees for education - first
> as youth, and later, as adults.

> ... two years of education and training
> on a voluntary basis for all... the
> provision of 'through routes' to further
> study on all existing courses, as part
> of the redesign of 16-19 curriculum and
> assessment.

> All training to be in real skills leading
> to nationally recognised qualifications.

> All training to lead to real jobs in
> socially useful work. (2)

Such recommendations not only involve teachers,
educationists, trade unionists and others in contest-
ing the unfamiliar terrain of vocational education,
but they also involve considering training schemes
which negate the vital interests of young people,
and which emasculate them. As one observer has
recently noted, it is not dole schools and work
experience that the young unemployed require now,
but "schools and (in a well known phrase) 'really
useful education' and rewarding, unexploitative
work" (Horne 1983). It is as a contribution to
this neglected aspect of the present debate about
training that this paper is addressed.

NOTES

(1)   In their different ways the MSC (1982)
and the FEU (1983) have sought to develop a more
integrated approach to training than the traditional
form of apprenticeship is seen to allow. As a
precursor to any form of specific vocational training
young people are expected to acquire a broad range
of skills. Hayes (1983) suggests that foundation

training ought to be widened to include a 'family' of
jobs and occupations. Here the task is to identify
the relationship between Occupational Training Families
(OTFs) and the way in which competence at work is
developed. The aim of such an approach is to ensure
that a broad range of skills are vested in the trainee
who can then adapt these skills in a variety of work
and non-work situations. However, the approach tends
to view jobs and occupations as 'given' with training
objectifying the basic skills connected with certain
occupations e.g. calculation, measurement, drawing,
communication, planning, problem solving and so forth.
The weakness of this causal approach is that such
'objective' skills avoids any real discussion of the
social relations which surround the operation of
those skills in the work situation.

(2) Adapted from The Youth Training Scheme:
A Strategy for the Labour Movement, Socialist
Society 1983.

REFERENCES

Anderson, D. (1982) Educated for Unemployment.
    Agenda for Debate No. 2, The Social Affairs
    Unit
Apple, M. (1979) Ideology and Curriculum, Routledge
    and Kegan Paul
Atkinson, P. et al (1983) 'Industrial Training for
    the Disadvantaged' in D. Gleeson (1983) Youth
    Training and the Search for Work, Routledge
    and Kegan Paul
Bowles, S. and Gintis, H. (1976) Schooling in
    Capitalist America, Routledge and Kegan Paul
Collins, R. (1979) The Credential Society, Academic
    Press, New York
Cohen, P. (1982) 'School for Dole', New Socialist,
    January/February
Department of Employment (1981) A New Training
    Initiative: A Programme for Action, Cmnd 8455,
    HMSO, London
Edgeley, R. (1978) 'Education for Industry', Radical
    Philosophy,19
Freeland, J. (1980) Where do they go after School:
    Youth Unemployment, Legitimation and Schooling,
    Department of Education, University of Sydney,
    Australia
Freshwater, M.R. (1982) Using a Basic Skills Check-
    list, Making the Most of Training Workshop
    Opportunities, vol. 1, Manpower Services
    Commission, London

FEU (1980) Developing Social and Life Skills, FEU,
    London
FEU (1982) Basic Skills, Further Education Curriculum
    Review and Development Unit, London
FEU (1983) Supporting YTS, FEU, London
Gleeson, D. (1983) Youth Training and the Search for
    Work, Routledge and Kegan Paul, London
Gleeson, D. and Mardle, G. (1980) Further Education
    or Training? (With the assistance of
    John McCourt), Routledge and Kegan Paul
Hargreaves, I. (1983) 'The Crisis that Growth Alone
    will not Solve', Financial Times, 7 January
    1983
Hayes, C. (1983) Training for Skill Ownership:
    Learning to take it with you, Institute of
    Manpower Studies, University of Sussex
Hoare, Q. (1967) 'Education: Programmes and Men',
    New Left Review, 32
Horne, J. (1983) 'Youth Unemployment Programmes:
    An Historical Account of the Development of
    Dole Colleges', in D. Gleeson (1983) op cit
Johnson, R. (1982) 'Learning for Life', Schooling
    and Culture, 12
Jones, I. (1982) 'The New Training Initiative: An
    Evaluation', National Institute Economic
    Review
Labour Party (1982) 16-19. Learning for Life, A
    Labour Party Discussion Document, January
Lempert, W. (1981) 'Perspectives of Vocational
    Education in West Germany and other Capitalist
    Countries', Economy and Industrial Democracy,
    2
Lenhardt, G. (1975) 'On the relationship between the
    education system and Capitalist Work Organisa-
    tion', Kapitalistate, no. 3
Lenhardt, G. (1978) 'Problems of Reforming Recurrent
    Education for Workers', Comparative Ed. Review,
    October
Lenhardt, G. (1981) 'School and Wage Labour',
    Economy and Industrial Democracy, 2, 1
Loney, M. (1983) 'School to What?' Times Educational
    Supplement, 7 January 1983
Meyer, J. (1977) 'The Effects of Education as an
    Institution', AJS, 83, 1
MSC (1981) A New Training Initiative: A Consultative
    Document, MSC, London
MSC (1982) Occupationally Based Training: YTS
    Guideline no. 3, MSC, London
MSC (1982a) Youth Task Group Report, Manpower Services
    Commission, London
MSC (1982b) Area office letter to local colleges,

22nd November 1982 (See Appendix 1), reported also in The Guardian, 29 November 1982

Moos, M. (1982) 'Voluntary Coercion', Schooling and Culture, 12

Moos, M. (1983) 'The Training Myth: A Critique of the Government's Response to Youth Unemployment and its impact on FE', in D. Gleeson (1983) op cit

Moore,R. (1983) 'Further Education, Pedagogy and Production', in D. Gleeson (1983) op cit

Newell, R. (1982) 'A Smokescreen over the Dole Queue', The Guardian, 12 October 1982

Offe, C. (1973) Unpublished mimeo. Max Planck Institute for Educational Research, Berlin. Quoted in Lenhardt (1975) op cit

Raffe, D. (1983) 'Education and Unemployment: Does YOP make a difference (and will YTS)?' in D. Gleeson (1983) op cit

Rees, T.L. and Atkinson, P. (1982) Youth Unemployment and State Intervention, Routledge and Kegan Paul

Rustin, M. (1983) 'A Right to Work', New Statesman, 4 February 1983 and New Left Review, February

Socialist Society (1983) 'The Youth Training Scheme: A Strategy for the Labour Movement', Socialist Society, Spider Web

Stafford, A. (1981) ' Learning not to Labour', Capital and Class, 15

Thurow, L. (1975) Generating Inequality, Basic Books

Whitty, G. (1982) 'Room to Move', Teaching London Kids, 19

Wickham, A. (1982) 'The State and Training Programmes for Women, in E. Whitelegg et al (1982) The Changing Experience of Women, Martin Robertson

New Vocationalism in Further Education and Training

APPENDIX 1

A copy of the Manpower Services Commission letter
sent to college principals. Headlined in The
Guardian report of 29 November 1982 "Colleges
warned about Politics in YOP courses"

Dear Trainer,

I am writing to you and other local trainers who are
running courses as part of the Youth Opportunities
Programme (YOP) to remind you that political and
related activities are not permitted within YOP.
Particular care should be taken if trainees are to
produce, as part of their course, magazines or other
literature for publication. Material with a
political or generally controversial content should
not be published.

Inclusion in the course of political and related
activities could be regarded as a breach of your
agreement with the MSC and could result in the
immediate closure of the course.

In the first instance it is for you to judge the
acceptability of material intended for publication,
but I shall be happy to advise you if you have any
questions either generally or in a particular case.

Yours sincerely

Area Manager

THE STATE AND THE INDEPENDENT SECTOR: POLICIES,
IDEOLOGIES AND THEORIES

Tony Edwards, Mary Fulbrook and Geoff Whitty

INTRODUCTION

'Public' day and boarding schools for boys remain
"remarkable in their social homogeneity".   Through
their close association with recruitment to positions
of conspicuous power and status, they retain "a
social importance out of all proportion to their
numerical place" (Halsey, Heath and Ridge 1980, pp.
28 and 51). (1)
          Those facts have dominated discussion of the
entire independent sector.   They have also ensured
that arguments over continued coexistence with publicly provided secondary education have ranged widely.
The Fleming Committee (1944), for example, concluded
that it was in "the widest national interest" to
make them more accessible.   The Public Schools
Commission, especially in its Second Report (1970),
echoed the views of the Minister (Crosland) who had
appointed it in judging the schools to be a main
cause of class consciousness.   It is now Labour
Party policy to abolish "an educational plutocracy
based on social and economic elitism", which is seen
as dividing society by enshrining privilege (Labour
Party 1980).   From the other side, those defending
the independent sector have been certain that its
survival both depended on and reinforced fundamental
individual rights, and that it provided an essential
defence against state manipulation of the school
curriculum (Conservative Pary 1983).   The whole
controversy is therefore seen as being about not
only educational excellence and diversity, but also
about "the whole nature of society" and whether "the
demands of freedom outweigh the demands of social
justice" (ISIS 1974).
          In the first part of this paper, we identify
some main positions in the controversy, concentrating

118

on attempts to link the public and private sectors
of which the latest has been the allocation (beginning in September 1981) of some 5,500 assisted places
a year to independent schools.   We then try to locate
support for private or independent educational provision within recent policy discourse in the Conservative Party.   Finally, we consider how different
theoretical perspectives might be compared for their
capacity to illuminate policy and policy-debate.   The
paper as a whole is based on preliminary work for our
study of the origins and consequences of the Assisted
Places Scheme.

INDEPENDENCE AND ASSOCIATION

Anticipating the arrival of state secondary education,
Sir John Gorst, then Vice-President at the Board of
Education, warned the 1901 British Association against
the dangerous tendency of public instruction "to
suppress or absorb all other agencies ... and substitute one uniform, mechanical system" (cit. Robinson
1971, p. 37).   As public provision of secondary
'instruction' expanded, many grammar schools certainly
chose to sacrifice or reduce their independence for
the sake of financial support from central or local
government.   The Labour Party might have been expected to encourage that choice, given its general opposition to the purchase of opportunities and its faith
in educational reform as a means of social reconstruction.   However, only in the sense of a general hos-
tility to the social exclusiveness of independent
schools is it true that the Party has "consistently
objected to their presence" (Labour Party 1980, p. 5).
Between the Wars, it largely ignored them (Parkinson
1970, pp. 96-7).   The Fleming Committee met at a
time when egalitarian ideas were unusually assertive,
and the TUC's evidence to it was intended to point
firmly to the conclusion that they should be entirely
absorbed within the national education system.   A
subsequent Labour Party deputation affirmed "the
broad democratic principle that all children of school
age shall be required to attend schools provided by
the State" (cit. Banks 1955, pp. 228-9).   Yet neither
the 1944 Act nor the legislative response to the
Fleming Report significantly affected the independent
sector.   As R.A. Butler reflected, the "first-class
carriage" was simply removed from view (1971, p. 120).
No radical policy emerged during the 1950s either,
mainly because of the priority given to improving the
public sector and partly because of uncertainty about
how to prevent the buying of educational services

from organisations which were operating within the law.   Only after the rejection of the Public Schools Commission's proposals for extensive reforms did Labour Party policy become consistently and specifically hostile.   The 1970 manifesto contained only a general declaration that "the educational system must not perpetuate educational and social inequalities". But by 1973, Gorst's 'dangerous tendency' was evident in the NEC's Programme for Britain, which included a commitment to "abolish fee-paying schools and bring all children of compulsory school age into the national system".

As the political challenge to its existence became more overt, so the independent sector became both more professional and more explicitly political in its own defence.   The task of the Independent Schools Information Service set up in 1972 was not only to provide information but also to "mobilise public opinion on behalf of freedom in education". Disclaiming any party-political ties, it sought support from all those who - "believe that a state monopoly in education is wrong ... that parents should be free to choose the kinds of education to be given to their children", and that "in a free society" efficient private schools had an incontrovertible right to exist.   Couched in such terms, resistance to the "growing threat to independence" was presented as a cause - a politically necessary reminder that "public authorities do not always know best" (ISIS 1974).

The threat had grown with the decline of hopes that the independent sector would wither away as the advance of state education reduced the temptation to pay.   Both the Fleming Committee and the Public Schools Commission sought to draw the more prestigious independent schools into some form of 'association' with, or 'integration' within, the public sector. The intransigently independent would then be progressively isolated until they and the still large category of "schools conducted for private profit" would diminish into an irrelevant enclave.   Indeed, the Public Schools Commission commented optimistically that its proposals were timely because the schools it intended to integrate had already passed the peak of their numbers and prestige.

That forecast has been confounded, and positions have since become much more sharply polarised.   The Commission's recommendations were rejected so flatly by the schools themselves as to remove any hope of thorough integration by agreement.   The 'public schools' saw the social and academic transformation

demanded of them as being much too extensive. Most
of the direct-grant schools, facing the prospect that
continued grants would be conditional on the abandonment of both fee-paying and academic selection, began
to prepare for complete independence. That eventual
decision by 119 schools added significantly to the
size and prestige of the independent sector. It
also removed what had long been presented as a 'bridge'
between public and private provision. The progress
of comprehensive re-organisation continued to sharpen
differences previously blurred by the meritocratic
successes of the grammar schools. It certainly
threatened to bring about what Crosland had predicted -
a sufficient flight from a public sector increasingly
lacking the attractions of academic selection to contradict the earlier optimism about a natural decline
and fall in private provision.

    It was in this context that the Labour Party
shifted from the integrationist approach dominant in
the 1960s to a policy of abolition. Outlining that
policy at the Party Conference of 1973, Roy Hattersley
also outlined the steps by which it was to be achieved.
The ending of the direct-grant list in 1976 was the
first main move. Attempts were made to enforce the
'self-denying ordinance' already followed by some
Labour-controlled LEAs, by limiting all recourse to
direct-grant or independent-day schools to cases where
the Authority could demonstrate to the Secretary of
State "a demonstrable absolute shortage of suitable
places" in its own schools. There was some whittl-
ing away of those sources of direct and indirect
support from public funds which Glennerster and
Wilson (1970) had estimated as contributing twenty
per cent of the total income of the independent
sector, although the obvious legal difficulty persisted of how to distinguish between charities which were
politically acceptable and those which were not. A
possible ban on fee-paying itself posed even greater
problems, despite Hattersley's 1973 comment that the
procedural details mattered less than a "demonstration
of political will" (cit. Rae 1979, p. 54).

    As he summarised it at that time, the political
case against the independent sector was that it consumed a disproportionate share of educational resources, diverted energies from the improvement of maintained schools, and was socially divisive. As
expressed more recently, and in more ideological form,
it is the last of those arguments which takes prece-
dence. The abolition of all private schools within
ten years, if necessary through a ban on the <u>charging</u>
of fees, is presented as an essential part of a

general assault on the reproduction of social and economic privilege (Labour Party 1980, Labour Party-TUC 1981). The independent sector has therefore been led to assert more strenuously than ever "the case for freedom" - the political importance of an alternative to state provision, the distinctive contribution of the independent schools to the formation of occupational elites, and the consequent advantages of retaining a mixed economy in educational provision in which those schools operate as "an equal and valuable partner" (ISIS 1976, 1981; Conservative Party 1983). It is to the ways in which that partnership has been defined and justified that we will now turn.

Defenders of the independent schools have often expressed concern that access to them should depend so largely on parents' capacity to pay the fees. The 'Old Toryism' discussed in the next section of the paper has been strongly represented among the leadership of the 'public schools', producing a frequent emphasis on the fostering of talent wherever it might be found and an expressed dislike of 'divisive' social policies (Dancy 1963, Howarth 1969, Rae 1979). When the 1979 Headmasters' Conference welcomed so enthusiastically the announcement of the Assisted Places Scheme, it attached two highly traditional conditions to that welcome. The Scheme should complement rather than compete with the public sector, and it should be so administered as to "benefit children who clearly have some form of need".

Given the special social prestige of the 'public schools' and the difficulty of claiming that they were academically superior to the maintained grammar schools, it is understandable that the form of association most commonly proposed has been in relation to the 'need' for more, and more equitably distributed, boarding education. Thus the initiative for the Fleming Committee came from a joint request by HMC and the Governing Bodies Association for an investigation of how the schools they represented "could be of service to a wider range of pupils". Fleming's scheme, however, went much further than the schools had envisaged. An initial annual intake of at least twenty-five per cent assisted pupils from elementary schools was to be reviewed every five years "with a view to the progressive application of the principle that (associated) schools should be equally accessible to all pupils, and that no child otherwise qualified should be excluded solely owing to lack of means" (1944, p. 66). Since the 'need' for boarding education would not be confined to children of high ability, and since the

Committee was adamantly against any segregation of the "particularly gifted" at the expense of maintained schools, its proposals threatened both the social and the academic exclusiveness of schools whose appeal to parents depended on both. The acceptance of those proposals 'in principle' by HMC and the GBA rested on a realistic appreciation that they were unlikely to be implemented extensively amid the turmoil of constructing 'secondary education for all'. Even in principle, they were rejected by the TUC on the grounds that "a system of educational privilege" was made no less objectionable by modifying the group on whom privilege was bestowed (cit. Banks 1955, p. 234).

The objection foreshadowed John Vaizey's dissenting comment that the Public Schools Commission was trying to solve the social problem presented by the public schools "by changing the bodies in their beds" (PSC 1968, p. 221). That solution had often been suggested before by those who saw in the opening-up of boarding education the means to a more important objective - that of "blurring hard-drawn class distinctions" which the public schools were thought to reinforce (Fleming 1944, pp. 53-5). Within the independent sector itself, some embarrassment at continuing to be what Fleming called "the preserve of a restricted class" brought several attempts during the 1950s to persuade the Government to introduce publicly-assisted places. And however impressed the Public Schools Commission generally may have been by Lambert's (1966) estimates of unsatisfied 'boarding need', there is no doubt that it seized on his research as supporting and justifying perhaps a last chance of achieving the social integration of those schools willing to provide the 'necessary' places. That purpose explains its warnings against scattering assisted places "over the face of the public schools like confetti" so that the schools' ties with "particular classes" would remain intact. Doubling the proportion of assisted places which Fleming had recommended would force integrated schools to transform themselves both socially and academically.

Whereas the Fleming Committee had managed to maintain unanimity over its recommendations, a minority of the Public Schools Commission rejected the majority diagnosis of social divisiveness as exaggerated and the majority remedy of fifty per cent assisted-place pupils as being too drastic. To implement that remedy was seen as threatening the distinctive qualities of the schools it was intended to integrate, and as dependent on a quite unacceptable level of government control. The schools them-

selves regarded the price of integration as much too
high. This was especially true of the direct-grant
schools, threatened with the simultaneous loss of
the fee-paying thought to guarantee a substantial
measure of independence, and the academic selective-
ness judged necessary to their continued academic
excellence.

Compared with the scope of the 1968 and 1970
proposals, the present Assisted Places Scheme represents a reversion to the earlier notion of 'association'. It certainly carries no equivalent 'costs'
for the 228 participating schools which the forms of
integration recommended by the PSC would have involved.
Pressure to conform to educational policy in the public sector, especially in relation to academic selection, is not only missing - its absence is an essential part of the Scheme's justification. Possible
LEA resistance to the loss of able pupils from their
own schools is avoided by denying them involvement
altogether. Parents approach a chosen independent
school directly, and even the initial LEA right to
block transfers at sixteen where these can be shown
to harm their own provision is to be taken away.
DES 'supervision' of the Scheme seems to be very
light, being confined largely to the financial
arrangements whereby schools reclaim from central
government the amount of the fees which they remit
to parents. The nature of the 'service' to be
provided by those schools is also defined quite
differently. To the regret of many within the
independent sector, there is no reference to the
'boarding need' which so dominated previous proposals
beyond some encouragement to schools to support the
boarding fees of some assisted-place pupils from
their own funds. There is no likelihood either
that the social homogeneity of participating schools
will be significantly modified. Judged by its own
criteria, and even by those of the Fleming Committee,
the Scheme would appear as what the Public Schools
Commission called "window-dressing" because in practice fewer than 4,500 places a year have been
"scattered like confetti" over so many schools. Very
few of those schools will have received even twenty-
five per cent of their intake through the Scheme,
so that no great social changes are required of them.

No academic change is required at all. The
most striking contrast with earlier proposals is the
reversal of arguments against 'creaming' the public
sector which even the independent schools themselves
had repeatedly employed. The Fleming Committee
rejected any segregation of the "particularly gifted".

124

The Public Schools Commission treated integration as inseparable from a widening of the ability-range to CSE and beyond, and insisted in its Second Report that assisted places should not be offered at all to schools "only willing to co-operate on academically-selective terms". The present Assisted Places Scheme explicitly supports academic selection. Participating schools were chosen for the size of their sixth forms and their academic results, and the criterion for assistance previously found in 'boarding need' is now found in the form of a 'ladder' from the public sector for able children whose parents cannot afford the full tuition fees. Comprehensive reorganisation in the public sector has coincided with what has often been described as an 'academic revolution' in the independent schools - a markedly stronger and more explicit emphasis on 'academic standards' and high rates of entry to higher education. Beginning as a response to the success of pupils from maintained grammar schools in competition for Oxbridge places and other prestigious contests, this academic bias intensified as an obvious and legitimate way of distancing the schools from the increasingly non-selective public sector (Glennerster and Wilson 1970, pp. 98-9, Lambert 1975, pp. 294-9, Gathorne-Hardy 1977, pp. 368-92, Rae 1979, pp. 154-9, Salter and Tapper 1981, pp. 157-88). It has therefore become possible to offer a strictly 'meritocratic' version of how public provision of secondary education should be complemented.

It has also made it seem possible to answer the charge that the worldly success of so many 'public school' pupils was no more than "an arbitrary conferring of advantages and power on an arbitrarily selected membership" (PSC 1968, p. 162). The charge of arbitrariness clearly depends on denying the schools themselves any special educational merits. That was a view expressed in 1961 by a Conservative Minister of Education, David Eccles, when he told the House of Commons that he could see no reason to "use public money to subsidise the transfer of boys" from the public sector when so many maintained grammar schools were academically superior to many independent schools (cit. Dancy 1963, p. 31). Belief in that superiority, and in the occupational opportunities available as a consequence to able working-class children, underlay the prolonged ambivalence in the Labour Party to 'common' secondary schools. Its eventual commitment to comprehensive re-organisation has been deplored as destroying the grammar schools' capacity to "circumscribe social-class power" by making entry to various elites more open (Musgrove 1979, pp. 92-118). It was certainly the determination to remain grammar schools which carried so many direct-grant schools into the independent sector (Kamm 1971, pp. 194-8, ISIS 1973). Throughout the 1970s, it has been argued with growing force that since 'real' academic education is impossible without selection, then comprehensive reorganisation was depriving many able children of opportunities once available in maintained schools with an 'academic tradition'. In so doing, it was also threatening to reduce the stock of educated manpower available to the nation (ISIS 1974, 1976). In this context, the Assisted Places Scheme has been presented as a meritocratic modification of the independent sector and a meritocratic complement to the public sector. What appeared from one side as a policy of "starving the maintained schools of funds and then rescuing the brightest children from the surrounding wreckage" (Labour Party 1980, p. 27), appeared from another to be a realistic appreciation of the difficulties of maintaining high academic standards in "schools catering for the majority" and a consequent offering of places "in what are acknowledged to be good schools" to able children "from all kinds of social background" (ISIS 1981, p. 14). That second view was expressed by Rhodes Boyson as the first assisted-place pupils were entering their schools:

> Once again the boy or girl from an
> inner-city area, where the aspirations
> and achievements of his local compre-
> hensive aren't such that he will be
> stretched the way he should be, can now
> once again join the ladders of social
> and economic mobility, and to me that's
> part of an open society. And I'm
> astonished anybody opposes it.

> (London Weekend Television, 'Starting Out',
> September 11, 1981.)

CONTINUITY AND CHANGE IN CONSERVATIVE DISCOURSE

The announcement of the Assisted Places Scheme in 1979 was one of the first declarations of educational policy by the new Conservative Government. The Scheme implemented what Party policy had promised since 1976, and that promise had been a somewhat delayed response to an approach made to Mrs. Thatcher (as 'Shadow' Minister for Education) by the direct-

grant committee of HMC. Its immediate origins,
then, lay in the reluctance with which direct-grant
school heads felt themselves forced into independence
by the Labour Government's insistence on tying continued financial support to the abandonment of academic selection, and their wish to restore the opportunities they saw as being lost by the imminent
abolition of the direct-grant list. By 1979, however, the Scheme had come to appeal strongly, and on
grounds of general principle, to a wide range of
Conservative Party politicians and theoreticians.
To this extent, it therefore constituted a broadly-
based policy preference rather than being merely a
pragmatic adjustment in educational provision (Dale
1983). Briefly, and we elaborate these points
later, the Scheme would support a form of educational
provision which was 'independent' of the state. It
would extend parental choice. It would contradict
what many saw as a process of 'levelling down' in
academic standards by restoring opportunities for
able and deserving children from modest backgrounds
in schools traditionally associated with academic
excellence, and indeed with traditional moral and
cultural values. As we have suggested already then,
the Scheme has to be located within long-standing
controversies over the relationship between the state
and private education, and those controversies have
often been argued in terms of fundamental principles
of individualism or collectivism, opportunity or
equality. In this section of the paper, we explore
the extent to which arguments of this nature lie at
the heart of contemporary debates about the future
of social policy in Britain and consider how far
shifts in educational policy discourse in general,
and that on state and private education in particular,
can be seen as related to changes in the broader
ideological climate.

Modern political parties are not only coalitions
of interests, they also have to represent themselves
in ways that appeal to reasonably broad constituencies.
Furthermore, the composition of particular parties
changes over time, as does the nature of the elector-
ates to which they appeal. Policy-making usually
entails the construction of an apparent unity between
different discursive elements, some of which may
appear contradictory when subjected to further analysis. At times, contradictions within the total
repertoire can remain more or less implicit. In a
period of relative economic growth, for example,
increased state expenditure on particular social
policies has been able to command widespread support,

often between as well as within parties, because the same policies can be justified in a variety of ways and be seen as occupying different places within a total policy package. The period of the so-called 'social democratic consensus' about education (Finn, Grant and Johnson 1977) can be seen in this way. It was exemplified in the main parties' agreement in principle that the independent schools should be more closely associated with the public sector.

In periods of crisis, however, when there is a clearer tension between state expenditure and the demands of capital for a real return on its investment, there is greater pressure to resolve ambiguities, establish priorities and find a new way forward. In most cases, this will involve the accenting of different elements within the total package, but there are also occasions when more resolute attempts are made to resolve some of the basic contradictions perceived within mainstream economic and social policies. As long as a commitment to electoral politics is maintained, occasions for sharp breaks with the traditional style of consensus politics will be rare (Gamble 1981, p. 223), though Gamble (1983) has recently argued that the immediate aftermath of the Falklands crisis could be seen as one of these in certain respects. At such times, especially if (as with the New Right) "the ground has been assiduously prepared over the last fifteen years" (Gamble 1981), particular political forces may try to win a political party to an ideologically more purist set of policies. Such tendencies have been evident recently in both the Conservative and Labour Parties, while the formation of the SDP might be seen as a recognition that the traditional style of consensus politics could no longer contain the 'extremes'.

In exploring how far the combination and balance between different elements in political discourse have altered over time in this way and influenced policy on state and private education, we concentrate in this paper on developments within the Conservative Party. We do so for the obvious reason that the Assisted Places Scheme is a Conservative policy introduced to contradict the policy of the previous Government by restoring in considerably modified form a traditional 'link' between the public and private sectors. But, as we have already intimated, an exploration of the origins of the policy, and the controversy surrounding it, brings into focus more fundamental ideologies about educational provision. In seeking to understand the broader contexts within which the Scheme might be understood, we begin with a general typology of positions offered by Room (1979, pp. 41-74), which identifies neo-Marxist, social democratic and liberal approaches to social policy. Of especial relevance to our own analysis is his distinction between 'market' and 'political' liberals. For the former, state provision that threatens the operation of a free market in which individuals or families compete without hindrance both constitutes an invasion of individual liberty and undermines the economic system most likely to maximise general prosperity and social integration. The main threat to both individual and public good is seen to lie in monopolistic welfare bureaucracies. From this perspective, state-organised social policies should not develop a distributive system at odds with the cash nexus, but at most provide a safety-net below which no citizen would be allowed to fall. Ideally, state subsidies should be to individuals and not to institutions. From a Friedmanite position, this points to an abolition of state educational provision, and the substitution of a system of vouchers which can be used in the market place (in combination with the individual's own resources) to purchase basic life-chances. Other market liberals accept state provision for those who cannot do better for themselves as a means of ensuring a necessary common minimum. Political liberals, on the other hand, being committed to the notion that industrialism can itself produce a more meritocratic and harmonious society, will tolerate a higher level of direct state provision in so far as it fosters meritocracy through the development of human capital and the opening up of opportunities for all who merit them.

For Room, the key characteristic which distinguishes the social democratic approach from both the liberal positions is its championing of social rights as opposed to individual civil rights. This is a distinction closely related to that between 'social justice' and 'freedom' which we touched on earlier. Individual civil rights are seen as an insufficient guarantee of equitable treatment, and involve the risk that the social costs of the economic system will be allowed to lie where they fall. Social rights substitute publicly defined and guaranteed life-chance outcomes, increasingly distributed through the state provision of social services. The minimum acceptable level of provision is therefore much higher than that recommended by market liberals. The social democratic approach also differs from the political liberals' notion of meritocratic distributive justice in seeing social rights not in terms of

merit but rather of need, a distinction which we
have already seen has important implications for the
grounds upon which educational selection is justified.
It also takes a less optimistic view of the convergence of self-interest and collective interest, arguing that the former must on occasions be subordinated
to the latter, and that social policy thus partly
involves fostering a moral commitment to collective
welfare.

As we argued earlier, political parties can
rarely be unequivocally committed to a purist position and still retain sufficient electoral support
to form a government. The modern Conservative Party
has itself always embraced market liberal, political
liberal and social democratic elements. But the
post-War 'consensus' over social and educational
policy was based upon agreement between political
liberals and social democrats in both the main parties
that the expansion and improvement of state provision
should be encouraged, whether it was to foster economic growth, equality of opportunity, equality or
social harmony. As long as such policies appeared
viable, and as long as there was no discernible likelihood of a real <u>reduction</u> in the extent of state
provision of services, contradictions between the
aspirations of different groupings within the consensus were obscured. At the same time, the alternative analyses of both market liberals and neo-
Marxists posed little threat to the capacity of the
leaderships of the main political parties to sustain
the consensus. It was a gradual disillusion with
mainstream approaches to social policy, exacerbated
by the effects of the mounting economic crisis on
levels of public expenditure, which enhanced the
appeal of these alternatives during the 1970s. This
encouraged shifts in the balance of forces within
the parliamentary parties, and in the elements of
their repertoires which were given prominence in
policy discourse.

We now wish to explore the extent of these
shifts within the Conservative Party in particular,
and to consider their effects on its policies towards
educational provision. For this purpose, the broad
analysis offered by Room needs to be supplemented and
refined. What Dale (1983) has sought to do in his
analysis of 'Thatcherism and Education' is to consider currently dominant positions in Conservative
Party policy discourse during a period when that
discourse has been marked by "a relative readiness
to own up to being ideological" (p. 233). In using
certain parts of Dale's framework, we should empha-

sise that we follow his usage of 'Thatcherism' as a
short-hand term to connote a currently dominant set
of positions within the Conservative policy 'repertoire'.   While its use in this sense has undoubtedly
become "an essential part of the vocabulary of British
politics" (Dale, p. 233), it carries the risk of imposing an artificial tidiness and uniformity on policy
descriptions.   In fact we agree with Dale that
'Thatcherism' should not be reified, since it is
neither internally consistent nor pervasively dominant.   Nevertheless, even a provisional identification
of positions is helpful in examining the larger questions implicit in a particular educational policy.
     Although the relationship of policy positions
to individuals and groups in and near the Party can
change with the changing balance of power within it
or even the particular constituency being addressed,
Dale's more detailed typology brings into view strands
neglected by Room - most notably, the benevolent pater-
nalism associated with what Dale calls the 'Old Tories'.
This approach, epitomised in contemporary references
to Disraeli, involves a concept of 'one nation' as a
community in which the responsibility of the rich for
the well-being of the poor can often be effectively
discharged through state provision of welfare and
educational services.   There are therefore points at
which the Old Tories seem to have more in common with
the Party's social democratic fringes than with its
now dominant market liberals.   This is perhaps demonstrated in Edward Heath's attacks on the policies of
his Thatcherite successors, especially on the issue
of education vouchers.   Another of Dale's groups,
the 'Industrial Trainers', stress the needs of industry and of investment in human capital, judge the
desirability of state intervention in terms similar
to Room's political liberals, and favour a modernisa-
tion of the humanist traditions supported by the Old
Tories (Williams 1961).   For Dale, Thatcherism
involves a downgrading of the influence of both groups
in relation to that of the 'Privatisers', the 'Populists' and the 'Moral Entrepreneurs'. (2)
     The Privatisers, closely associated with mone-
tarist economic theory, reassert faith in the power
of the free market, both economically and socially,
and thus seek to substitute social markets for sup-
posedly discredited social engineering by the state.
Their views are thus close to those of Room's market
liberals.   The Populists are seen by Dale as making
the ideological case for letting people stand on their
own feet rather than relying on the professional ex-
perts who sought to control our lives in the name of

social justice during the period of the social democratic consensus.   They are joined by the Moral
Entrepreneurs in seeking to re-establish the sanctity
of the family as the basic social unit fostering
traditional moral values.   Thatcherism is presented
as giving predominance in social policy to selectiv-
ity, self-help, individual freedom and choice.   It
draws its political strength from the capacity of
populist politicians such as Boyson to mobilise in
favour of market liberalism those groups who see
themselves as having been relatively disadvantaged
by the universalistic approaches to social and educational policy adopted by a statist social democracy
in the post-War period (Hall 1979, Taylor-Gooby 1981).
    Returning to policy in our own area of interest,
we can now explore how far the shift in the balance
of forces identified by Dale is discernible in the
Party's approach to state and private education.   As
we saw in the first section of this paper, there has
been general support for the retention of a small
private sector alongside an almost universal provision
of state primary and secondary education.   The availability of the private sector has satisfied a philosophical commitment to the pursuit of individual
liberty, and to parental choice as a check on a total
state monopoly.   Nevertheless, certainly after 1944,
the Party also demonstrated a commitment to state
provision for all who required it, and its policy
could not be seen generally as challenging the development of the public sector.   From the mid-1960s,
however, comprehensive reorganisation of state secondary education produced some diminution of bi-partisan
support for the public sector.   As we have seen, the
abolition of the grammar schools made it more possible
to argue that the private sector offered an educational
service (over and above that of meeting boarding need)
that the state was not providing.   Especially in the
aftermath of the Labour Government's abolition of the
direct-grant list, it justified the construction of a
ladder into the independent sector to ensure the
maximisation of talent from all sections of the community and to further the development of a truly meritocratic society.   In the early years of the Thatcher
government, the Assisted Places Scheme was thus justified in terms of the traditionally mixed repertoire
of post-War Conservative Party policy rather than as
heralding a new approach.   This was made clear in an
interview we conducted with one of the ministers involved in its introduction:

> It was definitely promoted ... as an
> opportunity through a scholarship
> scheme. Particularly in my mind
> always was that in inner-city areas
> for the children to benefit from the
> education that was available at places
> such as King Edward's (Birmingham),
> Bradford Grammar School and Manchester
> Grammar School. I didn't look upon
> it as a privatisation of the state
> system ... I didn't look upon it as
> a privatisation measure at all ...
> I did promote it on two points. One
> the basis of the scholarship idea ...
> and secondly as a general widening of
> choice for parents. Obviously, a
> widening of choice that was only
> available to the parents of children
> who had ability to pass any entrance
> exam., but to them it was a widening
> of choice ...
>
> (Interview, 16 November 1982)

He also added that, if widespread selective provision
had been available within the state system, the pressure for the Assisted Places Scheme would have been
considerably less and so would "the degree of priority"
given it by the Government, despite the commitment
made at the time when the direct-grant list was abol-
ished.

The early policies of the Thatcher government
on this issue could therefore command a considerable
degree of consensus within the party and among the
constituencies to which it then sought to appeal.
The continuing availability of a market sector, given
added legitimacy by an Assisted Places Scheme based
upon state subsidies for individuals rather than
institutions, appeased (though it did not satisfy)
the market liberals whose influence was growing (3),
while the challenge it offered to a totalising state
bureaucracy was particularly appealing to the populists. At the same time, the attempt to sponsor
talent from all sections of the community and enhance
meritocracy appealed to the political liberals/indus-
trial trainers, while the preservation of institutions
seen as pursuing excellence and maintaining traditional
standards enlisted Old Tory/moral entrepreneurial
support. The existence of a new but appropriately
limited route for elite recruitment provided by the
Scheme appealed to the Old Tories and, for different

133

reasons, to the populists. To some extent social democratic elements within the Party were rather more ambivalent in so far as they saw even this Scheme as implying the abandonment of a commitment to the fullest possible provision of opportunities within the state sector for all who wished to make use of them.

Recently, however, a rather different set of policies, less likely to command such a degree of consensus within the party, seems to have been placed on its agenda. Public attacks on the state system, alongside suggestions that a broader voucher scheme might replace Assisted Places, have led to the suggestion that the Privatisers are increasingly making the running in the formulation of educational as well as other social policies. Pring (1983) discerns an attempt to stimulate the privatisation of major parts of the education service while encouraging a return to the 'elementary school tradition' within a remaining non-privatised sector that will provide only basic socialisation for those families unable or unwilling to compete in the market. Making the major provision via the market in this way would encourage the idea that education is essentially a private matter of improving individual life chances through competitive struggle - a view that would clearly appeal to all three groups seen by Dale as constituting Thatcherism. Selective state subsidies within the private sector, especially when seen alongside cuts in the state sector, parallel other examples within social policy of using state money to re-stimulate market forces. They can therefore be interpreted as encouraging the re-commodification of education by supporting private provision at the same time as de-legitimating state education as an acceptable alternative, thereby enhancing the market appeal of the private sector in the long term. Any expansion of the Assisted Places Scheme has been seen in these terms by Peter Newsam of the ILEA, a leading opponent of the Scheme even in its original form. He characterised its potential impact as follows:

> A lot of people who send their children
> to the maintained system, and I suppose
> myself, could afford to send them to
> independent schools. Now, if they see
> a reasonable proportion of the ablest
> people of their comprehensive school
> going off somewhere else, they have a
> difficult choice because people of course
> put their children very properly first

> and they begin to say to themselves,
> well there seems to be a movement away
> from these schools, we are becoming
> something of a residue, perhaps we ought
> to join the movement in that direction
> ... (it could) really create a fee-
> paying grammar school system and a
> secondary modern maintained sector ...
>
> (London Weekend Television, 'Starting Out',
>   September 11, 1981)

An enhanced Assisted Places Scheme based upon
criteria other than 'merit' would widen the scope
for movement, while a cross-sector voucher scheme
could take the process still further.   In this
context, even some state provision above the minimum
implied by the elementary or secondary modern school
traditions would be acceptable to many market liberals
(and would certainly be a practical necessity in the
short term), so long as it competed for clients alongside the private sector through enhanced parental
choice.   All such provision would then be subject to
individual consumer competition, and thus be more
acceptable to the market liberals and their other
Thatcherite allies than the sort of state-run service
that encourages collective struggles for enhanced
universalistic provision.
     These developments would be unacceptable,
however, to any social democratic elements left
within the party, while even the Old Tories, as Dale
(1982) points out in his discussion of the dispute
between Boyson and Bogdanor, recognise that there is
a need to find a balance between "the freedom of the
market and the demand for equal rights in a democracy".
The political liberals/industrial trainers would
presumably want to judge events in terms of their
actual consequences for meritocracy and social
integration, though they are likely to be particularly suspicious of moves towards privatisation via a
voucher system which would appear to be justified
purely on ideological grounds and involve no immediate reduction in public expenditure.   For non-
Thatcherite Conservatives, this seems (rightly or
wrongly) to distinguish a voucher system from other
privatisation policies. (4)   As one of them put it
to us, with private health insurance " you are
actually promoting something the purpose of which is
to increase the resources available", whereas with
a voucher system "all you are doing is still saying
the money is provided by the state and dividing it up

in a different way" (Fieldwork interview, November 1982). Thus broad-based support for any policy going significantly beyond the existing Assisted Places Scheme is far from assured even within the contemporary Conservative Party.

Despite this, some Thatcherite commentators have tentatively moved towards the position that the future of the Assisted Places Scheme is tied up with the debate going on about even more radical reforms. Rhodes Boyson has been quoted as saying:

> If choice is a good thing and variety a good thing, which I obviously believe it is, then it should be open not only to academically able children but to all children ... That is why I moved towards the voucher system or contracting out or specialist schools in the long term, without denying the virtues of the assisted places scheme. But politically and philosophically I must move along those lines myself.

> (quoted Albert 1982)

In such pronouncements, it is possible to detect the preparation of the ground for a re-definition of the Assisted Places Scheme as the precursor of a radical new policy rather than a 'natural'extension of a .traditional one. Yet there has remained a considerable degree of diffidence in government circles about such a re-definition. The Assisted Places Scheme had been a limited attempt to translate the ideological preferences of the new Thatcher government into policy terms but had the advantage that groups holding rather different ideological preferences could support it for different reasons. It was also a relatively inexpensive scheme that posed no major administrative problems even to a bureaucracy geared largely to the administration of state provision. The same could not be said of the more radical proposals being canvassed by the 'New Right' outside Parliament during 1982 and early 1983 (see West 1982). Thus, for the government, the knowledge that the expansion of the Scheme into a fully-fledged voucher system would not command the same degree of consensus as the original scheme within the Conservative Party, and even less outside it, has combined with worries about its administrative and resource implications to counsel extreme caution. It would therefore be an exaggeration to claim that a market liberal

approach to educational provision gained ascendancy
over more traditional approaches even when Joseph
(a prime example of Dale's privatisers) and Boyson
(the leading populist) were together as ministers
at the DES.   Despite the fact that both had declared
a philosophical preference for educational vouchers
and an expanded private sector, their public pronouncements on government policy on the issue were
hedged with qualifications.   Thus Joseph stated in
a parliamentary answer on July 20, 1982, that, while
being "keen to find ways in which parental influence
and involvement in education might be taken yet
further than the point reached in the Education Act
1980", he was "not clear what part privatisation
might play in this".   Meanwhile, Boyson recognised
that, although education vouchers were being given
"serious consideration ..., at the moment things are
'up in the air'".   He was reported as saying that
much depended on the "climate of opinion", adding
"Nothing is more powerful than an idea whose time
has come" (Albert 1982).
    What became clear from discussions about Con-
servative education policy in the period leading up
to the 1983 General Election was that there was a
considerable lack of confidence even amongst those
ministers committed in principle to the idea of
vouchers that its time had actually come.   Indeed,
the ambivalence displayed by ministers on this issue
contrasted starkly with the government's so-called
'resolute approach' (5) in other areas of policy,
though there were some clear parallels in relation
to 'family policy'.   Tentative use of press leaks
indicated a continuing ambivalence and a need to
appease non-Thatcherite groups both inside and outside the party.   The possible voucher scheme outlined in the Daily Telegraph in November 1982 fell
far short of a major re-orientation of policy and
was, in many respects, a straightforward extension
of the Assisted Places Scheme of a kind that could
still command support from most sections of the party.
Yet this attempt to construct a policy that would
retain widespread support was made more difficult by
the impatience of Thatcherite groups outside the DES
for real progress towards a genuine cross-sector
voucher scheme.   The Daily Telegraph leader on the
November proposals condemned them as "a caricature
of the voucher idea, which would do far more to
discredit than to advance it" (November 8, 1982).
Even the more ambitious pilot experiments proposed
in January 1983 for possible inclusion in the forthcoming election manifesto were reportedly referred

back because Treasury ministers felt that they did too little to make state schools respond to market forces. Throughout consideration of the various possible schemes, ministers faced the dilemma that "too radical a scheme might alienate Conservative-controlled education authorities ... as well as frightening the electorate", while "too modest a scheme might not be worth doing at all". (6) Joseph continually stressed that it was "certainly not government policy at the moment" to introduce vouchers on a wide scale (e.g. BBC Television 'Nationwide', January 31, 1983) and, when the election campaign itself got underway in May, no clear and generally acceptable policy had emerged. The difficulties which this issue posed for the Conservative Party were symbolised in a minor controversy early in the election campaign over the fact that, although the party's election manifesto made no explicit reference to a voucher system, the candidates' notes issued by Central Office intimated that this was what the coded reference to "widening parental choice and influence over their children's schooling" might actually mean. (7)

The composition of the ministerial team at the DES after the landslide election victory in June 1983 suggests, however, that education policy will not be a major priority in the early years of Mrs. Thatcher's second term in office. (8) A small-scale voucher experiment or a relatively modest extension of the Assisted Places Scheme still seem the most likely policy initiatives in our field of interest in the immediate future. This should make us wary of attempting to 'read off' education policy from the general balance of power within a party or the ideological preferences of those groups that currently dominate it. More than this is involved, of course, in understanding the formulation and implementation of policy in any field, but it does seem that the formation that we have termed 'Thatcherism' faces some peculiar difficulties in translating its ideological preferences into specific education policy proposals of a sort that can command sufficient support to be feasible.

Nevertheless, it has certainly been suggested to us by a senior member of the Conservative Party that, while no voucher scheme of any sort would have commanded majority Cabinet support three years ago, this is no longer necessarily the case. This suggests that, although a market liberal philosophy has certainly not yet prevailed in the field of education, a significant change has taken place in the way the state education service is viewed within government circles. As we have suggested, even limited proposals for voucher experiments or an extension of the Assisted Places Scheme would be likely to encourage an expansion of the private sector and, by presenting entry to it as a legitimate aspiration for all, they could have a potentially powerful backwash effect on the status of public sector provision. Such initiatives would also help to foster a climate in which a more full-blown attempt at privatisation would become a real possibility should the balance of forces within the party change still further and wider support seem more attainable. The fact that the term 'privatisation' can now be used so freely in discussions of educational provision when only a few years ago it was restricted to housing, refuse collection and the more profitable parts of the Health Service, demonstrates just how much progress has been made towards constructing a climate favourable to a predominantly market liberal approach to social policy. It has never been more clearly on the agenda this century, even if a final decision on its feasibility within education has been deferred. So it is clear that traditional Labour Party hopes of the 'withering away' of the private sector are now balanced by a Conservative policy option of a 'withering away' of state provision at least beyond a basic minimum.

THEORETICAL PERSPECTIVES AND EDUCATIONAL POLICY

Turning now to our own investigation of the Assisted Places Scheme, we want to conclude this paper with a brief discussion of the relevance of research of this nature to theoretical debates within the sociology of education. This is in no sense an attempt to present 'findings', which would be an entirely inappropriate exercise at this stage of the research, but rather an exploration of the scope for theorising within a particular policy-oriented study. The issues are complicated in this case by the fact that the three principal researchers come to their task with distinctly different theoretical predilections. Initially, we felt that it would be feasible to design the research in such a way as to agree on the nature of the data in which we were interested, and to use that data to test some of the claims made for and against the policy at the time of its inception. At the same time, we attempted to identify some middle-range theories which, although themselves informed by broader theories, could be interrogated with this same data. We suggested, for example, that it could

be used to probe more general claims such as -
(a) that the scholarship 'ladder' is a way of enhancing equality of opportunity and so producing a
genuine meritocracy, (b) that the scholarship 'ladder'
is a means whereby leading elements of the working
class may be co-opted into the service of the ruling
class, (c) that urban comprehensive schools are becoming inheritors of the elementary school tradition,
and (d) that state provision of services is being
reduced to the minimum compatible with the reproductive needs of capital while other state resources are
diverted to stimulate the private sector.

   We were, however, quite explicit in our initial
project proposal that "research of this nature cannot
be used to establish or refute the varieties of high-
level functionalist, Marxist and Weberian theories
that are characteristically used to account for (the
relationships between education, state and society)".
Nevertheless, although that view of the extent to
which the project might adjudicate between competing
theoretical positions has not altered, internal
debates within the research team often seem to focus
on the relationship between the data being generated
and our broader theoretical interests. We felt
therefore that the conference would be an appropriate
context in which to explore some of the wider issues
involved in developing a relationship between policy
studies in education and sociological theorising.
The question we would like to pose is this. Is there
any empirical material that might be generated by a
policy study of this sort that might lead us to adopt
one rather than another theoretical perspective, or
can the issues with which we are dealing be equally
well accounted for in the differing terms of mutually
incompatible frameworks?

   Theoretical paradigms in the social sciences
differ in at least four respects: they employ
different vocabularies, or sets of terminology; they
involve different presuppositions about relationships
among conceptually constructed elements of society;
they rest on differing philosophical anthropologies,
particularly concerning the relationships of structure
and agency in human history; and they are inspired
by different 'knowledge-informing interests'. Although
the possibility of a theory-neutral data language can
be discounted, is there some empirical method of
adjudicating among competing approaches?

   To some extent, it is proving possible to gather
data relevant to the claims generated by proponents
and antagonists in the political debates; but even
the 'raw' data thus gathered is framed in terms of

certain concepts, categories, and assumptions, and there is perhaps a limit to the extent to which such data may be translated into the terms of different theoretical frameworks. (An obvious case in point is the interpretation of different occupational categories in terms of different theories of 'class' and class structure.) Nevertheless, some further reflections on the issue of the compatibility between the sort of data we are gathering and various different sociological theories may be worthwhile even at this preliminary stage of our project.

The theoretical approaches we shall consider are structuralist Marxism, class-theoretical Marxism, and Weberian sociology. Structuralist Marxism is of course associated with the names of Althusser (1969, 1979; Althusser and Balibar 1970) and of Poulantzas (1973). The mode of explanation is implicitly functionalist, focusing on the relationships among levels in a complexly articulated totality; the analytic focus is on the logic of functioning of a given mode of production; the role of agency is demoted in favour of structure, humans appearing as the 'bearers of structures' rooted in a specific mode of production. Attempts by these structuralist writers to theorise the relationship between mode of production, social formation and the class struggle in a more complex way have only marginally modified their approach. Class-theoretical Marxism is a broad category including a range of neo-Marxist positions which share certain fundamental departures from the structuralist approach. The category would range from instrumentalists like Miliband (1973) to the recent work of Jessop (1983), Dale (1982), Johnson (1979) and others, whose focus is more clearly on class struggle and human agency. These writers place more emphasis on the historically variant nature of the social formation, and allow for considerable autonomy for the role of culture. This gives their work a more voluntaristic, activist flavour. The mode of production is seen more as 'setting limits' and 'exerting constraints' than as determining in any strong sense the course of historical change. The Weberian approach, although sometimes inaccurately characterised as 'idealist', is also aware of the brute facts of structural constraints on action, both political and economic. Weber himself was quite pessimistic in his search for the maximisation of freedom within the 'iron cage'. In contrast to Marxism, however, the Weberian approach involves no a priori presupposition about the causal priority of the mode of production or the material base.

Rather, empirical analysis of contingent relationships among elements of complex historical configura-
tions is required in order to impute causal significance (e.g. Weber 1968). (9)

How can these approaches be applied to the
material we have already presented? There are a
number of elements involved in the policies and issues
considered above which may be differently interpreted
according to the preferred theoretical framework, and
it would obviously be impractical to consider all of
these here. For the present purposes, we shall focus
in this section specifically on the typology of recent
Conservative educational policy discourse presented
above, and consider in particular questions about the
origins and consequences of the ideological clusters
depicted there. We identify some of the questions
raised by this typology and explore how empirical
answers to these questions might be differently
incorporated in the different ideological frameworks
under discussion.

First, the question is raised of the relationship between identifiable social groups and the ideological clusters or categories delineated by Room
and Dale. There is some ambiguity in the use of
labels to characterise modes of discourse, or repertoires, which may be combined in complex ways by
single individuals, and their use to refer to particular groups of people (the 'privatisers', the 'populists', and so on), who may together combine in
different political alliances. To take the analysis
further, one would have to determine which groups
held what range of positions and in what circumstances,
and to consider both the social origins of those
holding certain combinations of views and the social
interests which those views might serve. Findings
on social origins and on social interests could be
accommodated, in differing ways, by the three theoretical frameworks under consideration. The question
of social origins has become less important in the
analysis of ideologies since Mannheim's day, but is
still important in some theories of the state -
notably that of Miliband, who is perhaps closest to
the Marxian notion of the state as the "executive
committee of the bourgeoisie", and is particularly
salient in considering the independent sector as a
mode of recruiting able children into the elite.
None of the three approaches assumes a close fit
between ideologies and specific social groups,
although they have different methods of conceptualis-
ing the looseness of fit. These range from concepts
of hegemony and false consciousness in the Marxist

traditions to Weber's notion of elective affinity
(or Wahlverwandschaft). The question of social
interests may appear to differentiate more clearly
among the various approaches. For Marxism, social
interests play an important role in explanation, since
the theoretical 'knowledge-informing interests'
revolve around the issue of the reproduction or otherwise of the capitalist mode of production. Thus the
consequences of an ideology, and the social interests
it serves, are central to the analysis. This retrospective angle of interest can lend a somewhat functionalist slant even to class-theoretical Marxism,
although, unlike structuralist Marxism, it cannot
treat agents' intentions, ideas and perceptions as
being largely irrelevant to the explanation of
historical outcomes. The Weberian approach would
differ from both sorts of Marxism in that the consequences of an ideology (its effects on reproduction
or transformation), while historically interesting,
are not integral to the explanation. The 'warring
of the Gods', of mutually irreconcilable value-
systems, cannot be explained in terms of the social
interests being served, as these refer to the functioning of a specific socioeconomic system. For
Weberians, that system does not exhaustively explain,
or solely set the limits and constraints upon, the
complexity of historical determinations and eventua-
tions. It might be argued, of course, that the same
can be said of class-theoretical analyses of particular
historical conjunctures (e.g. Johnson 1979, Dale 1983)
and we return later to the compatibility of such
Marxist analysis with Weberian sociology.

The second question raised by our political
typology is - why do particular political coalitions
of particular views become dominant at specific points
in time? Some explanation is required both of the
rise of 'Thatcherism' at the expense of older Tory
traditions during the 1970s, and of its continued
popularity when economic recession and rising unemployment might have been expected to lower the esteem
in which any government was held. The more deterministic versions of Marxism would presumably see
'Thatcherism' as the necessary ideological means of
restructuring British capitalism in crisis. Weberians
might posit a purely contingent relationship between
the ideological phenomenon and the economic crisis
of the late 1970s and early 1980s. Class-theoretical
Marxism might adopt some combination of these approaches, though the question then arises of how 'soft'
its determinism can become while still retaining, in
any meaningful sense, distinctively Marxist presuppo-

143

sitions about relationships among elements in societal structure, reproduction and change. (9)

That broad question may itself be approached through a third and more specific question arising from our characterisation of 'Thatcherism' and education. Against what opposition were particular policies introduced? Taken alone, the typology might suggest that policy emanates from certain powerful political actors, in apparent isolation from any intrinsically important context of conflict, debate, or opposition. In this sense, it would suggest a minimal and one-sided interest group theory with most of the salient interest groups left out. In considering the wider context of policy construction, formulation and legislation, all three approaches might implicitly employ some sophisticated form of pluralism as part of the analysis. When such pluralism does not presuppose (a highly hypothetical and unlikely) equality of power and resources among competing interest groups, and does not ignore structural constraints on action, it can play an important part in both Marxist and non-Marxist analyses (although it is unclear how analysis of competition between interest groups can be meaningfully related to the wider metatheoretical tenets of structuralist Marxism). In this respect we might expect considerable formal convergence, or indeed compatibility, between the Weberian and class-theoretical accounts, though the terms and characterisations employed in the analysis would differ according to the preferred theoretical vocabulary and its associated assumptions.

Finally, there is the question - one which forms the thrust of much of our current empirical work - of the historical outcomes of policies, of the translation of legislative act into social fact. How unintended are the social consequences of social policies? How do outcomes compare with intentions? And what are the implications of empirical findings, in relation to the varying claims initially made by political actors, for theories concerning social and cultural reproduction and for assumptions about structure and agency in societal change? Marxism might regard any particular policy development as irrelevant to its central 'knowledge-informing' interests. Insofar as the issue is perceived retrospectively as being relevant, structuralist Marxism can account for whatever outcomes we may find in terms of structural determinations irrespective of the agents' acknowledged intentions. Class-theoretical Marxism, by allowing greater importance to the role of agency

144

and struggle, may interpret outcomes partly incompatible with the reproduction of the capitalist mode of production in terms of oppositional intervention and resistance. Yet given the wide range encompassed by the general category, there are many possible variations in this theoretical area. In one view, abolition of the Assisted Places Scheme by any future Labour government, perhaps followed by an assault on the independent sector generally, might be seen as a progressive step in the direction of attacking the capitalist class structure and the 'closed' recruitment of elites. But in another view, such a victory for parliamentary socialism would represent merely another step in the incorporation of the working class in advanced capitalism and the bourgeois democratic state, since assaults on the visibly privileged independent sector would serve solely to disguise the continued inequalities in the social relations of production. In that sense, a genuinely comprehensive system of secondary education might seem to serve the meritocratic ideologies of social democracy and the capitalist welfare state more than the sharpening of class awareness and class struggle. The Weberian approach, with its somewhat different 'knowledge-informing interests', would consider outcomes in wider terms than their functionality or otherwise for the reproduction of the capitalist mode of production. Such an account would rather be couched in terms of the transformations of social action in particular sets of structural circumstances which constrain and influence the development of historical outcomes, as the irony of history distorts (often tragically) the initial goals and intentions of actors motivated by both ideal and material interests.

What are the implications of these reflections? Explanatory accounts in all three theoretical frameworks would be retrospective, rather than predictive, in intention; one could not expect to 'test' or 'falsify' approaches at this general, metatheoretical level as one might with more specific substantive hypotheses. As we have indicated, there are differences among the approaches in vocabulary, analytic focus, philosophical anthropology, and knowledge-informing interests. While refinements and developments in each of these areas may take place within the particular theoretical tradition, it is not clear whether there are means of mutually acceptable adjudication among the traditions on particular sets of metatheoretical assumptions. An adequate consideration of competing accounts in relation to a specific policy would in any case require much lengthier dis-

cussion than we have been able to give here, and might
raise the question of whether Conservative policies
towards private education would constitute appropriate
material for such an examination anyway. Nevertheless
those working in the sociology of education do employ
different assumptions in their analyses, and even our
own preliminary reflections raise some important
general questions. It appears from our account that
structuralist Marxism probably differs more from both
class-theoretical Marxism and Weberian sociology than
do either of the latter from each other on the fundamental issue of structure and agency. The crucial
difference between the class-theoretical and Weberian
approaches arises from the former's focus as inspired
by knowledge-informing interest on the mode of production. The central focus of both forms of Marxism
clearly derives from their concern with social reproduction and the possibilities for social transformation. Yet recent critiques by Marxists of deterministic interpretations of historical materialism, and
consequent attempts to assign a causal role to culture
in the development of a particular mode of production,
raise questions about whether it remains possible to
identify either a distinctively Marxist political
economy, or a wider Marxist historical sociology. (10)
To this extent, the most diluted forms of class-
theoretical Marxism are formally more compatible with
Weberian sociology than they might wish to acknowledge.
     Perhaps we can end with some further questions.
Given that competing approaches can give what are on
their own terms valid retrospective accounts of the
particular problem being analysed, on what grounds
should we prefer one approach rather than another, and
adopt its terminology and assumptions rather than those
of another, for reasons other than initial moral and
political preference or indeed arbitrary patterns of
taste? If we can formulate no empirical means of
adjudicating among approaches on this particular substantive issue, in what sense can our 'academic'
interpretations of the material claim a status different from the arguments and ideologies current in the
general political debate which we are analysing? Our
research itself constitutes an intervention in the
social processes under analysis in a variety of ways
which pose methodological problems of their own. But
we must also ask - will our social scientific interpretations of our findings also constitute interventions in the political debate which differ only in
being better informed empirically than the current
ideological assertions and arguments? Would the
accumulation of a large number of studies in a similar

genre make it easier to resolve such issues?   We
hope to have some clearer answers to these questions
in a few years time!

ACKNOWLEDGEMENTS

The authors gratefully acknowledge the support of the
Social Science Research Council for the research
which they are currently undertaking.   They would
also like to thank the following people for their
helpful comments on an earlier version of this paper:
Madeleine Arnot, Len Barton, Gerald Bernbaum, Roger
Dale, Gordon Hogg, Stephen Walker and participants
in the Westhill Conference, January 1983, at which
the original version was first presented.

NOTES

(1)   Halsey, Heath and Ridge had to limit their
observations to boys' public schools as their data
concerned only male respondents.   Our own work will
explore the significance of the education of boys
and girls outside the state system.
(2)   Given the government's continuing sponsor-
ship of the Manpower Services Commission, it is argu-
able that Dale exaggerates the decline of the
Industrial Trainers.   Nevertheless, even there, an
attack on the more corporatist aspects of the MSC
has been evident under the Thatcher government.
(3)   For a discussion of the limitations of the
present Assisted Places Scheme from this perspective,
see West (1982).
(4)   Even Sir Geoffrey Howe, architect of many
Thatcherite policies and a long-standing proponent
of educational vouchers, has acknowledged this as a
problem and has accepted that if a voucher system
"were tried now most of the money would be given to
parents who already pay for education" (The Guardian,
May 24, 1983).   Whether or not a voucher system
would save public expenditure in the medium to long
term remains a matter of intense controversy even
amongst those who favour it.   Nevertheless, the
long-term aim of the market liberals is that it should
do so.
(5)   This was the term adopted by the Conservative Party to characterise its approach to government
and used in its publicity campaigns during 1981/83.
(6)   See Passmore's article on the "tameness"
of the voucher scheme then under consideration,
Times Educational Supplement, February 11, 1983.

(7)　See The Conservative Manifesto 1983,
Conservative Central Office, May 1983, and a report
in The Times, May 20, 1983.
(8)　See Times Educational Supplement, June 17
1983.　See also The Guardian for June 16, 1983 on
the likely abandonment of any large-scale introduction
of vouchers.
(9)　There is wide scope for debate concerning
what might constitute 'distinctively Marxist' tenets
or a 'distinctively Marxist' theory of history.　For
a broad survey of a range of Marxist traditions, see
Kolakowski (1981).　For a strong interpretation of
Marxist theory of history, see Cohen (1978).　For
differences among contemporary Marxist interpretations,
see for example Thompson (1978) and Anderson (1980).
Obviously these matters cannot be dealt with in the
present paper.
(10) As Marxism is a continually developing
tradition, by no means limited to the repetition of
'received wisdom', the notion of what is or is not
'essentially' Marxist may itself be debated and
frequently is within our own research team.

REFERENCES

Albert, T. (1982) 'The cheapest way to help the
　　　brightest and best', The Guardian, 23 November
　　　1982
Althusser, L. (1969) For Marx, Penguin Books,
　　　Harmondsworth
Althusser, L. (1971) Lenin and Philosophy and Other
　　　Essays, New Left Books, London
Althusser, L. and Balibar, E. (1970) Reading Capital,
　　　Random House, New York
Anderson, P. (1980) Arguments within English Marxism,
　　　New Left Books, London
Banks, O. (1955) Parity and Prestige in English
　　　Secondary Education, Routledge and Kegan Paul,
　　　London
Board of Education (Public Schools Committee) (1944)
　　　The Public Schools and the General Education
　　　System (The Fleming Report), HMSO, London
Cohen, G. (1978) Karl Marx's Theory of History: A
　　　Defence, Clarendon Press, Oxford
Conservative Party (1983) Independent Schools:
　　　Speakers' Notes, Conservative Central Office
Dale, R. (1982) 'Education and the capitalist state:
　　　contributions and contradictions', in Apple, M.
　　　(Ed.), Cultural and Economic Reproduction in
　　　Education, Routledge and Kegan Paul, London

Dale, R. (1983) 'Thatcherism and education', in
    J. Ahier and M. Flude (Eds.), Contemporary
    Education Policy, Croom Helm, London
Dancy, J. (1963) The Public Schools and the Future,
    Faber, London
Finn, D., Grant, N. and Johnson, R. (1977) 'Social
    democracy, education and the crisis', Working
    Papers in Cultural Studies Number 10, Centre
    for Contemporary Cultural Studies, Birmingham
Gamble, A. (1981) Britain in Decline, Macmillan,
    London
Gamble, A. (1983) 'The rise of the resolute right',
    New Socialist, 9, pp. 7-14
Gathorne-Hardy, J. (1977) The Public School Phenomen-
    on, Hodder and Stoughton, London
Glennerster, H. and Wilson, G. (1970) Paying for
    Private Schools, Allen Lane, London
Hall, S. (1979) 'The great moving right show',
    Marxism Today, January, pp. 14-20
Halsey, A., Heath, A. and Ridge, J. (1980) Origins
    and Destinations: Family, Class and Education
    in Modern Britain, Clarendon Press, Oxford
Howarth, T. (1969) Culture, Anarchy and the Public
    Schools, Cassell, London
ISIS (1973) What is a Direct-Grant School?, ISIS,
    London
ISIS (1974) The Case for Independence, ISIS, London
ISIS (1975) If the Grant Goes: The threat to the
    Direct-Grant and Grant-Aided Schools of
    Britain, ISIS, London
ISIS (1976) Selection: Modern Education's Dirty Word,
    ISIS, London
ISIS (1981) The Case for Collaboration: the Indepen-
    dent Schools and the Maintained System, ISIS,
    London
Jessop, Bob (1982) The Capitalist State, Martin
    Robertson, Oxford
Johnson, R. (1979) 'Three problematics: elements of
    a theory of working-class culture', in
    J. Clarke, C. Critcher and R. Johnson (Eds.),
    Working Class Culture, Hutchinson, London
Kamm, J. (1971) Indicative Past: A Hundred Years of
    the Girls' Public Day Schools Trust, Allen and
    Unwin, London
Kolakowski, L. (1981) Main Currents of Marxism (3
    volumes), Oxford University Press, Oxford
Labour Party (1980) Private Schools (A Discussion
    Document), Labour Party, London
Labour Party (1981) A Plan for Private Schools,
    TUC-Labour Party Liaison Committee, London
Lambert, R. (1966) The State and Boarding Education,

Methuen, London

Lambert, R. (1975) *The Chance of a Lifetime*,
     Weidenfeld and Nicolson, London

Miliband, R. (1973) *The State in Capitalist Society*,
     Quartet Books, London

Musgrove, F. (1979) *School and the Social Order*,
     Wiley, London

Parkinson, M. (1970) *The Labour Party and the
     Organisation of Secondary Education*, Routledge
     and Kegan Paul, London

Poulantzas, N. (1973) *Political Power and Social
     Classes*, New Left Books, London

Pring, R. (1982) 'Privatisation', *Where*, No. 186
     (March) pp. 9-14

Public Schools Commission (1968 and 1970) *First
     Report* and *Second Report*, HMSO, London

Rae, J. (1979) *The Public School Revolution*, Faber,
     London

Robinson, G. (1971) *Private Schools and Public
     Policy*, Department of Social Science and
     Economics, Loughborough University

Room, G. (1979) *The Sociology of Welfare*, Martin
     Robertson, London

Salter, B. and Tapper, T. (1981) *Education, Politics
     and the State*, Grant McIntyre, London

Taylor-Gooby, P. (1981) 'The New Right and social
     policy', *Critical Social Policy*, 1, 1, pp. 18-
     31

Thompson, E.P. (1978) *The Poverty of Theory*, Merlin
     Press, London

Weber, M. (1968) *Economy and Society*, Bedminster
     Press, New York

West, E.G. (1982) 'Education vouchers - evolution
     or revolution', *Journal of Economic Affairs*,
     3, 1, pp. 14-19

Williams, R. (1961) *The Long Revolution*, Chatto and
     Windus, London

PART TWO

CRISIS IN RESEARCH

ON THE APPLICATION OF QUALITATIVE RESEARCH TO THE
POLICY PROCESS: AN EMERGENT LINKAGE

Ray C. Rist

> There is no body of methods;   no
> comprehensive methodology for the
> study of the impact of public policy
> as an aid to future policy.
>
> James Coleman, 1972

INTRODUCTION

A decade later, Coleman's now famous quote still
rings true.   Indeed, one can argue that in the
intervening years, the tendency in policy research
and analysis has become even more centrifugal,
spinning off more methodologies, more conceptual
frameworks, and more disarray among those who work
under the rubric of 'policy studies'.   A number of
thoughtful critics of the current scene of policy
studies and the attendant methodologies have argued
that any improvements in the techniques of policy
research have not led to greater clarity about what
to do or what to think.   Instead, these improvements
have led to a greater sense of complexity and confusion (cf. Cohen and Weiss, 1977).   More charitably,
it could be argued that the multiplicity of approaches
to policy research should be welcomed as they bring
different skills and strengths to what are admittedly
difficult and complex educational issues.
    Regardless of whether one supports or challenges
the contention that policy research has had a centrifugal impact on the knowledge base relevant to
decision making, the bottom line remains much the
same: what policy researchers tend to consider as
improvements in their craft have not significantly
enhanced the role of research in policymaking.
Instead, the proliferation of persons, institutes
and centres conducting policy-related work has led

153

to more variation in the manner by which problems are defined, more divergence in the way in which studies are designed and conducted, and more disagreement and controversy over the ways in which data are analysed and findings reported. The policymaker now confronts a veritable glut of conflicting research information.

A sobering but provocative counterintuitive logic is at work here: increased personnel, greater allocation of resources, and growing sophistication of methods have not had the anticipated effect of greater clarity and understanding of the policy issues before us. Rather, current efforts have led to a more complex, complicated, and partial view of the issues and their solutions.

While one may grant that early policy work in education, for example, was frequently simplistic and not especially sophisticated in its designs or application of methods, the inverse does not, in and of itself, work to the advantage of the policymaker. To receive a report resplendent with 'state of the art' methodologies and complex analyses that tease out every nuance and shade of meaning on an issue may provide just as little guidance for effective decision making as did the former circumstances. Stated differently, a fixation on the technical adequacy of policy research without a commensurate concern for its utilisation is to relegate that work to quick obscurity (cf. Chelimsky, 1982).

If this admittedly brief description of the current state of policy research approximates the reality, then a fundamental question arises: What ought to be the role of research in informing the policy process? This question I take to be central to the focus of our deliberations here over the next several days. I should like, in the pages of this paper, first to address certain generic aspects of both policy decision making and policy research, and second, to address the several contributions of ethnographic research in particular to effecting a linkage between the two.

THE NATURE OF POLICY DECISION MAKING

Policy decision making is multidimensional and multifaceted. Research is but one (and often minor at that) among a number of often contradictory and competing sources that seek to influence what is an ongoing and constantly evolving process. I stress here the term 'process' because I should choose to describe policy decision making as more or less unbounded, as characterised by actors who arrive on the scene (often unannounced) and leave again, as not delimited by clearly defined constraints of time and location, and as often as not neither purposeful nor calculated. Such a description suggests the antithesis of the conventional understanding of decision making. In this latter, more traditional approach, decision making is understood as a discrete event, undertaken by a defined set of actors working in 'real time' and moving to their decision on the basis of their analysis of alternatives.

Weiss has nicely summarised this notion of 'decision making as an event' when she writes (1982: 23):

> Both the popular and the academic literature picture decision making as an event; a group of authorized decision makers assemble at particular times and places, review a problem (or opportunity), consider a number of alternative courses of action with more or less explicit calculation of the advantages and disadvantages of each option, weigh the alternatives against their goals or preferences, and then select an alternative that seems well suited for achieving their purposes. The result is a decision.

She also nicely demolishes this view when she writes (1982:26):

> Given the fragmentation of authority across multiple bureaus, departments, and legislative committees, and the disjointed stages by which actions coalesce into decisions, the traditional model of decision making is a highly stylized rendition of reality. Identification of any clear-cut group of decision makers can be difficult. (Sometimes a middle-level bureaucrat has taken the key action, although he or she may be unaware that his or her action was going to be - or was - decisive.) The goals of policy are often equally diffuse, except in terms of 'taking care of' some undesirable situation. Which opinions are considered, and what set of advantages and disadvantages are assessed, may be impossible to tell in the interactive, multiparticipant, diffuse process of formulating policy. The complexity of governmental decision making often defies neat compartmentalization.

Of particular relevance here is that the focus on decision making as an ongoing set of adjustments, or mid-course corrections, eliminates the bind of having to pinpoint the event - that is, the exact time, place, and manner - in which research has been influential.   Parenthetically, because the specifics can seldom be supplied, the notion that research should impact on decision making events seems to have become more and more an article of faith.   That researchers have so persistently misunderstood deci-sion making, and yet constantly have sought to be of influence, is a situation deserving of considerably more analysis than it receives.   So long as researchers presume that research findings must be brought to bear upon a single event, a discrete act of decision making, they will be missing those cir-cumstances and processes where, in fact, research is and can be useful.   However, the reorientation to 'process decision making' and away from 'event decision making' necessitates looking at research as serving an 'enlightenment function' in contrast to an 'engineering function' (cf. Janowitz, 1971; Weiss, 1977).   Policy research can illuminate, it cannot dictate.

I should emphasise here that these comments ought not to be taken as a diatribe against research or an argument that knowledge counts for nought. Quite the contrary.   Research is an important and necessary component of the decision making process. Its relevance and usefulness will not become appar-ent, however, unless there is a reconsideration of what is understood by policy decision making.   A redefinition is needed of the context in which to look for a linkage between knowledge and action. It is my position that a shift from quantitative to qualitative research methodologies is integral to this redefinition.

RESEARCH FOR POLICY'S SAKE

Succinctly, the linkage between policy research and policy decision making is a tenuous one.   On both sides, there are differences in philosophy, in func-tion, in self-definition, and in criteria by which worth and success are measured.   Given that these two domains - knowledge and action - do not necessar-ily overlap and often are mutually contradictory, it is not surprising that their engagement period has been such a difficult one.   The effort to wed these two very dissimilar functions has not come easily.

Policymakers view themselves as flexible,

decision oriented, pragmatic, and able to thrive in
settings of high pressure and conflict.   These
characteristics are not part of the self-definition
of researchers, nor are they attributed to them by
others.   Chelimsky has described researchers in the
following way (1979:21):

> Researchers tend not to be very flexible.
> They have a design, they want to adhere
> to it, and they snarl if someone tries to
> tamper with their efforts in ways which
> they think are going to hurt or weaken
> their results.   A typical researcher is
> not a pragmatist, he can't be.   He's a
> seeker after truth, a knowledge fanatic,
> a juste, as the French would say.   When
> he works with government officials and
> program managers or practitioners, he seems
> like a sort of Robespierre unleashed in a
> world of unsuspecting Dantons.   Perhaps
> the most annoying thing about him is that
> he doesn't always understand those Dantons
> and doesn't realize that he doesn't under-
> stand.   He certainly doesn't always approve
> of them either, and he makes that quite
> clear.   He feels that they want things to
> be simple whereas he knows them to be com-
> plex.   To many researchers, in fact,
> social programs often seem to be expressions
> of faith, of wishful thinking: the 'hope
> springs eternal' of the political process.

There is also the need here briefly to distinguish between two levels of policy decision making.
The first level involves the establishing of the
broad parameters of government action, e.g. providing national health insurance, establishing a national energy policy, or restructuring the national
immigration laws.   At this level and in these instances, policy research input is likely to be quite
small, if not nil.   The setting of these national
priorities is a political event, a coming together
of a critical mass of politicians, special interest
groups, and of persons in the media to generate the
attention and focus necessary for the items to reach
the national agenda.   While one or another research
study might be quoted during this phase of agenda
setting, the initiative simply is not very reliant
on research findings or implications.
   At the second stage, however, when there is some
agreement among a sizeable sector of the policy

establishment that action ought to be taken, programs initiated, target populations identified, and resources allocated, the opportunities for policy research are much enhanced. At this stage, certain questions are amenable to influence from policy research - for example, questions of program performance, program improvement, delivery of services, comparisons among different program strategies, and decisions on where to allocate demonstration and model program funds.

To be amenable is but a precondition. The eventual utilisation of policy research is something quite different.

The researcher cannot dictate the use of policy research findings, but it can be argued that the researcher is able to influence the eventual reception and use of policy research, in two broad ways: through emphasis on technical adequacy and on usefulness. The researcher's concern with both is perhaps as much as can in good conscience be done in the hope of providing information and analysis that will be considered in the decision making process. Chelimsky (1983, forthcoming) suggests that the technical adequacy component can be subdivided into three parts: (1) the appropriateness of the study design for answering the questions posed within the time and cost parameters assigned; (2) the appropriateness of the execution of the study in terms of the design selected and the resources allocated; and (3) the absence of major conceptual errors, the misapplication of technical procedures, and the drawing of improper or unwarranted conclusions and inferences. Likewise, she suggests a number of subparts to the usefulness component of a policy study. These include (4) relevance, (5) timeliness, (6) presentation, and (7) impact.

If the researcher takes these seven aspects of a policy study together (and is concerned with each of them during the course of the study), the likelihood of utilisation should be considerably enhanced. But in the end there are no guarantees of influence and use with policy research; there are only opportunities that one more or less prepares for.

Much the same tenuousness characterises the situation of the policymaker. He or she cannot guarantee that sponsored policy research will be used, even if that research meets the tests of technical adequacy and usefulness. The degree to which the policymaker is able to use policy relevant research depends on a number of considerations, some of which are in his control, others of which are not. Where there is considerable pressure to create a program in concert with the philosophy of government in power at the time, research findings may be of little use. Likewise, where there are multiple constituencies organised against a particular policy initiative, quality report after quality report can have little impact on the eventual accommodation that must be achieved. Alternatively, in those instances where the policymaker has more discretion and is able to shape a newly authorised program, the opportunity for the use of policy research is heightened. The same can be said for those circumstances where there is an ongoing program that is perceived as weak, mismanaged or simply not having the desired outcomes. A manager given the mandate to rethink and reorganise such a program also creates a situation conducive to the use of policy research.

THE CONTRIBUTION OF QUALITATIVE RESEARCH

Two remarkable and interrelated events have occurred in policy research in the past ten years. The first is the dissolution of the natural science model of inquiry as the pre-eminent model in policy studies. This approach, frequently referred to as 'the scientific method', was lauded by Campbell and Stanley in 1963 as "the only available route to cumulative progress". The hegemony of this approach has dissolved as researchers have come to realise that there are multiple routes and multiple destinations for their efforts.

The causes of this recognition include the inability of the 'scientific' approach (1) reasonably to address many of the most pressing issues, for example, in education or health or employment training; (2) to respect the fluidity and change in social environments; and (3) to address the question of program processes instead of program outcomes. In addition, the outright antagonism of many practitioners and policymakers to the sterile empiricism characterising much of current research has forced new reflections on current practices. The limitations in the view that 'what cannot be measured cannot be important' have become apparent for all to see.

The second of the changes, and related to the first, is that the conceptual vacuum created by the retreat of quantitative methods into an intellectual cul-de-sac has been filled by a growing and vigorous interest in qualitative methods. Many researchers are now looking beyond simply expanding computer software capacity as the answer on how to 'do' science. The grip that the experimental model has

had on policy research has been loosened. No longer
is there overwhelming agreement that experimentation
is "the only way for settling disputes regarding
educational practice, the only way of verifying
educational improvement, and the only way of establishing a cumulative tradition in which improvement
can be introduced without the danger of a faddish
discard of old wisdom in favor of inferior motives"
(Campbell and Stanley, 1963:2, emphasis added). Two
pithy phrases suggest the reorientation of much
current policy research: "generalisations decay",
and "statistical realities do not necessarily coin-
cide with cultural realities".

The qualitative perspective (synonymous terms
used elsewhere include ethnography, ethnographic
research, field work, field studies, naturalistic
studies, and case study methodology) leads the investigator in quite different directions from those
predicated upon experimental and quasi-experimental
designs. Rather than presuming that human environments and interactions can be held constant, manipulated, treated, scheduled, modified or extinguished,
qualitative research posits that the most powerful
and parsimonious way to understanding human beings
and the social environments they have created is to
watch, talk, listen and participate with them in
these environments (cf. Rist, 1977, 1979, 1981, 1982b).
This is quite the opposite of claiming 'to know'
about human behaviour by fracturing it into small,
atomistic components that are then subjected to
intensive scrutiny (as if teacher-pupil interactions
and the internal structure of DNA both can be
approached using the same logic of inquiry). Qualitative research focusses on a different way of knowing - one based on experience, empathy, and involvement. These differences are caught in the German
language with two terms for knowing - wissen and
kennen, the former implying a quantitative and the
latter a qualitative perspective on knowledge.

If one holds that generalisations decay, one
can only reluctantly presume that policy research
can, through the application of any research strategy,
match the natural science goal of constructing theory
and formulating theorems and laws. Indeed, qualitative perspectives would suggest that such a goal is
quixotic at best and extremely destructive at worst.
The qualitative perspective would contend that to
understand any social program or social setting, one
must describe and analyse in an ecologically valid
manner the values, behaviour, settings, and interactions of the participants. An additional strength

of the qualitative approach comes in the emphasis on a longitudinal perspective, tracing out over time these values, behaviours and interactions. Asking the question, "What is going on here?" is at once disarmingly simple and incredibly complex. It is to the answer of this question that qualitative research addresses itself.

From the advent of the 'Great Society' program under President Johnson until recently, there was an unchallenged presumption that the answers to the 'big questions' in U.S. policy research were to be found in 'big studies'. The Coleman Report of 1966, Equality of Educational Opportunity, for example, was but one among many such large studies, based on data collection with literally tens of thousands of students. Quantitative methods, employing computerised data bases, were used to address pressing problems in the policy arena. Much of the work done in this mode, however, was soon seen to be ephemeral. For some policymakers, it resulted in disenchantment with policy research and generated claims that research has no role in the policy process.

The rush to measure outcomes in programs that were themselves little understood (or not at all) meant that the findings from these large studies frequently were of little or no utility. As policymakers became more and more dissatisfied with material they were receiving from the research community, they began pushing to refocus the efforts. Central to this push was the concern to learn exactly what program was in place and whether the implementation resulted in anything approximating the intentions of the policymakers who created and funded the effort. Once policymakers and researchers suspended the presumption that what had been anticipated did occur in fact, they had to refocus attention on finding out what 'really' was going on. Policymakers have come to realise that it is politically and administratively dangerous to rely on outcome measures of program impact while they are still guessing at the processes that produced those outcomes.

FORGING THE LINK

The task remaining is to make specific what has heretofore been general, to give examples of areas where qualitative research can inform the decision making process. I should like to suggest at least four such opportunities for linking qualitative policy research and decision making. These four are not meant to exhaust the possibilities, only to indicate the ways in which contributions are possible.

A RESPECT FOR DIVERSITY

It is a truism in social science research that the perceptions, values and attitudes one holds about various issues are highly influenced by one's location in the social structure. Stated differently, not everyone holds to the same definitions of reality. While this may at first glance appear somewhat facile, the multiple ways in which the world might be viewed and understood have direct implications for policy-making and program operation. To wit: while a policymaker may assume that intervention X will have impact Y, the recipients of that intervention may have understood and interpreted the actions quite differently, thus responding so as to create outcome Z - which for them was highly adaptive and successful. For the program administrator or policymaker, outcome Z was not anticipated or desired. Outcome Y was their goal, and in its absence, the program would most likely be judged a failure.

Quantitative work has been particularly unhelpful when shifts in understandings of program objectives or procedures have occurred. In a research mode where the outcomes are anticipated and predefined, 'good research' becomes an effort at rigorously measuring whether the outcomes actually appeared. Lipsey et al. (1981:304) have noted:

> The standards of the profession are based
> on a statistical inference model in which
> the null hypothesis assumption of no
> program effect provides the starting point
> for evaluation. The burden of the research
> is to show contrary evidence. For this
> approach to be justified, we must have
> confidence that the actual program effects
> will be registered in the measures chosen
> and will emerge through the noise and
> confoundings associated with the implemen-
> tation of research designs under field
> conditions. This is a large burden for
> a few measures and a 'one shot' research
> design to carry. The frequency of null
> findings in evaluation research may be, in
> part, because this burden is too great.

The quantitative approach is a hindrance to answering questions of concern to policymakers when the program in question was implemented in ways quite different

from those anticipated. The null hypothesis of no
program effect can in these instances be easily proven
because of the hiatus between what the researcher
anticipated and what in fact was implemented. But
is this conclusion of assistance to the policymaker
when the impacts that did emerge are ignored?

Currently, many policy researchers are reacting
against this mindset of assuming a priori the outcomes that are relevant and how they are to be
measured. Stating 'no effect' is really quite
different than stating 'effects were different from
what we anticipated and were able to measure'.

Qualitative research is appropriate to the
articulation of the multiple ways in which people
understand their world and react to it. By paying
attention to the manner in which program recipients
themselves define the situation and their needs, the
policymaker can check these perceptions against his
own. This is not to argue that the policymaker
ought to take on and ascribe to the views and values
of the participants, but only that this diversity
should alert the policymaker to the competing definitions of the situation and/or problem.

Several key dimensions of qualitative research
are germane to this contribution. First, qualitative research is longitudinal. It is predicated
upon spending time - considerable amounts of time -
with the various participants in a social setting.
It works to build trust and familiarity with the
persons involved so that the researcher can go, in
Erving Goffman's term, "backstage" to participate in
events, discussions and activities that never meet
the public eye. A longitudinal perspective also
allows the researcher to observe events over time.
This vantage, in contrast to the cross-sectional
approach of most survey and attitudinal research,
respects the fact that the values, beliefs, and
behaviours of individuals can and do change. What
quantitative research has to treat as static, qualitative work can treat as fluid and constantly evolving.

A second aspect of qualitative research that
contributes to this most complex (but, one hopes,
more accurate) mosaic of a social setting or intervention is that behaviours and beliefs are examined
in their context. This is particularly critical,
for example, in developing school-to-work transition
programs that accurately reflect the diversity of
ways in which young people come into adulthood. To
develop programs that presume a uniformity in the
young is to guarantee that many young people will not

benefit from them.   Answering the question of 'what
works best for whom' necessarily suggests a diversity
of strategies and of outcomes as well.   Indeed, we
have so little understanding of the cultures of the
young and the ways in which they are constantly adap-
ting that we find ourselves striving to rediscover
the wheel as we create education and employment
training programs for them (Berg, 1971; Rist, 1982a).

A third important contribution from committing
oneself to a longitudinal perspective in research is
that the presence of the observer at the site allows
for a continuity and ability to document the processes
of change as they occur.   The belief that intermit-
tent or 'hit and run' forays into the field are
sufficient to chronicle the changes in the setting
are presumptuous - unless, of course, one is content
with brief surface descriptions, a presumption that
leads to being surprised when situations turn out
differently from what a quick glance might suggest.

The problem with this approach is that policy-
makers do not like to be surprised.   They sponsor
policy research so as to enhance their information
base and be able to anticipate problem areas that will
require their attention.   It is this continuous relation to the field that gives the qualitative researcher
a sense of patterns, of what is predictable, of how
change is likely to be received (or rejected), and of
what factors precipitated acceptance or resistance.
Not to have this information leaves the policymaker
to guess what the settings are 'really like' or
simply to dismiss differences and assume that settings
elsewhere are like his own.   Either assumption carries
with it built-in risks - and the likelihood of more
surprises.

MULTIPLE LINES OF EVIDENCE AS A CHECK ON STATISTICAL
PORTRAYALS

Beyond the open question in quantitative research of
whether there is shared understanding of the concepts
and measures that are employed, there is the concern
with interpretation.   Statistical data can often
lead to mathematically correct but socially ludicrous
conclusions (Sieber, 1973).   Qualitative data can
provide an important 'validity check' on statistical
data.   Predicating a policy response upon a statistical definition of the situation can badly miss the
mark if the statistics obscure or miss important
dimensions of the setting.

Qualitative research thus becomes a key component
in multi-method studies.   So many policy studies are

predicated upon the single design, single method
approach of gathering and analysing quantitative data,
that qualitative work can provide an important counter-
weight to analysis generated solely from statistical
inference. Lipsey, et al. see this approach as not
only aiding the policymaker, but the field of policy
research as well. They write (1981: 303):

> We believe that the state of the art in
> evaluation research will advance more
> rapidly through increased use of multiple
> research designs and multiple lines of
> evidence within individual studies than
> through any foreseeable technical improve-
> ments in design and analysis or any futile
> hope that evaluators will suddenly be able
> to limit themselves to randomized experi-
> ments. An additional strength of evalu-
> ation through multiple lines of evidence,
> in our experience, is that it requires
> a much closer integration of quantitative
> information with qualitative information.
> Selection of multiple measures and designs,
> data probes and stratifications, and
> supplementary data collections must neces-
> sarily be based on an intimate understand-
> ing of program functioning, client response,
> and the vagaries of recordkeeping.

In contrast to strict statistical portrayals,
qualitative research is in a distinct position to
capitalise on the 'human dimension' that pervades
the political milieu in which policymaking occurs.
Qualitative data can give the policymaker a 'feel'
for the setting, the program, and the participants
that reams of statistical printouts can never match.
Computer printouts are difficult mechanisms by which
to convey the nuances of a setting or program, the
enthusiasm of the participants or the problems that
have led the program to the brink of disintegration.
The political arena in which policy is formulated is one where the key actors are not researchers.
They are politicians or generalists, individuals
who, of necessity, must 'stay in touch', 'cover
their bases', 'stay close to the folks back home',
and any number of other such stock phrases. As a
group, politicians function as arbitrators, mediators,
reconcilers and referees over the allocation of our
collective resources. Qualitative research can
speak to them with an authenticity, with a sense of
'how things really are' that can allow them to utilise

information relevant to their policymaking roles.

EXAMINING THE UNANTICIPATED

The earlier discussion on respecting the complexity
of the social world challenged the view that policy
researchers can hold the world still long enough to
maintain their experimental controls. The fact that
such rigour is ever elusive allows for events, situations and outcomes to emerge that are not under
'control'. In short, there are opportunities for
unanticipated consequences. Program managers know
that confronting the unanticipated is an incessant
part of their daily effort. Putting out brush fires
is but another way of acknowledging that events,
persons and situations have a tendency to go their
own way, not to act as predicted, and not according
to the original script.
     Research strategies not sufficiently flexible
and open-ended to accommodate this ever-present
serendipitous aspect of human behaviour are doomed
to reflect only that which stood still long enough
to be measured in conventional ways. The irony of
this is that these static aspects of the environment
are often the least interesting, the least critical,
and the least amenable to change (Bronfenbrenner,
1979). Research methods that can capture only the
stationary because of the epistemological assumptions
upon which they are built are strategies, as I have
said, in an intellectual cul-de-sac.
     Qualitative research puts no such constraints
upon itself. The observation and study of behaviour
in natural settings emphasises nonintervention, a
willingness to use any setting as a research site,
and allows events to go as they will. It is in this
way that the noncontrived aspects of situations can
be studied. Unanticipated events occur. Some are
episodic and marginal. Others take on a central and
profound importance. A close-in and longitudinal
familiarity can not only document that such unanticipated events do indeed occur, but can also determine
the relative importance of these events upon the long-
term adaptation and response of persons and organisations.

PROGRAM IMPLEMENTATION

In their 1978 assessment of previous large scale
efforts in the United States to address the problems
of youth unemployment, Mangum and Walsh posed the
following question (1978:11):

166

> It seems fair to ask whether the assumptions
> upon which past youth programs were based
> were faulty, or whether the programs them-
> selves were poorly designed or mismanaged.

The answer, as they themselves later suggest, is quite
unknown.   In large part this is because the research
was not conducted to answer a simple but necessary
question: what youth programs were actually implemented?

The process of moving from policy objectives to
program results by means of effective implementation
is one where most program managers are woefully unin-
formed.   Indeed, Hargrove (1975) sees it as the
"missing link" between policy formation and program
operation.   This view is supported by the Rand
Corporation study of federal program implementation.
The findings are quite consistent that federal programs are seldom implemented as they were designed
(Berman and McLaughlin, 1978).   The clean and crisp
organisational charts developed by new programs often
start to disintegrate before the ink is dry.   Any
number of unanticipated events or circumstances tend
to deflect the program in other directions.   The
complexities of program administration seldom conform
to the Weberian models drawn from 19th century Prussian
bureaucracies.

Successful program implementation necessitates
an ability to postulate a causal chain of sequences
that will allow the original policy objectives to be
translated into program realities.   Pressman and
Wildavsky have described it as follows (1979:XXI):

> Policies imply theories.   Whether stated
> explicitly or not, policies point to a
> chain of causation between initial conditions
> and future consequences.   If X, then Y.
> Policies become programs when, by authori-
> tative action, the initial conditions are
> created.   X now exists.   Programs make
> the theories operational by forging the
> first link in the causal chain connecting
> actions to objectives.   Given X, we act
> to obtain Y.   Implementation, then, is the
> ability to forge subsequent links in the
> causal chain so as to obtain the desired
> results.

Qualitative research is well suited to the study
of the implementation process.   The three examples
of the application of qualitative research to policy-

167

making noted in this section - respecting the complexity of the social system, providing a check on statistical interpretations, and studying the unanticipated consequences of social change - all are appropriate in the analysis of implementation. Each can contribute important insights into research that addresses how existing conditions, desired or otherwise, are obtained. The more the realisation that the implementation process has to be treated as an independent variable in any program assessment, the more imperative a qualitative perspective.

POSTSCRIPT

The policy process is incremental and interactive. Perhaps ninety per cent of the issues which a policymaker confronts are issues that have been faced before and will be faced again. They recur time and again. The policy process is seldom one of addressing new and uncharted problems. Rather, time is spent continually adjusting and responding to conditions in the society that demand a response from the public sector. In this context, those involved in providing information and analysis ought to quickly disabuse themselves of the notion that any one study or one report is likely to have a 'major' impact. Perhaps some very few do, but they are clearly the exceptions. As noted in the introduction, increased sophistication and application of policy research leads to an increased understanding of the complexity of the problem, but not to an increased capacity for decision making. The tension between knowledge and action is not resolved. The actual linkage between research input and policy output remains tenuous.

Policy research is not social engineering, nor can it aspire to be. It is best suited to enlighten. Cronbach and his associates (1980:47) have recently written that "instead of promoting single definitive studies that promise unquestionable guidance on a narrow issue of policy, evaluations should be contributing to the slow, continuous, cumulative understanding of a problem or intervention". They also note, "What is needed is information that will facilitate negotiation of a compromise rather than information that can be cranked into a decision rule"(1980:16).

Qualitative research is the antithesis of research predicated on prefabricated and furtive encounters. Understanding the dynamics of program implementation, for example, will demand a long-term commitment to the in-depth study of multiple social programs. These kinds of demands are the raison d'etre of qualitative work. By taking us inside the social settings and organisations of our societies, it informs us of existing conditions as they are, not as we might hope them to be. Substituting understanding for presumption is no mean feat.

NOTES

*) The views expressed here are those of the author and no endorsement by the US General Accounting Office or the United States Congress is intended or should be inferred.

(1) Though the focus is on the 'process', not the 'event', decisions still do get made. Weiss offers a number of undirected strategies that can result in a decision (1982:26-27): reliance on custom and implicit rules; improvisation; mutual adjustment; accretion; negotiation; move and countermove; a window for solutions; and indirection. Each of these she suggests can result in policy outcomes without "considered review or rational assessment".

REFERENCES

Berg, I. (1971) Education and Jobs: The Great Training Robbery, Beacon Press, Boston
Berman, P. and McLauglin, M.W. (1978) Federal Programs Supporting Educational Changes, Vol. VIII, The Rand Corporation, Santa Monica, CA
Bronfenbrenner, U. (1979) The Ecology of Human Development, Harvard University Press, Cambridge, MA
Campbell, D.T. and Stanley, J.C. (1963) Experimental and Quasi-Experimental Designs for Research, Rand McNally, Chicago, IL
Chelimsky, E. (1979) 'The Research Perspective', in E. Chelimsky (Ed.), Symposium on the Institutionalisation of Federal Programs at the Local Level, The MITRE Corporation, Arlington, VA
Chelimsky, E. (1982) 'Making Evaluations Relevant to Congressional Needs', The GAO Review, 17, 1
Chelimsky, E. (1983, forthcoming) 'Some Thoughts on the Nature, Definition and Measurement of Quality in Program Evaluation', in R. St. Pierre (Ed.), New Directions in Program Evaluation, Jossey-Bass, San Francisco, CA
Cronbach, L. (1982) Designing Evaluations of Educational and Social Programs, Jossey-Bass

Cohen, D.K. and Weiss, J. (1977) 'Social Science and
    Social Policy: Schools and Race', in R. Rist
    and R. Anson (eds.), Education, Social Science
    and the Judicial Process, Teachers College Press,
    New York
Hargrove, E. (1975) The Missing Link: The Study of
    the Implementation of Social Policy, The Urban
    Institute, Washington, DC
Janowitz, M. (1971) Sociological Methods and Social
    Policy, General Learning Press, New York
Lipsey, M.W., Cordray, D.S. and Berger, D.E. (1981)
    'Evaluation of a Juvenile Diversion Program:
    Using Multiple Lines of Evidence', Evaluation
    Review, 5, 3
Mangum, G. and Walsh, J. (1978) Employment and
    Training Programs for Youth: What Works Best
    For Whom?, Employment and Training Administra-
    tion, United States Department of Labour,
    Washington, DC
Pressman, J.L. and Wildavsky, A. (1979) Implementation
    (Second edition), University of California Press,
    Berkeley, CA
Rist, R.C. (1977) 'On the Relations Among Educational
    Research Paradigms: From Disdain to Detente',
    Anthropology and Education Quarterly, 8, 2
Rist, R.C. (1979) 'On the Means of Knowing:
    Qualitative Research in Education', New York
    University Education Quarterly, 10, 4
Rist, R.C. (1981) 'On the Utility of Ethnographic
    Research for the Policy Process', Urban Educa-
    tion, 15, 4
Rist, R.C. (1982a) Earning and Learning: Youth
    Employment Policies and Programs, Sage Publica-
    tions, Beverly Hills, CA
Rist, R.C. (1982b) 'On the Applications of Ethnogra-
    phic Inquiry to Education: Procedures and
    Possibilities', Journal of Research in Science
    Teaching, 19, 6
Sieber, S. (1973) 'The Integration of Fieldwork and
    Survey Methods', American Journal of Sociology,
    78, 6
Weiss, C.H. (1977) 'Research for Policy's Sake:
    The Enlightenment Function of Social Research',
    Policy Analysis, 3, 4
Weiss, C.H. (1982) 'Policy Research in the Context
    of Diffuse Decision Making', in R.C. Rist (ed.)
    Policy Studies Review Annual, Sage Publications,
    Beverly Hills, CA

ETHNOGRAPHY AND SOCIAL POLICY FOR CLASSROOM PRACTICE

Andrew Pollard

INTRODUCTION

There are two fundamental questions which have to be answered when considering the relationship between sociological research, education and policy formation. Firstly ... 'should the sociology of education seek to be policy-relevant?' If so, the second question follows ... 'has the sociology of education at present got anything to offer?'
I want to argue in this paper that we should make positive responses to both questions, an argument which is based unashamedly on a combination of political commitment and academic optimism. In so doing I shall be primarily concerned with ethnographic work and with its potential influence on classroom practice, as befits a recent classroom teacher. In this respect I shall focus on social policy at micro level - on the social policies which teachers adopt in their classrooms - which I take to be very important but which are often barely considered in discussions of public policy. I shall also focus on the potential influence of ethnographic work on the education of teachers, an issue which I take as a case study to illustrate more general arguments and which is clearly of professional importance to many of us.
These arguments are embedded in a more fundamental philosophical and theoretical position which sees both historical development and social processes in dialectical terms. Thus the dualities of action and constraint, the individual and social structure are seen as being constantly in process, events at the micro level are regarded as being powerfully influenced by factors at the macro level but they in turn are seen as exerting a creative influence back on to the social structure. Of course this theoreti-

cal position is well established, indeed it relates
directly to the early work of Marx (e.g. Marx 1970).
In terms of the sociology of education the dialectical model has, in the past, yielded critiques of
both the idealistic relativism of some interpretive
sociology and the pessimistic determinism of some
structural Marxist accounts.   More recently, however,
it has been applied to 'the crisis' by Michael Apple
(1982).   He writes that:

> Behind the ups and downs of the 'business
> cycle' and beyond the turmoil in education
> our daily lives and the lives of millions
> of people throughout the world are caught
> up in an economic crisis, one that will
> probably have lasting cultural, political
> and economic effects.   In fact, it is at
> the intersection of these three spheres of
> social life, how they interact, how each
> supports and contradicts the others, that
> we can see the crisis in its most glaring
> form.   The structural crisis we are
> currently witnessing - no, living - is not
> really 'explained' only by an economy,
> therefore (that would be too mechanistic),
> but by a social whole, by each of these
> spheres.   As Castells (1980) puts it, this
> is the case because:

>> the economy is not a 'mechanism'
>> but a social process continuously
>> shaped and recast by the changing
>> relationships of humankind to the
>> productive forces and by the class
>> struggle defining humankind in a
>> historically specific manner.

>   (Apple 1982: 1/2)

This then is where this paper starts, from a
belief that many recent developments in society are
divisive, regressive and unjust.   Indeed they
properly merit the term 'crisis'.   I start, too,
though from a belief that more positive developments
will only occur as the result of increased awareness
and action by people from many walks of life.
Two areas towards which I feel some particular
responsibility here are those of ethnography and
teacher education - hence this paper which is essentially about how to obtain an appropriate quality
and focus in ethnographic research so that it might

be more likely to have some influence on teacher consciousness and on the social policies which are adopted in classrooms.

PART ONE: SHOULD THE SOCIOLOGY OF EDUCATION SEEK TO INFLUENCE SOCIAL POLICY?

We must begin with the question of values, a question which is inescapable, particularly in the context of the political, economic and social crisis to which this volume addresses itself and one which is currently providing fascinating contrasts and debate between neo-Marxists - such as Madeleine Arnot and Geoff Whitty (1982), Michael Apple (1982), and the work of the Centre for Contemporary Cultural Studies (CCCS 1981) - and their recent critics, notably Andy Hargreaves and Martyn Hammersley (Hargreaves 1982, Hargreaves and Hammersley 1982). Hargreaves, for instance, claims that recent Marxist work is "distorted and incoherent" because of its political commitment, and he advocates a new commitment to "value-free science".

A discussion of this sort could clearly get out of hand quite quickly. The use of the concept of 'value freedom' is, to say the least, provocative; since in the opinion of many sociologists it has been consistently unmasked as a legitimating ideological device associated with inherently conservative positivist researchers. Alvin Gouldner (1970), for instance, was scathing in his attack on 'objectivity', describing it as "the ideology of those who are alienated and politically homeless", and as "the way one comes to terms and makes peace with a world which one does not like but will not oppose". Andy Hargreaves claims however, following Keat (1981), that a position of value-freedom is "consistent with socialist theory and practice" (1982: 122), but it is not immediately clear how he reconciles what appears to be a call for a lack of political commitment with such a statement.

The probability is that Hargreaves and Hammersley are simply making methodological points, in which case greater distinctions between the various stages of research work would help clarify matters. In an ongoing research project it is perfectly reasonable to expect the rigorous empirical testing of theory and a willingness to interpret results openly. Accurate, reliable, valid, generalisable research is a legitimate and necessary goal but we should be clear that such a goal reflects a concern with the quality of research rather than with its purpose or implica-

tion.   It is when we think about these two other
stages in particular, the <u>selection</u> of research topics
and the <u>dissemination</u> of results, that the influence
of political commitment is, in my view, legitimately
felt.

For sociologists, as for any other individuals
in society, to question and exert influence over the
aims and possible consequences of their own actions
seems to me to be entirely reasonable.   Of course,
if 'Science' could be separate from life, then we
might decide to retreat to our ivory towers without
undue concern.   The reality of the situation though
is rather different and we should recognise it.   We
cannot expect the world to stop while we attempt to
work out a scientifically 'pure' understanding of
"social life in general".   We are in a society,
indeed in a society in crisis, and cannot pretend
not to be.   This takes up the well-known position
of Gunnar Myrdal (1958) who wrote:

> The value connotation of our main concepts ...
> gives direction to our thoughts and signi-
> ficance to our inferences.   It poses the
> questions without which there are no answers
> ... and ... the value premise should not be
> chosen arbitrarily: it must be relevant
> and significant to the society in which we
> live.

> (Myrdal, 1958)

My own view then is that we need to separate
the various stages of research work far more clearly.
In the identification of problems and, to some
extent, in the design of research projects, I would
argue that the involvement of values is not only
unavoidable but is responsible and necessary.   There
is no shame in having a particular committed rationale
for undertaking research, indeed from many perspectives it is a social obligation.   Having said that,
I do take the Hargreaves/Hammersley argument that
there is little point in then misleading oneself by
failing to test one's thesis thoroughly with evidence
or by drawing conclusions perhaps because of 'political optimism'.   Such practices could not advance
any cause, but would simply lead to later confusion
and disappointment.   'Openness' is thus important
for the sound development of social analysis of whatever type but in my view it does need to be put in
its place.

I wonder too if there isn't an even more funda-

174

mental issue embedded here concerning different views on the nature of sociological research as such. The neo-Marxist school clearly see it as informing political action, whilst Hargreaves and Hammersley appear to put a priority on "developing social scientific understanding" as such. His position even leads Hammersley to advocate research at particular levels of analysis only, as part of an analytical division of labour - a position which is clearly anathema to those who view each 'part' of society as only being understandable in terms of the 'whole', and a position which makes the drawing of political inference much more difficult. I recognise the difficulties which are posed by the micro-macro problem but I take the issue to be fundamental to the nature of sociology and crucial if sociology is to provide incisive forms of critical social analysis. The macro-micro problem may well delay us but I doubt if we would have the same sociological or ethical integrity if we do not attempt to face it, be it with specific regard to gender, class, race or even age.

Now, if the arguments above are basically those of 'conscience', then a second, but no less important, set might be termed 'pragmatic'. In the first place it is clearly the case that policy decisions will be taken at all levels of social life whether sociologists participate or not. If we do not then we run a particular risk, for the work which we do in the name of 'social science' is always liable to be used or interpreted by others in ways which we may not have anticipated and might not want to endorse. Of course, research findings must be published to make them open to criticism, but once publication occurs the material in a sense becomes public property, it may be institutionalised and politicised, and to a great extent we may lose control over it. This, in my view, reinforces the importance of recognising the particular social responsibility which is involved in being a member of the academic community. The production of knowledge and the exercise of power are clearly related. We thus have a duty not only to select socially relevant problems and issues to investigate, but also to clarify, and publish, the social consequences of our analyses with a clear eye on their possible implications. Nor is this necessarily a potentially dangerous course of action for a community of professional sociologists to undertake.

It has sometimes been suggested that academic purity and academic irrelevance have been linked far too often and in this respect perhaps it would be of positive benefit for us as sociologists if we were to address ourselves more directly to aspects of social policy. There are difficulties and dilemmas here of course for we must avoid "regression" as Bienkowski (1981) argues ... "to working out the equivalent of astrological horoscopes for (our) rulers" (Bienkowski 1981: 25). This could be the cost of seeking to make more overt policy contributions for, particularly with funded research, would he who pays the piper call the tune? If so then we could soon be back to Seeley (1966) and the distinction between the 'taking' and 'making' of problems, and it is worth remembering what Michael Young had to say in 1971. He wrote:

> On the whole, sociologists have 'taken' educators' problems, and, by not making their assumptions explicit, have necessarily taken them for granted. These implicit assumptions might be adequately characterised by what Dawe (1970) has called an 'order' doctrine which ... leads to explanations in terms of a system perspective ... starting from a loosely defined consensus on goals and values.

> (Young, 1971:1)

The dangers are clear. However, we are in a different position now to that in the 1960s when the sociology of education was struggling to establish itself and perhaps the notion of 'academic freedom' contains sufficient contradiction to make action possible within those institutional bases that are left to us after the cuts. We are also more alert to the issue now and, as Bienkowski (1981) suggests, although awareness of the danger of contributing to social reformism in the interests of an oppressive state does not remove that danger, it does clearly help to prevent such a 'slide' and constantly points the way to the need to actively protect the scientific and social conscience of sociology. Sociologists must then do what they can.

This basically concludes my answer to this first question - the Sociology of Education should seek to be policy relevant - but it should do so on its own terms and with its own integrity and independence. Given such a position, if we as sociologists are able to present adequate evidence to support our analyses then we have nothing to fear from critics. It is when we gloss such methodological issues that we leave ourselves vulnerable, and this of course leads us to the second question.

This second question, concerning the ability of the Sociology of Education to make any such contribution to policy formation, is more difficult and I want to focus my attention on interpretive sociology and more specifically on ethnographic work.

PART TWO: CAN ETHNOGRAPHY AND THE SOCIOLOGY OF EDUCATION MAKE A POLICY IMPACT?

It is a fact that interpretive work as a whole has made very little impact on policy in the last decade and it is also the case that many academics have been disappointed at the lack of coherent advance in the theoretical development which is ostensibly part of the ethnographic enterprise. Yet I want to be optimistic in this paper and argue that, in the area of classroom studies at least, ethnographers are faced with many opportunities at the present time. The dilemma which faces us is that many of these opportunities are themselves a partial product of the crisis so that to be clear about commitment is essential if ethnography is not to slide into becoming a means towards unexplored and taken-for-granted ends. This has always been a particular danger for interpretive research on education because from a non-sociological educationalist point of view, such work sometimes appears simply to offer possible ways of achieving educational goals in micro-contexts more 'efficiently'.

In order to appreciate fully the present situation regarding the development of ethnographic work it is useful to consider how it, and interpretive studies in general, have evolved during the last decade and here I particularly note the relationships between interpretive sociology and various aspects of teacher education and classroom practice - themes which will be picked up later.

In 1971, in the introduction to Knowledge and Control, Michael Young expressed the hope that his collection of papers would "open up some alternative ... and fruitful directions for sociological enquiry into education" (Young 1971: 2). Following this bold declaration the flow of interpretive studies was hardly overwhelming, nevertheless the endeavours of the 'new' interpretive sociologies of education received positive endorsement from several significant sources. One of course was the mainstream academic sociology which had spawned them and there was a brief period in the early 1970s when action theory, phenomenology, symbolic interactionism and ethnomethodology seemed to be becoming new orthodoxies to which the sociology of education could clearly make some contribution. This was a time of considerable excitement and exploration.

In a very different context, that of teacher education, it was the time of the James Report (DES 1972) with attention being particularly drawn to links, or the lack of them, between theory and practice. Gorbutt (1972) had already seen the potential of the new sociology of education for developing "professional awareness". As he put it, the new sociology of education "challenges prevailing practices and assumptions in colleges and schools" (Gorbutt, 1972:7) and he developed this argument more systematically at the North East London Polytechnic in his notion of teachers as "self-critical problem-solvers" (Gorbutt 1975). Lawrence Stenhouse (1975) at the Centre for Applied Research in Education (CARE) identified the same potential and, building on the work of Walker, Elliott, Adelman and others in the Ford Teaching Project and the concept of 'teacher as researcher', he inspired a significant movement of action-based classroom researchers.

Even representatives of the mainstream political arithmetic tradition in the sociology of education came, somewhat grudgingly perhaps, to the conclusion that interpretive accounts could be useful, in that they might illuminate their 'black box'. As Karabel and Halsey (1977) wrote:

> Interpretive sociology ... focuses precisely on those classroom processes that must be understood if there is to be any chance of reducing the class and racial differentials in academic achievement that concern the administrators of the Welfare State ... The possibility of an interpretive sociology of education aligned with the interests of educational policy-makers is thus apparent.
>
> (Karabel and Halsey, 1977:60/1)

Of course the alignment which Karabel and Halsey foresaw has remained little more than a 'possibility', with very little interpretive work being taken up by policy makers.

Sociologists' expectations in the early '70s regarding interpretive work were in fact short-lived, and in the sociology of education Sharp and Green's (1975) critique asserting the importance of material and structural factors clearly struck home. The structuralist Marxist analysis of Bowles and Gintis (1976) and Althusser (1971) seemed to be particularly influential in the mid '70s and interpretive work appeared to be increasingly construed as of relative insignificance. Indeed, the thought that it might 'fade away' prompted David Hargreaves in 1978 to ask 'whatever happened to symbolic interactionism?' and to put up a spirited defence of the approach.

Another area in which the early interpretive work was poorly received was that of 'teaching studies' in which positivist designs and systematic observation methods predominated (e.g. Flanders 1970). The behaviourist base and the fragmented empiricism of that work was criticised (e.g. Hamilton and Delamont 1974) but counter-claims that interpretive work was subjective and non-generalisable seemed to lead to the demarcation of clear and relatively non-negotiable positions.

The first decade of interpretive work in the sociology of education thus evoked both expectation and scepticism, despite which a steady stream of specifically ethnographic work was published. As we know the expectations have now drifted away and have left even ethnographers taking a hard analytical look at themselves. This is very relevant to the main questions which we can now direct to ethnography - is it in a position to contribute to policy; is it methodologically sound, has it a coherent analysis to put forward? Some of the recent attempts to review the present state of ethnographic work in education are clearly important here.

The development of ethnography and the sociology of education has been reviewed by Delamont (1981), Hargreaves, D. (1981) and Woods (1984). These accounts are incisive and useful but, in that they essentially document the failure of ethnographic work to achieve cumulative growth and also the theoretical incoherence of the sociology of education as a whole, they essentially communicate disappointment.

I want to argue that we should be more optimistic. The first stage in overcoming any problem is often to achieve an accurate analysis of its nature and a realistic assessment of available options for action. The papers by Hargreaves, Delamont and Woods provide us with just such an appraisal of the state of ethnographic work, from which it is possible to argue that the developments which are necessary to reinvigorate the contribution of ethnography to our social scientific understanding are very close to those which are necessary to make it a more effective source of informed policy.

In the first of these papers, David Hargreaves (1981) argues that in the sociology of education we have a proliferation of theories particularly associated with various forms of neo-Marxism but that these are notable for their "extremely weak link to supporting empirical evidence" (1981: 9). On the other hand we have too much a-theoretical empirical work, often ethnographic, which is perhaps grafted onto fashionable theoretical perspectives but which does not represent a form of rigorous testing of theory by which the discipline might be developed. Following from these points Hargreaves identifies the non-cumulative nature of both theory and research and also the fact that very little of recent sociological work is of any direct use to policy-makers. As he puts it

> A reluctance to indulge in hasty or
> superficial policy relevance is surely
> to be applauded, but our distaste of
> policy relevance is not to be wholly
> explained by such proper caution.

> (Hargreaves, D. 1981:11)

Hargreaves does not elaborate but it is implicit that he feels that sociologists of education have little which is coherent to offer. The other point which is embedded here but again is not drawn out concerns values and the reluctance of many sociologists to contribute to the formation of what might be construed as 'reformist' policies, particularly in the academic climate which had been produced by structural-Marxist analyses.

Sara Delamont's paper (1981) is not concerned with policy but suggests that ethnography has had little impact on the sociology of education for two reasons. Firstly it has been blinkered and parochial, failing to draw on comparative studies of different cultures and on studies of different substantive areas. Secondly it has "failed to make the familiar strange" - failed to produce analyses which are significantly different from accounts which might be produced by pupils, teachers or advisers - failed in other words to be sufficiently analytical and theoretical.

Peter Woods would agree with her. In his paper (Woods 1984) he suggests that it is possible to distinguish two 'phases' in the development of ethnographic work. In 'Phase One' he includes most of the work of the last ten years. This has been largely descriptive and concerned with "fine-grained detail" which reflects an apparent priority on providing empirically grounded and valid accounts of the perspectives of actors in the settings studied. It has also been based on a number of relatively disparate case studies which have accumulated as a product of attempts to 'cover the ground', given the size and complexity of the substantive area involved. Woods claims that these features have "actually gone against the realisation of (ethnography's) promise in the area of theory". What we need therefore are more 'Phase Two' projects which "use existing ethnographic studies as a launching pad, (are) more theoretically conscious in the early stages, and engage in theoretical sampling, hypothesis formation and testing". (Woods, 1984: 14) Such studies will be based on "less fieldwork and rather more armchair reflection" and Woods appeals for more "theoretical creativity" and openness to collaborative work and to the incorporation of alternative theories and methodologies.

Woods seems to me to be thinking here almost exclusively of the necessary developments for ethnography as part of social scientific activity designed to analyse and increase our understanding of schools and school processes. He appears to share this priority with Sara Delamont and, unlike David Hargreaves, makes no explicit reference to possible policy applications of ethnography. Yet his argument is of considerable relevance to the policy issue. Sara Delamont however will explicitly have no truck with such a practical intent. She calls for "differentiation" between sociologists and practitioners and accuses the team at the Centre for Applied Research in Education in East Anglia, for instance, of "moving away from being social scientists towards a quasi-therapeutic role in education" which is, she implies, "pointless". (Delamont 1981:80)

Clearly, among other things, different positions are being taken here on the purpose of educational research and we are back to the first question - should sociology seek to be policy-relevant? I have answered in the affirmative but that still does not mean that we have anything to contribute and the analyses of Hargreaves, Delamont and Woods are implicitly pessimistic on this point because of the lack of empirically supported theoretical development. However, there is another way to approach the issue by looking at it from the perspective of policy-makers themselves and an interesting analysis from

this direction has been provided by Marten Shipman
(1984) in a paper specifically on ethnography and
public policy.

Shipman begins by describing policy-makers as
being "hungry for evidence" and he regards ethnographic
work as having a clear potential role by virtue of
the inadequacies of previous work.   As he puts it:

> One ... general point has to be made about
> social research in general and its relation
> to policy.   The track record so far has
> been poor.   Much of the justification for
> ethnographic ... approaches to research
> comes from the failures of the positivists
> to deliver evidence on which policy-makers,
> including teachers in their classrooms,
> could depend.
>
> (Shipman, 1984)

However, ethnography lacks the 'objective' image
of other research methods and suffers, in Shipman's
view, from a disadvantage "in looking similar to
methods used by other professionals in the education
service" - the same point made by Delamont in her
claim that ethnography should be more "clearly
different" because it should contribute more clearly
to Social Science.   Shipman suggests that because of
the lack of clear difference ethnographic analysis is
unlikely to be able to claim privilege over other
types of account and sources of evidence which are
available to policy-makers from HMIs, teachers or
journalists.   Following from this Shipman argues
that it is particularly important that the methods
which ethnographers employ must be carefully controlled
and clearly stated if official policy-makers are to
evaluate such work positively.

Clearly not all ethnographic work satisfies these
criteria but we should note that Shipman is stressing
methodological points relating to assessment for
possible policy application which are identical to
those stressed by D. Hargreaves (1981) and Woods
(1984) with regard to the needs of the theoretical
development in the sociology of education as an
academic area.   The conclusion which can be drawn
is that there is no necessary incompatibility between
the attributes of research which may have policy
implications and research which may have theoretical
implications.   In either case it is the quality of
the work which is of paramount importance.   This is
an important point because it opens up the possibility

that, given a careful choice of topic and an acute awareness concerning research design, it may be possible to conduct studies which are relevant in both spheres.

With regard to ethnography the detailed methodological objections of policy-makers, be they government officials or teachers, are no doubt many; but perhaps they can be seen to relate to the three classic areas - reliability, validity and generalisability. There is a large literature now on fieldwork methods, Bob Burgess' on Field Research (1982) being the latest, and in my view there is every reason to be more confident than of most methodologies that the validity of ethnographic data can be high. However, the individualistic nature of the enterprise has always made the question of reliability an awkward one and it is by no means certain that the recent interest in the inclusion of autobiographical details in methodological accounts (Burgess 1984) will allay the fears of sceptics. Nor has the question of generalisability been easy to answer given a case-study base. However, if Woods' projected 'Phase Two' materialises, it could answer some of these points. It would be incorporative work drawing on a range of studies carried out by a number of researchers and such a version of Glaser and Strauss' (1967) "constant comparative method" would clearly increase reliability and generalisability. The greatest increase in generalisability however would come from the growth in the analytical and theoretical refinement from which abstractions could be drawn. These could be applied to other contexts precisely because of their reduced grounding in specific cases alone. We would be moving from the 'generation' towards the 'verification' of theory.

This is of considerable interest, for again it seems that in this instance the concerns of academic development and the needs of policy development are not in conflict. Although it could be argued that a fully developed and scientific understanding should precede any sort of application, 'Phase Two' analyses need not only be a "springboard for further empirical and theoretical work" as Woods suggests. They may also have enough 'respectability' to be taken seriously by policy-makers and, as I suggested earlier, in my view it is the responsibility of the academic community to ensure that this happens.

There seems to me though to be another fundamental problem with ethnographic work and its relationship with policy beyond the methodological ones considered by Shipman. This concerns the tendency of ethnographic work to focus on processes. In one sense this is a great strength but those policy-makers who are primarily concerned with the deployment of resources are also likely to require output measures of one sort or another. Two recent research studies have satisfied these criteria only through a combination of methods, including some qualitative work and may be showing us the way forward. Dave Reynolds' study of schools in South Wales (1976 and 1979) has been taken up enthusiastically and interpreted by many as being concerned with the influence of school management strategies on delinquency rates. In its combinations of process and output analysis it has clear policy implications which have been drawn despite the other concerns of its author. Similarly the Oracle project team have seen fit to include ethnographic analyses in the final stages of their study of primary school classrooms. However dubious one might be about the ways in which this was done (Galton and Delamont 1984) this combination of methods is clearly intended to strengthen the study and take it beyond quantitative description. It seems likely that ethnographically inspired studies will have to adopt similar strategies if they are to make much impact on the formulation of public policy, and this could well involve changes in typical research designs and the increasing use of methodological triangulation and multiple data sets. It may well be that ethnographers are not interested in making such changes to their previously independent, individualistic and exploratory styles of research but it does appear to be one way forward. Again these are precisely the type of measures which Woods (1982) claims are required for theoretical advance - collaboration, comparison and openness both to other theories and methodologies. A clash of interests between developing 'scientific' understanding and contributing to policy is thus by no means clear when it comes to actually carrying out the research. This issue is also of particular interest to me because one work which Woods cites as an example of 'Phase Two development' happens to be my own teacher-pupil coping strategies (Pollard 1982) which is one part of a cumulative series of studies by a variety of people (Westbury 1974, Lacey 1977, Woods 1977, 1980a, 1980b, Hargreaves, A. 1978) and to which I will return.

We should not lose sight either of the fact that some of the 'weaknesses' of ethnography which Shipman identifies, when thinking of government policy-makers, are also related to unique strengths, particularly when thinking of practitioner policy-makers such as teachers. Because ethnography stems from a 'humanistic' paradigm rather than a 'scientific' paradigm, if we can use such terms, it can address itself to a different range of questions. It is interesting, for instance, in the HMI discussion paper on the training of secondary school teachers (DES 1981) to note a concern with the "quality of students' learning-experience". This theme also occurs in CNAA literature and has always been an issue for committed and aware teachers and of course for children. An ethnographic approach would clearly be more appropriate for investigating this type of issue than more rigid, less empathic, methodologies. Ethnography also seems to me to carry with it as a method a potentially democratic capacity which we could take advantage of. Because of its fundamentally appreciative attribute it can articulate the perspectives of particular groups and present them forcefully in much the same way that a good union might do. This is particularly relevant for work with pupils. The analytical way in which ideas may be presented provides protection for individuals and also makes it difficult for those called upon to act to evade the arguments put forward.

In making such an argument the issue of 'social policy for whom' is raised sharply. This is the moral issue again but there are strategic aspects to it, including a decision about which level to focus on. Should we be aiming at government policies, at classroom policies, or at policies for levels in between? In my view we should exert influence where we can but it is perhaps realistic to expect to make more impact at the micro level because of the nature of ethnographic work. Michael Apple (1982) clearly thinks this is the correct strategy anyway because of the need to develop counter-hegemonic activity as a social movement within such work places as schools and classrooms. I will come back to this issue but before that I want to highlight the dangers which are inherent in becoming more involved in policy application by considering certain recent developments in the areas of teaching studies and teacher education.

PART THREE: ETHNOGRAPHY, TEACHER EDUCATION AND CLASSROOM PRACTICE

Teacher education provides a case study of the increasing application of ethnographic work to an area of educational policy and practice. Of course

the present situation in teacher education is fragmented, depressed and confused, as one might expect
in the context of economic and political crisis, but
there are still patterns which can be discerned.

At the present time there are some professional
educationalists in colleges and schools who seem to
be taking a relatively broad view regarding what the
aims of teacher education should be, and this increasingly includes a role for ethnography. Meanwhile
the Government in the shape of the Secretary of State
takes a far narrower, more traditional view. The
HMI seem to vacillate in between. Let me trace some
of these developments in more detail.

The sociology of education has been regarded for
many years now as one of the main contributing disciplines to the study of 'education'. Sociology has
also been a popular 'main subject', but the new situation in which we find ourselves is that the ethnographic element of the sociology of education is
being introduced into <u>professional</u> courses. Should
we be concerned at dangers of distortion, or delighted
at the new opportunities which are being presented?

The Dangers

The potential application of ethnographic work in
professional work was seen early on by Gorbutt (1975)
and the Ford Teaching Project team, but more recently
the argument has been taken up by people from quite
unexpected quarters.

Donald McIntyre, whose work on classroom behaviour
in a systematic observation mould has an international
reputation, recently wrote:

> As recently as 1970 some of us ... thought
> that the findings of (systematic) research
> on teaching could form the basis of a body
> of ⸢theoretical knowledge which would ...
> generate prescriptive principles which
> could form the core of a theoretical/
> practical teacher education programme.
> We were wrong.

> (McIntyre 1980: 296)

McIntyre goes on to recommend a new dialogue between
researchers and teachers and he suggests that "teacher
education could be best facilitated by <u>interpretive</u>
and action research designed to elucidate, examine,
explain and extend teachers' working knowledge"
(1980: 293). In the same tradition we also have the

influential paper by McNamara and Desforges (1978) arguing for the "objectification of craft knowledge", but perhaps even more surprising is the intervention of Stones (1982) who, although renowned for his work on psychopedagogy, has not routinely shown much interest in sociology. However, in one of his most recent papers to the Council for National Academic Awards (CNAA), he writes:

> Of at least as much importance as the development of systematic pedagogical skills is the development of the ability to make a systematic and critical analysis of the context of teaching. ... Students ... must be helped to escape from the utilitarian mode of perceiving teaching practice as one in which they learn to accommodate to the prevailing ideology of the schools in which they find themselves. Equipping them with the tools to make a critical analysis of context is therefore an essential aspect of their course. This 'ethnographic' work complements their pedagogic work and the two are mutually supportive.

> (Stones 1982: 7)

Stones clearly sees what he calls 'ethnographic work' to be an essential part of teacher education. In other contexts related arguments are being presented. Robin Alexander, the Chairman of a Primary Teacher Training Sub-Committee on CNAA has written on the need for 'practical theorising'. As he puts it:

> While academic research and speculative theory have a great deal to contribute, good teaching depends less ... on the quality of such theory than on the quality of the teachers' everyday theorising - the way he observes, interprets and analyses situations, postulates hypotheses ... explores alternative solutions, evaluates them. Teaching is an intensely theoretical activity.

> (Alexander 1982: 25)

This has resonances with the view put forward by the National Union of Teachers policy document on teacher education (NUT 1981) and as developed by the then

President, Dick Chambers (Chambers 1981). The same
emphasis was clear at a recent national conference
on teacher training held by the National Association
for Primary Education (NAPE 1982). It is also one
of the arguments of the recent Department of Education
and Science discussion paper on the training of
teachers for secondary schools (DES 1981) and is
reflected again in the new HMI call to involve teachers in teacher-training course construction and
again in the expansion of IT-INSET programmes
(Henderson et al. 1982). Such developments are
reviewed more extensively by Isaac (1983) who again
sees an important role for ethnographic studies as
a means of educating reflective, self-critical
teachers.

Of course this argument comes as nothing new to
those who, for many years, have operated within the
teacher-based action research mode, for instance at
CARE and the Cambridge Institute. Again though
there are signs of an expansion of interest in that
type of work, indicated most obviously by the publication of a Teacher's Guide to Action Research
(Nixon 1981) and by the continued growth of the
Classroom Action Research Network (CARN) both nationally and internationally. As if to underline the
point, the latest bulletin of CARN (Elliott and
Whitehead 1982) is specifically focussed on "action-
research for professional development and the improvement of schooling".

Sociologists clearly have to take a position
regarding these developments. The first reaction I
suspect is likely to be, like Sara Delamont's reaction
to CARE, one of scepticism and withdrawal. I share
the concern, for it seems clear that interpretive
work has been identified as being 'useful' in the
training of teachers in the interests of 'improvements'
in professional competence. It is being regarded as
a 'means' to that 'end', whatever 'improvement' may
mean. It is being used as a means of analysis of
classroom or institutional situations without any
necessary awareness of macro-contexts. In a sense
it is being 'hi-jacked' and removed from its context
in sociological theorising and analysis. This is
where the danger of separating the micro from the
macro becomes particularly apparent because studies
which focus on the micro level alone are particularly
vulnerable to being used in ways which may have been
quite unexpected by their authors.

I personally find this worrying, and as I
suggested earlier, my concern stems essentially from
a value position which asserts firstly that sociology

loses its integrity as a discipline if it does not
continually struggle to relate macro and micro levels
of analysis and secondly that we can no longer afford
the academic luxury of detachment from the 'real
world' in schools and the education service generally
in which decisions are being taken and life chances
being affected without there being serious contributions to the debate from sociologists, including
ethnographers. As Barton and Lawn (1980-1981) put
it in their critique of CARE's work:

> Faced with the conservative re-structuring
> of the British educational system, the
> economic depression forecast for at least
> a decade, and the severe pruning of educa-
> tional institutions, will the CARE ideology
> survive the polarisation of thought and
> action that is being created? ... CARE may
> have to accommodate itself more openly to
> the new grassroots educational militancy.

(Barton and Lawn 1980/1:11)

Much the same will, in my view justifiably, be said of
more mainstream ethnographers if we are not careful.
But it is possible to be more positive.

The Opportunities

The other way of looking at recent developments is as
an emerging area of opportunity. Interestingly, this
takes us back to the new movement of culturalist neo-
Marxists. However great the misgivings which A.
Hargreaves and Hammersley might have about their
methodology, there is no mistaking the political
commitment and the new theoretical structure which
is being put forward. In the 'new' Marxism the
influence of structuralist analyses with determinist
assumptions (Althusser 1971, Bowles and Gintis 1976)
has passed. Now we have Apple (1982) and others
picking up where Gramsci, Marx's early work and Mills
left off and developing analyses which specifically
attempt to link ethnography and history, social structures and individual action. This has had radical
implications for the conceptualisation of teachers
and classrooms. Thus teachers are no longer inevitably cast as the unwitting agents of capitalism but
it is acknowledged that positive forms of praxis can
be developed in classrooms. Similarly classrooms
are no longer regarded as the settings in which ideological determination and the structural correspon-

189

dence of social relations are played out but are
regarded as potential sites of struggle and resistance. The model in use here is a dialectical one
in which the individual and society, macro and micro
factors are seen to be in constant interaction and
in a relationship of mutual influence.

Now it may be necessary to point out that there
is a macro-macro problem as well and that Weberian
analyses at the structural level may have much to
offer, but I am not sure that such an awareness of
pluralist diversity does not actually reinforce the
points which Apple, for instance, makes regarding
action at the micro level. Reflecting his new
optimism and commitment Apple writes:

> We need to be aware of possibilities for
> action. For just as this crisis generates
> contradictions and tensions that are emerg-
> ing at all levels of our social formation,
> so too will these emerge in schools. ...
> What can progressive educators and others
> do about this situation?

(Apple 1982: 8/9)

This seems to me to be the key point. What can
sociologists do given that there are things which
can be done? Whether these are made possible by
'contradictions and tensions' or by 'pluralist
diversity' is not necessarily crucial. The point
is to act.

In the area of teacher education a general
direction for such action is indicated by some of
the work of Kenneth Zeichner and his colleagues at
Wisconsin, work which utilises the tensions and
contradictions in the practical-theorising arguments
reviewed earlier, just as Apple advocates.

In a series of papers (Zeichner 1981-2, Zeichner
and Teitelbaum 1982, Zeichner and Grant 1981) Zeichner
argues that teacher education is not normatively neutral. Drawing on the analyses of Greene (1978),
Popkewitz (1979) and Giroux (1980) he suggests that:

> ... the dominant forms of teacher education
> today largely encourage acquiescence and
> conformity to the status quo, both in
> schooling and in society.

(Zeichner and Teitelbaum 1982:101)

... which picks up themes brought up in a British

context some time ago by Hooper and Johnston (1973) and Bartholomew (1976). The Wisconsin team have also noted the power of school experience (Tabachnik, Popkewitz and Zeichner 1979-80) to distort course objectives in much the same type of analysis as that provided by Denscombe (1982) regarding the 'hidden pedagogy' of classroom experience.

The problem then is that teacher education programmes tend to lead, remorselessly it seems, to the development of utilitarian teaching perspectives in students in which "teaching is separated from its ethical, political and moral roots" (Zeichner and Teitelbaum 1982: 102). This is the outcome of 'personalised' teacher education programmes which focus on the survival concerns of the students and have been particularly developed in the USA at the University of Texas (Fuller 1971) and of course, of craft or skill based courses which seem to be more popular in Britain (e.g. Wragg 1981). Zeichner argues that to counter this some "conception of social and economic justice" is an essential constituent of every teacher's education. The means by which he suggests this can be achieved is through what he calls an 'inquiry-oriented approach' to student education. The inquiry-oriented approach picks up many of the ideas present in the 'practical theorising' literature reviewed earlier but it is far more clear about 'ends'. The type of reflectivity which is sought is not simply 'technical' or 'practical' but is 'critical' (Van Manen 1977), it

> legitimates a notion of inquiry where
> education students can begin to identify
> connections between the level of the
> classroom (e.g. form and content of
> curriculum, classroom social relations)
> and the wider educational, social,
> economic and political conditions than
> impinge upon and shape classroom practice.

> (Zeichner and Teitelbaum 1982:104)

The primary vehicle for achieving such critical reflectivity is seen as being through carefully structured courses in which the study of macro-contextualised ethnographies is interspersed and integrated with study and teaching in schools. The clear purpose of this is to pre-empt the pragmatic orientation which seems to stem from the immersion of students in schools for long periods of time. School practices are thus continually related to reflection on possible social consequences, thus promoting not merely self-critical awareness but a socially-critical consciousness.

As far as I know evaluations of the success or otherwise of such programmes have not been completed and clearly this is important. Nevertheless we have an example of a direct application of sociological work in ways which could be, in my view, socially progressive and the present interest in the use of ethnographic work in teacher education programmes in this country represents an opportunity to raise similar issues. This use of ethnographic work could therefore be productively followed up by sociologists and with it we should take every opportunity to pose questions about the social consequence and moral basis of practical action in classrooms as well as merely contributing to discussions about pedagogic efficiency. This of course is precisely what it is alleged is not done in the work of CARE despite its other qualities (Reynolds 1981-82, Barton and Lawn 1980-81).

There is, however, much to admire in the work of CARE and in the philosophy of the classroom action research movement. The ethical priority and the facilitating policies of the professional researchers has led to an unusual degree of collaboration, openness and team work among teachers and social scientists. Arguably such work illustrates a viable and suitable democratic means of developing more sociologically informed action. In the course of such activity the lesson is that teachers should be worked 'with', not 'at'; perhaps, as Smith and Knight (1982) advocate, following up the contradictions already existing in liberal educational philosophies to foster progressive practice. I am optimistic about this for it seems to me that a basic tenet of the 'sociological imagination', that processes in such sites as schools are both reproductive and productive, has enough resonance in 'common sense' to provide a working relationship between a great many teachers and researchers, and indeed the professional commitment of many teachers is often based on an optimism which is partially legitimated by the dialectical model. As at CARE, work with teachers could easily form a part of in-service courses, although the provision of suitably written texts is also a necessity.

Ethnography of schools and classrooms thus seems to me to be in a position to make an immediate and particular contribution to social policy. The social policy, that is, which is adopted by every

teacher in the micro-social system of their cl...
room whether they are aware of it or not. Class...
are as significant a site of praxis or of social
renewal as any other and the personal policies of
teachers are of paramount importance. Being with
teachers, talking to teachers, working with teachers -
these are essential if sociologists wish to influence
school practices and such practical action seems to
me to be no less valuable than research or abstract
theorising.

On the other hand of course there is also plenty
of necessary research work to be done - among other
things the macro-micro problem is not going to go
away. I suggested earlier, however, that through
the careful selection of research topics we could
identify projects which would be both socially relevant and contribute to social scientific understanding as such. One such project I believe is the
study of coping strategies precisely because of the
macro-micro articulation of the concept with Andy
Hargreaves (1978), identified in his paper to the
Westhill conference five years ago and which I,
among others, have tried to develop (Pollard 1981,
1982, 1983).

Knowledge about coping strategies is certainly
socially relevant if the work with teachers and
student teachers which I have advocated is to be
followed up. If teachers are to move anywhere near
towards the adoption of more socially aware or
radical forms of pedagogy, such as that advocated
by Richer (1981-82) for instance, then it is crucial
that we know more about the constraints which they
face, the typical perspectives which they bring to
the situation and the ways in which such factors are
played out in the school and through interaction with
pupils. Nor are such socially relevant projects
incompatible with theoretical development. With
that in mind Sara Delamont called for more comparative studies and more studies of the unusual; Peter
Woods called for more theoretical sampling. Following those ideas we could have much to learn from the
study of radical teachers and their coping strategies
in the same way that studies of deviance have always
been able to cast light on conceptions of 'normality'.
Similarly a study of the relationship between coping
strategies and particular types of classroom organisation could be worthwhile, particularly if some
index of social consequence were taken as an output
measure. Clearly some strategies are more socially
divisive than others but we need more knowledge about
such factors. Not only could the product of such

...erable implications for teachers,
...ght enlist their support and col-
...ney could also provide further
...the micro-macro linkage which the
models claim to reflect.

...NCLUSION

I hav...   ...that the sociology of education <u>should</u>
involve ...   ...lf in the formation of social policy,
indeed, I have suggested that it is socially irres-
ponsible not to do so. At the same time though, I
have suggested that we need to safeguard our integrity
as sociologists and scrupulously avoid any seduction
into forms of reproductive social engineering. The
key safeguard for interpretive work here seems to me
to be to recognise the necessity of macro linkages,
however difficult to delineate these may be.

Regarding ethnography in particular, I have
suggested that it <u>can</u> attempt to influence policy
formation and that a particular opportunity exists
with regard to teacher education and classroom practice. Methodological adequacy, theoretical accumulation and coherence remain important in this, both
for our future social scientific understanding of
particular substantive areas and as a crucial influence on the impact which we can make on policy. A
high quality of work is necessary in both spheres and
I have argued that, given such quality and careful
choice of research issues, then studies which contribute to both concerns are possible.

This is a committed and optimistic conclusion
but I don't see much point in sociology if it does
not take on this role as a constructive social critic.
A time of crisis is a time of change, a time in
which there are <u>opportunities</u> as well as difficulties
and depression. I am suggesting that we should take
them.

REFERENCES

Alexander, R.J. (1982) 'Class Teacher, Child and
    Curriculum: Some Issues for Primary Teacher
    Education', Paper given at the National
    Association for Primary Education Conference,
    Roehampton Institute, October.
Althusser, L. (1971) 'Ideology and the Ideological
    State Apparatuses', in <u>Lenin, Philosophy and
    Other Essays</u>, New Left Books, London
Apple, M. (1982) <u>Education and Power</u>, Routledge and
    Kegan Paul, London

Arnot, M. and Whitty, G. (1982) 'From Reproduction to Transformation: Recent Radical Perspectives on the Curriculum from the USA', British Journal of Sociology of Education, 3, 1

Bartholomew, J. (1976) 'Schooling Teachers: The Myth of the Liberal College', in G. Whitty and M. Young (eds.) Explorations in the Politics of School Knowledge, Nafferton, Driffield

Barton, L. and Lawn, M. (1980/81) 'Back Inside the Whale: A Curriculum Case Study', Interchange, 11, 4

Bienkowski, W. (1981) Theory and Reality, Allison and Busby, London

Bowles, S. and Gintis, H. (1976) Schooling in Capitalist America, Routledge and Kegan Paul, London

Burgess, R.G. (1982) Field Research, Allen and Unwin, London

Burgess, R.G. (1984) 'Autobiographical Accounts and Research Experience', in R. Burgess (ed.) Field Methods in the Study of Education, Falmer, Lewes

Castells, M. (1980) The Economic Crisis and American Society, Princeton University Press, Princeton

Centre for Contemporary Cultural Studies (1981) Unpopular Education, Hutchinson, London

Chambers, J. (1981) 'The Role and Function of Advanced Study in Professional Development', in R.J. Alexander and J.W. Ellis (eds.) Advanced Study for Teachers, Society for Research into Higher Education, Guildford

Gorbutt, D. (1972) 'The New Society of Education', Education for Teaching, 89, 3

Gorbutt, D. (1975) 'Redesigning Teacher Education at North East London Polytechnic', British Journal of Teacher Education, 1

Delamont, S. (1981) 'All too Familiar? A Decade of Classroom Research', Educational Analysis, 3, 1

Denscombe, M. (1982) 'The "Hidden Pedagogy" and its Implications for Teacher Training', British Journal of Sociology of Education, 3, 3

DES (1972) Teacher Education and Training, HMSO, London

DES (1981) Teacher Training and the Secondary School, HMSO, London

Elliott, J. and Whitehead, D. (eds.) (1982) Action Research for Professional Development and the Improvement of Schooling, Classroom Action Research Network Bulletin, no. 5, Cambridge Institute of Education, Cambridge

Flanders, N.A. (1970) Analysing Teacher Behaviour,

Addison Wesley, London

Fuller, F. (1971) <u>Relevance for Teacher Education:
A Teacher Concerns Model</u>, University of Texas,
Austin

Galton, M. and Delamont, S. (1984) 'Speaking with a
Forked Tongue? Two Styles of Observation in
the Oracle Project!' in R. Burgess (ed.) <u>Field
Methods in the Study of Education: Issues and
Problems</u>, Falmer Press, Lewes

Giroux, H. (1980) 'Teacher Education and the Ideology
of Social Control', <u>Journal of Education</u>, 162

Giroux, H. (1981) <u>Ideology, Culture and the Process
of Schooling</u>, Falmer, London

Glaser, B.G. and Strauss, A.L. (1967) <u>The Discovery
of Grounded Theory</u>, Weidenfeld and Nicholson,
London

Gouldner, A.W. (1970) <u>The Coming Crisis of Western
Society</u>, Heinemann, London

Greene, M. (1978) 'The Matter of Mystification:
Teacher Education in Unquiet Times', in
<u>Landscapes of Learning</u>, Teachers College Press,
New York

Hamilton, D. and Delamont, S. (1974) 'Classroom
Research: A Cautionary Tale', <u>Research in
Education</u>, 11

Hammersley, M. (1980) 'Classroom Ethnography',
<u>Educational Analysis</u>, 2, 2

Hargreaves, A. (1978) 'The Significance of Classroom
Coping Strategies' in L. Barton and R. Meighan
(eds.) <u>Sociological Interpretations of Schooling
and Classrooms</u>, Nafferton, Driffield

Hargreaves, A. and Hammersley, M. (1982) 'CCCS GAS! -
Politics and Science in the Work of the Centre
for Contemporary Cultural Studies', <u>Oxford
Review of Education</u>, 8, 2

Hargreaves, A. (1982) 'Resistance and Relative
Autonomy Theories: Problems of Distortion and
Incoherence in Recent Marxist Analyses of
Education', <u>British Journal of Sociology of
Education</u>, 3, 2

Hargreaves, D.H. (1978) 'Whatever Happened to Symbolic Interactionism?' in L. Barton and
R. Meighan (eds.) <u>Sociological Interpretations
of Schooling and Classrooms</u>, Nafferton, Driffield

Hargreaves, D.H. (1981) 'Schooling for Delinquency'
in L. Barton and S. Walker (eds.) <u>Schools,
Teachers and Teaching</u>, Falmer, Lewes

Henderson, E.S. et al. (1982) <u>Teacher Education in
the Classroom</u>, Croom Helm, London

Hooper, D. and Johnston, T. (1973) 'Teaching Practice:
Training or Social Control?', <u>Education for</u>

Teaching, Autumn

Isaac, J. (1983) 'Teacher Education and the Future', in M. Galton and R. Moon, Changing Schools; Changing Curriculum, Harper and Row, London

Karabel, J. and Halsey, A.H. (eds.) (1977) Power and Ideology in Education, Oxford University Press, New York

Keat, R. (1981) The Politics of Social Theory, Blackwell, Oxford

Lacey, C. (1977) The Socialisation of Teachers, Methuen, London

Marx, K. (1970) The German Ideology, Lawrence and Wishart, London

McIntyre, D. (1980) 'The Contribution of Research to Quality in Teacher Education', in E. Hoyle (ed.) The World Yearbook of Education, Kegan Paul, London

McNamara, D. and Desforges, C. (1978) 'The Social Sciences, Teacher Education and the Objectification of Craft Knowledge', British Journal of Technical Education, 4, 1

Myrdal, G. (1958) Value in Social Theory, Routledge and Kegan Paul, London

National Association for Primary Education (1982) 'The Future of Primary Professional Training', National Association for Primary Education Conference, Roehampton Institute, London, October

Nixon, J. (1981) A Teacher's Guide to Action Research, Grant McIntyre, London

National Union of Teachers (1981) Initial and In-Service BEd Degrees, National Union of Teachers, London

Pollard, A. (1981) Coping with Deviance: School Processes and their Implications for Social Reproduction, Unpublished PhD thesis, University of Sheffield

Pollard, A. (1982) 'A Model of Coping Strategies', British Journal of Sociology of Education, 3,1

Pollard, A. (1983) 'Coping Strategies and the Multiplication of Social Differentiation in Infant Classrooms', British Journal of Educational Research, Autumn

Popkewitz, T. (1979) 'Teacher Education as Socialisation: Ideology or Social Mission', Paper to the American Educational Research Association, San Francisco, April

Reynolds, D. (1976) 'The Delinquent School' in M. Hammersley and P. Woods (eds.) The Process of Schooling, Routledge and Kegan Paul, London

Reynolds, D. and Sullivan, M. (1979) 'Bringing Schools
    Back In' in L. Barton and R. Meighan (eds.)
    Schools, Pupils and Deviance, Nafferton,
    Driffield
Reynolds, D. (1980-81) 'The Naturalistic Model of
    Educational and Social Research: A Marxist
    Critique', Interchange, 11, 4
Richer, S. (1981-82) 'Towards a Radical Pedagogy'
    Interchange, 12, 4
Seeley, J. (1966) 'The "Making" and "Taking" of
    Problems', Social Problems, 14
Sharp, R. and Green, A.G. (1976) Education and
    Social Control, Routledge and Kegan Paul, London
Shipman, M. (1984) 'Ethnography and Policy' in
    R. Burgess (ed.) Field Methods in the Study of
    Education, Falmer Press, Lewes
Smith, R. and Knight, J. (1983) 'Liberal Ideology,
    Radical Critiques and Change in Education: A
    Matter of Goals' in British Journal of Sociology
    of Education, 3, 3
Stenhouse, L. (1975) An Introduction to Curriculum
    Research and Development, Heinemann, London
Stones, E. (1982) 'Some Notes on Practical Teaching
    with Especial Reference to the PGCE Course',
    Paper for CNAA, January
Tabachnik, B.R., Popkewitz, T. and Zeichner, K.
    (1979-80) 'Teacher Education and the Professional
    Perspectives of Student Teachers', Interchange,
    10
Van Manen, M. (1977) 'Linking Ways of Knowing with
    Ways of Being Practical', Curriculum Enquiry, 6
Westbury, I. (1973) 'Conventional Classrooms, "Open"
    Classrooms, and the Technology of Teaching',
    Journal of Curriculum Studies, 5
Woods, P. (1977) 'Teaching for Survival' in P. Woods
    and M. Hammersley (eds.) School Experience,
    Croom Helm, London
Woods, P. (1980a) Teacher Strategies, Croom Helm,
    London
Woods, P. (1980b) Pupil Strategies, Croom Helm,
    London
Woods, P. (1984) 'Ethnography and Theory Construction'
    in R. Burgess (ed.) Field Methods in the Study
    of Education: Issues and Problems, Falmer Press,
    Lewes
Wragg, E.C. (1981) Class Management and Control,
    Macmillan, London
Young, M.F.D. (1971) Knowledge and Control, Collier-
    Macmillan, London
Zeichner, K.M. and Grant, C.A. (1981) 'Biography and
    Social Structure in the Socialisation of Student

Teachers', <u>Journal of Education for Teaching</u>,
<u>7</u>, 3

Zeichner, K. (1981-82) 'Reflective Teaching and
Field-Based Experience in Pre-Service Teacher
Education', <u>Interchange</u> 12

Zeichner, K. and <u>Teitelbaum</u>, K. (1982) 'Personalised
and Inquiry-Oriented Teacher Education: An
Analysis of Two Approaches to the Development
of Curriculum for Field-Based Courses', <u>Journal
of Education for Teaching</u>, <u>8</u>, 2

CLASSROOM CONTROL AND INITIAL TEACHER TRAINING:
THE CONTRIBUTION OF ETHNOGRAPHY

Martyn Denscombe

For a long time teacher training programmes have
been criticised by teachers and trainees alike for
their lack of relevance to the real world of teaching.
(1)   Particularly in terms of secondary schooling
it has been alleged that initial teacher training
(ITT) simply does not prepare the trainees adequately
for the things they need to do in the classroom.
According to the HMI Report 'The New Teacher in the
School'(1982b), for instance, one quarter of new
teachers are not adequately prepared for the job
they actually take up when they enter the profession.
Some of the lack of preparation concerns the level of
proficiency in the subject discipline and some of it
the match between subject qualification and the kind
of job the new entrant first takes up in school.
Significantly, though, much of the anxiety concerns
the preparation of newcomers to deal with matters of
classroom organisation, management and control.
There are clear indications that the HMI would like
to see more attention given to such skills in the
content of ITT (HMI 1982a) because where new teachers
struggle in class it frequently appears to be due to
a lack of control (HMI 1982b).   Summarising the
nature of the least successful lessons they had witnessed, the HMI point out that the

> Characteristics most commonly associated
> with lessons of low quality included ...
> poor relationships and class control,
> particularly in the secondary schools,
> where occasionally these seriously
> inhibited the teaching and rendered
> meaningless any comment on other aspects.

> (HMI 1982b p. 23)

Efforts to improve the preparation of new teachers on matters of classroom control, then, would seem to warrant high priority on the agenda for improvements in ITT and the purpose of this paper is to point out how ethnographic work can make useful, empirically grounded comment both on this perceived need for improvements and the proposed measures to achieve them. This is not to suggest that it can offer a panacea to control problems but rather to indicate that it can complement existing lines of enquiry by focusing on an area that is crucial to the analysis of the problem and to do this the paper draws on a variety of ethnographic studies, particularly those concerned with teacher perceptions of classroom control. (2)

Teacher perceptions of classroom control are regarded as primarily important because teachers hold a crucial position in the education system, standing at the interface between formal visions of what needs to be accomplished and practical visions of what is feasible under the prevailing circumstances. In a sense they stand between pedagogy and pupil, between theory and outcome, acting as a gatekeeper to the pupils' experience of schooling (King 1973).

As a result, there is no shortage of advice on what teachers ought to be doing. Politicians and industrialists pontificate on the kind of end-product teachers should be striving to achieve while professional educationists provide the teacher with plans for pedagogic innovation and suggestions on how to do the job effectively. What is remarkable about these deliberations and prescriptions on teacher activity, however, is the relatively little amount of attention given to what the teachers themselves feel about the aims of education and the methods to be employed. What are their priorities and what is their view of the situation? Why do they operate in a particular manner and why do they favour certain approaches?

This is where ethnography has a vital contribution to make. Using observation or participant observation backed up by interviews, questionnaires and documentary evidence, ethnography provides detailed studies of specific settings to show how the participants think and act, and what reasons they put forward to explain their beliefs and actions. It is, first and foremost, interested in members' understandings of the situation in which they operate and the factors that contribute to this understanding (Hammersley 1978, Stebbins 1981). It examines the perspectives used by those involved in the situation, their negotiation of interests, the strategies employed and the careers of personal identity (Hammersley 1980, Woods 1983). (3)

By its very nature,then, ethnography is not happy to leave the phenomenon of classroom control in an unexplored state. In fact, the unique contribution of ethnography is that, unlike other approaches to the problem of classroom control where writers have tended to assume that what teachers regard as classroom control is obvious and have then proceeded to concentrate on the causes and remedies, (4) it does not assume that what constitutes classroom control is self-evident. Rather than take it for granted, <u>ethnography deliberately focuses on how participants in classrooms understand the phenomenon</u> and how they recognise, interpret, establish and/or challenge the existence of classroom control.

II

Ethnography's description of the phenomenon of classroom control has some value in its own right for ITT because it meets the need for greater attention to matters of classroom control within the content of ITT programmes (cf HMI 1982a, 1982b, Wilson 1981). Specifically where ethnography focuses on teachers' perceptions of the reality of achieving classroom control it can be used as practical advice to newcomers about the situations they might meet and the methods they might be able to adopt to cope with these situations - offering the trainee some insight to the phenomenon as viewed from the stance of 'the practitioner'. In a broad way, it presents the trainees with the 'teacher context' version of classroom control, how it is recognised, how it is achieved, how it gets threatened and why it is crucial to the job. And on the available evidence, this is just the kind of input the trainees value. Being anxious about their ability to manage a class, they are likely to appreciate the chance to pick up hints on 'how to do it' since this appears to be their overriding concern during training. It might allay some of the 'control anxiety' that, as we see later in the paper, is a characteristic of trainee teachers and a major baulk to the effectiveness of ITT.

Pulling together the strands of this perspective from a variety of ethnographic studies we can identify twelve facets to the phenomenon of classroom control as experienced by teachers which could be used to illuminate trainees' perceptions of the job.

1.   As teachers see it, <u>classroom control is a crucial part of the job</u>. (5)   It is elementary in the sense of being the first thing on which their competence is judged and it is elementary as well in the sense that it is a basic precondition for success as a teacher (Denscombe 1977, Kohl 1970).   There can be little doubt, in fact, that teachers see classroom control as a necessary (though not sufficient) condition for putting over the subject content of a lesson.   In their eyes

> The teacher who has 'lost control' of his class, as the expression goes, cannot compensate for that deficiency by doing an especially good job of evaluation or by spending extra time with his remedial reading group.   In an educational sense, when group control is lost, all is lost.
>
> (Jackson 1968, p. 106)

2.   It is also clear that teachers' concern with control is <u>not entirely the product of free choice</u> on their part.   There are (i) legal obligations and (ii) directives from the local education authority as well as a variety of less formal expectations from (iii) colleagues, (iv) pupils and (v) the school organisation which reinforce their expectation that classroom control is an essential part of the job. (6)

3.   Teachers are conscious that <u>problems of classroom control will be localised in their severity</u>. There are 'pockets of resistance' resulting from things like the motivation of the pupils in the school or class, the time of day, week or term, the weather, and the subject of the lesson; each can affect the severity of the problem.   The severity of the problem, in terms of the extent to which individual teachers experience control difficulties, is, in this sense, 'localised' because not all teachers face the same problem. (7)   The impact of streaming and timetabling are crucial in this respect as the findings of Hargreaves (1967) and Lacey (1970) demonstrate.

4.   Having said this, it is also true that, as teachers see it, the problem of classroom control is not limited to particular times and particular places. The problem is actually a <u>routine feature of the job</u> facing most teachers in most lessons even though it clearly becomes more acute under certain circumstances. This feature of teachers' understanding of classroom control is worth emphasising.   From their point of

view, the problem is not restricted to the explosive instances that occur occasionally - the serious incidents involving violence or extreme verbal abuse. What troubles teachers more are the minor irritations and minor challenges to their authority that occur as a routine feature of lessons. (8)

This says something about the nature of the 'control problem' as a phenomenon. As Boyson, an unlikely ally in this context, suggests:

> It is possible that it is not the figures
> for violence and arson which are the
> greatest threat to schools but the lesson
> resisters of the classroom. A teacher
> can be undermined as efficiently by dumb
> insolence, time wasting and non-cooperation
> of pupils as by physical threats or obscene
> insults.

> (Boyson 1975, p. 13)

5. From ethnographic work on classrooms (e.g. Smith and Geoffrey 1968, Jackson 1968, Woods 1979), it is evident that, because control problems arise as a normal feature of classroom interaction, the remedies used by teachers need to be fast-acting with an immediate effect. The decisions that are effective are seen as the ones that are (a) proximate, in the sense that they are geared to the circumstances most intimately connected with the classroom in question, and (b) instantaneous in the sense that they constitute immediate remedial action. Whilst upon reflection teachers might see the cause of disruptive behaviour as lying in the historical development of their role, cultural domination, family breakdown or the emotional disturbance of the pupil, for practical purposes control demands decisions that are orientated to the immediate circumstances and that offer some kind of immediate relief. For this reason, teachers use 'strategic action' to accomplish the truce that passes for classroom control (Hargreaves 1978, 1979, Pollard 1982, Woods 1977, 1978, 1979).

Such strategies are interchangeable to the extent that they provide teachers with alternative ways of coping with the same thing. Each kind of strategy effectively tries to routinise charisma and thus help those teachers - the vast majority - who have not got the personality to command the class on the strength of charisma alone. Rather than rely on charisma, the strategies appeal either to institutional authority/tradition, to the demands of classwork, or to the pupils' own interests as the source of legitimacy for control - i.e. factors that locate the demand for control outside the auspices of the individual teacher who requests it. The strategies exist in the first place because the "low technology" classroom typical of today places heavy emphasis on interpersonal skills, man-management techniques and "personality" style teaching (Westbury 1973). For this reason, new forms of technology in the classroom might be expected to have a marked impact as control becomes depersonalised and embedded in the hardware/software packages of microcomputers or pre-programmed teaching packages coupled with audio-visual aids (cf Blau and Schoenherr 1971). New technology in the classroom, in other words, might be expected to reduce the need for teachers to rely on existing strategies as ways of depersonalising the demand for control.

6. The widely used strategies available to teachers share other qualities as well. They aid control by reducing uncertainty and unpredictability in the lesson and this tells us something else about teachers' perceptions of classroom control. It tells us that teachers regard uncertainty and unpredictability as hazards to control which, though inherent features of classroom life, need to be contained and limited if control is going to be exercised (Smith and Geoffrey 1968, Kounin 1970).

7. The strategies also tend to combine the appearance of control with the appearance of covering syllabus material - a point made clear by Hoetker and Ahlbrand (1969) and Westbury (1973). This suggests that though control is seen as fundamental to the practice of teaching, there is still considerable anxiety amongst teachers to be seen to be covering the content of the particular syllabus. In most cases, teachers do not lose sight of their avowed intent - to impart knowledge to the pupils - and thus they favour those strategies that foster control and cover work simultaneously.

8. Contributions by ethnographers further make it clear that control is a negotiated phenomenon and not simply the unilateral imposition of a situation by one party (teacher) on the other (pupils). What Woods (1978, 1979), Hargreaves (1978, 1979), Pollard (1982), Stebbins (1981) and Denscombe (1980b) inter alia have clearly demonstrated is that control has to be negotiated and constantly achieved through interaction between teacher and pupils. In no sense is control simply a question of teachers imposing a set of rules by virtue of their positional authority or

legal duty to operate 'in loco parentis'. To achieve control teachers need to overcome the pupils' ability to mobilise resistance and to do this teachers have to negotiate a set of ground rules that are tacitly or explicitly recognised by both parties (cf Hargreaves et al 1975).

9. The fact that control is a negotiated rather than an absolute phenomenon means that <u>the recognition of classroom control is quite a complex interpretive skill on the part of teachers</u>. The negotiated rules that cover the existence of control generally depend on <u>specific contexts</u> - specific parts of the school, specific times of the day, specific phases of a lesson The context needs to be taken into account by the teacher in the course of identifying acts as a threat (or otherwise) to control. Teachers need to be sensitive to the <u>intent</u> behind the action and need to adjust their responses according to whether the pupil activity is perceived as malicious or otherwise. Similarly they need to be sensitive to the <u>repercussions</u> of any efforts they make to remedy the situation since the intervention itself might cause more trouble than it cures (cf Stebbins' (1970) notion of the 'avoidance of provocation').

10. To compound the complexity of recognising and acting upon control problems, teachers must also be aware of the <u>outcome</u> of pupil actions and, specifically, their implications for the appearance of classroom control to those not immediately involved. It is interesting, on this point, that under the prevailing circumstances in secondary schools, teachers appear to be particularly sensitive to noise in classrooms - especially noise created by pupils and noise that permeates the walls of the classroom to become audible to colleagues working in adjacent classrooms. Such noise contains an implicit threat to the teacher responsible for the classroom from which it emanates because it is easily identified as a symptom of a lack of control in the class. The noise provides a source of information about events behind the closed classroom doors and such information, in view of the paucity of alternative sources, tends to assume considerable significance because it can be used to <u>infer</u> whether or not control is being exercised (Denscombe 1980a, McPherson 1969). This explains why it is that teachers tend to recognise 'disruptive behaviour' primarily through the noise it entails (cf Dumont and Wax 1969).

Without suggesting that teachers only recognise disruptive behaviour through the medium of noise, what is suggested by this is that, amongst the

variety of pupil behaviours that might be deemed
'disruptive', it is the noisy disruptive behaviour
that will be regarded as the most urgent and one
that will receive priority treatment.   And it seems,
here, that if schools were designed to minimise the
prospect of noise travelling between classrooms - by
added attention to soundproofing of classrooms - we
might expect a reduction in teacher sensitivity to
noisy pupil behaviour as the prime threat to control.
　　11.　The symbolic value of quiet orderliness
during lessons owes something to another facet of
teaching in the closed classroom: teacher autonomy.
Because teachers operate in circumstances that
isolate them physically and visually from colleagues,
and because they are generally expected to operate as
individuals rather than teams, they have come to place
great store by the degree of autonomy they have.   The
combined influences of 'classroom architecture',
'organisational delegation of responsibility' and
the 'occupational culture of teachers' provide
mutually reinforcing factors that stress the importance for teachers of gaining classroom control by
themselves without assistance from colleagues.
　　Working under the conventional circumstances of
the closed classroom, then, teachers appear to be
sensitised to the idea that there are two prime
threats to the impression of control that 'leak'
from their classroom: pupil initiated noise and the
need to call on outside help to cope with matters in
'their own' lesson.   We ought to acknowledge, of
course, that this sensitivity is largely a response
to the specific closed classroom context that characterises secondary schooling in Britain and that where
alternative contexts exist they are likely to promote
a different set of priorities in the minds of the
teachers.   Where teachers operate as teams, where
they operate in open-plan classrooms, even where they
operate in gymnasiums, laboratories, art rooms and
playing fields, the expectations about control might
not be quite the same.   Ethnographic research would
suggest, indeed, that alternatives to the closed
classroom such as open-plan classrooms, especially
where teachers operate in teams, can have a quite
definite impact on teacher perceptions of control by
creating a context that fosters a corporate approach
to the job rather than the radical individualism
generated by the conventional classroom. (9)   In
other words, there is nothing immutable about the
sensitivity to noise and autonomy despite the fact
that they appear to provide a prevalent and persistent concern of teachers currently working in

secondary education.

12. Last, but far from least, we should note
that, whatever teachers' understanding about control
and its significance for the job, it owes relatively
little to the process of initial teacher training.
Shortly after completing training and embarking on
their careers as fully fledged teachers, their
attitudes on matters connected with classroom control
reveal little legacy of their tutors' wisdoms (Hoy
1969, Morrison and McIntyre 1967).   They owe more to
'common-sense' versions based on their experience as
pupils in the classroom and on the support such
versions receive in practice in schools from the
expectations of colleagues and the practical realities
of classroom life as a teacher (Petty and Hogben 1980).

In essence, this is because teachers' understanding of classroom control is shaped by a 'Hidden
Pedagogy' - a knowledge of the teacher's job which is
rooted in classroom experience rather than pedagogic
theory. (10)   This classroom experience, of course,
starts in the thirteen years that most trainees have
spent in schools as pupils.   Having witnessed
teachers at work over a protracted period they can
hardly avoid developing a picture of what makes some
teachers 'good' and what makes other teachers 'bad'.
Indeed, evidence shows that newcomers arrive at
college with fairly firmly established notions of
what the job is all about and manage to resist the
thrust of sociological and psychological work that
has a bearing on the job (Hogben and Petty 1979).

As a result, the main anxiety of trainees is
not what is classroom control?, nor, even 'what
methods are needed to achieve it?'   For them, the
main anxiety appears to revolve around the implementation of the known methods towards the known goals -
the experience and confidence of putting them into
practice in the real-world setting.   They know that
their success as a teacher depends initially on their
ability to maintain classroom control and what they
are concerned with is not so much the theory of
teaching as the opportunity to practise the techniques.
This frame of mind, of course, promotes an inertia
to the work of teaching (a) because conceptions of
the task depend largely on what has been witnessed
prior to training and (b) because the 'control
anxiety' experienced by trainees predisposes them to
the practical side of their training at the expense
of the theoretical inputs and innovative ideas
originating in the content of the ITT programme.

III

This ethnographic account of classroom control, necessarily schematic as a result of the confines of a short paper, goes some way towards mapping a detailed explanation of how control is perceived and exercised in practice by experienced members of staff. The value of this, as we have already suggested, is that it can contribute to the professional training of teachers by providing a picture of the job as practised by competent, seasoned teachers. Its value, however, is not restricted to specific content inputs to programmes of ITT - even though such content is currently being advocated by HMI and schools alike. As well as this, the ethnographic account of classroom control points to factors that are of central concern to the whole organisation of ITT programmes and, therefore, has particular implications so far as any proposed changes in ITT are concerned.

The important point to recall here is that ethnographic research on teachers points to the existence of a 'control anxiety' which is particularly prevalent in trainees. Whilst trainees already have a substantial vision of the job they feel that they lack experience at actually mastering classroom control. The result is (a) a preference for the practical side of training courses rather than inputs on sociology, psychology and philosophy, and (b) a preference for the 'wisdoms' of teachers in schools rather than tutors based in colleges. However, the ethnographic account of control problems in the classroom not only suggests that ITT is being inhibited in its effectiveness by this concern of trainees about their competence to control a class, it also provides clues to ways of overcoming this 'control anxiety' because it tells us:

(a)   why, and how, assumptions about classroom control are built into teacher culture,

(b)   why trainees quite rationally prefer practice in classrooms to theory in the college lecture theatre and why they tend to resist the implications of sociology, psychology and philosophy, and,

(c)   why newcomers to teaching soon forget any ideas of control picked

> up during training that do not
> match the ideas of colleagues (and
> pupils) or the situational impera-
> tives they confront in the class-
> room.

It provides some solid, empirical basis on which to
work when considering the reorganisation of ITT and
suggests certain key directions to be taken to enhance
the impact of ITT on the practice of trainees during
their training programme as well as in the longer
term when they become established teachers.

The major factor to be taken into consideration
here is the <u>isolation of newcomers</u> - an isolation
which reflects both the rampant individualism of
teachers' approaches to their work and the use of
closed classrooms in schools.   The result, as
Dreeben points out, is that

> Unlike medical training institutions,
> institutions that train teachers do not
> provide anything approaching a system of
> supervised apprenticeship; thus many new
> teachers start their first job green -
> and then go it alone. ... Immediately
> following graduation (or even before)
> students embark on the first job, one
> entailing full classroom responsibilities,
> ecologically isolated from experienced
> colleagues, but subject to sporadic super-
> vision from school administration, super-
> vision that even if helpful cannot be
> based on prolonged observation.   Hence
> the portrait of the beginning teacher:
> cut off from the sources of knowledge
> underlying his work, isolated from
> colleagues and superiors, left alone to
> figure out the job - discover, correct or
> repeat his own errors - through his own
> experience.

> (Dreeben 1970 pp. 64, 128-9)

Given the same responsibility in the classroom
as senior staff, the beginners' problem is not only
that they are pretty 'green' but that, right from
the start, they are left very much to their own
devices, as Lortie (1968) puts it, "to sink or swim".
In the absence of attempts to overcome the isolation,
trainees (and probationers as well) show a distinct
willingness to resort to ad hoc measures or to the

strategies they used to observe when they themselves were pupils in classrooms. In other words, where there are no systematic efforts by senior personnel to guide the newcomer's practice there will tend to be an <u>inertia of approaches</u> to teaching - an inertia that stems initially from the 'control anxiety' of trainee teachers.

Team teaching offers one solution to this. Where trainees, and probationers for that matter, start their teaching experience as part of a group of teachers they can look to senior colleagues for direct guidance and assistance with their work, not least on the matter of classroom control (Shaplin and Olds, 1964). The very presence of established teachers alongside the newcomer can be expected to reduce the prospect of the newcomer suffering difficulties of control and will thereby reduce the level of control anxiety experienced by the novice. On the basis of observation and interviews with trainees and probationers starting in a team teaching situation in a Leicestershire comprehensive (Denscombe 1981), there certainly appears to be support for the idea that such group-based induction reduces 'control anxiety'. In general, the newcomers said that they received implicit support, occasionally direct support from the more experienced members of the team and this made their initial teaching experience less fraught with tension and anxiety. This support could be observed in the way experienced team members reacted when they were joined by a trainee or probationer. On one occasion, for instance, when a team that had been observed over five double periods was joined by a student teacher who replaced one of the regulars, the lesson started with an uncharacteristic outburst from one of the regulars demanding work and "no mucking about this lesson". The other team regular went on to operate with his group behind a partition, whilst the 'task-master' worked alongside the student teacher. Though they worked with separate sets of pupils his presence and occasional admonishments to his own set seemed to have a ripple effect on the student's set of pupils. When the situation was discussed later, the regular team member said that his actions were consciously those of the 'team heavy'. As most of the Humanities staff recognised, it generally fell to one of the team members to become the 'team heavy' who took the burden of responsibility for control in the group. As this particular member of staff put it:

> One person often gets to be the 'team
> heavy' - an uneasy role. The role will
> be more of a responsibility for the
> experienced teacher - and it's good for
> the less experienced who get sheltered a
> bit.

By 'coming on heavy' he felt he could show the student
how to 'make your presence felt' and 'get things
moving' whilst, at the same time, giving the student
a chance to settle down and get some confidence. The
student appreciated these motives and said she felt
that:

> As an inexperienced teacher, it's a great
> help to be 'alongside' more experienced
> colleagues, especially in a course which
> makes heavy demands.

There was a price to pay for this support,
however, and it was a price that worried some.   The
mistakes the newcomer made were visible to experienced
colleagues and this could prove an embarrassment which
the newcomer would be less likely to face in the
closed classroom.   Nevertheless, the predominant
view of trainees, probationers and experienced teachers
alike was that the team situation reduced the newcomers
anxiety about controlling pupils.
     If the possibilities of induction via groups
were limited to situations where team teaching in
open-plan classrooms already existed, there would be
little scope to exploit the practice simply because
team teaching is quite uncommon.   Fortunately, there
are other opportunities to use group-based induction:
trainees can start their classroom experience as part
of a group of trainees rather than being isolated
from contact with those experiencing the same anxieties and problems.   An example of such a group-
based induction is to be found on the PGCE Art and
Design Education course at Leicester Polytechnic
which has endeavoured to induct trainees via groups
since its initial validation in 1975.   Student
teachers are assigned to schools in groups of three
or four and these groups form the core component of
classroom experience during the first two terms.
They are the basis for regular tutorial meetings in
the schools and the initial encounters with classes
are on a group basis where the trainees share the
responsibility for taking the lesson.
     It would be unrealistic, though, to suppose
that group-based induction contains all the answers

212

to the newcomers' 'control anxiety'. It does not, and the main reason it does not is because the trainees 'control anxiety' originates in places other than the training experience itself (Denscombe 1982). This point was clearly demonstrated by the reactions of the Art and Design PGCE students to their group-based induction. Responses to interviews and a questionnaire administered in June 1983 revealed that, whilst the trainees tended to value group induction in terms of developing their own teaching skills there was a slight feeling that it could prove unmarketable in terms of the practical demands of teaching in normal conditions, and in effect, could jeopardise their job prospects. To quote two of the student teachers:

> During interviews, I have found that
> it is experience in solo teaching
> that is required and I have seen
> very little interest shown in group
> teaching.

> I have had the experience of being
> in an interview for a job where the
> interviewing panel seriously
> questioned my (or anyone else's)
> ability to teach solo when such a
> large proportion of my experience
> of teaching was in a group situation.

Group induction, in other words, whilst it would appear to possess certain key benefits for the trainee, can expect to be met with caution because there is still a question mark in the eyes of trainees about the extent to which such induction prepares the newcomer for the real world of teaching. Specifically, in the present context, the implication is that whilst solo teaching allows trainees to confront their 'control anxiety' - to practise the skills of control, make mistakes, learn from them and thus gain confidence in their ability to survive in class - group-based induction largely side-steps the issue by reducing the extent to which newcomers experience the realities of coping alone in the classroom. As a result, the adoption of group-based induction without concomitant changes in the expectations of both trainees and employers is unlikely to eliminate the 'control anxiety' completely.

In terms of the organisation of ITT, another major factor to be taken into consideration is the amount of <u>time available to the trainee during ITT to gain experience in classrooms</u>. It seems reasonable to suggest that a reduction in the amount of 'control anxiety' experienced by trainees might be achieved simply by extending the period of training and, thereby increasing the amount of time spent in classrooms by the trainees. The trainees' additional experience in classrooms would give them added opportunity to practise the skills of classroom management and hence increase their confidence at this vital part of the job. This would not only improve the trainees' preparedness for the existing real world of teaching, it would also make them more receptive to the ideas that sociology, psychology and philosophy might bring to bear on the work of teachers.

As with group-based induction, though, extending the period of time that trainees spend in schools turns out to give no guarantee in its own right that the trainees will be freed from acute control anxiety. It is not just a question of time spent in school, it is the amount of <u>time spent in classrooms</u> practising the necessary control techniques which is crucial and the content of ITT, therefore, needs to be careful to include experience of teaching as a deliberately quantified element of the school experience provided for trainees.

The case for three or four year training courses would seem strong on this point and certainly there is evidence that:

> In terms both of their mastery of a range of teaching skills (as evidenced by the work observed) and of their confidence in the effectiveness of their training, ... teachers who had followed a B.Ed course are generally superior in their first year.

(HMI 1982b, p. 83)

Some caution is needed on this point, though, because the actual amount of time spent in schools by B.Ed trainees is not a great deal longer than that spent in schools by PGCE students.   As Yates (1982) discovered recently, "the average length of teaching practice over a three-year teacher training course was 17.2 working weeks, i.e. 86 working days".   This might be significantly longer than the period spent in schools by university sector PGCE students - prompting the HMI (1982a) to recommend increases in the length of one-year training programmes from thirty to forty-four weeks, most of the extra time to be devoted to more school experience.   But, as Smith (1982) makes the point quite forcefully, it is overlooked all too often that "approximately fifty per cent of PGCE students are in institutions other than university departments or schools of education" (p. 11).   CNAA validated courses are already normally thirty-five weeks in duration and contain a minimum of sixty days school experience.   In Smith's research twenty-six per cent of CNAA PGCE courses devoted around seventy-eight to ninety days to school-based experience and the majority contained sixty-six to seventy-seven days in schools.   The differences between B.Ed and PGCE courses, in other words, is not as great as the time-span of the course would immediately imply.

There is another reason why additional time in school might not actually promote the ideas and aims of those who design the ITT course - in effect a third consideration of significance for reorganisation of ITT courses.   Because new teachers are generally anxious to win the approval of the established staff and are prepared to slot-in with their approach rather than cling to ideas gathered from training or else- where (Hanson and Herrington 1976, Leacock 1969 , McPherson 1972), it is the rare exception indeed who stands out against established school practices during training or in the probationary year.   And when we consider, too, that pupils exert considerable pressure on newcomers and experienced teachers alike to fit in with established conventions, in particular the need to assert control, it is not surprising that if the newcomer is conscious of any inconsistency between approaches suggested at college and those advocated by colleagues, it is the ideas of teacher colleagues which carry the day.   Just as Hanson's (1975) research revealed:

> The contrast between (the need for control)
> and the radical rhetoric at college creates

> no great tensions for most students. What
> matters most to them is what is seen to
> matter most to senior colleagues.

Yates (1982), basing his research on a random sample
of 500 trainees, 100 supervising teachers and 100
college tutors throughout Britain, finds firm support
for the idea that (a) trainees treat the school
teachers as their reference group, (b) that supervising teachers in schools see colleges as relatively
unconcerned with developing teaching 'skills' and
(c) that college tutors and supervising teachers both
see the latter as primarily responsible for oversee-
ing the development of the trainees' 'skills' at class
management, organisation and control. In essence,
college tutors were seen as assessors and evaluators,
whilst supervising teachers were the main source of
support.
    This division of labour, according to Webster
(1983), has its roots in nineteenth century conceptions of university education which accord far lower
status to practical skills than they do to abstract
knowledge. The legacy is clear:

> The one aspect of teacher-education (he
> argues) which teachers emphasise most but
> which teacher-educators tend to neglect
> is the development of practical teaching
> skills or 'pedagogy'. The university
> tradition which elevates subject knowledge
> far above practical skills appears to be
> the underlying cause.

> (Webster 1983, p. 1)

    Responsibility for developing this part of the
trainees' competence is more or less delegated to
the supervising teacher in the school through some
implied kind of contract. But, as Webster proceeds
to argue, this 'contract' is one that warrants
serious reconsideration if ITT is to become more
effective. Rather than college tutors simply acting
as final arbiters of the trainees' performances there
should be a partnership between college tutors and
supervising teachers. The point is an important one.
Without a change in the relationship between the two
a simple addition of classroom experience will only
exacerbate the tension that already exists between
the college tutors' emphasis on the subject knowledge-
base/possibilities for change and the supervising
teachers' emphasis on pedagogic skills/coping with

existing reality (Allison 1982, Inman et al 1983, Smith 1982).   And it is, remember, the latter that tends to hold sway over the trainees' thinking.
Partnership between college tutors and supervising teachers would bring the training of teachers more into line with the training of other professions where practitioners have greater influence over the whole process of recruitment and training.   In the case of ITT, such a partnership would entail three things.
1.   The involvement of teachers in the selection of those to enter ITT.   As the HMI (1982b) stressed, "training institutions should carry out a more effective process of 'quality control' to ensure that only those who have the qualities of personality and temperament as well as the academic and professional skills needed for teaching are awarded teaching qualifications" (p. 18).   Involving teachers in the recruitment of trainees might bolster such a 'feet on the ground' approach that looks at personal qualities as well as academic eligibility.
2.   The involvement of teachers in the assessment procedures.   The supervising teachers would formally gauge the performance of the trainees and be represented on the examining body that awards the qualification.
3.   The involvement of supervising teachers in the development of teaching skills at a formal rather than informal level.   Their contribution to the process of training, in other words, would need to be formally recognised by the training institution and the school.
These factors require a lot of attention to the quantity and quality of communication between training institutions and schools so that both parties understand the aims of the other and the particular problems they face (McCullough 1983).   They would even seem to call for more resources to the extent that the supervising teachers need time freed from their school duties to involve themselves in the ITT programme and, possibly, to embark on some specialist training.   Some advances in this direction have been achieved by the PGCE in Social Studies at Goldsmiths' College, London, where the ILEA actually release a number of teachers for about a day a week so that they can become co-tutors on the course (Inman et al 1983).
Most obviously, perhaps, they support a call for ITT in the form of School-Based Studies (SBS) rather than the conventional college based course interspersed with teaching practice (cf HMI 1981).   To achieve the amount of school/classroom experience

required and to generate increased collaboration between college and school in the recruitment of trainees and the design, implementation and evaluation of teacher training, there is a need for training which is based on concurrent and inter-related studies in schools and in the training institution. This is precisely the kind of requirement which has been recognised by the PGCE Art and Design Education operating at Leicester Polytechnic. Since its inception in 1975 it has been an SBS course where students spend eighty-two days in schools and where there is explicit emphasis on using the students' school experience as the cornerstone of the training programme. It is also an explicit feature of the autumn term of the PGCE in Social Studies at Goldsmiths' College referred to above and no doubt other schemes exist or will emerge that organise teacher training on different lines than the conventional college based studies plus teaching practice. Indeed, interest in SBS is now being fostered by the DES who are funding an investigation of four pilot SBS projects at Leeds Polytechnic, Roehampton Institute, Leicester University (Northampton Annexe) and Sussex University. These SBS courses are to start in 1983/ 84 in a fully operational form (though Sussex has had an SBS PGCE running for some years) and the project as a whole is to be monitored by Furlong and Hirst at Cambridge University. The point to be borne in mind, however, is that ethnographic research provides support for the rationale behind such changes in organisation specifically where they involve SBS because the conventional arrangements would seem to do little to alleviate the trainees' 'control anxiety' and do little to shift the trainees' dependence on school teachers and classroom experience as the basic reference points for competent teacher activity.

IV

Summary and Conclusion

It has been argued that ethnographic research on teachers in classrooms has a distinct contribution to make to our understanding of classroom control and that this contribution can provide a basis for policy recommendations in education. In particular, we have looked at the way in which ethnographic work can be significant for the nature of ITT. First, at a descriptive level, it provides a detailed and empirically-grounded account of the way teachers understand classroom control, where they learn this understanding and how they cope with problems of control thrown up by life in classrooms. This account has a straightforward value as an input to ITT that can help to explain to trainees the nature, source and centrality of the problem of classroom control to their future work, plus pointing to some of the coping strategies currently employed by teachers in classrooms.

Second, ethnography points to a major feature of the trainees' understanding that limits the impact of ITT on their thinking. As a result of the 'Hidden Pedagogy' of classroom experience they suffer an acute 'control anxiety'. Ethnographic research suggests some possible remedies to this control anxiety.

These remedies are not novel. In fact, as the discussion has shown, they are part of the current debate that involves teachers, the unions, HMI and the DES. Substantially, ethnographic work would support moves towards SBS and group-based induction to teaching because, despite some caveats, there is reason to believe they will go some way towards reducing 'control anxiety' and hence open up the trainees' receptiveness to the ideas of sociology, psychology and philosophy of education as they have a bearing on the work of teachers. The potential to enhance the influence of ITT on the preparedness and quality of new entrants to the profession, nevertheless depends on the creation of some partnership between college and school if trainees are to be weaned away from a blinkered dependence on classroom experience as the source of their beliefs about the realities and possibilities of teaching.

V

The description and analysis of existing classroom practices, along with its use to 'improve' teacher training programmes, faces a rather thorny problem, however, because at first glance this focus of attention, and the purpose to which the data is put, would seem to engulf ethnography within existing social relations. Because its focus is deliberately on a description and analysis of the existing situation rather than dynamics of change it is easy to dismiss the enterprise of ethnography as one that lacks a critical perspective and one that reinforces a blinkered vision of what is possible. As Apple (1979) suggests along these lines, such a depiction of the situation is far from ideologically neutral. And because the data can be used as the foundation for prescriptions to aid teachers' control of the classroom the thrust of any such research would seem automatically to bolster the social control function

of both the teachers and those who train them.
Indeed, the very choice of topic itself - the problem
of classroom control for teachers - would seem to
pre-empt the way in which the data is used. By
focusing on the problem of classroom control from the
teachers' point of view it would seem to be an exercise that inherently denigrates the pupils' perspective, their status, power and rights.

There are, in other words, grounds for arguing
that ethnography's unique and practical contribution
to the issue of classroom control serves to perpetuate
the status quo. First, it seems to concern static
pictures rather than dynamic relations. Second, its
use in teacher training only improves the effectiveness
of the school as a social control mechanism and thereby serves the interests of the dominant minority.
Third, and related, the focus on a 'teacher problem'
makes the research, implicitly or explicitly, a
management exercise. Such allegations deserve
serious consideration.

It is true that ethnography does not contain
within its own method and perspective the kind of
overview provided by macro theories such as those
associated with marxist sociology of education.
There is no idea of social formation to be derived
from ethnography other than the ones contained in the
perception of the subjects. Ethnography, according
to this line of argument is inherently conservative
because it lacks the potential for generating a
coherent critique of society; it lacks any unifying
theme and its selections of phenomena to be studied
are potentially haphazard and fragmentary.

This is a forceful criticism but one that can be
answered in two ways. First, ethnography can, and
I would argue should, be conscious of contemporary
macro theory in its direction and choice of topic.
The relationship between micro and macro, as Hammersley
(1980) indicates, is not at all straightforward or
simple. As he puts it:

> While it may be almost impossible in a
> single study satisfactorily to relate
> micro and macro analysis, as a whole
> ethnographic work on the classroom does
> provide the basis for a model of class-
> room process which is both sensitive to
> the complexity of social interaction and
> at the same time provides links with
> macro level analysis.

(Hammersley 1980, p. 49)

Certain social relationships are posited by macro theory and ethnography's choice of topic can be deliberately directed towards investigating the existence of those relationships at an interactional level. There are, for instance, a host of such topics currently awaiting investigation as a result of theorising connected with class, gender and racial inequalities and how they are generated by classroom interaction.

Two examples of this contextualising of ethnographic work within macro theory are the work of Davies (1978) and Fuller (1983). Davies' study of secondary school girls was inspired by the need to investigate the nature of sex-role stereotyping in schools, how it occurs and how effective it is. As she concludes from her ethnographic work:

> (The girls') awareness of the contradictions and discontinuities in school life suggests ... that school is an incomplete reproducer of social and sexual divisions in society.
>
> (Davies 1978, p. 103)

Similarly, Fuller uses ethnographic research to examine some elements of macro theory about the underachievement of girls in schools. In her case the ethnographic research led her to reject the view that girls are less critical of the schooling they receive than boys. She argues that girls are just as critical, if not more so, but are inclined to 'bottle' their criticism if success at school offers them some prospect of alleviating the oppression they experience from social relations located outside school - repressive parents and/or the sexism/racism of wider society. Both studies are clearly inspired by, and comment upon, an analysis of social structure which itself is not 'ethnographic'. This does not mean, of course, that the ethnographer is constrained to furnish evidence in support of the relationships suggested by macro theory. What is being suggested is not the subordination of ethnography to parameters established by macro theory (cf Sharp and Green 1975) but a symbiotic relationship between empirical ethnographic research and macro theory in the true spirit of scientific investigation.

The second answer to the point is that, in practice, ethnographic accounts of classroom life rarely involve a static description of the situation without adding to that picture some analytic framework that 'locates' it within wider social relations and social forces. As Hammersley has retorted to this kind of allegation, far from "neglecting the conditions in which, and constraints under which, teachers work ... this issue has been at the forefront of the ethnography of schooling for the past five years" (Hammersley 1981, p. 168). Whilst it is certainly true that the major concern of ethnography is to depict the members' understanding of a given situation, contemporary ethnography within the British sociology of education has hardly presented a decontextualised picture. Indeed it is interesting to note that when the contexts are identified they are treated in a way that actually promotes the prospects of change because the "research does not treat those conditions and constraints as simply given, but rather, as themselves in need of explanation" (ibid.).

The second allegation concerning the use to which such accounts can be put is equally answerable. To argue that an ethnography of classroom control can be used to make social control more efficient without recognising that it can also be used to sensitise teachers and trainees to the wider implications of their efforts to secure control seems, to say the least, partial. By indicating why control figures so prominently in the work of teachers, by indicating the way in which limited resources and architectural legacies put pressure on them to operate in a certain fashion, trainees might actually be spurred towards a critical stance on their practice and away from a passive acceptance of common-sense assumptions about the need for classroom control in the work of teaching. Obviously, the ethnographic data has the potential to be used in either fashion and the crucial factor is the way it is used by teacher trainers rather than any inherent quality of the data per se.

The third point, that focusing on a teacher problem makes ethnography inherently a management exercise, certainly has some substance. Yet by focusing on the teacher problem the research also contains a particular potential for change precisely because it is 'consumer orientated'. After all, the recommendations of social scientists have had relatively little direct impact on the decisions of those in strategically powerful positions and one of the main reasons for this lack of impact has been the lack of a 'consumer orientation'. (11) The 'control problem' is one of central concern to teachers since the burden of responsibility for achieving control rests with them and, with this point in mind, an ethnographic account of the problem of classroom

control which focuses on their perception of the
problem might hope to be productive in terms of
applied findings simply because it is 'consumer
oriented'.

Bearing all this in mind, it seems reasonable
to suggest that, in the case of ethnography's contribution to the issue of classroom control and ITT, any
accusation of conservative bias would be nullified
where the use of ethnographic data to guide and help
the practice of trainees was coupled with:

   (i)   awareness of how the issue is related to
        broader theoretical concerns currently being
        examined within the sociology of education,
  (ii)   guidance on the social, legal and organisa-
        tional genesis of the need for classroom
        control, and
 (iii)   equal consideration of the pupils' methods
        and rationale for challenging teacher control.

NOTES

   (1)   See, for example, Williams (1963), Cornwell
et al (1965), Wiseman and Start (1965), Taylor and
Dale (1971) and Hannam, Smyth and Stephenson (1976).
   (2)   The ethnography of classroom control
naturally involves pupils' perceptions as well as
the teachers' and considerable work is emerging on
pupils' view of classroom control: e.g. Corrigan
(1979), Davies (1978, 1979), Fuller (1983), Furlong
(1977), Marsh et al (1978) and Willis (1977). For
present purposes attention is focused on teacher
perceptions because of their relevance to ITT, though
the implications of this selection are discussed
later in the paper.
   (3)   Added to this, ethnography is also
distinguished by its particular sensitivity to the
reflexivity of the research process and the implications this has for 'capturing' the members interpretations and meanings in their natural setting
(Hammersley 1978, 1983).
   (4)   This is evident in recent texts on classroom control such as Francis (1975), Gillham (1981),
Gnagey (1975, 1981), Haigh (1979), Marland (1975),
Millman et al (1981), O'Leary and O'Leary (1977),
Saunders (1979) and Sloane (1976). Docking's (1980)
useful account, whilst recognising the need to grapple
with the question of how control is understood by
teachers (chapter 3), does not actually take the
matter as a central issue and, consequently, does
not actually take the matter very far or provide

substantial answers. Studies which do focus on members' understandings include Stebbins (1970), Hargreaves et al (1975), Woods (1977), Denscombe (1980a, 1981).

(5) This is recognised by a number of texts on the basics of teaching (e.g. Marland 1975, Gnagey 1975).

(6) See, for instance, the pressure put to bear by pupils (Corrigan 1979, Hanson and Herrington 1976), the pressure exerted by colleagues (Denscombe 1980a, McPherson 1972) and the legal pressures on teachers (Barrell 1978).

(7) It is worth noting that the great majority of teachers work in schools where control would not appear to be a desperate problem. As the HMI (1979) conclude having investigated 384 secondary schools, it was only in 6 per cent of cases that indiscipline could be seen as a 'considerable problem' and in less than 1 per cent of the schools was it a 'serious problem'.

(8) See Lawrence et al (1977), Laslett (1977), Mills (1976), Wilson (1981) and Dierenfield (1982) for further evidence on this point.

(9) Shaplin and Olds (1964), inter alia, consider the repercussions of team teaching in principle. Empirical research reports exist, for example, in Denscombe (1980b, 1981) and Martin (1975).

(10) The concept of the 'Hidden Pedagogy' is explored in Denscombe (1982).

(11) This is one of the points to emerge clearly from the book 'Social Science Research and Public Policy-Making' (NFER-Nelson 1982) based on the proceedings of an international seminar on the subject held in Holland.

REFERENCES

Allison, B. (1982) 'Persistent dilemmas in teacher education with particular reference to Art and Design education', paper presented to Department of Education and Science course N4 "Art and Design: Visual Education in Teacher Training", October 1982

Apple, M. (1979) Ideology and the Curriculum, Routledge and Kegan Paul, London

Barrell, G.R. (1975) Teachers and the Law, Methuen (Fifth edition), London

Blau, P.M. and Schoenherr, R. (1971) The Structure of Organisations, Basic Books, New York

Boyson, R. (1975) The Crisis in Education, The Woburn Press, London

Cornwell, J. et al (1965) The Probationary Year, University Institute of Education, Birmingham

Corrigan, P. (1979) Schooling the Smash Street Kids,
    Macmillan, London
Davies, L. (1978) 'The view from the girls',
    Educational Review, 30, 2, pp. 103-109
Davies, L. (1979) 'Deadlier than the male? Girls'
    conformity and deviance in school' in L. Barton
    and R. Meighan (Eds.) Schools, Pupils and
    Deviance, Nafferton, Driffield
Denscombe, M. (1977) The Social Organisation of
    Teaching, unpublished Ph.D. Thesis, University
    of Leicester
Denscombe, M. (1980a) 'Keeping 'em quiet: the
    significance of noise for the practical activity
    of teaching' in P. Woods (Ed.) Teacher Strategies,
    Croom Helm, London
Denscombe, M. (1980b) 'Pupil strategies and the open
    classroom' in P. Woods (Ed.) Pupil Strategies,
    Croom Helm, London
Denscombe, M. (1981) 'Organisation and innovation in
    schools: a case study of team teaching' in
    School Organisation, 1, 3, pp. 195-210
Denscombe, M. (1982) 'The "Hidden Pedagogy" and its
    implications for teacher training' in British
    Journal of Sociology of Education, 3, 3,
    pp. 249-265
Dierenfield, R. (1982) 'All you need to know about
    disruption' in Times Educational Supplement,
    29.1.1982
Docking, J.W. (1980) Control and Discipline in Schools,
    Harper and Row, London
Dreeben, R. (1970) The Nature of Teaching, Scott,
    Foresman, Glenview, Illinois
Dumont, R.V. and Wax, M.L. (1969) 'Cherokee school
    society and the intercultural classroom',
    Human Organisation, 28, 3, pp. 217-226
Francis, P. (1975) Beyond Control? A study of
    discipline in the comprehensive school, George
    Allen and Unwin, London
Fuller, M. (1983) 'Qualified criticism, critical
    qualifications' in L. Barton and S. Walker
    (Eds.) Race, Class and Education, Croom Helm,
    London
Furlong, V. (1977) 'Anancy goes to school' in
    P. Woods and M. Hammersley (Eds.) School
    Experience, Croom Helm, London
Gnagey, W.J. (1975) Maintaining Discipline in Class-
    room Instruction, Macmillan, New York
Gnagey, W.J. (1981) Motivating Classroom Discipline,
    Macmillan, New York
Haigh, G. (Ed.)(1979) On Our Side: Order, Authority
    and Interaction in School, Maurice Temple Smith
    London

Hammersley, M. (1978) 'Data collection in ethnographic research' in Research Methods in Education and the Social Sciences (part 3 block 4 DE304), Open University Press

Hammersley, M. (1980) 'Classroom ethnography', Educational Analysis, 2, 2, pp. 47-74

Hammersley, M. (1981) 'The Outsider's advantage: a reply to McNamara' in British Educational Research Journal, 7, 2, pp. 167-171

Hammersley, M. (Ed.) (1983) The Ethnography of Schooling, Nafferton Books, Driffield

Hannam, C., Smyth, P. and Stephenson, N. (1976) The First Year of Teaching, Penguin, Harmondsworth

Hanson, D. (1975) 'The Reality of classroom life' in New Society, 4.9.1975

Hanson, D. and Herrington, M. (1976) From College to Classroom: the probationary year, Routledge and Kegan Paul, London

Hargreaves, A. (1978) 'The significance of classroom coping strategies' in L. Barton and R. Meighan (Eds.) Sociology Interpretations of Schooling and Classrooms, Nafferton, Driffield

Hargreaves, A. (1979) 'Strategies, decisions and control: interaction in a middle school classroom in J. Eggleston (Ed.) Teacher Decision-Making in the Classroom, Routledge and Kegan Paul, London

Hargreaves, D.H. (1967) Social Relations in a Secondary School, Routledge and Kegan Paul, London

Hargreaves, D.H. et al (1975) Deviance in Classrooms, Routledge and Kegan Paul, London

Her Majesty's Inspectorate of Schools (1979) Aspects of Secondary Education in England, HMSO, London

Her Majesty's Inspectorate of Schools (1981) The Postgraduate Certificate in Education in the Public Sector: a discussion document, HMSO, London

Her Majesty's Inspectorate of Schools (1982a) Content of Initial Training Courses for Teachers, HMSO, London

Her Majesty's Inspectorate of Schools (1982b) The New Teacher in the School, HMSO, London

Hoetker, J. and Ahlbrand, W. (1969) 'The persistence of the recitation' in American Educational Research Journal, 6, 2, pp. 145-167

Hogben, D. and Petty, M.F. (1979) 'Early changes in teacher attitude' in Educational Research, 21, 3, pp. 212-219

Hoy, W.K. (1969) 'Pupil control ideology and organisational socialisation' in School Review, 77, pp. 257-265

Inman, S. et al (1983) 'Theory and practice in teacher training - the way forward?' Social Science Teacher, 12, 3, pp. 86-88

Jackson, P.W. (1968) Life in Classrooms, Holt, Rinehart and Winston, New York

King, R. (1973) School Organisation and Pupil Involvement a study of secondary schools, Routledge and Kegan Paul, London

Kohl, H. (1970) The Open Classroom, Methuen, London

Kounin, J.S. (1970) Discipline and Group Management in Classrooms, Holt, Rinehart and Winston, New York

Lacey, C. (1970) Hightown Grammar, Manchester University Press

Laslett, R. (1977) 'Disruptive and violent pupils: the facts and the fallacies' in Education Review, 29, 3, pp. 152-162

Lawrence, J. et al Disruptive Behaviour in a Secondary School, Goldsmiths' College, London

Leacock, E. (1969) Teaching and Learning in City Schools, Basic Books, New York

Lortie, D. (1968) 'Shared ordeal and induction to work' in H.S. Becker et al (Eds.) Institutions and the Person, Aldine, Chicago

McCullough, M. (1983) 'School experience: the roles of college tutors and the schools' in SCETT News, 3, NATFHE, London

McPherson, G. (1972) Small Town Teacher, Harvard University Press, Cambridge, Mass.

Marland, M. (1975) The Craft of the Classroom, Heinemann, London

Marsh, P. et al (1978) The Rules of Disorder, Routledge and Kegan Paul, London

Martin, W.B.W. (1975) 'The negotiated order of teachers in team teaching situations' in Sociology of Education, 48, 2, pp. 202-222

Millman, H.L. et al (1981) Therapies for School Behaviour Problems, Jossey-Bass, Hollywood, Ca.

Mills, W.C.P. (1976) The Seriously Disruptive Behaviour of Pupils in Secondary Schools in One Local Education Authority, unpublished M.Ed thesis, University of Birmingham

Morrison, A. and McIntyre, D. (1967) 'Changes in opinions about education during the first year of teaching' in British Journal of Social and Clinical Psychology, 6, 3, pp. 161-163

O'Leary, K.D. and O'Leary, S.G. (1977) Classroom Management: the successful use of behaviour modification, Pergamon (Second edition), Oxford

Petty, M.F. and Hogben, D. (1980) 'Explorations of semantic space with beginning teachers: a study of socialisation into teaching' in British Journal of Teacher Education, 6, 1, pp. 51-61

Pollard, A. (1982) 'A model of classroom coping strategies' in British Journal of Sociology of Education, 3, 1, pp. 19-37

Saunders, M. (1979) Class Control and Behaviour Problems, McGraw-Hill, London

Shaplin, J. and Olds, H.F. (Eds.) (1964) Team Teaching Harper and Row, New York

Sharp, R. and Green, A. (1975) Education and Social Control, Routledge and Kegan Paul, London

Sloane, H.N. (1976) Classroom Management: remediation and prevention, Wiley, New York

Smith, L.M. and Geoffrey, W. (1968) The Complexities of an Urban Classroom, Holt, Rinehart and Winston New York

Smith, R.N. (1982) 'Towards an analysis of PGCE courses' in Journal of Further and Higher Education, 6, 3, pp. 3-12

Stebbins, R. (1970) 'The meaning of disorderly behaviour' in Sociology of Education, 44, (Spring), pp. 217-236

Stebbins, R. (1981) 'Classroom ethnography and the definition of the situation' in L. Barton and S. Walker (Eds.) Schools, Teachers and Teaching, Falmer Press, Lewes

Taylor, J.K. and Dale, J.R. (1971) A Survey of Teachers in their First Year of Service, Bristol University Press

Webster, H. (1983) 'Practical Teaching and Partnership with Teachers' in SCETT News No. 3, NATFHE, London

Westbury, J. (1973) 'Conventional classrooms, "open" classrooms and the technology of teaching' in Journal of Curriculum Studies, 5, 2, pp. 99-121

Williams, R.N. (1963) 'Professional studies in teacher training' in Education for Teaching, 61, pp. 29-33

Willis, P. (1977) Learning to Labour, Saxon House, London

Wilson, J. (1981) Discipline and Moral Education: a survey of public opinion and understanding, NFER-Nelson, Windsor

Wiseman, S. and Start, K.B. (1968) 'A follow-up of teachers five years after completing their training' in British Journal of Educational Psychology, 35

Woods, P. (1977) 'Teaching for survival' in P. Woods

and M. Hammersley (Eds.) <u>School Experience</u>,
Croom Helm, London
Woods, P. (1979) <u>The Divided School</u>, Routledge and
Kegan Paul, London
Woods, P. (1983) <u>Sociology and the School: an
interactionist viewpoint</u>, Routledge and Kegan
Paul, London
Yates, J.W. (1982) 'Student teaching: results of a
recent survey' in <u>Educational Research</u>, <u>24</u>, 3,
pp. 212-215

THE PARADIGMATIC MENTALITY: A DIAGNOSIS

Martyn Hammersley

> The initial impression one has in reading
> through the literature in and about the
> social disciplines during the past decade
> or so is that of sheer chaos. Everything
> appears to be 'up for grabs'. There is
> little or no consensus - except by members
> of the same school or subschool - about
> what are the well-established results,
> the proper research procedures, the impor-
> tant problems, or even the most promising
> theoretical approaches to the study of
> society and politics. There are claims
> and counterclaims, a virtal babble of
> voices demanding our attention.
>
>   (Bernstein 1979, p. xii)

There is little doubt that ... the level of
theoretical sophistication has risen out of
all recognition in the contemporary sociology
of the last decade. But sociologists'
contributions to the understanding of the
world outside their study have, on the other
hand, been remarkable for paucity, not to
say poverty.

These two situations are not just accidental
or paradoxical conjunctures: they are
interconnected. They reflect, that is,
the socialisation of the young into a
pluralistic sociological universe, in which
they are systematically, as never before,
exposed to several varieties of theorising.
The usual claim ... is that this is a
liberating experience, and it can be. But
it can also be quite demoralising. The

(British) sociological universe once resembled
the more thinly-populated reaches of outer
space, with Fabian empiricism, primitive
Marxism, and structural-functionalism as
the only visible heavenly bodies of theory.
Today, there is a coruscating explosion of
new and glittering stars: structuralism
and Marxism in various forms and combinations,
symbolic interactionism, and now phenomenology, especially in its ethnomethodological
variants ...

The rate of change of theoretical fashion
is now such, indeed, that whereas it took
a decade or so before the demolition of
functionalism ... became a ritual part of
any self-respecting curriculum, theories
are nowadays demolished before the ink of
their manifestos has dried.

(Worsley 1974)

There is a rather old joke which tells of someone
travelling abroad asking one of the locals for
directions to a nearby town.   The reply comes back:
'If I were going there, I wouldn't start from here'.
That story provides an analogy for the phenomenon
I want to discuss: the idea that where you start
from determines where you can get to.
Over thirty years ago Robert Merton berated his
fellow sociologists for their premature pursuit of
all-embracing, unified sociological theory. He
traced the impulse to construct 'grand theory' back
to the beginnings of the discipline, suggesting that
it had been inherited from the system-building which
dominated philosophy in the nineteenth century. He
goes on to remark that:

Within this context, almost all the pioneers
in sociology tried to fashion his own system.
The multiplicity of systems, each claiming to
be the genuine sociology, led naturally enough
to the formation of schools, each with its
cluster of masters, disciples and epigoni.
Sociology not only became differentiated from
other disciplines, but it became internally
differentiated. This differentiation,
however, was not in terms of specialization,
as in the sciences, but rather, as in
philosophy, in terms of total systems,
typically held to be mutually exclusive

and largely at odds.

(Merton 1967, p. 46)

One of Merton's main targets in his critique of 'grand theory' was of course the work of Parsons. Twenty years later Parsons' influence is much less than it was. However, on this side of the Atlantic at least, the pursuit of 'total systems of sociological theory' is if anything even more feverish, and the fragmentation of the discipline into different schools to which that leads has grown apace. This process has been particularly far-reaching in the sociology of education over the last decade.

For many of us in the sociology of education, and in sociology generally, the late 1960s and early 1970s were an exciting time of new horizons and possibilities. The old sociology was to be swept away and replaced by more relevant alternatives, truer to what we took to be the real nature of humanity and society. One of the guiding lights here was Dawe's (1970) discussion of order and control doctrines; the one legitimating oppression, the other inspiring liberation.

Today we are in a good position to look back and assess the 'new sociology of education', and that in one sense is what I shall be doing in this paper (for other assessments see Whitty 1974, Pring 1972, Bernbaum 1977, Karabel and Halsey 1977). However, my motive is far from being a matter of mere nostalgia or antiquarian interest. It seems to me that our work today still owes much to that 'new paradigm' of the 1970s.

It has sometimes been claimed that the new sociology of education had a demoralising effect on teachers exposed to it (Simon 1974). In the early years this new approach was often taken to imply that any attempt on the part of teachers to shape what pupils learned represented a suppression of pupils' culturally given abilities and a denial of their rights. Later, the complaint was heard that teachers could be forgiven for concluding from our work that their plight was hopeless since whatever they did would lead to the reproduction of capitalism, and the persistence of all those ills customarily ascribed to that type of society by sociologists. These accusations have some justification, but I believe that the new sociology of education has had an even more damaging effect on sociologists of education themselves, and that this effect is as strong today as it has ever been.

The Paradigmatic Mentality: A Diagnosis

The predominant impression when I look back over the last decade or so is one of disappointment and frustration. It seems to me that we have a lot less to show for our efforts than we expected to have and indeed than we could have been justified in expecting. I am not talking here of the realm of political change, though that was certainly where many of our hopes lay. Rather, I refer to the limited contribution we have made to the understanding of educational structures and processes. We have produced plenty of theoretical ideas and many descriptive studies. But what is lacking, I suggest, is any significant cumulative development of knowledge. In particular, we have few powerful theories which would allow us to explain those aspects of educational phenomena which are of concern to us. I shall propose that one major reason for this is that there is a central element of the new sociology of education that was, and indeed still is, antithetical to any such theoretical development.

Of course, I am not denying the benefits which the new sociology of education brought. It constituted an important corrective to the narrow theoretical and methodological orientation of the earlier political arithmetic tradition. It opened up whole new areas of investigation and reintroduced important theoretical and methodological ideas. Nevertheless, I shall claim that one of its central elements was not only fundamentally mistaken but also seriously detrimental to the development of the discipline. Indeed, I would go so far as to suggest that, to some degree at least, the discipline's current political difficulties, such as right wing attacks on left wing bias, arise from it and are thus to an extent self-inflicted.

THE PARADIGM ARGUMENT

What I want to challenge is a set of ideas which trades under many different names. By friend and foe it is often identified with the sociology of knowledge, though it by no means exhausts nor is necessary to that discipline. I shall call it the paradigm argument. Currently, this doctrine pervades sociology; and increasingly, it seems, it is to be found in other social sciences too. Nevertheless, the effects of the acceptance of this argument are most obvious within sociology and especially within the sociology of education.

The basic premise of the paradigm argument is that all knowledge is founded upon epistemological,

> materialist framework under consideration
> is 'What functions do particular theoretic
> products serve in particular societies?'
> This question (and it does not preclude
> answers being given in terms of discovering
> or producing the real world) at once becomes
> both the focus of epistemological investi-
> gation, while also providing a means whereby
> we can make viable judgments of critical
> preference between competing interpretations,
> theories and research programmes.

> (Harris 1979:60)

The origins of this argument are many and varied.
The work of Kuhn (1962) was a major resource, not
least in providing a concept of 'paradigm' which
could be used in this way. Kuhn, Lakatos (1978) and
Feyerabend (1975) and other contributors to post-
empiricist philosophy challenged the conventional
positivist accounts of science which treated the
assessment of theories against facts as the feature
which distinguished science from non-science (Newton-
Smith, 1981, Tudor 1982). These authors emphasise
the theory-laden character of all observations and
point to other criteria than empirical testing as
necessary and legitimate grounds for the acceptance
and rejection of theories. Also influential has
been the revival or importation into Anglo-American
sociology of a whole variety of alternatives to
positivism - symbolic interactionism, phenomenology,
structuralism and Frankfurt Marxism - all of which
stress the active character of knowledge production
as against the empiricist idea that knowledge arises
simply from the impression made on one's senses by
the world.
Within sociology, versions of the paradigm
argument were developed by a number of writers,
notably Gouldner (1970) and Phillips (1977). Sociology
has increasingly come to be taught, in higher education and in schools, in terms of multiple perspectives
Moreover, the paradigm argument has provided a powerful rhetorical device in arguments for and against
different kinds of sociological work.

THE PARADIGMATIC MENTALITY AND ITS CONSEQUENCES

Central to the new sociology of education was a
challenge to the claims of conventional sociologists
to be engaged in the value-free pursuit of objective
knowledge. That sociology had not been and could

theoretical and political assumptions which are not
open to test, so that any knowledge must be regarded
as framed within, and thus relative to, a particular
paradigm. Paradigms not only indicate what is
relevant and important, how to go about investigating
it, and what can be taken for granted, they also lay
down the criteria for determining what is true and
false, real and unreal. On the basis of this idea
it is argued, or implied, that sociology and other
social sciences are _necessarily_ composed of several
incommensurable if not mutually antagonistic paradigms, perspectives or problematics founded upon
competing political interests.

One rarely finds this argument clearly and fully
expressed, usually it is implicit. Here, though,
are two of the more explicit declarations:

> Through its focus on the link between social
> structural interests and the production of
> ideas, sociology is putting forward an
> overtly political view of knowledge. It
> would be consistent with this position to
> argue that 'no knowledge is neutral', and
> that criteria of truth, rationality and
> plausibility are similarly related to the
> social interests underlying them.
>
> (Esland 1977:11)

> Once the social dimension of knowledge
> production is recognised and emphasised,
> the role and the extent of social practice
> and social interests in the very produc-
> tion of knowledge emerge clearly as
> central issues in evaluating the theoretic
> product (or knowledge). In evaluating
> theories, interpretations or knowledge,
> it becomes both relevant and necessary to
> consider which particular interests are
> being served in the production and promul-
> gation of any particular theory, in what
> ways particular social interests are being
> served in any process of production, and
> how the various interests concerned are
> interrelated (and, if necessary, disguised).
> These considerations are not merely
> necessary for evaluating knowledge or
> theory; they are crucial: for, given
> the social dimension to the production of
> knowledge, the key question that we find
> embedded in and arising from the particular

not be value-free was treated as a foregone conclusion
on the basis of arguments such as those of Gouldner
(1962). But what made the new sociology of education
particularly significant was its denial of the claim
that sociologists (or indeed anyone else) can produce
objective knowledge about the world. (1)
    Bernbaum (1977:59) highlights this difference
between the new and the old sociology:

> In both kinds of sociology of education ...
> ideological elements are to be found.
> There is, however, an important difference.
> The old sociology of education contained,
> also, a commitment on the part of its
> practitioners to the possibility of arriving
> at truth ... Within the new sociology of
> education and particularly the general
> sociological standpoints from which it
> develops, it is very difficult to make the
> distinction between 'ideology' and 'science'.

The new sociologists argued that different cultures
have different criteria of truth and falsity, indeed
different logics (Keddie 1973), and that, for example,
positivist sociology simply represented a vehicle
for the imposition of western, white, middle class
values and beliefs on other groups. Since all
knowledge, including that concerning truth criteria,
is founded on fundamental assumptions and political
interests, the argument ran, it can only be judged
in terms of the interests which motivate it or the
functions which it serves. It was claimed that,
given a commitment to human liberation (Young 1973),
what is required in a society characterised by
domination and alienation is to challenge the assumptions built into social institutions, including
sociology itself. Only by the rejection of such
assumptions, it was believed, could people take
control of society rather than being dominated by it
(Dawe 1970).
    The new sociology of education was never a
coherent and well-integrated set of ideas and it was
not long before it began to split into competing
approaches whose proponents became increasingly at
odds with one another. The major division which
arose was between those concerned with macro-theory
and those engaged in micro-focused research on
schools. But this was by no means the only division,
further fragmentation occurred within both macro and
micro camps. It was in this context that what I
shall call the paradigmatic mentality, a set of

236

attitudes to sociological work deriving from the
paradigm argument, flourished.

One aspect of this mentality concerns our
attitudes to the ideas associated with other paradigms.
At first sight it might be assumed that the paradigm
argument would encourage tolerance. One of its
implications is that disagreement among social
scientists is inevitable, given the existence of
multiple paradigms grounded in conflicting assumptions and interests. And since paradigms are valid
in their own terms, it might be concluded that one
should simply accept that others think differently.

In practice, however, the paradigm argument
encourages intolerance. This is most obviously true
in the case of attitudes towards those who refuse to
accept the paradigm argument itself, claiming that
their knowledge at least approximates to the truth.
They have felt the full brunt of attack, being
accused, for example, of adopting 'a lofty pose of
being above the battle'. Their views are dismissed
as arrogant and empiricist. However, the paradigm
argument has encouraged little tolerance even towards
others who also accept it. Much as Weber argued
that people could not tolerate the strain of trying
to live their lives on the basis of strict Calvinist
beliefs, so it seems that it is difficult to be a
sociologist while yet accepting that any sociological
view is as good as any other. From this perspective
sociological work seems pointless. In practice,
paradigm members tend to treat their own assumptions
as true and to reject those of other paradigms as
necessarily false. And, of course, given the
paradigm argument, other paradigms cannot be subjected
to rational criticism. Rather, they can only be
dismissed, on the grounds that they draw on assumptions
different from those built into one's own paradigm.

There are many examples of this. For instance,
in advocating a Weberian perspective, Ronald King
writes as follows:

> One of the forms of Marxism to be found
> in the recent sociology of education is the
> structuralist variety of Althusser and of
> Bowles and Gintis which draws upon the
> political economy of the 'mature' Marx
> (another of the emanationist theories
> dismissed by Weber). This shows an
> interesting convergence with the structural
> functional analysis of education ...

237

> Weber considered that rational actions were
> in the ascendancy in the modern world, but
> as Eldridge points out, Weber was referring
> to the subjective intentions of individuals
> directed to means regarded as correct for a
> given end.   Classical Marxism proceeds by
> the application of its own (economic)
> rationality, and where the behaviour of
> people is at variance with their imputed
> 'true interests' they are suffering from
> false consciousness.   Having carried out
> lengthy 'probing' interviews with three
> teachers and the headteacher of a primary
> school, Sharp and Green virtually dismiss
> their accounts of their actions (made, for
> the most part, at a high level of abstrac-
> tion remote from classroom events) in
> pursuit of 'progressive' ideals, and, by
> the application of a Marxist perspective,
> conclude that such education contributes
> to the preservation of the existing social
> order.   There is little to choose between
> being the cultural dope of functionalism
> or suffering from the false consciousness
> of Marxism.
>
> (King 1980:10)

Here the argument against Marxism is two-pronged.
Firstly, King points to its similarities with
functionalism, trading on the ritual rejection of
functionalism by members of other paradigms, including Marxists.   The second element of the argument,
hardly disputable though not as clear-cut as King
suggests, is that Marx's mode of explanation is
different from Weber's.   But the question of which
approach is correct, or most useful, is treated as
self-evident;   even though sophisticated arguments
have been deployed on the other side (for example
Lukes 1974).

In much the same manner, Sharp (1981) criticises
a long stream of authors in the sociology of education
from Durkheim to Michael F.D. Young on the grounds
that they do not conform to her interpretation of
Marxism.   She makes little attempt, however, to
demonstrate that her perspective is the most fruitful
one.   That is an assumption from which she starts
and which she expects her readers to accept on faith.

The effect of the paradigm argument, then, is to
reduce us either to debilitating uncertainty about
the justification for our work or to political and

theoretical dogmatism. The paradigm argument not only divides sociological work up into different paradigms it also threatens the very possibility of rational debate among representatives of the different approaches. One simply must accept one or another set of assumptions about the nature of the social world as a matter of commitment or faith. Other paradigms can only be rejected on the grounds that they are other paradigms, though rhetorical force can be added to such rejections by explaining away alternative views in terms of interests or functions claimed to underlie them. The concept of 'ideology' which has of course become very popular among sociologists of education in recent years is ideally suited to such a task (Hammersley 1981).

Much time is thus expended in fruitless polemic in which the concepts employed are progressively drained of cognitive meaning. The all-purpose insults 'positivist', 'empiricist' and 'liberal' are only the most obvious examples. We can get some sense of how empty such terms have become by comparing how they are used by representatives of different paradigms. Thus, Sharp (1982:50) claims that

> ... despite its self-concept as embodying a methodological procedure which overcomes the blindness of positivism with its empiricist fetishization of the 'objective' fact, ethnography's own method is equally empiricist. In place of 'the facts' as objectified in a computer printout, appear the facts of the raw data of consciousness, of the motivations, purposes and creative projects of active intending minds in interaction with other minds, and of events and happenings as these are subjectively constructed and mediated through everyday encounters and relationships. Ethnography follows a classic empiricist inductivist method: observable phenomena are recorded, ordered, and classified; this collating process gives rise to empirical generalizations and hypotheses. Evidence is then sought to further substantiate such empirical generalizations which are then used deductively in explanation to produce plausible interpretations.

From a very different perspective, that of ethnomethodology, Hitchcock (1983:21) also charges ethnography with failing to break with positivism.

239

He cites Rist's (1973:241) claim to have found 'an interlocking pattern of institutional arrangements descending from the macro-level of the city-wide school system ... to the various stratification techniques employed by individual teachers in their classrooms' as an example. Yet he claims that Rist's approach is positivist precisely because the latter does <u>not</u> do what Sharp sees as characteristic of positivism:

> we are left in the dark about exactly <u>how</u> Rist was able to manage deductions about the relationships between phenomena at different levels, about how he came to his conclusions.

Here we have arguments about practical methodology dressed up as epistemological issues through loose talk of 'positivism' and 'empiricism'. This is a widespread phenomenon. (2)

Even where the arguments of each side address substantive issues, theories deriving from different paradigms are often regarded as mutually incompatible, on no strong evidence. For example, Collins (1972 and 1979) treats as competitors functionalist and conflict explanations for the increasing levels of qualifications demanded by North American employers, and seeks on the basis of inadequate evidence to demolish the former in order to make way for the latter. Yet the two theories are certainly not logically incompatible, and it may well be that each provides a partial explanation for the phenomenon with which Collins is concerned.

The defects of particular theories or studies are often treated as symptoms of the general worth-lessness of the paradigm from which they derive, rather than as an opportunity for further research. For example, on the grounds that some versions of structural functionalism have been less than convincing in their explanations for social change, functionalism is often assumed to be <u>incapable</u> of explaining change and is dismissed as conservative. Similarly, because interactionists have sometimes neglected to investigate the material constraints which operate on actors, this is taken as conclusive evidence that interactionism is idealist and thus simply liberal ideology. Only rarely do the critics try to develop the theories they criticise to discover whether the attributed faults are intrinsic or contingent; and thus whether they can be overcome. Generally, it is assumed that the theories are incapable of such development. (3)

Part and parcel of this is the assumption that political assumptions are logically tied to particular theoretical views and perhaps even to certain empirical claims about the world. For example, it is often assumed that interactionists necessarily view western societies as characterised by "democratic pluralism" and that they look on this feature favourably. Conversely, both functionalism and "deterministic" forms of Marxism are accused of failing "to treat people seriously" and thus by implication of being linked to repressive forms of politics (Hargreaves 1978:73).

Of course, the most common response to work in other paradigms which the paradigm argument induces is sheer neglect. Huge tracts of the sociological literature are ignored. One sign of this is that those who study the same area from the point of view of different paradigms draw on completely different literatures. Some years ago I had occasion to compare the indexes of two books appearing at the same time both dealing with what we might call 'rebellious youth': Willis's Learning to Labour and Marsh, Rosser and Harré's The Rules of Disorder. The entries listed in their indexes under 'A' and 'B' are by no means untypical:

accounts, 15,17,21-2,117; see also football fans, schoolchildren: accounts
actions, social, 3,14-17, 21-2,25-6,64,118,121, 131; rule-governed, 15,18, 29,121
acts, social, 15,21,25-6, 29,121
aggression, 27-8,128,130; ritualized, 24,26-8,91, 125-8,131,133-4; social management, 97,128-9, 131, 134
aggro, 118,121,125,127-30, 133-4; definition, 28, 68n; leader, 68-70,74, 77-9,82,97,116; outfit, see dress
animals' behaviour, 127-8
Ardrey, Robert, 129n

Alienation 143
Althusser, L. 137, 183
Anderson,P., 170
Ashton,D.N., 141
Auld, R. 86
Autonomous Work groups 179-183

Balibar,E. 137
Barthes,R. 115
Bennett, 193
Bourdieu,P. 128,142
Braverman,H. 142, 180,183
Brighton Labour Process Group 142

(Willis 1977)

Becker, Howard, 10-11
Bernstein, Basil, 6,19
biological factors, 27-8,
   109,118,129-30
Blackpool FC, 70
Bullshitters, 68-9,124
Burrell, Joanna, 5

(Marsh, Rosser and Harré 1978)

Despite their similar focus these books show virtually no overlap in the references they cite. Each appeals to a quite different literature and probably, of course, to a quite different audience. (4)

Up to now I have considered the external relations of paradigms, how we deal with work which we take to represent other paradigms than our own. Equally damaging, though, are the attitudes which the paradigm argument encourages us to take towards the ideas which make up our own paradigm. Given that there is no rational basis in terms of which those ideas can be doubted, they have to be treated as true a priori. Moreover, this is reinforced by the effects of the foreign policies of paradigms. As already implied, these tend to reduce the audience for any piece of work to those who view it as deriving from their own paradigm. The result is that, as writers, not only are we rarely required to try to justify our paradigm assumptions, often we do not even have to think about them, they become second nature.

In any event, to question these assumptions is, of course, to threaten one's identity as a paradigm member and to open oneself up to the attributions of ulterior motive and ideology deployed against representatives of other paradigms. This comes out clearly in the following extract from a review of Willis's Learning to Labour by Michael Apple. Having pointed out that reproduction theory is "a bit incorrect", Apple goes on to remark:

> Before my colleagues on the left grow
> uncomfortable, let me clarify what I
> mean. There is no lack of evidence
> to support the claim that schools act
> as agents in the economic and cultural
> reproduction of an unequal society.
> Nor is there any lack of evidence about
> the power of the hidden curriculum in
> schools in teaching norms and values
> to students that are related to this

> unequal society. What I mean to contest
> here is a particular assumption - that of
> passivity - one which tends to overlook
> the fact that both students and workers
> are creatively acting in ways which often
> contradict these expected norms and
> dispositions which pervade the school and
> workplace.

> (Apple 1979:101-2)

Here Apple clearly finds it necessary to guard against
the possibility that he might be thought to be casting
doubt on the basic premises of the neo-Marxist paradigm. He hastily reassures his readers that "there
is no lack of evidence" for these, that he is only
modifying one of the minor premises. (5)

The treatment of certain political and theoretical assumptions as articles of faith has a number of
effects. One is the encouragement of speculation
and the neglect of systematic checking of theories
and facts. After pointing out the similarities
between order and control theories of schooling,
Edwards (1980:67) notes their common weakness: "the
practice of constructing a description of how things
'are' from a theoretical analysis of how things 'must
be' to maintain the social system, thereby avoiding
the chore of observation". And later (p. 71) he
notes that "some of the bleakest accounts of schooling seem to follow the American Declaration of Independence in presenting their 'truths' to be self-
evident".

Unlike King, Edwards does not claim, however,
that this feature is intrinsic to these paradigms.
And indeed in my view it stems rather from the paradigm argument in general, not from the content of
particular paradigms. Evidence for this comes from
the fact that, despite the frequent criticisms of
interactionism as 'empiricist', this perspective also
rarely leads to the rigorous assessment of empirical
claims. While interactionist ethnographers show no
reluctance to employ data, their treatment of this
data is often highly speculative relying not on
systematic checking of interpretations but on a
general appeal to be in touch with reality through
naturalistic research methods (Hammersley and
Atkinson 1983). And those who most strongly insist
upon the paradigmatic purity of interactionism often
reject those few methodological procedures built into
ethnography which are designed to test accounts, such
as triangulation and analytic induction (Williams 1976).

The Paradigmatic Mentality: A Diagnosis

As a result of the way in which the paradigm argument discourages empirical checks on theories, other criteria come to be used for choosing among theoretical ideas. Thus, for example, the assumed political implications of explanations may become an overriding consideration (Hargreaves 1982). Giroux (1981:3) provides an example:

> In stressing the primacy of either the state or political economy in educational theory and practice, radical theories of reproduction have played a significant role in exposing the ideological assumptions and processes behind the rhetoric of neutrality and social mobility characteristic of both conservative and liberal views of schooling. Yet while such theories represent an important break from idealist and functionalist paradigms in educational theory, they still remain situated within a problematic that ultimately supports rather than challenges the logic of the existing order. The point here is that there are some serious deficiencies in existing theories of reproduction, the most important of which is the refusal to posit a form of critique that demonstrates the theoretical and practical importance of counter-hegemonic struggles both within and outside of the sphere of schooling.

The comprehensiveness of a theory is also sometimes given great weight. For example, it is sometimes claimed that a theory is superior if it can not only explain the phenomena under study, but also why others might adopt different explanations (Sharp 1980). Within interactionism, the 'richness' of data, and the extent to which findings contradict conventional or official views, have come to be major criteria for judging ethnographic accounts.

In this section I have outlined what I see as the major features of the paradigmatic mentality. What I have presented is very much an ideal type. I am not claiming that this set of attitudes totally dominates the sociology of education. We are not all locked into membership of closed, self-interacting paradigms. Nevertheless I think the paradigm argument, in one form or another, has been extremely influential and that as a result the paradigmatic mentality has to a considerable extent become

244

institutionalised in our intellectual and social
relations. Moreover, in my view this has had a
disastrous effect on the development of our discipline.
It is one of the major reasons why the sociology of
education has shown very little cumulative development
of knowledge over the last ten years or so, why we do
not have a body of knowledge on which much reliance
can be placed in formulating policy, either at the
national or the classroom level. Not only does the
paradigm argument undercut attempts to develop
objective knowledge through the systematic development
and testing of theory, the mentality to which it leads
sabotages this process through secondary effects: for
example the dismissal of much of the existing literature as worthless and the encouragement of speculation
presented as fact.

One important consequence of our failure to
'produce the goods' is that it opens the sociology
of education up to economic and political attack, as
we have recently discovered. But the paradigmatic
mentality leaves us vulnerable to such attacks in
another way too. If we claim that our findings stem
from the political and theoretical assumptions built
into our paradigms, we can hardly plead innocence to
charges of political bias. Nor can we legitimately
complain when those holding different political
commitments refuse to finance our work. Presumably,
were the roles reversed, we would do the same. The
costs of the paradigmatic mentality have been high,
and they could rise still further.

THE PARADIGM ARGUMENT ASSESSED

Now, if the paradigm argument were valid, we might
simply have to live with its consequences. Fortunately, there are good grounds for thinking that it
is not. The paradigm argument is founded upon
relativism, and relativism is logically incoherent.
If it were true that the validity of all knowledge
claims is relative, this would also apply to the
argument for relativism itself. But this leads to
the paradoxical conclusion that there are, after all,
some knowledge claims which are not relative. In
other words, relativism undercuts its own claim to
truth:

> Truth, says the cultural relativist, is
> culture-bound. But if it were then he,
> within his own culture, ought to see his
> own culture-bound truth as absolute. He
> cannot proclaim cultural relativism without

rising above it, and he cannot rise above
it without giving it up.

(Quine 1975:327-8) (6)

Rejecting the paradigm argument as incoherent
does not force us to deny that all knowledge is
subject to value biases and that all facts are
dependent on the validity of theories. But these
are not the novel claims that they are often presented as being by proponents of the paradigm argument.
Weber was perfectly well aware of the first when he
argued for sociology to be value-neutral. He did
not claim, as seems to be widely assumed, that one
could produce sociological knowledge unaffected by
values. Rather, he was arguing that we should try
to minimise the effect of practical values (i.e.
those other than the search for truth) on the execution of our research procedures (Keat and Urry 1973
chapter 9). By contrast, Gouldner (1973) simply
implies that since knowledge can never be unaffected
by values, there is no point in trying to control
their effects. But this is to treat a matter of
degree as if it were all or nothing. The implication is that all ideals should be abandoned since,
by their very nature, they are unattainable.
    As the Marxist historian Eugene Genovese (1968:4)
points out "the inevitability of ideological bias
does not free us from the responsibility to struggle
for maximum objectivity". Moreover, the justification he provides for this is very much the same as
Weber's: objective knowledge aids principled and
effective political action (Roth and Schluchter 1979):

> In fact what we (socialist historians) stand
> for is the realization that all historical
> writing and teaching - all cultural work -
> is unavoidably political intervention, but
> that ideologically motivated history is bad
> history and ultimately reactionary politics
> ... In each case the demand for ideological
> history for 'class truth', for 'partisan-
> ship in science', has ended in the service
> of ... a new oppressor.
>
> (Genovese 1968:5-10) (7)

Moreover, if one looks at the relationship
between political standpoints and theoretical assumptions, one finds that these are weak at best. For
example, neither side of the argument about whether

the education system is relatively autonomous from
the economy is logically tied to any general political
viewpoint. Its political implications depend critically upon how the economy is conceptualised. While
relative autonomy has become a catchword for Marxists
wishing to avoid the political pessimism induced by
direct reproduction theories (Hargreaves 1982), the
latter need not be pessimistic from a socialist point
of view nor does relative autonomy necessarily offer
hope regarding effective socialist interventions.
If the mode of production is regarded as itself shot
through with contradictions and conflict, according
to reproduction theory these would be reflected within
the education system. Under these conditions relative autonomy would not be needed to allow for the
possibility that workers in the education system
might make political headway. Indeed, in this case
relative autonomy might well diminish the effects of
economic contradictions on schools, and thus reduce
the possibility of significant educational change.

However, even in the absence of contradictions
within the mode of production, relative autonomy does
not necessarily imply that 'radical' social change,
in whatever direction, is easier or more likely than
it would be if direct reproduction theories were
correct. This is because while relative autonomy
implies that change within the limits set by forces
outside the education system is easier, the obverse
of this is that any change lying beyond these limits
is likely to be more difficult to bring about since
it requires change in other relatively autonomous
sectors. Whereas, in a tightly integrated system,
change in one area tends to lead to change throughout, in a system where the parts enjoy relative
autonomy, change in one sector may have little effect
elsewhere in the system. There is no longer a single
point of leverage by which, given appropriate circumstances, social change can be brought about. The
battle has to be fought on many different fronts each
no doubt requiring very different strategies. The
task of bringing about change may thus be more difficult in a system characterised by relative autonomy
than in one in which direct reproduction obtains.

The paradigm argument leads us to neglect such
possibilities - it hitches up sets of theoretical and
political assumptions and presents them as though they
necessarily belong together. Yet quite clearly they
do not. Marxist theories are often functionalist
(Cohen 1978, Giddens 1979), sometimes differing from
structural functionalism in little more than the
evaluations made of the processes described and

explained.   Equally, the Weberian character of much
recent Marxist theorising has been noted (Hargreaves
1983) and there have even been claims that Marxism
and interactionism share much in common (Goff 1980,
West, this volume).   Quite clearly, there is strong
evidence against the claim that we have internally
consistent and mutually exclusive paradigms in
sociology.

The fallacy of treating matters of degree as
though they were all or nothing alternatives also
underlies the paradigm argument's treatment of the
relationship between theory and evidence.   It often
seems to be assumed that because all facts are theory-
dependent the empirical testing of theory is impossible.   One simply has to take paradigmatic assumptions on trust:

> The theory-ladenness of investigation
> gives rise to a large number of method-
> ological issues and problems, and it is
> hardly our purpose to discuss these here.
> On the other hand, it is our purpose to
> undertake an investigation, and this we
> shall do by ... casting our investigation
> into the context of a research programme
> (or problematic) wherein certain basic
> or 'hard core' hypotheses and proposi-
> tions are accepted as being secure and
> inviolable for the purpose of operating
> or working with the research programme.
>
> (Harris 1983:29)

But the theory-laden character of facts does not
rule out their use in assessing the validity of
theories, it simply means that such assessments can
never be absolutely conclusive.   Moreover, while
there may be no 'pure facts', one can nevertheless
range statements along a theoretical-empirical
continuum (Kaplan 1964, Newton-Smith 1981, Quine
1981).

We are not faced with a choice between naive
empiricism on the one hand and the paradigm argument
on the other.   There have been many attempts by
philosophers to resolve the epistemological issues
which surround the relationship between theory and
evidence.   Their work no more suggests that the
paradigm argument is the solution than it recommends
naive empiricism.   Few philosophers have adopted
either of these positions, and for good reasons. (8)
But the strongest argument of all against accepting

the paradigm argument is that, like all forms of relativism, it denies the very possibility of knowledge (Newton-Smith 1981). Of course, it may be that our everyday experience of the world is wholly an illusion, but we have no way of judging that claim nor is it clear that it would make any difference to our everyday judgements about what is and is not true if it were the case. Certainly, the fact that relativism undercuts claims to truth has not prevented those who use the paradigm argument from making strong claims about the world.

CONCLUSION

Even if the effects of the paradigm argument on the sociology of education have been damaging and it is also false, the question of what the alternative is remains to be answered. There have, of course, been many critics of paradigm divisions, and especially of that separating macro and micro research (Bernstein 1975, Banks 1978, Hargreaves 1978). The remedy recommended has often been that the paradigms be put together in some kind of synthesis.

In many ways this is an appealing idea. It seems to involve an even-handed approach in which the strengths and weaknesses of each perspective are recognised and treated as complementary. The paradigm argument is side-stepped through the construction of a single, all-embracing paradigm. This strategy combines the emotional satisfaction of visiting a plague on both houses with a more constructive process of reconciling differences and making peace.

However, in my view the search for synthesis is misdirected. In many ways it compounds the damaging effects of the paradigmatic mentality. Two or more sets of paradigm assumptions about the nature of the social world are put together, but since these are of uncertain validity in the first place, combining them carries few advantages. Moreover, the task of formulating revisions to these assumptions to make them mutually consistent comes to consume all our energies, at the expense of efforts to develop and test theories. Comprehensiveness remains a key criterion in judging theoretical ideas, and because the paradigm argument has not been directly challenged attempts to produce empirically valid findings are still discouraged.

In trying to find a way out of this cul-de-sac, we can do worse than return to Kuhn. It is curious that one of the major sources of the paradigmatic mentality should have been a study of the natural

sciences, given that another influential source was
the rejection of these as a model by such theoretical
traditions as interpretive sociology and Critical
Theory. But it seems clear that despite his protesta-
tions to the contrary, Kuhn's account of the incommen-
surability of paradigms does lapse into relativism.
And his conception of 'paradigm' is notoriously vague
and contradictory. Still, most of his account of
science can be preserved while rejecting relativism
(Masterman 1970, Newton-Smith 1981). Furthermore, the
core meaning of 'paradigm' has become much clearer in
his responses to critics than it was in the first
edition of The Structure of Scientific Revolutions
(Kuhn 1968, 1970a and 1970b). Of course, even in that
first edition Kuhn made clear his view that the social
sciences were pre-paradigmatic. This becomes even
more obvious once the root meaning of 'paradigm' is
identified as an exemplar: a particular study or set
of studies which establishes the importance of a
problem and demonstrates how that problem, and others
like it, can be effectively solved (Barnes 1982).

One aspect of this conception of paradigm which
it is particularly important to note is that it treats
the sciences as organised principally around research
problems and not around conflicting world-views.
Ironically, the pre-paradigmatic character of sociology (in Kuhn's terms) may stem in large part from
the fact that it has typically been organised around
paradigms (in the sense of conflicting political
philosophies).

The paradigmatic mentality represents an un-
healthy exaggeration of traits to be found in normal
science. Our knowledge is always founded upon
assumptions and open to the influence of our values.
As a result it is never absolutely certain. But we
should not draw the conclusion from this that any
'knowledge' is as valid as any other, and that prior
commitment is the only basis on which selection among
theories can be made. The fact that we can never
attain absolute certainty in the sociology of education does not mean that we cannot come to rational
conclusions about the validity of our descriptions
and theories on the basis of empirical evidence.
And indeed, unless we are prepared to accept defeat,
to call what we do 'social studies' rather than
'social science', and to look for work elsewhere, we
must reject the paradigm argument. Quine (1975:34)
neatly sums up the alternative I am recommending:

> We make do with what we have and improve
> it when we see how. We are always talking

within our going system when we attribute
truth; we cannot talk otherwise. Our
system changes, yes. When it does, we
do not say that truth changes with it; we
say that we had wrongly supposed something
true and have learned better. Fallibilism
is the watchword, not relativism.

NOTES

(1) This claim is rarely presented in clear
form, for obvious reasons. Thus, for example, in
the extract from Harris (1979) quoted earlier he
retains the possibility that whether theories
discover or produce the real world might be used as
a criterion for choosing between them. Yet in his
attack on empiricism and his adoption of Althusser's
distinction between theoretic and real objects he
undercuts any possibility of making claims about the
world.

(2) Particularly instructive as regards Sharp's
critique of empiricism is Hudelson's (1982) cogent
argument that Marx himself was an empiricist.

(3) There is evidence of this in my own work.
See, for example, Hammersley 1980 and Hammersley and
Turner 1980.

(4) For an account of external relations among
paradigms in another area of sociology which identifies a similar range of attitudes see Bradley and
Wilkie (1980).

(5) In fact the evidence he cites is very
meagre. For the most part it consists of other
studies expressing a commitment to but providing
little empirical support for reproduction theory.

(6) For further discussion of relativism, see
Trigg (1973), Meiland and Krausz (1982), Hollis and
Lukes (1982). Mackinnon (1976) assesses the
relativistic arguments of the new sociology of
education.

(7) Mackinnon (1977) and Keat (1981), provide
useful discussions of the fact-value issue.

(8) One of the most persuasive treatments of
the problem is that of Charles Peirce (Reilly 1970,
Rescher 1978, and Almeder 1980).

REFERENCES

Almeder, R. (1980) <u>The Philosophy of Charles Peirce</u>,
     Blackwell
Apple, M.W. (1979) 'What Correspondence Theories of
     the Hidden Curriculum Miss', Review of Education,
     Spring

The Paradigmatic Mentality: A Diagnosis

Banks, O. (1978) 'School and Society' in L. Barton and R. Meighan (Eds.) Sociological Interpretation of Schooling and Classrooms: A Reappraisal, Nafferton

Barnes, B. (1982) T.S. Kuhn and Social Science, Macmillan

Bernbaum, G. (1977) Knowledge and Ideology in the Sociology of Education, Macmillan

Bernstein, B. (1975) 'The Sociology of Education: A Brief Account' in B. Bernstein Class Codes and Control, Vol. 3, Routledge and Kegan Paul

Bernstein, R.J. (1979) The Restructuring of Social and Political Theory, Methuen

Bradley, D.A. and Wilkie, R. (1980) 'Radical Organization Theory - A Critical Comment', British Journal of Sociology, 31, 4

Cohen, G.A. (1978) Karl Marx's Theory of History: A Defence, Oxford University Press

Collins, R. (1971) 'Functional and Conflict Theories of Educational Stratification', American Sociological Review, 36

Collins, R. (1979) The Credential Society, Academic Press

Dawe, A. (1970) 'The Two Sociologies', British Journal of Sociology, XXI, 2

Edwards, T. (1980) 'Schooling for Change: Function, Correspondence and Cause', in L. Barton, R. Meighan and S. Walker (Eds.) Schooling, Ideology and the Curriculum, Falmer Press

Fay, B. (1975) Social Theory and Political Practice, George Allen and Unwin

Feyerabend, P.K. (1975) Against Method, New Left Books

Genovese, E. (1971) In Red and Black: Marxian Explorations in Southern and Afro-American History, Allen Lane

Giddens, A. (1979) Central Problems in Social Theory, Macmillan

Giroux, H.A. (1981) 'Hegemony, Resistance and the Paradox of Educational Reform, Interchange, 12, 2-3

Goff, T. (1980) Marx and Mead, Routledge and Kegan Paul

Gouldner, A. (1970) The Coming Crisis of Western Sociology, Basic Books

Gouldner, A. (1973) 'Anti-Minotaur: The Myth of a Value-Free Sociology' in A. Gouldner For Sociology, Allen Lane

Hammersley, M. (1980) 'On Interactionist Empiricism' in P. Woods (Ed.) Pupil Strategies, Croom Helm

Hammersley, M. (1981) 'Ideology in the Staffroom?

A Critique of False Consciousness' in L. Barton and S. Walker (Eds.) Schools, Teachers and Teaching, Falmer

Hammersley, M. (1983) 'Social Relations in Hightown Comprehensive', unpublished

Hammersley, M. and Turner, G. (1980) 'Conformist Pupils?' in P. Woods (Ed.) Pupil Strategies, Croom Helm

Hammersley, M. and Atkinson, P. (1983) Ethnography: Principles in Practice, Macmillan

Hammersley, M., Scarth, J. and Webb, S. (1983) 'Developing and Testing Theory', paper given at conference on Qualitative Research in Educational Settings, Whitelands College, London

Hargreaves, A. (1978) 'The Significance of Classroom Coping Strategies' in L. Barton and R. Meighan (Eds.) Sociological Interpretations of Schooling and Classrooms: A Reappraisal, Nafferton

Hargreaves, A. (1982) 'Resistance and Relative Autonomy Theories: Problems of Distortion and Incoherence in Recent Marxist Analyses of Education', British Journal of Sociology of Education, 3, 2

Hargreaves, A. (1983) 'The Myths of Multicausality: Ideological Influence on Weberian Accounts of Educational Change', paper delivered at conference on Social Crisis, Educational Research and Social Policy, Westhill College, Birmingham, January

Harris, K. (1979) Education and Knowledge, Routledge and Kegan Paul

Harris, K. (1982) Teachers and Classes: A Marxist Analysis, Routledge and Kegan Paul

Hollis, M. and Lukes, A. (1982) Rationality and Relativism, Blackwell

Hudelson, R. (1982) 'Marx's Empiricism', Philosophy of the Social Sciences, 12

Kaplan, A. (1964) The Conduct of Inquiry, Chandler

Karabel, J. and Halsey, A.H. (1977) Power and Ideology in Education, Oxford University Press

Keat, R. and Urry, J. (1975) Social Theory as Science, Routledge and Kegan Paul

Keat, R. (1981) The Politics of Social Theory, Blackwell

Keddie, N. (1973) Tinker, Tailor, Penguin

King, R. (1980) 'Weberian Perspectives and the Sociology of Education', British Journal of Sociology of Education, 1, 1

Kuhn, T.S. (1962) The Structure of Scientific Revolutions, University of Chicago Press

Kuhn, T.S. (1970a) The Structure of Scientific Revolutions, second edition

Kuhn, T.S. (1970b) 'Reflections on my Critics' in I. Lakatos and A. Musgrave, Criticism and the Growth of Knowledge, Cambridge University Press

Lakatos, I. (1978) The Methodology of Scientific Research Programmes, Cambridge University Press

Lukes, S. (1974) Power: A Radical View, Macmillan

Mackinnon, D. (1976) 'The Curriculum and the Sociology of Knowledge' in Unit 5 of Open University Course E203, Curriculum Design and Development, Open University Press

Mackinnon, D. (1977) Unit 24, Open University Course E202, Schooling and Society, Open University Press

Marsh, P., Rosser, E., and Harre, R. (1978) The Rules of Disorder, Routledge and Kegan Paul

Masterman, M. (1970) 'The Nature of a Paradigm' in I. Lakatos and A. Musgrave, Criticism and the Growth of Knowledge, Cambridge University Press

Meiland, J.W. and Krausz, M. (1982) Relativism: Cognitive and Moral, Notre Dame, University of Notre Dame Press

Merton, R.K. (1967) On Theoretical Sociology, Free Press

Newton-Smith, W.H. (1981) The Rationality of Science, Routledge and Kegan Paul

Phillips, D.L. (1977) Wittgenstein and Scientific Knowledge, Macmillan

Pring, R. (1972) 'Knowledge Out of Control', Education for Teaching, Autumn

Quine, W.V. (1975) 'On Empirically Equivalent Systems of the World', Erkenntnis, 9

Quine, W.V. (1981) 'The Pragmatists' Place in Empiricism' in R.J. Mulvaney and P.M. Zeltner Pragmatism: its Sources and Prospects, University of South Carolina Press

Reilly, F. (1970) Charles Peirce's Theory of Scientific Method, Fordham University Press

Rescher, N. (1978) Peirce's Philosophy of Science, University of Notre Dame Press

Roth, G. and Schluchter, W. (1979) Max Weber's Vision of History: Ethics and Methods, University of California Press

Sharp, R. (1980) Knowledge, Ideology and the Politics of Schooling, Routledge and Kegan Paul

Sharp, R. (1982) 'Self-Contained Ethnography or a Science of Phenomenal Forms and Inner Relations', Boston University Journal of Education, 164, 1

Simon, J. (1974) '"New" Direction Sociology and Comprehensive Schooling', Forum, 17

Trigg, R. (1973) _Reason and Commitment_, Cambridge
    University Press
Tudor, A. (1982) _Beyond Empiricism_, Routledge and
    Kegan Paul
West, W.G. (This volume) 'Phenomenon and Form in
    Interactionist and Marxist Qualitative
    Educational Research'
Whitty, G. (1974) 'Sociology and the Problem of
    Radical Educational Change', in M. Flude and
    J. Ahier (Eds.) _Educability, Schools and
    Ideology_, Croom Helm
Williams, R. (1976) 'Symbolic Interactionism: Fusion
    of Theory and Research' in D.C. Thorns (Ed.)
    New Directions in Sociology, David and Charles
Willis, P. (1977) _Learning to Labour_, Saxon House
Worsley, P. (1974) 'Sociological Babel', _The Guardian_,
    13 June 1974
Young, M.F.D. (1973) 'Taking Sides Against the
    Probable: Problems of Relativism and Commitment
    in Teaching and the Sociology of Education',
    Educational Review, 25, 3

PHENOMENON AND FORM IN INTERACTIONIST AND NEO-MARXIST
QUALITATIVE EDUCATIONAL RESEARCH

W. Gordon West

INTRODUCTION

In the last few years, on both sides of the Atlantic,
ethnography has enjoyed a remarkable popularity boom
as an educational research method.   Offering stimulating insights into microlevel classroom interaction
(e.g. Woods and Hammersley 1977), being theoretically
open to examining failures of educational reforms
(e.g. Corrigan 1979), examining the lived meaningful
consciousness of students and teachers (e.g. Willis
1977), it has offered analyses of 'what really goes
on' in everyday educational experience, offering the
possibility of research taking practitioners' problems seriously.   Attempts by neo-positivists to make
it rigorous (e.g. Smith 1979) and by neo-Marxists to
insist on situating particular ethnographies within
wider structural accounts (e.g. Willis 1977) have
offered the hope of such research being not only
relevant to practitioners, but scientifically accurate,
generalisable, theoretically engaged, critical and
policy-related (Arnot and Whitty 1982).
     Not surprisingly, such grand hopes have not been
entirely fulfilled, in part, say some critics, (e.g.
Hargreaves 1982, Delamont 1981:73, Rock 1979a, Woods
1979) because the ethnography has not been done
adequately;   others (Hargreaves 1982, Hammersley and
Woods 1977:3, Hammersley 1980b:205) have raised the
more basic question of the fundamental epistemological
viability of such an enterprise as neo-Marxist ethnography.   If ethnography is centrally concerned with
phenomenal microlevel experience, is empiricist,
theoretically open, and value-free, then how can it
be combined with the macro-level system-oriented,
objectivist, value-committed approach of Marxism?
     In this paper, I want to press an argument which
may not please doctrinaire diehards in either the

256

ethnographic or neo-Marxist camps, but may force some dialogue (following, with differences, Hargreaves 1980, and Hammersley 1980a, 1980b). On the one hand, I agree with the 'purist' ethnographic critics that it must be admitted that many 'sins of omission' are all too painfully apparent in the neo-Marxist ethnography which has been done to date; yet it seems to me there are no intrinsic reasons why such relatively technical problems could not be rectified by better utilisation of ethnographic techniques. On the other hand, I believe the epistemological criticism of the very attempt at neo-Marxist ethnography is incorrect; not only is such synthesis possible around the shared concept of form, it is eminently desirable and justifiable on epistemological grounds alone, leaving aside its political and substantive utility. But it is, of course, exactly the potential political utility of research which is both true to educators' lived experience and embedded in theoretically sophisticated and cogent systemic policy issues which makes establishing intellectual grounds of such research important.

CRITICISMS OF EXEMPLARY NEO-MARXIST ETHNOGRAPHY: LEARNING TO LABOUR

A brief but detailed examination of Willis' Learning to Labour will illustrate these issues. The first half of this book is clearly ethnographic. The segments of description and analysis of Willis' lads' activities around such topics as "having a laff", defying authority, engaging in fights, sexism, and racism are gems in their own right. Willis traces these (often objectionable) behaviours as manifestations of underlying structural problems in working class adolescent lives, emphasising how the lads draw upon their parental working class culture for guides. Their realistic assessment of their employment futures causes them to see little use for extended formal schooling, to downgrade intellectual learning and admire physical prowess (and hence look down on weaker women and immigrants), encouraging them to leave school early, which then ironically locks them into the worst jobs.

The last half of Learning to Labour then jumps to abstract discussions of Althusserian structuralism and neo-Marxist cultural reproduction theories. Willis notes how the lads see through much of their situation (e.g., that schooling won't provide better jobs for them), but remain entrapped by the limitations of their understanding (e.g., failing to take seriously

257

that racial minorities share their fate).   Rather
than a dominating ideology being simply imposed, the
lads actively participate in their own demise at the
same time that their anti-intellectualism and sexism
gain them some space.   Ideology thus acts in a complicated way, confirming or dislocating local cultural
interpretations.   This conceptualisation allows the
research to penetrate surface appearances, widening
understanding, and juxtaposing immediate issues with
some more general theories.   All this is not to
indicate that Learning to Labour is without problems.

(a)   Difficulties of Technique and Substance
Although it might detract somewhat from the aesthetic
interest aroused by the sense of transcendental insight resulting from methodological mystery, it would
have been clarifying to know just how Willis got into
this research, what his expectations and presuppositions were at that time, and what biassing commitments
were involved and what surprises he encountered (West
1980a).   We learn that Willis associated closely
with the lads in their informal activities, and hence
was able to present a worldview closer to theirs than
ethnographers with different ties (e.g. Hargreaves
1967).   It would be nice to know how this affected
Willis' relations with school staff, however, and in
turn perhaps led to him interpreting teachers' viewpoints less well.
        Although passing mention is made of five
"comparison groups", Willis reports directly on only
a dozen lads from the West Midlands (with many quotes
from "Joey" alone), and the "comparison groups" are
not much used in the analysis, being referred to only
in the interview material from three "ear 'oles".
The description of the dozen lads and the cultural
form of their working class adolescent subculture is
rich, but of less certain wider representativeness
and hence the external validity of the research is
not clearly established when comparative sampling
could have been done (Glaser and Strauss 1967).   As
Willis admits, he should have paid more attention to
the experience of being female or ethnic (McRobbie
1980), and he has attempted to rectify this in his
recent course unit on Cultural Studies for the Open
University (1982:52).
        There is a relative lack of serious examination
of institutional or organisational mediations between
capital and the classrooms experienced by the lads.
Although other CCCS work does begin to address such
issues of educational policy, professional alliances,
etc. (CCCS Education Group 1981), we still have little

idea of how such national policy issues and processes connect to schools and classrooms, and how the latter connect to groups such as the lads.

How do we know Willis' conceptualisation and interpretation of his data is better than possible others? Surely "penetrations" are more than just those occasions when the lads agree with Willis' more structural analysis and "limitations" where they disagree (Menzies 1979). Why is the lads' misbehaviour conceived as "resistance"? Could it not (at least sometimes) just be precocious assertion of adulthood (as Werthman argued regarding similar San Francisco youths 1976, and I have argued regarding Chicago youngsters 1979). Is the "havin' a laff" syndrome not as much an example of Goffman's theory about establishing character in a situation of risk (e.g., Goffman 1967, West 1979). Could "nationalism" have been cited as an equally prominent limitation? Or "individualism"? If so, then how does one justify the focus on patriarchy and racism as the prominent "limitations" (see Cohen 1980)?

At the risk of sounding like a cranky old schoolmaster presumptuously reprimanding a pupil more brilliant than himself for doing his homework sloppily (even if he did get perfect on the test), there really is little excuse for not doing ethnography properly. Central to that is recounting the procedures used. Participant observation does have some standard techniques and approaches, with standard issues and difficulties, and standard ways of addressing them given in standard textbooks (McCall and Simmons 1969, Glaser and Strauss 1967, Filstead 1970, Becker 1970, Bogdan and Taylor 1975, Spradley 1980, West 1977, Shaffir, Stebbins, Turowetz 1980, Hammersley 1979a, 1979b). If we are to substantiate any serious and sustained claim that ethnographic research is relevant to any kind of social policy-making in this crisis, we must at the very least recognise and incorporate the previous half-century's methodological groundwork for such research. I also think such rigour would improve its utility, a point to which I will return in the last section.

(b) Epistemological Difficulties

Willis asks: "What are the basic determinants of those cultural forms whose tensions, reversals, continuities and final outcomes we have already explored?" (1977:119)

> ... the basic material of the cultural
> is constituted by varieties of symbolic

> systems and articulations ... I suggest
> that these things are produced at least
> in part by real forms of cultural pro-
> duction quite comparable with material
> production ... Finally I suggest that
> cultural forms provide the materials
> towards, and the immediate context of,
> the construction of subjectivities and
> the confirmation of identity.

(Willis 1977:172-3) (1)

Willis himself has later stated (1982:4) that he was
interested in describing the cultural form of the
white male counter school subculture. The subcul-
tural form is seen as mediating dominant ideologies
(such as "working hard for good grades, a certificate
and a good job") at the conjunction of subordinate
age and class, providing the means to kids for understanding and living out their social position. Stable
working class communities are seen as the locational
site, with partial disintegration and wider market
forces providing change.

Willis' descriptions thus speak in some way to
important theoretical issues within the on-going
British debate about educating working class kids.
Learning to Labour actually does attain some considerable substantive and conceptual coherence between its parts I and II. Willis convincingly shows
how racial, gender and mental/manual divisions are
limitations for the lads, expressed in their activities (such as "havin' a laff"). He clearly argues
for the non-reducibility of the cultural to the
economic (1977:171); the analysis is one of cultural
production, the ethnography is cultural.

However, although he later argues that Learning
to Labour specifically critiqued reproduction theories
by showing how social reproduction depended upon acti-
vistic always contingent production of cultural forms
by groups such as the lads, the rejection of an
Althusserian functionalist determinism (see Fine 1979)
is not nearly so clear in the original book. The
reconciliation of micro and macro, liberty and determinism, functional requisite and action, remains
ambiguously unstated. Without a closer articulation
of the ethnography and the analysis, Learning to
Labour remains open to the charge of having "spot-
welded" a Marxist analysis together with its descriptive material (Atkinson 1979). The central methodological issue thus consists of articulating exactly
how such ethnographic work links with wider theory

in general and neo-Marxist theory in particular (see Butters 1976).

As it stands, Learning to Labour's loose ends and gaps are as irritating and frequently difficult as they are tantalising and stimulating. Just how do the descriptions relate to the major analytic categories of "penetrations" and "limitations", "confirmations" and "dislocations"? From where do such concepts derive, a priori deductive structural-ist theorising about production and reproduction of ideology (Althusser 1971) or a posteriori inductive grounded theory (à la Glaser and Strauss 1967). In a structuralist manner, Willis seems to view the ethno-graphic description as simply an illustration of more real underlying processes. (2) An ethnographic des-cription could neither prove nor refute such theory within the structuralist problematic dominant at the Birmingham Centre at the time (CCCS 1978) (3). A crucial failure of Althusserian epistemology is its over-reliance on a coherence theory of knowledge, without satisfactory acknowledgment of the issue of demonstrating correspondence (see, e.g. Thompson 1978); Learning to Labour is equally silent on correspondence. Yet elsewhere Willis advocates ethnography for its capacity to surprise and presumably refute (Willis 1976/1980), but even here he is far from the attemp-ted tabula rasa of grounded theory (Glaser and Strauss 1967), which he criticises as incipient empiricist positivism. (4) A decided ambivalence lies at the heart of the analysis of Learning to Labour, hidden only by the brilliance of the ethnography and the cogency of the theorising.

By displaying the process of analysis more explicitly, the conceptualisation could be more open to evaluation and possible revision. I believe that Willis' major difficulty in articulating the two halves of Learning to Labour is located in the need-lessly Althusserian version of social structure and theorising (CCCS 1978), compounded with the needlessly epiphenomenal view of ethnography, with both of which he was implicitly wrestling at the time. (5)

ONTOLOGY AND EPISTEMOLOGY IN SYMBOLIC INTERACTIONIST PARTICIPANT OBSERVATION

The most crucial of these charges against neo-Marxist ethnography is the second one, concerning the very possibility of its being done, and I will spend most of the rest of this paper arguing that there is at least one ethnographic epistemological resolution which not only allows an analysis of structures to be combined with describing phenomenal events, but, from a critical viewpoint, actually demands it: Chicago School symbolic interactionism. Although cited in various reviews as influencing British educational ethnography (e.g. Delamont and Atkinson 1980, Hammersley and Woods 1977:3), it has almost always been accompanied by phenomenology and ethnomethodology (e.g. Atkinson 1977:10, Fletcher 1975, Woods 1977:23). (6) Given the relative lack of British direct familiarity with symbolic interactionism, and the strong British interest in the latter two perspectives, I believe it fair to state that British ethnography has traditionally relied upon and been seen as phenomenology and ethnomethodology when challenged (e.g. Sharp and Green 1975). (7)

As a result, ethnographic techniques were initially adopted without recognition of their cognate epistemological and ontological bases. Rather like Sergio Leone's "spaghetti westerns" starring Clint Eastwood, wherein the essential story-line and characters of the indigenous American western are adapted into a grandiose and exaggerated operatic style, this "fish and chips" ethnography underwent a similar transformation in its recent re-adoption in the UK whereby the techniques have been stylised (e.g. into just hanging on the corner or just observing in classrooms), emphasising phenomena and subjectivism to the point where structure and situation have been dissolved, precluded, or obviated (Hammersley 1980a:66); use of quantitative data has been regarded as illegitimate and contaminating; any alliance with macrostructural research has been seen as impossible. When recently challenged regarding validity, etc. (e.g. Reynolds 1981, Evans 1983), some British school ethnographers seem to have quite abandoned any pretence of holding a symbolic interactionist stance distinct in its ontology and epistemology (cf Rock 1979), and instead have surprisingly (given Woods 1977) but revealingly taken rather neo-positivist positions regarding the fact-value split, independence of data from theory, testing, etc. (see Hammersley, 1980, 1983, Hargreaves 1982, 1983). I believe it is such an ambiguous and bastardised view of participant observation which would preclude any integration with Marxism.

In this section, then, I want to outline the theoretical and epistemological roots of classic Chicago School participant observation, drawing on the work of Simmel (1971), Park and Burgess (1921), Hughes (1971), and Becker (1970). In this tradition, I will argue, the notion of form is as central as

that of content, structure as that of phenomenon. (8)
Since it is British ethnography's lack of attending
to the analysis of form which causes the difficulties
under discussion in this paper (9), I want to emphasise that Chicago School symbolic interactionism was
as reliant on Simmel (through Park's studying under
him) as on Mead, Dewey and the pragmatists. Simmel
translations appeared from the beginning (1895) in
the American Journal of Sociology, and he claimed
more entries than any other author in the Park and
Burgess key text (1921), on which a whole generation
of American sociologists were raised.

Simmel's central concerns arose within the
debates of late nineteenth century German social
science dominated by issues originating in Kant,
Hegel and Marx. (10) Most sociologists are familiar
with symbolic interactionism's connection with
American pragmatism (Kaplan 1963, Greer 1969); perhaps the Hegelian philosophical roots of this are
less clearly seen. "By discarding the idea of an
antecedent reality which may be somehow known, Dewey
and Mead gave birth to a theory of knowledge which
anchored the truth in praxis alone" (Rock 1979b:69-
70). With such an instrumentalist theory of knowledge, truth claims are judged by their effectiveness
in realising practical ends, including the obtaining
of scientific results. A Darwinian notion of evolving progress is discernible.

Consistent with this, philosophical pragmatism
was augmented (and I will argue later, perhaps tainted)
by American liberalism and social reformism. Burgess
and Park (the former newsreporter) managed to get
sociology rolling as a going research concern by
seeing their city as a social laboratory throwing up
social problems for analysis. From its inception,
the University of Chicago was deeply enmeshed in its
local society; social gospelism, settlement house
work, policy consultation, etc. are clearly inter-
twined with research in the early decades of its
sociology department. (11)

Simmel's Germanic theoretical problematic is
also central to Chicago School symbolic interactionism.
If one accepts the historicist argument that culture
must be analysed in such a way as to take into account
the (often biased and ignorant) beliefs and evaluations of its human originators and carriers, how can
one do valid scientific analysis of it (see Bergner
1981)? Borrowing directly from Kant's (1929) epistemological resolution of the difficulties for
natural science knowledge posed by Hume (1962),
Simmel asked "how is society possible?" (1963). He

answered that, as with natural science knowledge, we
can only know phenomena (including other persons),
through use of categories. As such knowing is essential for social interaction, we can only create and
maintain society through formal categorisation; such
categorisation always incompletely captures the
inchoate stuff of social life, just as the noumenal
world can never be directly presented in our phenomenal experience of it; and finally he suggested that
society is unlike the natural world in that it is
both external to us, confronting actor and analyst
with its obdurateness, yet also internal, existing
only through our activities as actors and knowers.
Ontologically, sociation was possible via forms,
although social life is always more than the forms.
Acting subjects inherit, internalise and re-enact
such forms; for Simmel, unlike Kant, they may also
abandon them and create new ones (Levine 1971:XV).
     This is not an ontology which would easily
allow behaviourist or positivist methods; it is
dialectical, and so is interactionism's epistemology.
"Valid knowledge is held to reside neither in the
subject nor in the object, but in the transactions
that unfold between them" (Rock 1979a:61). Since
society is only possible by the 'shaping' of the
flux through forms, and these are not only enacted
but also carried conceptually by actors, social
researchers can understand the organisation of society
through themselves being actors and thus sharing social
concepts. Adequacy is indicated by successful accomplishment of interaction (Glaser and Strauss 1970).
Participating in language use, therefore, gives the
researcher as actor access to the knowledge of the
formal structure of the society: interactively, the
language shapes the action, and social action shapes
the language. In contrast to Kant's dualism in
natural science knowledge, in Simmel's social science
the subject-object split is dissolved into a unity,
at least regarding forms (if not content). (12) The
very 'subjectivity' of the construction of the social
world permits an intimacy of knowledge not achievable
in the natural sciences. (This is quite different
from Weber's notion of ideal types being fundamentally
ideal constructions by the observer/analyst only, and
not realised in the lived world: for Simmel, forms
were more or less actually realised.)
     The participant observation style for which
interactionism is famous flows directly from this
ontology and epistemology. The researcher's immersion in the field, negotiation of access, fashioning
roles, collecting data through multiple methods,

writing field notes, etc., all follow. In social research, one attempts to replicate more self-consciously the same processes of knowing which all humans basically pursue.

But besides rich or thick description which is the hallmark of ethnography, good Chicago school participant observation since the twenties has been explicitly concerned with the analysis of forms: their interrelations and preconditions. (13) The outline by Robinson (1952) of step by step procedures for analytic induction is proto-typical. Starting with a sensitising concept (Blumer 1969) or topic area, the researcher attempts a rough first definition of the phenomenal form to be explained, ideally drawing upon subjects' understanding of key issues or problems in their worlds. After collecting relevant data, the researcher then groups this information into categories, if necessary redefining terms, and specifying indicators. These categories are linked into propositions specifying the conditions under which the central forms of interest occur. As with all empirical claims, such propositions must be explicitly and logically non-tautologous, i.e., open to empirical refutation. The investigator then returns to the field, collecting more data by purposely theoretically seeking and sampling negating evidence to put his or her propositions to the toughest test, explicating richly and delimiting scope or generalisability (referred to as constant comparison by Glaser and Strauss 1967). This forces modification of the definitions of the forms or their conditions, or reformulations of the hypotheses to account for all cases encountered (see Table 1). The procedure is repeated in conscientiously seeking each new piece of data, until no further modification occurs nor seems likely ('saturation' is reached). At this point, the investigator may choose to write up a relatively delimited report on one or a few forms, or may research further in attempting to interrelate different forms. The write-up concludes a movement from substantive to formal theory (Glaser and Strauss 1967).

TABLE 1

	Phenomenon/ Form	No Phenomenon/ Form
Conditions specified	X cases	? or O cases
Non-conditions specified	O cases	X cases

- adapted from Robinson (1952)

Such sampling, while differing from the more familiar probability sampling of survey researchers, allows the logical possibility of checking alternative or rival explanations, and thus can address issues of both internal and external validity (Berk 1970). Indeed, one might suggest that immersion in the field leaves the participant observer most open to the unanticipated discovery of triangulating chance outcroppings of data (Webb et al 1966), whereas the rigidity of survey and experimental designs explicitly seek to allow maximum researcher control, while leaving subjects more free to dissimulate as they are removed from their everyday constraints (Becker 1970). Moreover, the participant observer is likely to be more conscious of sampling concepts, propositions, data collection methods, situations and sites in space and time, interactions, social relations and groups rather than just sampling the individual respondents which concern his survey colleagues.

I do not want to leave the impression that analytic induction is a procedure without problems. These range from technical ones (14) to more fundamental ones partly arising from the procedure's relative isolation from wider philosophy of science debates.(15) Yet to admit that there are live methodological issues within participant observation reinforces rather than detracts from my main point: that the central tradition of sociological ethnography has not been concerned simply with description of phenomenal social life, but rather has consistently involved analysis through some fairly widely accepted, rigorous, and demanding procedures. Furthermore, such epistemological procedures only make sense if accompanied by an ontology which includes the notion of form as the major organising component without which sociation would not be possible. Rather than being antithetical to the analysis of social structure, then, Chicago School participant observation has actually demanded it, albeit in its own way, with its own view of structure.

If Learning to Labour and other neo-Marxist attempts at ethnography had more self-consciously followed some of these traditional procedures, they would have precluded many of what I have called technical problems. More crucially, admission of precisely this formal aspect of traditional participant observation research seems to me to open up the possibility of engagement with at least some kinds of neo-Marxism, and hence the possibility of a defensible neo-Marxist ethnography. In order to draw out such similarities (and some differences), I will now turn to a brief analysis of Marx's method.

FORM IN MARX'S ANALYSIS (16)

The recent rediscovery and English translation of
Marx's early work (especially 1844/1964, 1846/1977,
1857-8/1973) has forced a re-interpretation of the
'late Marx' of Capital, including our understanding
of what he regarded as correct social scientific
method.   If one takes the position that fundamentally there was no epistemological break between the
early and late work, but rather an evolving consistency, neither the narrow economism and positivist
scientism of the Second International and Soviet
Marxism, nor the arid structuralism of Althusser and
Balibar (1970) are the only Marxisms possible. Other,
at least equally defensible and more attractively
persuasive Marxisms greatly lessen the divergence
from interactionism (see, e.g. Colletti 1972, Bologh
1980, Sayer 1979, 1975, Smith 1974, Smart 1976,
Geras 1972, Mepham 1979). (17)   I am arguing that
the extension of so-called humanist or neo-Marxism
combined with a renewed proper recognition of form
in interactionist analysis narrow the gap to allow
a reconciliation, at least in terms of central
methodological procedures.   Minimally, such an
integration is not logically precluded, and its
potential advantages should at least be considered.
For Marx was clearly engaged in an attempt to analyse
both formal and phenomenal aspects of social reality.
Indeed, the central argument of Capital is now seen
as turning on his analysis of the form of commodity
production under capitalism, relying upon a basic
logic which I believe is very similar to analytic
induction: the exploration and identification of
the basic conditions for the realisation of a particular form.
        Let me immediately make clear that I am not
claiming that there are no differences between mainstream Marxism and symbolic interactionism as traditionally practised.   But elements of voluntarism or
at least a notion of soft determination (cf Matza
1964), historicity, concern with lived experience,
a dialectic between such lived experience and conceptualisation of it, and notions of praxis not
radically divergent from pragmatism - all these are
found in the early manuscripts, and suggest the
necessity of reconceptualising traditional Marxist
dogmas (e.g. re materialism; see West 1983, for a
lengthier discussion).
        As in interactionism, the social relations

necessary for sustaining human life are recognised
by Marx as gradually attaining the relatively fixed
patterns of social forms.

> The social structure and the state are
> continually evolving out of the life
> process of individuals ...

> (Marx 1867:72)

Indeed, scattered throughout <u>Capital</u> and other works,
Marx regularly uses the term "form" (e.g. Marx 1867:
81n).
   Furthermore, Marx defines social forms as the
sole proper subject matter of political economy
(Sayer 1979:chapter 5).   This is not to claim that
Marx self-consciously devoted extended, thematic
consideration to the nature of forms per se, as
Simmel did;   rather, I simply want to claim both
shared this notion of the fundamental nature of social
ontology;   both saw forms giving an obdurate structure
of patterned repetitions to the flux of human life
processes.   Marx saw with Simmel that such crystalli-
sation, sedimentation, or formalisation also allowed
the possibility of a social science.   The attainment
of the money-form for exchange, for instance, allows
human relations to be congealed into a thing measur-
able at the interval level.
   It is directly on the topics of conceptualisation and explanation that Marx's early writings have
wrought a changed understanding of his project which
most directly allows the methodological congruence
for which I am arguing. (17)   From the early manuscripts onwards, there is a clear sense of the form
of social organisation being replicated in the categories by which society is understood, much as in
symbolic interactionist accounts.

> The production of ideas, of conceptions,
> of consciousness, is at first directly
> interwoven with the material activity
> and the material intercourse of men, the
> language of real life ...

> Language is as old as consciousness,
> language is practical consciousness
> that exists also for other men, and
> for that reason alone it really exists
> for me personally as well. ... The
> ruling ideas are nothing more than the
> ideal expression of the dominant

> material relationships grasped as
> ideas; hence of the relationships
> which make the one class the ruling
> one, therefore, the ideas of its
> dominance.
>
>> (Marx and Engels 1846/1977
>> 47; 51; 64)

This statement from the German Ideology can be
regarded not only as referring to dominant ideas as
mystifying, but also as enlightening - precisely in
that they reference the dominant material relationships.
From the 1850s onwards, in his search to comprehend society, Marx turned to the study of political economy, not in a positivist or economistic sense
of taking it at its face value, but because he now
believed that this most advanced bourgeois social
science extracted and refined from lay thought and
practice concepts that indeed identified key relations
in capitalist society.

> The categories of bourgeois economy
> consist of such like forms. They are
> forms of thought expressing with social
> validity the conditions and relations
> of a definite, historically determined
> mode of production, viz., the production
> of commodities.
>
>> (Marx 1867:76)

> (Categories) arise ... from the
> relations of production themselves.
> They are categories for the phenom-
> enal forms of essential relations.
>
>> (Marx 1867:537)

There admittedly is no direct parallel identification
of central social forms or essential concepts in
Simmel or interactionism but otherwise the view of
the relation of concepts to lived social reality is
almost exactly the same.
Precisely because of their connectedness to
particular social relations, particular categories
generally are not appropriate across epochs and
cultures, as positivists might claim (see also
Sayer 1975:785).

> Even the most abstract categories,
> despite their validity - precisely
> because of their abstractness - for
> all epochs, are nevertheless, in the
> specific character of this abstrac-
> tion, themselves likewise a product
> of historic relations, and possess
> their full validity only for and
> within these relations.

(Marx 1858/1973:105)

In this sensitivity to cultural and temporal bounded-
ness, Marx again anticipates interactionism, although
he is much less hesitant to propose theoretical over-
views and transhistorical categories, as Rock points
out (1979b).

For Marx as for Simmel, forms and formal concepts inevitably are selective; they both reveal and
hide aspects of the social world. But whereas for
Simmel, following from Kant, it is the non-formalised
content of human activity which could not be known,
Marx develops a particular notion of ignorance:
formal ignorance or ideology. Where Simmel and
interactionism revel in alternative conceptions, world-
views, etc. for their diversity, and encourage comparative sampling for clarification (Glaser and Strauss
1967), Marx goes beyond this to recognise that some
viewpoints (e.g. political economy) become definitive,
attain dominance and override others in a mystifying
way which precludes the perception of alternatives
or of their own foundations:

> The ideas of the ruling class are in
> every epoch the ruling ideas, i.e.,
> the class which is the ruling material
> force of society, is at the same time
> its ruling intellectual force.

(Marx and Engels 1846/1977:64)

This notion of contradictory formal knowledge-and-
ignorance also clearly goes far beyond the traditional
view of false-consciousness and ideology:

> First, if as Marx contends, phenomena
> can be deceptive and phenomenal cate-
> gories in some sense inadequate, the
> inadequacy is not simply one of subject-
> ive perception. It isn't a matter of
> people seeing the world 'wrong'; on
> the contrary, if conceptions correspond

> to experiences, then the 'inadequacies'
> must lie at the level of experience
> itself.   Illusoriness then becomes a
> matter of the forms in which the world
> 'presents itself' to experience, and not
> a matter of inadequate perception of
> these forms.   Secondly, and conversely,
> it is evident that phenomenal categories
> cannot be totally inadequate; they must
> allow people to make sense of their
> experience ...

> (Sayer 1975:783-4)

Following Marx, then, we must seek some way to
be able to interrogate dominant or taken-for-granted
categories, including lay concepts, but especially
including received social scientific and governmental-
administrative ones.   Marx does not merely _do_
political economy, he _critiques_ it, thereby developing a critique of the social order it, as a science,
comprehends.

> Political economy begins with the fact
> of private property; it does not ex-
> plain it. It conceives the _material_
> process of private property, _as this_
> occurs in reality, in general and
> abstract formulas which then serve
> it as laws.   It does not _comprehend_
> these laws; that is, it does not
> show how they arise out of the nature
> of private property ...
> Classical Political Economy borrowed
> from everyday life the category 'price
> of labour' without further criticism,
> and then simply asked the question,
> how is this price determined?

> (Marx 1867/1967:537)

For Marx, then, use of both social scientific
and lay concepts should not just organise data into
refutable propositions; they must be thought through
as a central part of any analysis, for the data are
not self-evident.   It is precisely in the recently
re-examined fragmentary passages (e.g. the 'early'
1857 Introduction to _Grundrisse_, and also the 'late'
Marx 1880:198) that Marx most explicitly and extensively discusses his methodology as centring on
conceptual analysis, whereby the central task is to

271

unearth the preconditions for such categories as
'commodity' to be viable within a society (see also
Sayer 1975:783-4, Hall 1973:6). (18)   In all science,
one must "uncover the reality behind the appearance
which conceals it" (Geras 1972:285). Furthermore,
as Sayer argues:

> ... This much, at least should by now
> be clear. Marx's historical categories,
> the ones in which he grasps 'real his-
> torical stages of production', are genera-
> ted neither from 'simple abstraction' in
> general nor from transhistorical categories
> in particular. They are emphatically
> a posteriori constructs, arrived at pre-
> cisely by abstraction from the 'real and
> concrete'. Marx has no mysteriously
> privileged starting-point. Like the
> rest of mankind, he starts from phenomenal
> forms of our 'what is given'. What
> differs, perhaps, is what he does with
> these forms. For ... he holds them to
> be far from transparent and demands that
> they be accounted for. If, then, Marx's
> science is founded upon any 'coupure',
> it must reside in the method of this
> accounting, of which his new conceptual
> lexicon is but the end-product.

(Sayer 1979:102-3)

This argument has particular relevance for
ethnography. For where traditional Marxists have
relied on a misconstrued notion of materialism to
utilise mainly official statistics of economic
production for whole societies as their data base
for theorising, ethnography has not been seen as a
relevant mode of data collection. But The German
Ideology provides what can be interpreted as a clear
justification of the utility of fieldwork (see Smith
1974, 1981) rather than rationalist or structuralist
deductive speculation:

> The premises from which we begin are not
> arbitrary ones, not dogmas but real
> premises from which abstraction can only
> be made in the imagination. They are
> the real individuals, their activity and
> the material conditions under which they
> live, both those which they find already
> existing and those produced by their

activity. These premises can thus
be verified in a purely empirical way ...
The fact is, therefore, that definite
individuals who are productively active
in a definite way enter into these
definite social and political relations.
Empirical observation must in each
separate instance bring out empirically,
and without any mystification and speculation, the connection of the social and
political structure with production.

(1846/1977:42, 46-7)

The strong emphasis on the need for comprehension of
concrete mundane activities, including both their
behavioural and mental aspects, and a distrust of
received theory is echoed in interactionism (e.g.
Glaser and Strauss 1967). Subjects' consciousness
as a basis for scientific concepts occupies a much
more important place within neo-Marxist analysis in
order to reveal the inadequacy of the received,
ideologically dominant theories.

SOME IMPLICATIONS FOR EDUCATIONAL POLICY ANALYSIS

I have argued that British educational ethnography
has failed to recognise adequately the more formal
aspects of its heritage. I believe this is attributable to the dominance of anthropological and
phenomenological justification for British ethnography; a reaffirmation of ethnography's sociological roots in symbolic interactionism would not only
make ethnography more defensible, but would also
offer a better basis for cross-fertilisation with
neo-Marxism. As I hope to have shown, Chicago
School fieldwork is as concerned with form as it is
with phenomenon. The central methodological procedure of analytic induction has been examined to
illustrate this. I submit that neo-Marxist and
interactionist formulations of conceptual analysis
have much in common (Robinson 1952, Sayer 1979,
especially pp. 114ff). There is the same search for
necessary relationships, and the same allowance for
history, will, and political action to provide the
real sufficient conditions. There is the same
relative disinterest in particular contents, the
same search for underlying structure. Furthermore,
both neo-Marxism and interactionism rely upon a
claimed isomorphism of subjects' categories (or
ideology) and social behaviour and social form. In

273

a very real sense, the 'micro-macro' split is dissolved.
    I have been arguing that although mainline
symbolic interactionism and Marxism have traditionally
been regarded as incompatible, the advent of neo-
Marxism allows at least a conciliatory dialogue on
many issues of contention. Throughout the discussion
above, however, I have tried to note where some of
the major epistemological differences might remain.
Even within neo-Marxism there are concerns most interactionists would find unacceptable or at least beyond
adequate warrant: the continuing notions of analysing
beyond phenomenal forms and critiquing false-conscious
ness (Nicholaus 1973:30-1, Marx 1858:255); being
value committed; and especially postulating a totality (Geras 1972:305) with central determinants
(Nicholaus 1973:80). But these differences would
seem to be more ones of style and elaboration than
logical incompatibilities: interactionists also
analyse beyond subjects' understanding; pragmatism
has always recognised value commitment; and the very
choice of research topic itself implies sampling from
a wider universe and a claim to the importance and
relevance of particular research. I believe such
extensions can be made without compromising interactionist fundamentals (cf Rock 1979b).
    Furthermore, such an integration of inter-
actionism and neo-Marxism not only provides a more
clearly articulated epistemology for research that
is both ethnographic and structural, phenomenal and
formal, but also allows clearer substantive analysis
of our present educational crises, and the advocacy
of social policy. I have mentioned interactionism's
pragmatist roots, wherein science is seen as arising
in experienced problems. The populist policy rela--
tedness of the early Chicago School seems to have
been gradually abandoned, perhaps as its naively
ameliorist liberal notion of piecemeal accumulative
social change was frustrated and professional
pressures to appear scientific and detached increased. The interactionists' underplaying of power,
and lack of self-consciousness as social science has
been incorporated into advising the powerful is connected with their traditional refusal to designate
central or determining dominant social forms. Demanding such explicitness is essential in any policy
analysis, which assumes that problems are systemic;
only with such explicitness can ethnography become
policy relevant.
    Reasserting that one test of the truth of an
analysis is its utility in effecting social change

also has political relevance.   It would force ethnographers to extend their considerations of praxis
beyond the narrow notion of "field tests of hypotheses"
(Glaser and Strauss 1970), and force clarification of
the political context of all research.   In any case,
almost all social research, and certainly that so
lavishly funded by state agencies, has always been
concerned with the utility of theories; it has only
been when such state agencies or bureaucratic elites
haven't controlled the value commitments and feedback
of research to practice that they accuse researchers
such as ethnographers of contamination of the object
of study or being biased (Becker 1970).
     Social crises and policy issues become known in
lived experience through actors' categories and concepts.   A methodology attuned to analysing social
crises must take those conceptualisations seriously,
in a return to traditional pragmatism.   Studying such
issues from the viewpoint of ordinary pupils, parents
and teachers would provide alternative formulations
to those provided by state bureaucrats (e.g. Smith
1983).
     In such a sociology of educational politics (as
opposed to simply policies), there are exciting iso-
morphisms with recent theoretical analyses of the
state form (e.g. Holloway and Picciotto 1978, Sarup
1982).   Most directly, such theoretical developments
suggest the need to study the powerful as well as the
traditionally oppressed subjects of ethnographic
research.   Questions are raised in a new way as to
"whose side are we on" (Becker 1970).   Theoretically
embedding our ethnographies and a more explicit concern with such technicalities as sampling would identify the potential for political action of the class
fractions being researched.   As Willis has recently
admitted, it is quite possible the "ear 'oles" may be
ultimately more seriously radical than the lads (1982:
52); romanticisation of working class delinquents has
perhaps all too often blinded ethnographers to considering linkages with more organised oppositional
groups, such as teachers, parents, and progressive
political tendencies.   A more serious examination of
such politics of ethnographic research must be done
if it is to contribute substantively to progressively
resolving our present educational crises.

ACKNOWLEDGMENTS

My sincere thanks to Vivian Crossman and Millie Landry
for typing assistance.   Numerous people have contri-
buted, although probably all of the following would

disagree with some of my formulations: Howard S.
Becker, Northwestern; Eldon Bennett, York
(Toronto); George Smith, Dorothy Smith, Diane
Gerin-Lajoie, and the Critical Pedagogy and Cultural
Studies Workgroup at OISE and especially John Clarke,
Jeff Evans, Jock Young, Nigel South and Mike McKenna
at Middlesex; Sheila and Phil Scraton at Edgehill;
Philip Stone at South Bank; Roger Dale and John Fitz
at the Open University; Sara Delamont and Paul
Atkinson at Cardiff; Paul Willis at Birmingham CCCS;
Paul Rock and David Downes at LSE; Frank Pearce at
Toronto; and Phil Corrigan at London Institute of
Education. A special thanks to Wally Seccombe at
OISE, students in all the field research classes at
the above named institutions, and to Middlesex Poly-
technic, the London School of Economics, and the Open
University for the stimulating study leave which
started this paper in 1979.

FOOTNOTES

(1) Cf Interactionists on the construction of
the self (e.g. Rock 1979, chapter 4)!
(2) "The essential meaning of the analysis in
Part II was precisely that cultural forms cannot be
understood with respect to themselves and upon their
own base. In order to understand the counter-school
culture we had to go to alternative starting points
and construct the culture partly from outside: from
the nature of labouring in modern capitalism, from
general abstract labour; from sexism, from ideology"
(Willis: 1977:186, also 119-121)
(3) He clearly had a different notion of
analysis than that involved in analytic induction,
which he maintains even later:

> More theoretical methods tend to 'abstract out'
> of many situations the common strands of the
> theoretical focus - new ... forms, new language,
> new media, etc. ... Ethnography is inherently
> 'messier' than this and can give some grounds
> for investigating the 'theoretical' themes
> combined in a concrete case. (1982:5, 13)

(4) Probably thinking of Glaser and Strauss's
(1967) absurdly non-Kantian polemic, Willis accuses:

> The first principle of PO, the postponement
> of theory, compounds the dangers of ... covert
> positivism. It strengthens the notion that
> the object can present itself directly to

the observer.   (Willis 1976/1980:90)

(5)   Stuart Hall (1980) mentions first an
interest in verstehen, Berger and Luckmann's phenomenology, Schutz and ethnomethodology; afterwards,
he mentions interactionism being sensitive to lived
experience and using a qualitative methodology (p.23-
24).   This is continued in an "Introduction to Ethnography at the Centre" (Grimshaw, Hobson, Willis 1980:
74, 5-6).
No Chicago School ethnographer would care to
claim such a motley collection of parents!   Willis'
later definition of ethnography limits it to data
gathering and there is no mention of qualitative
research being connected with distinct analytic
procedures, such as analytic induction (1982:11).
Admittedly, there was clearly some knowledge
of and interest in Chicago school participant observation (see Roberts 1976 and Butters 1976).   Their
methodological concerns, however, are not very adequately followed up or addressed in accompanying
ethnographies (Hall and Jefferson 1976).
(6)   This conflation is most clear in the
middle seventies.   After stating "the theoretical
position adopted in this block is, broadly speaking,
an interactionist one" (1977:3), Hammersley and
Woods go on to describe not only symbolic interactionism, but also dramaturgy and ethnomethodology as
theoretical background to ethnography (see also
Hammersley and Woods 1976).   In a context citing
Weber and followed by a reading from Schutz, Woods
states:

> Most of these theoretical developments
> lie within the framework loosely known
> as 'symbolic interactionism', which
> embraces various diverse schools of
> thought ... and I shall therefore look
> at the prominent features of three of
> the most important of them: (a) symbolic
> interactionism, (b) dramaturgy, (c) ethno-
> methodology.   (Woods 1977:23)

Atkinson similarly allies them (1977:10).
The more recent methodological writings by these
interactionist ethnographers (especially Hammersley
1979a, 1979b) are clearer on the Chicago school
(formal) aspects of ethnography, but, as with the
neo-Marxists' failure to take Butters (1976) seriously
in their substantive work, so too with the British
interactionists, to this point at least.
(7)   I believe Rock acutely points to the

difficulty being interactionism's unusual oral tradition; without such personal tutorship, it has not been fully understood in Britain. (Rock 1979b, chapter 1). Hammersley, in reviewing the mid-70s literature in British classroom ethnography, admits as much:

> ... while the general direction that research should take was clear, more specific guidance was not available. Researchers were forced to find their own way in the field, making what use they could of the theoretical and methodological resources at their disposal. (Hammersley 1980a:48)

(8) In stressing the interactionist tradition's concern with form, I hasten to state that of course participant observation has also been concerned with description of surface phenomena, the voluntaristic development of self, and "telling the news" (Hughes 1971).

(9) In a recent text (1981), Menzies goes so far as to maintain that interactionism denies itself when it attempts to deal with form or structure, arguing it must stick to thick description only.

(10) There are obviously great differences in epistemology among these, which I do not have space to explicate here; the interested reader can refer to: Levine 1971, Sayer 1979, Ruben 1979, Colletti 1972, Bergner 1981. As will become apparent, I side with Levine and take issue with Bergner who, while correct in identifying Simmel as neo-Kantian, is quite mistaken in failing to understand how Simmel differed from Weber; I also clearly am opting for Sayer's and Colletti's "Kantian" interpretation of Marx, and am opposed to Ruben's interpretation.

(11) See Faris (1970) for listings of how the early theses and dissertations at Chicago were frequently concerned with religious or social problem questions.

(12) The similarity to Lukacs (1971) is not coincidental: the two were in contemporary contact (cf Bergner 1981).

(13) The central procedures have gone under various names as outlined by Robinson (1953), Becker (1970), Blumer (1969), Glaser and Strauss (1969), or Schatzman and Strauss (1973). For examples of use, see Becker et al (1960, Becker et al (1968), Cressey (1953), Becker (1963), West (1979, 1979/1980, 1980b).

(14) For elaborations, see Robinson (1952), Denzin (1970), Glaser and Strauss (1967), Matza (1964,

1969), Turner (1953), and West (1983).

(15) Consider, for instance, the implications of the Kuhn-Popper debate in Lakatos and Musgrave (1970).

(16) The following analysis owes much to Sayer (1975, 1979), Smith (1974, 1983), Geras (1972), and Hall (1973).

(17) I realise there are a host of issues in this claim, and the authors cited are not entirely in agreement, but space does not permit an explication here. The general direction, however, should be clear enough.

(18) For further elaboration, see especially the authors in footnote (16), and McQuarrie (1978), Nicolaus (1973:36), Carver (1975).

REFERENCES

Althusser, L. (1971) 'Ideology and Ideological State Apparatuses', in Lenin and Philosophy and Other Essays, New Left Books, London

Althusser, L. and Balibar, E. (1970) Reading Capital, New Left Books, London

Arnot, M. and Whitty, G. (1982) 'From Reproduction to Transformation', British Journal of Sociology of Education, 3, pp. 93-103

Atkinson, P. (1977) 'Research Design in Interpetive Research', Research Design, Open University, Milton Keynes

Atkinson, P. (1979) Personal Communication.

Becker, H.S. (1970) Sociological Work:Method and Substance, Aldine, Chicago

Becker, H.S. et al (1960) Boys in White, University of Chicago, Chicago

Becker, H.S. (1963) Outsiders, Free Press, Glencoe, Ill.

Becker, H.S. et al (1968) Making the Grade, Wiley, New York

Bergner, J. (1981) The Origin of Formalism in Social Science, University of Chicago, Chicago

Berk, R. (1974) 'Re: Qualitative Methodology', Northwestern Sociology, Evanston, Ill., USA (xerox)

Blumer, H. (1969) Symbolic Interactionism, Prentice-Hall, Englewood Cliffs, N.J.

Bogdan, R. and Taylor, S. (1975) Introduction to Qualitative Research Methods, Wiley, New York

Bologh, R. (1980) Dialectical Phenomenology: Marx's Method, Routledge, London

Butters, S. (1976) 'The Logic of Enquiry of Participant Observation' in S. Hall and T. Jefferson

(Eds.), Resistance Through Ritual, Hutchinson, London

Carver, T. (Ed.) (1975) Karl Marx: Texts on Method, Basil Blackwell, Oxford

Centre for Contemporary Cultural Studies (1978) On Ideology, Hutchinson, London

Centre for Contemporary Cultural Studies, Education Group (1981) Unpopular Education, Hutchinson, London

Clarke, J. (1979) 'Capital and Culture' in J. Clarke et al, Working Class Culture, Hutchinson, London

Cohen, S. (1980) Folk Devils and Moral Panics, Martin Robertson (Second Edition), London

Colletti, L. (1972) From Rousseau to Lenin, New Left Books, London

Corrigan, P. (1979) Schooling the Smash Street Kids, Macmillan, London

Cressey, D. (1953) Other People's Money, Free Press, Glencoe, Ill.

Delamont, S. and Atkinson, P. (1980) 'The Two Traditions in Educational Ethnography', British Journal of Sociology of Education, 1, 2, pp. 139-52

Delamont, S. (1978) 'Sociology and the Classroom' in L. Barton and R. Meighan, Sociological Interpretations of School and Classrooms, Nafferton, Driffield

Delamont, S. (1981) 'All Too Familiar? A Decade of Classroom Research', Educational Analysis, 3, 1, pp. 69-84

Denzin, N. (1970) The Research Act, Aldine, Chicago

Evans, J. (1983) 'Criteria of Validity in Social Research' in M. Hammersley (Ed.) The Ethnography of Schooling, Nafferton, Driffield

Faris, R.E.L. (1970) Chicago Sociology 1920-1932, University of Chicago, Chicago

Filstead, W. (1970) Qualitative Methodology, Markham, Chicago

Fine, B. (1979) 'The Theory and Politics of Michel Foucault', Capital and Class, 9

Fletcher, C. (1975) Beneath the Surface, Routledge, London

Geras, N. (1972) 'Marx and the Critique of Political Economy', in R. Blackburn (Ed.) Ideology in Social Science, Fontana, London

Glaser, B. and Strauss, A. (1967) The Discovery of Grounded Theory, Aldine, Chicago

Glaser, B. and Strauss, A. (1971) 'Discovery of Substantive Theory', in W. Filstead, Qualitative Methodology, Markham, Chicago

Goffman, E. (1967) 'Where the Action Is' in his
    Interaction Ritual, Doubleday Anchor, Garden
    City and New York
Gramsci, A. (1971) Selections from the Prison Note-
    books, Q. Hoare and G.N. Smith (Eds.), Laurence
    and Wishart, London 1967
Grimshaw, R, Hobson, D. and Willis, P. (1980) 'Intro-
    duction to Ethnography at the Centre' in S. Hall
    et al, Culture, Media, Language, Hutchinson,
    London
Greer, S. (1969) The Logic of Social Inquiry, Aldine,
    Chicago
Hall, S. (1980) 'Cultural Studies and the Centre', in
    S. Hall et al, (Eds.), Culture, Media, Language,
    Hutchinson, London
Hall, S. (1973) 'A Reading of Marx's 1857 Introduction
    to the Grundrisse', Centre for Contemporary
    Cultural Studies, University of Birmingham,
    (stencilled paper)
Hall, S. and Jefferson, T. (1976) Resistance Through
    Rituals, Hutchinson, London
Hammersley, M. (1983) 'The Paradigmatic Mentality',
    (this volume)
Hammersley, M. and Woods, P. (1977) 'Introduction'
    in P. Woods, The Ethnography of the School,
    Units 7-8, Course E202, The Open University,
    Milton Keynes
Hammersley, M. (1979a) 'Data Collection in Ethno-
    graphic Research', Part 3, Block 4, Data
    Collection Procedures, DE304 Research Methods,
    The Open University, Milton Keynes
Hammersley, M. (1979b) 'Analysing Ethnographic Data',
    Part 1, Block 6, Making Sense of Data, DE304,
    Research Methods, The Open University, Milton
    Keynes
Hammersley, M. (1980a) 'Classroom Ethnography',
    Educational Analysis, 2, 2, pp. 47-74
Hammersley, M. (1980b) 'On Interactionist Empiricism'
    in P. Woods (Ed.), Pupil Strategies, Croom
    Helm, London
Hargreaves, A. (1982) 'Resistance and Relative
    Autonomy Theories', British Journal of Sociol-
    ogy of Education, 3, 2, pp. 107-126
Hargreaves, A. (1983) 'The Myths of Multicausality'
    Conference Paper, Westhill College, January 1983
Hargreaves, A. (1980) 'Synthesis and the Study of
    Strategies', in P. Woods (Ed.) Pupil Strate-
    gies, Croom Helm, London
Hargreaves, D. (1967) Social Relations in a Second-
    ary School, Routledge, London

Heap, J. (1977) 'The Problem of Order in the Problematic of Social Science', Xerox, OISE

Hebdige, D. (1979) Subculture: The Meaning of Style, Methuen, London

Holloway, J. and Picciotto, S. (1978) 'Introduction' to their edited State and Capital, Edward Arnold, London

Hughes, E.C. (1971) The Sociological Eye, Aldine, Chicago

Hume, D. (1962) Hume on Human Nature and Understanding, (A. Flew, Ed.), Collier, New York

Kant, I. (1929) The Critique of Pure Reason, Macmillan, London

Kaplan, A. (1963) The Logic of Inquiry, Chandler, Chicago

Kuhn, T. (1964) The Structure of Scientific Revolutions, University of Chicago, Chicago

Lakatos, I. and Musgrave, A. (1970) Criticism and the Growth of Knowledge, Cambridge University Press, Cambridge

Lawn, M. and Barton, L. (1981) 'Recording the Natural World', Interchange, 11, 4, pp. 13-25

Levine, D. (1971) 'Introduction' in his edited Georg Simmel on Individuality and Social Forms, University of Chicago, Chicago

Lukacs, G. (1971) History and Class Consciousness, Merlin, London

Marx, K. (1844/1964) The Economic and Philosophical Manuscripts of 1844, McGraw Hill, New York City

Marx, K. and Engels, F. (1846/1977) The German Ideology, International, New York

Marx, K. (1858/1973) The Grundrisse, Penguin, Harmondsworth

Marx, K. (1867/1967) Capital I, Progress/International New York

Marx, K. (1859/1970) A Contribution to the Critique of Political Economy, Progress /International, New York City

Marx, K. (1880) 'Notes on Adolph Wagner' in T. Carver (Ed.) 1975, Karl Marx: Texts on Method, Basil Blackwell, Oxford

Matza, D. (1964) Delinquency and Drift, Wiley, New York City

Matza, D. (1969) Becoming Deviant, Prentice-Hall, Englewood Cliffs, New Jersey

McCall, G. and Simmons, J. (1969) Issues in Participant Observation, Addison-Wesley, Reading, Mass.

McQuarrie, D.V. (1978) 'Marx and the Method of Successive Approximations', Sociological Quarterly, 19, 2, pp. 218-33

McRobbie, A. (1980) 'Settling Accounts with Sub-
     cultures: A Feminist Critique', Screen
     Education, 34, pp. 37-49
Menzies, K. (1979) Personal Communication
Menzies, K. (1981) Sociological Theory in Use,
     Routledge, London
Mepham, J. (1979) 'From the Grundrisse to Capital:
     The Making of Marx's Method' in J. Mepham
     and D.H. Ruben (Eds.) Issues in Marxist
     Philosophy, Vol. 1, Harvester, London
Nicholaus, M. (1973) 'Forward' in his edited,
     K. Marx Grundrisse, Penguin, Harmondsworth
Park, R. and Burgess, E. (1921/1970) Introduction
     to the Science of Sociology, University of
     Chicago, Chicago
Popper, K. (1959) The Logic of Scientific Discovery,
     Basic, New York
Reynolds, D. (1981) 'The Naturalistic Method of
     Educational Research - A Marxist Critique',
     Interchange, 11, 4, pp. 77-89
Roberts, B. (1976) 'Naturalistic Research into
     Subcultures and Deviance' in S. Hall and
     T. Jefferson (Eds.) Resistance Through Ritual,
     Hutchinson, London
Roberts, B. and Cohen, P. (1978) Knuckle Sandwich,
     Penguin, Harmondsworth
Robinson (1952) 'The Logical Structure of Analytic
     Induction' in G. McCall and J. Simmons (Eds.)
     Issues in Participant Observation, Addison-
     Wesley, Reading, Mass.
Rock, P. (1979b) The Making of Symbolic Interaction-
     ism, MacMillan, London
Rock, P. (1979a) 'The Sociology of Crime' in D.
     Downes and P. Rock, Deviant Interpretations,
     Martin Robertson, London
Ruben, D.H. (1979) Marxism and Materialism,
     Harvestor, Brighton
Salamini, L. (1974) 'Gramsci and Marxist Sociology
     of Knowledge', Sociological Quarterly, 15,
     pp. 359-80
Sarup, M. (1982) Education, State and Crisis,
     Routledge, London
Sayer, D. (1975) 'Method and Dogma in Historical
     Materialism', Sociological Review, 23, 4,
     pp. 779-810
Sayer, D. (1979) Marx's Method: Ideology, Science,
     and Critique in Capital, Harvestor, London
Schatzman, L. and Strauss, A. (1973) Field Research,
     Prentice-Hall, Englewood Cliffs, New Jersey
Shaffir, W. et al (1980) Fieldwork Experience,
     St. Martin's, New York

Shaffir, W. and Green, T. (1975) Education and
    Social Control, Routledge, London
Simmel, G. (1971) Georg Simmel on Individuality and
    Social Forms, University of Chicago, Chicago
Simmel, G. (1963) 'How is Society Possible?' in
    M. Natanson (Ed.) Philosophy of the Social
    Sciences, Random House, New York
Smart, B. (1976) Sociology, Phenomenology and Marxian
    Analysis, Routledge, London
Smith, D.E. (1983) 'Institutional Ethnography:
    Feminist Method', OISE, xerox
Smith, D.E. (1981) 'On Sociological Description: A
    Method from Marx', Human Studies, 4, pp. 313-37
Smith, D.E. (1974) 'The Ideological Practice of
    Sociology', Catalyst 8
Smith, L.B. (1979) 'An Evolving Logic of Participant
    Observation' in L. Shellman (Ed.), Review of
    Research in Education, Peacock, Chicago
Spradley, J. (1980) Participant Observation, Holt
    Rinehart Winston, New York
Thompson, E.P. (1978) The Poverty of Theory, Merlin,
    London
Turner, R. (1953/1969) 'The Quest for Universals in
    Social Research' in G. MacCall and J. Simmons
    (Eds.) Issues in Participant Observation,
    Addison-Wesley, Boston
Webb, E. et al (1966) Unobtrusive Measures, McNally,
    Chicago
Weber, M. (1947) The Theory of Social and Economic
    Organisations, Free Press, Glencoe, Ill.
Werthman, C. (1976) 'Delinquents in Schools' in
    B. Cosin et al (Eds.) School and Society,
    Routledge, London
West, W.G. (1983 in press) 'The Possibility of
    Critical Field Research' in Psychology and
    Social Theory
West, W.G. (1981) 'Education, Moral Reproduction,
    and the State', Interchange, 12, 2-3
West, W.G. (1979/80) 'Trust Among Serious Thieves',
    Crime et/and Justice, 7/8, 1-2
West, W.G. (1980a) 'Access to Adolescent Deviants
    and Deviance' in W. Shaffir et al, Fieldwork
    Experience, St. Martin's, New York City
West, W.G. (1980b) 'The Short Term Careers of Serious
    Thieves' in R. Silverman and J. Teevan (Eds.)
    Crime in Canadian Society, Butterworths,
    Toronto
West, W.G. (1979) 'Adolescent Autonomy, Education and
    Pupil Deviance' in L. Barton and R. Meighan
    (Eds.) Schools, Pupils and Deviance, Nafferton,
    Driffield

West, W.G. (1977) 'Participant Observation in Canadian Classrooms', Canadian Journal of Education, 3, 2

West, W.G. (1975) 'Participant Observation Research on the Social Construction of Everyday Classroom Order', Interchange, 6, 4

Whitty, G. (1981) 'Ideology, Politics and Curriculum, Unit 8, Block 3, The Politics of Cultural Production, Course E353, The Open University, Milton Keynes

Williams, R. (1976) 'Base and Superstructure in Marxist Cultural Theory' in R. Dale et al (Eds.) Schooling and Capitalism, Routledge, London

Willis, P. (1977) Learning to Labour, Saxon House/ Teakfield/Gillis, Westmead, Farnborough, Hants. (1981 edition: Columbia, New York City)

Willis, P. (1978) Profane Culture, Routledge, London

Willis, P. (1976/80) 'Notes on Method/The Man in the Iron Cage', in S. Hall et al /Eds.), Culture, Language, Media, Hutchinson, London

Willis, P. (1982) 'Structures and Forms in Cultures of Resistance in the School', Unit 30 of Popular Culture, Course E203, The Open University, Milton Keynes (xerox

Wilson, S. (1977) 'The Use of Ethnographic Techniques in Educational Research', Review of Educational Research, 47

Woods, P. and Hammersley, M. (Eds.) (1977) School Experience, Croom Helm, London

Woods, P. (1977) The Ethnography of the School, The Open University, Milton Keynes

Woods, P. (1979) 'Review of P. Willis Learning to Labour', Research in Education, 19, pp. 87-90

RELATIVE AUTONOMY RECONSTRUCTED

David Reynolds

> The truth does not lie mid way between
> extremes but _in_ both of them. (Newman)

The early 1980s are seemingly a highly inopportune
time to argue that the educational system possesses
a 'relative autonomy' from the need to perpetuate
existing capitalist economic and social relations.
Attempts to 'tie' the educational system towards a
concentration on subjects necessary for industrial
production, towards a concentration on merely
'cognitive' outputs and towards a concentration on
the development of high ability children is widely
argued (Ahier and Flude, 1982) to have been a characteristic of educational policies under both Labour
and Conservative governments since 1976.   The notion
that schools could potentially be sites of 'transformative' practice - a hope clearly associated with
the theory that schools have the certain 'freedom'
as stated in the relative autonomy thesis - is also
apparently difficult to square with the increasing
de-radicalisation of the curriculum, the threat
posed to progressiveness in the pedagogical area
and the current threats posed to potentially radical
developments such as the 'new' sixth form.   All the
evidence available at present seems to support the
thesis that the educational system is being used to
reproduce, not change, the existing set of economic
and social relations.
    It seems that the belief that the system has
'relative autonomy' and that it therefore could be
potentially 'transformative' is only now being
argued and asserted mostly because of what can only
be called an 'aberration' - the popularity of neo-
Marxist correspondence theories over the last
decade.   Given the popularity of the thesis that
sees complementarity in the social relations of

schools and in the requirements of the economy, it
has simply taken a considerable time for any idealistic
notions that grant freedom to schools to have any
professional space in the discipline of sociology of
education.   Since - to use David Hargreaves' description - we have been both captivated by and captured
by neo-Marxism, the pervasiveness of what are
probably highly erroneous views about education/
society correspondence unfortunately coincided with
those years - the late 1960s and early 1970s - when
schools were probably corresponding _least_ with the
needs of the economy.

FROM THE CORRESPONDENCE THESIS TO THE RESISTANCE PARADIGM

To outline developments briefly, correspondence theory
drew from an Althusserian determinism in which capitalism reproduced itself through an R.S.A. (Repressive
State Apparatus), and an I.S.A. (Ideological State
Apparatus).   Teachers who tried to change the system
were doomed to be heroes, conventionally meeting
tragic ends.   Bowles and Gintis (1976) took the notion
of the educational system as _controlled_ from Althusser,
added Jencksian (1971) notions that related the qualifications pupils obtained from school to their social
class background, added the profoundly non-Jencksian
notion that it was the discriminatory power and huge
influence of the schooling system that had these
effects - (Bowles and Gintis were in effect the first
theorists that asserted that schools made a difference)
- and dressed up the whole theoretical edifice around
the notion of the complementarity of the structure
and organisation of schooling and the broader
requirements of the capitalist mode of industrial
production.
   The thesis has of course been bitterly contested.
It has been argued that evidence about within school
practices which are dysfunctional for capitalism has
been simply ignored (O'Keefe, 1981).   The thesis
concentrated on examining only the structure or
vessel of the school, rather than upon any curricular
content which may equally have hegemonic properties.
Many school systems also, it is suggested by historical analysis (Ramirez, 1981) ante date the arrival of
capitalism and societies can be found with both
high levels of literacy and so called capitalistic
organisational forms in feudal, pre capitalist or
even agrarian societies.   The specific links between
capitalism and schooling appeared unproven and unclear
to a large number of observers.   Furthermore, the

thesis was monocausal in its assertions as to the
determining nature of solely economic influences
upon the educational system and did not allow for
other influences such as religious factors, cultural
factors, gender relations or systemic factors themselves as determinants of educational form.   The
precise links between the economic base, the State
apparatus of which education formed a part and the
nature of the educational system were furthermore
left completely unspecified.

The thesis had undoubted popularity however.
As I have suggested elsewhere (Reynolds and Sullivan,
1980), it appeared to explain the failure of social
engineering to attain more than a minimal success in
affecting the outputs of the educational systems in
both Britain and America.   Its emphasis upon
'reproduction' related to the 'cultural reproduction'
hypotheses of the system/society relationship
propounded by both Bourdieu (1977) and Bernstein (1977)
although both the latter permitted substantial and in
some assessments total autonomy of the world of the
cultural from the material economic base.   The thesis
was furthermore in tune with the structurally determinist forms of neo-Marxist thinking which had such
an influence in political science, in sociology and
in other disciplines such as urban studies and media
studies.   Even though the thesis was based primarily
upon American evidence, it was taken to apply in its
virtual entirety (see for example the Schooling and
Capitalism reader) to the British educational system.
Whilst more sensitive socialist analysis still left
a place for human agency as a potential change agent
of the system (e.g. Young and Whitty (1977)), both
enthusiasts and critics (Musgrove, 1981) view the
correspondence thesis as being the dominant paradigm
of the last decade within British sociology of
education.

The original somewhat simplistic and crude
correspondence theories have in recent years however
been substantially modified.   The discovery in
Willis's (1977) work of resistance, contestation and
rebellion within schools has led to an appreciation
that there may exist within schools a 'culture of
opposition' amongst pupils who may not necessarily
be leaving school with the abilities, attitudes or
moral codes supportive of the wider capitalist
economy.   Some pupils - as suggested by Willis -
may reject mental labour and desire the manual as a
symbolic gesture of their working classness.   Even
though such rejection of school may in the short term
be functional for capitalism, since they are 'needed'

to perform manual tasks, the culture of their world has in its perceptions and 'penetration' of capitalism a clearly dysfunctional, potentially transformative role, the more so if it can be developed, sharpened and linked with the insights of intellectuals and others from outside the system.   Interest in the contested nature of reproduction and in the potentially transformative nature of pupil resistance is evident in the well known ethnographic work of Anyon (1979; 1980; 1981), in the more recent work of Apple (1980; 1981; 1982) and in the writings of Giroux (1980; 1982), who argues that "... what is crucial about these contradictions is that they highlight the relative autonomy characteristic of cultural institutions such as schools.   It is this relative autonomy that provides the space for institutions in the ideological realm to serve as more than agents of reproduction" (1980, p. 234).

The resistance paradigm has, though, been subject to considerable criticism, most notably in A. Hargreaves (1982).   Only some varieties of pupil behaviour are accorded resistance status.   The quantity of resistance by comparison with conformity is left uncharted and unstated.   Whether the resistance itself is school caused or reflects merely the influence of extra-school factors (Hargreaves, 1981) is also unclear.   Whether the pupils – especially women and blacks (Apple, 1980) – in whom faith is placed as agents of transformation are actually capable of such socialistic purpose also seems doubtful, particularly since they may lack a clear understanding of the nature of the world around them.   Since according to some American authorities, low stream rebels resemble more of a peasantry than anything else (Garbarino and Asp, 1982), the prospects for their 'conscientisation' must be seen as limited.

Perhaps one of the more remarkable things about relative autonomy/resistance theory is, though, that it appears to have become influential in the United States, where it seems less than valid but has not been received with enthusiasm in Britain, where its tenets seem to accord much more closely with the empirical reality of a continuing lack of fit between the British education system and the needs of the British economy.   American schools seem in most accounts pressed by their local communities to perform functions of skill development and talent nurturing, with a curriculum that seems to be generally supportive of capitalism.   American local State involvement – involving basic competency testing for example – has similar reproductive aims.   Whilst the articulation

between the American Federal Government, the States
and the schools themselves is clearly different from
Britain, the Federal Government's recent activities
in such areas as curriculum and pedagogy appear linked
to the same attempt to encourage schools to be supportive of the economy.   The increasing role of central
government throughout the 1960s and 1970s in generating
'liberal' pressure on subjects like pre-school education, racial integration, the elimination of sexist
practices and teacher education used policy means
whereby additional sums of money were 'tied' to these
specific policies and innovations - the tying of
money is now much more an attempt to inculcate real
knowledge about (and relevant to) the industrial world.
As one authority comments (Male, 1974, p. 21) "Now the
only choice left to many school boards is whether or
not to participate in programs designed by the federal
government or by wealthy private foundations.   The
lure of outside money makes the matter of participation a foregone conclusion ...".

Relative autonomy theory is popular then -
perhaps as a simple way of reviving rather dashed
liberal hopes - in a society which even many of the
theory's adherents believe to be exhibiting increasingly less of it, since "relative autonomy may be
breaking down today", (Apple, 1980, p. 16).   In
Britain, its adherents are few, with the exception of
some tentative and exploratory formulations by Whitty
(1982), myself (1979) and Dale (1982).

RELATIVE AUTONOMY THEORY NOW

To its critics, the thesis is "incoherent" in its
explanations, is clouded by a "theoretical fog" and
"has not classified the relationship between schooling
and society but only added to the confusion by asserting contradictory or unclear arguments ..." (all
quotations from Hargreaves, 1982, p. 119).   It is
also alleged that in their assertions that schools
are both dependent on wider social pressures and yet
independent of them, those who adhere to the thesis
merely rush 'to have their cake and eat it'.

Certainly, many such as Apple and Giroux wish to
somehow marry together neo Marxist base/superstructure
determination and the evidence of pupil resistance by
asserting the independence of the <u>pupil</u> subcultures
yet the dependency of the <u>system</u> on outside forces.
Linked with this device is a related attempt by these
authors and others to hang on to 'material determination in the last instance', which of course is the key
constituent of a specifically Marxist form of social

analysis.   Both Whitty (1982) and Dale (1982) seem
to be in this position, particularly the latter who
perceives a complex, interactive relationship between
a poorly designed, rather ill equipped State apparatus
and the economic base, which in the last instance is
still heavily determinate.
    The specificity of the political - the notion
that the political sphere of civil society has an
influence upon State actions separate from and perhaps
in contradistinction to the economic sphere - has
been of course suggested by Poulantzas (1978) and
others (Bowles and Gintis, 1980), yet the possibilities of relative autonomy from the economic base that
this may suggest for the State has been argued to be
severely limited by other Marxists (e.g. Mouzelis,
1976).   Poulantzas himself argued - perhaps appropriately from his death bed - that he too believed in
economic determination 'in the last instance' and
therefore in a highly circumscribed relative autonomy -

> One must know (he argued) whether one
> remains within a Marxist framework or not
> and if one does, one accepts the determinant
> role of the economic in the very complex
> sense ... In this sense, if we remain in
> the conceptual framework, I think that the
> most that one can do for the specificity
> of politics is what I have done.   I am
> sorry to have to speak like that.   (In
> Block, 1980, p. 227.)

In all formulations except for that of perhaps
Williams (1976) - where the mode of production is no
longer merely economic but also cultural - Marxist
analysis leaves little room for the independence of
the educational system or the State from the needs
to reproduce existing economic and social relations.

CORRESPONDENCE THEORY DESTRUCTED

Most adherents to a relative autonomy thesis continue
to argue then that the autonomy of the educational
system is severely limited, constrained by the
demands of an economic base which is in the last
instance determinate, a view which is only different
in degree from earlier Althusserian notions of
complete determination of superstructure by base.
The potentially transformative role of the educational
system - rather than that of the pupils who reject
it - is in these formulations also severely limited.
    Four major developments within British social

science over the last decade suggest however a rather
different form of relative autonomy thesis, one that
grants considerable freedom to the educational system
within British society to act either in a reproductive
or transformative fashion.   Since these developments
are only marginally appreciated within the British
sociology of education, they will be examined here in
some detail.

1.   The Limited Fit Between Education and the Economy
The first set of evidence concerns the massive evidenc
of lack of fit between what the educational system
produces and the needs of the British economic
structure.   The amount of resistance, of rejection
of the mental and of searching for the manual is
clearly far more than is functionally necessary for
the recruitment of the numbers of workers needed to
form the unskilled working class population.   Large
numbers of pupils still leave school with no qualification whatsoever - over 20 per cent in Wales for
example.   In non-cognitive areas, the failure of
adolescents to acquire the moral codes supportive of
the wider structure of society are evidenced by the
high rates of official delinquency (involving one
child in five by age seventeen) and international
studies which show British youth as much more likely
to engage in antisocial conduct than those of any
other industrial society surveyed.   Indeed, one
major cross cultural study (Bronfenbrenner, 1972,
p. 286) concluded that

> It is noteworthy that of all the countries
> in which my colleagues and I are working ..
> the only one which exceeds the United
> States in the willingness of children to
> engage in antisocial behaviour is the
> nation most close to us in our Anglo-Saxon
> traditions of individualism.   That country
> is England.

Whilst there may well be family factors and wider
social class influences responsible for school
failure in both the cognitive and affective areas,
much evidence suggests that it is the workings of
the educational system itself that is responsible
for much pupil alienation.   The existence of certain
rules, the ethos of schools, their curricula and
their pupil/teacher relations have all been suggested
as school factors that are implicated (Reynolds, 1975;
1976).   It is simply very difficult to see how
capitalism is in any way served by an educational

292

system that generates these outputs.

Secondly, there is evidence suggesting the very limited extent to which the organisation of schools 'corresponds' with capitalism's needs. By contrast to American high schools where classroom life is heavily individualised through use of graded tests and materials that are different from child to child and with a guidance system designed to facilitate individual differentiation, British schools still appear as more 'collectivist' in orientation, since learning is still heavily group or class based. Although there are hints that this may be changing in some comprehensive schools (D. Hargreaves, 1982), the predominance of streaming or banding as against setting and the absence of much use cf individually determined work programmes suggest the continuing existence of a collectivist ethos, instead of an ethos preparing for the individualised worker/plant relationships that capitalism is said to 'need'.

Thirdly, the limited correspondence between school organisational form and the requirements of capitalism extends to curricular content also. The survival in schools of a liberal, humanities based curriculum, the emphasis upon the acquisition of knowledge for the purposes of intellectual self betterment rather than collective material gain, the limited swing to science within higher education, the continuing high status of 'pure' disciplines as against work related applied knowledge, the decline in commercially important foreign language courses at sixth form level and the continuing presence in schools of a 'cultural' world of sexist practices that effectively isolates many able girls from doing industrially relevant courses in science and technology all suggest lack of correspondence.

This lack of fit between the outputs of the educational system and the 'needs' of the economy is probably due to a structural looseness in the wider relationships between aspects of the State and the economy. Britain has a heavily decentralised locus of power in the educational system that is rare in a European context, where central government intervenes more in the areas of both pedagogy and curricular content. There has also been - until its emergence quite recently - no comparable citizen or community involvement (as in the United States) that would act as a populist check upon non reproductive functioning and system outputs.

The system then - probably more than any other in the industrialised world - is autonomous. The tradition of headteacher autonomy in decision making,

the absence of any centrally imposed core curriculum,
the inadequate procedures for monitoring, evaluation
and feedback of information upon inputs, processes
and outputs, the substantial autonomy of LEA's
again confirmed by the 1977 Tameside decision and the
huge variability between schools that are outwardly
subject to the same pressures and outwardly aiming
at attainment of the same goals all suggest a highly
autonomous educational system, with substantial
variation in practice within it.

Although it could be that this autonomy merely
exists because the system can be relied upon to
reproduce capitalism without any need for direct State
involvement, the exercise of that autonomy has often
been by people who do not wish merely to reproduce
existing class relations. The large number of
radicals who have been attracted into teaching, the
presence amongst many of a liberal, educational
orientation rather than a training orientation, the
attraction of teaching to those with high autonomy
needs and the ways in which schools are a refuge for
those with high security needs (Derr and Delong,
1982) do not suggest an overwhelming orientation
amongst those in education to generate in their school
crucibles in which industrially relevant skills and
characteristics are forged. There is I suspect as
much or more evidence that the system is staffed by
those with an anti industrial bias as there is
evidence of pro industrial bias.

Apart from being used sometimes to stand against
the demands of the wider society, the autonomy of the
system has been used in an attempt to satisfy educational practitioners' own class or status interests in
ways again that are not necessarily functional for
the wider capitalist enterprise. The influence of
the National Union of Teachers in, for example,
limiting the areas of school outputs to be assessed
by the Assessment of Performance Unit, in changing
the provisions for the publication of school examination results in the 1980 Education Act and in opposing
any professional disciplinary body for teachers, as
examples, suggest the important influence of educators
in moulding the system to suit their own definitions
of the situation, definitions which may not be
functionally in accord with the economic interests of
capitalism.

2.   Recent Developments in Social Science/Social Policy Studies

It is important to realise that many of these influences have passed by the British sociology of

294

education because of its long standing tradition of
an intellectual location within broader <u>sociological</u>
paradigms to the exclusion of developments in other
related fields, a tradition unknown in the United
States for example where policy sciences, the educational management tradition and mainstream sociology
of education are both inter linked and inter penetrated. We have missed then developments in political
science and particularly in social policy field
(Hall et al., 1975) associated with the 'bounded
pluralism' thesis, which in summary holds that the
economic base imposes major constraints upon State
actions but that there is a degree of freedom within
these constraints to respond to demands from other
spheres of influence such as the political, the
cultural or the religious for example.

Within the field of social policy again, we have
missed developments that see the State and its
managers as capable of acting as historical subjects,
generating policies beneficial to themselves, as in
analysis of the medical profession (Parry and Parry,
1976), the growth of the Manpower Services Commission
(Blunckett, 1983) or social work practice (Hall, 1976).

Further developments in thinking about how
within State decision making takes places (Hall, op.
cit.; Crossman, 1970) shows the processes as 'muddling
through', as the politics of administrative conven-
ience, as potentially disjunctive incrementalism and
as supportive of the 'cock up' theory of history,
which argues the State to be fragmented, uncoordinated
and precedent bound in its actions, totally attached
to pattern maintenance, coping and mere survival as
its major goals.

Finally, historical scholarship (e.g. Simon,
1975) suggests that the State itself may be the
outcome of struggle whereby the working class may
evoke - because of the independence of the rights
granted in individuals by the political 'site' -
concessions which range beyond what is strictly
economically necessary for the requirements of
efficient production.

3. The Partial Penetration of Capitalism in Britain

The extent to which the 'cultural' world of values
and the functioning of key British institutions may
in fact be 'capitalist' in orientation has also been
the subject of recent somewhat controversial analysis
(Wiener, 1982). The public schools of the nineteenth
century, for example, actually aimed to 'civilise'
children from the new commercial and industrial middle
classes away from holding 'capitalist' values about the

importance of science, technology, business and commerce - many authorities would argue (Jackson and Marsden, 1962) that the imitation of the private education system by the State schools generated in grammar schools for example very similar organisational values. Gentlemen, it seemed and perhaps still seems, should not try too hard and within schools and also outside

> the dominant collective self image in
> English culture became less and less
> that of the world's workshop. (...)
> These standards and images supported
> a very attractive way of life, geared
> to maintenance of a status quo rather
> than innovation, comfort rather than
> attainment, the civilised enjoyment of,
> rather than the creation of, wealth
> (Wiener, 1982, pp. 158-159)

Given the strong anti-industrial, somewhat Luddite and pre-industrial rural echoes that are found even in the British Labour party, the strong suggestion must be of a lack of penetration of capitalist economic values in British culture, key British institutions such as schools and within the political 'site'.

4.   The Independence of the School

Perhaps the last major set of empirical evidence which suggests a degree of autonomy for the education system is the growing body of knowledge that focusses upon the individual school's substantial freedom to determine the nature of its educational output. Our own past work into the functioning of secondary modern schools shows huge variation in the means employed to deliver the attainment of common goals, means which had implications for the characteristics of their outputs of pupils. Comprehensive schools also seem to have had clearly specified goals but an absence of clearly specified organisational means to attain them and the precise ways in which they have attempted to meet the demands to generate more talent, involving a concentration upon the higher streams, combined with an increased coercion of the former secondary modern pupils, seems to have generated outputs of pupils more developed cognitively but in many ways more unsocialised into mainstream core values. Schools in our work we have seen as determining the nature of the wider society as well as being determined by it, in an interactive relationship with the economic and political 'sites' of the wider society (see Reynolds and Sullivan, 1982).

RELATIVE AUTONOMY THEORY RECONSTRUCTED

To summarise so far, we have seen that the existing
body of relative autonomy theory has grown out of a
dissatisfaction with the complementarity of the
education system and the economy proposed by adherents
to the correspondence thesis.   Whilst as a theory it
is seemingly more popular in America than in Britain,
American society seems at present to evidence more
correspondence than autonomy.   Recent formulations
of the theory propose only severely limited autonomy,
together with a continuing economic determination in
the last instance.
    Using British evidence, it is suggested that
evidence for a 'stronger' relative autonomy theory
exists, evidence that makes it difficult to propose
any determinate relationship between capitalism's
economic base and the nature of the educational
system's functioning or the nature of its outputs of
pupils.   There is a lack of 'fit' in the organisation
of schools, the content of the curriculum and in the
ways that educators have tailored the system to meet
their own perceived needs.   The system has substantial autonomy, is part of a State apparatus poorly
co-ordinated to serve capitalism and may reflect in
part the results of struggle by working people for
transformation of their lives by means of education.
Capitalism itself may not have penetrated either
British culture or key British institutions to the
extent hitherto assumed.   Schools appear to be
active participants not merely in the reproduction
of existing sets of productive relationships but in
actually re-making - utilising their freedom on
means - the forces that influence them in a complex,
interactive relationship between 'superstructure'
and 'base'.
    Our evidence about the interrelationship between
the British educational system and the British
economic base would suggest a theoretical position
as follows:-

1.   There exist important but not completely
determinate economic constraints upon the educational
system that prescribe certain types of pedagogy and
practice as functional, given the requirements of the
capitalist economic base to further capital accumulation.   These constraints can be seen as broad limits
outside of which practice is unlikely to extend.

2.   A range of other non-material influences -
religious factors, historical tradition and gender
relations for example - also have influence upon the
precise nature of the educational system, the
practices employed within schools and the nature of
the outputs which the system generates.   These
influences determine exactly where educational practice becomes located between the constraints of the
economic sphere.

3.   The high degree of autonomy granted to the
system grants it power to be reproductive or transformative in its effects upon the economic base.
Certain practices - training for technology for
example - may be reproductive;   others - such as a
radical social studies curricula - may be transformative, the precise mix of practice depending upon the
strength and range of non-economic influences and the
precise nature of the practice desired by those
educators who staff the system.

4.   The precise mix of policies adopted will
have effects upon the constraints of the economic
base and upon the nature of the economic and other
influences in a complex system of 'interactive feedback' between system, economic base and other 'sites'.
The economic base is therefore crucially seen as
changeable by the way in which the system chooses to
utilise its autonomy and is in no sense merely
determinate but also determined.

There may well be those from existing theoretical
positions who do not regard such versions of relative
autonomy theory as outlined here as in accord with
empirical reality or who do not view the theory as in
any way a 'progressive problemshift'.   This formulation does accept a large degree of economic determination of the system as given, which may not be
generally acceptable to Weberians for example.   It
accepts that the primary role of the system is a
reproduction of existing sets of economic and social
relations.   It does not accept economic determination
in the last instance, which may make it unacceptable
to neo-Marxists, seeing the base as in part open to
determination as well as determining.   It does not
attempt to argue that all phenomena - cultural,
sexual, political and social - are merely epiphenomena
of the economic and grants these variables partial
independence.   It does accept feedback from superstructure to base and it does accept a 'looseness of
fit' between educational system and economic structure

In all these respects, it will be open to attack from
those who inhabit existing entrenched theoretical
positions.
  There is no doubt also that this multi-causal
theory, unlike monocausal vulgar Marxism, requires a
precise determination of the range of influences upon
the system and their precise relative strengths as
determinants of practice. The extent of material
influences - as opposed to non-material - needs to be
validated and assessed. The extent of the systemic
autonomy also needs careful investigation, as does
the nature of the systems of feedback from educational
system to economic base. This is of course a major
intellectual task and there is no reason to expect
that it will be one on which many people in the
discipline will ever become engaged. In spite of
the evident fact that relative autonomy theory has
utility, that it explains disparate findings and that
it begins to explain the somewhat complicated, confused and complex nature of British late capitalism,
there are likely to be numerous blocks upon its
future development as a useful middle range theory.
Most important of these is our continuing disciplinary tendency for the macro end of the discipline to
be peopled by structural determinists and the micro
end by ethnographers who - implicitly if not explicitly - see human behaviour at classroom level as
unconstrained. Very few people - save only the
contexted interactionists or structured interactionists - occupy a 'both/and' position on human
development that is similar to the 'both free/and
constrained' nature that is the relative autonomy
position.
  Crucially, there are such a small number of
people operating and researching at the level of the
educational system or at the level of the individual
school itself that very few sociologists of education
can ever see directly the sort of data which leads,
in my view, inexorably towards a relative autonomy
position. If one sees schools all beset with similar
policies to reproduce the existing pattern of class
relations and with similar intakes ultimately
generating very different processes and outputs, or
if one sees LEA's responding differently and using
their autonomy to utilise different sets of means to
attain stated Governmental or State goals - if one
sees those things happen, one can have no position
other than that of relative autonomy. Until more
people return to study the school and the educational
system, rather than focussing on the macrostructural
or micro-interactional levels, few will have the

potential of seeing both freedom and constraint in
operation, as educators utilise different strategies,
coping mechanisms and procedures to mediate the
common extra-school factors of economic, political
and social life into that classroom and school
experience that in turn affects the nature of the
schools' output.

The relative autonomy theory - if it can be
developed and particularly if the notion of the
school as both determined and free can be utilised
by more researchers - has immense promise.   It is
an organising framework to link together apparently
disparate phenomena.   In our situation of continuing
paradigmatic confusion, there is something for both
micro and macro ends of the spectrum in its thesis.
At a basic level, it does actually make possible a
sociology of education, whereas determinist Marxism
reduces our discipline to being merely the educational
implications of economic or political structure, an
epiphenomena of economics or politics.   It also
makes links between the old sociology of education -
most of whom were closet relative autonomists - and
those who have forged the developments of the last
decade.

Crucially, it makes possible a link between
sociology of education and the educational system's
practice, a link that has been defined out of existence by determinist Marxism's emphasis upon the
determination of the educational by the economic and
by that form of resistance theory which saw only
pupil potential independence.   At a time when the
system itself is lost, uncertain of direction and
badly in need of fresh intellectual input after the
collapse of those policies associated with the
liberal or Fabian dream, it seems more desirable than
ever that this intellectual reorientation takes place
for the sake of those who staff the system.   For the
discipline's sake too an involvement in the day to
day problems of 'policy' has advantages - it moves us
away from the somewhat endless relativistic philosophical problems with which the sociology of
knowledge has disabled us ever since Michael Young
shattered the discipline's old paradigms and moves
us towards a concentration upon the practical and
towards a concentration upon what is practicable.
Every social scientific or scientific discipline
that has made progress in its infancy has done so
through a close alliance with practical problem
solving, as physiology did in the last century through
its close allegiance with clinical medicine, simply
because such an allegiance with the practical prevents

quasi philosophical or metaphysical speculation of a kind that generates no certainties. A concentration upon questions that can be answered seems preferable to an obsession with those that by their nature cannot generate answers.

Our reorientation towards the concern with the more practical matters of educational policy that the relative autonomy theory makes possible is also clearly linked with the ongoing search for transformative practice, a search which has again preoccupied the American sociology of education but which has been curiously neglected at a practical level within Britain. The socialist philosophical position that 'socialistic' transformative practice should be encouraged and fought for is clearly not one that is shared by all members of the discipline, many of whom would regard political commitment of this kind as intellectually undesirable in its effects upon scholarship.

Yet ultimately the way to understand something as complex as a school is probably to attempt to change it, since the change attempts as they encounter blocks, facilitators or linkages between various process factors will reveal the complexity of the institution. Whilst one should be cautious about commitment to a transformative practice of only one (socialistic) variety, the close involvement in action that this would give the discipline is again something that is likely to advance rather than retard our knowledge of schools.

CONCLUSION - WHITHER NEO-MARXISM?

In this paper, an attempt has been made to suggest that relative autonomy theory has utility or usefulness. It attempts - as formulated here - to explain how the educational system is both constrained and free in its actions. The system is seen as facing external constraints but as having freedom - through its variety of coping strategies and internal processes - to determine the precise ways in which it will react. The site of the school - where structure is mediated through to the individual child and where the individual child influences that structure in turn - is argued to be an important location for sociological work, together with a renewed emphasis upon practical educational matters permitted by relative autonomy theory and encouraged by a search for transformative practice.

Perhaps the most important group for whom relative autonomy theory has utility is, however, neo-Marxists themselves. Whilst it would be erroneous to assume that a highly heterogeneous group within the discipline had completely common beliefs and tenets, the Marxist 'enterprise' as Musgrove labelled it does seem open to a number of highly damaging criticisms.

Neo-Marxism's monocausal economic determinism, monolithic view of the State, correspondence view of the educational system/society relationship and assertion of limited superstructural freedom fly in the face of much empirical scholarship and have intellectually greatly harmed Marxism, since disconfirmatory evidence has usually either been ignored, or, if noticed, dismissed. The theoretical position of neo-Marxism seems increasingly to owe more to a commitment to a certain theoretical view of what empirical reality ought to be, rather than to a sensitively grounded appreciation of what empirical reality actually is.

For a body of theory that is increasingly intellectually discredited, relative autonomy theory is not only useful in permitting a theoretical reorientation - one suspects that it is also far closer to classical Marxism in its tenets. The economic determinism of neo-Marxism - with which relative autonomy theory is clearly at intellectual odds - is not in tune with classical Marxism, for whilst Marx saw 'the mode of production' as the foundation of human society since economic activity is essential and indispensable, nowhere does Marx argue that independent of time and culture the mode of production is 'universally decisive' in determining the various forms of society. As Zeitlin (1981, p. 15) notes "It is strictly a matter for empirical investigation whether economics, politics, religion or whatever will be the decisive element for change or non change in any particular case". Classical Marxism - like relative autonomy theory - saw the economic structure as changeable over time, particularly of course by means of an educational inculcation that related to the empirical reality of society. In its notions of the society being determined yet changeable, relative autonomy theory seems to this author at least to be reflecting the historical tenets of Marxist scholarship.

One suspects, then, that relative autonomy theory may be a helpful method by which Marxists may cope with the empirical reality of the British educational system/economy relationship. It suggests not that humans are <u>either</u> free <u>or</u> determined but that there are both determinations and freedoms. It sees humans as influenced and influencing. It may just be the organising framework around which to build an empirically valid, intellectually coherent and policy relevant British sociology of education.

REFERENCES

Ahier, J. and Flude, M. (1982) Contemporary Education Policy, Croom Helm, London
Anyon, J. (1979) 'Ideology and United States History Textbooks', in Harvard Educational Review, 41
Anyon, J. (1980) 'Social Class and the Hidden Curriculum of Work', in Journal of Education, 162, part 1
Anyon, J. (1981) 'Elementary Schooling and Distinctions of Social Class', in Interchange, 12, 2-3
Apple, M. (1980) Ideology and the Curriculum, Routledge and Kegan Paul, London
Apple, M. (1981) 'Social Structure, Ideology and Curriculum', in M. Lawn and L. Barton (eds.), Rethinking Curriculum Studies, Croom Helm, London
Apple, M. (1982) Education and Power, Routledge and Kegan Paul, London
Bernstein, B. (1977) 'Aspects of the Relations Between Education and Production', in Class, Codes and Control, 3, Routledge and Kegan Paul
Block, F. (1980) 'Beyond Relative Autonomy', in R. Miliband and J. Saville (eds.), The Socialist Register 1980, Merlin Press, London
Blunckett, D. (1983) 'The Manpower Services Commission', in Critical Social Policy, 2, 3 pp. 86-88
Bourdieu, P. and Passeron, J.C. (1977) Reproduction In Education, Society and Culture, Sage, London
Bowles, S. and Gintis, H. (1976) Schooling in Capitalist America, Routledge and Kegan Paul, London
Bowles, S. and Gintis, H. (1980) 'Contradiction and Reproduction in Educational Theory', in L. Barton, R. Meighan and S. Walker (eds.), Schooling, Ideology and the Curriculum, Falmer Press, Lewes
Bronfenbrenner, U. (1972) 'Another World of Children', in New Society, 10th February, pp. 278-286
Crossman, R.H.S. (1970) Inside Politics, Hamish Hamilton, London
Dale, R. (1982) 'Education and the Capitalist State: Contributions and Contradictions', in M. Apple (ed.) Cultural and Economic Reproduction in Education, Routledge and Kegan Paul, London

Derr, B.C. and Delong, J.T. (1982) 'What Business Management Can Teach Schools', in H.L. Gray (ed.) The Management of Educational Institutions, Falmer Press, Lewes

Hargreaves, A. (1982) 'Resistance and Relative Autonomy Theories: Problems of Distortion and Incoherence in Recent Marxist Analyses of Education', in British Journal of Sociology of Education, 3, 2, pp. 107-126

Hargreaves, D. (1981) 'Schooling for Delinquency', in L. Barton and S. Walker (eds.), Society, Schools and Teaching, Falmer Press, Lewes

Hargreaves, D. (1982) The Challenge for the Comprehensive School, Routledge and Kegan Paul

Garbarino, J. and Asp, C.E. (1982) Successful Schools and Competent Students, D.C. Heath, Lexington, Mass.

Giroux, H. (1980) 'Beyond the Correspondence Theory: Notes on the Dynamics of Educational Reproduction and Transformation', in Curriculum Inquiry, 10, 3

Giroux, H. (1982) Ideology, Culture and the Process of Schooling, Falmer Press, Lewes

Hall, P. (1976) Reforming the Welfare, Heinemann, London

Hall, P. et al. (1975) Change, Choice and Conflict in Social Policy, Heinemann, London

Jackson, B. and Marsden, D. (1962) Education and the Working Class, Routledge and Kegan Paul, London

Jencks, C. et al. (1971) Inequality, Allen Lane, London

Male, G.A. (1974) The Struggle for Power, Sage, London

Mouzelis, N. (1976) 'Capitalism and Dictatorship in Post War Greece', in New Left Review, March 1976

Musgrove, F. (1981) School and the Social Order, John Wiley, Chichester

O'Keefe, D. (1981) 'Market Capitalism and Nationalised Schooling: The Socio Economy of Education in Liberal Society', in Educational Analysis, 3, 1, pp. 23-36

Parry, N.C.A. and Parry, J. (1976) The Rise of the Medical Profession, Edward Arnold, London

Poulantzas, N. (1978) State, Power, Socialism, New Left Books, London

Ramirez, F.O. (1981) 'Comparative Education: Synthesis and Agenda', in J.F. Short (ed.), The State of Sociology, Sage, London

Reynolds, D. (1975) 'When Pupils and Teachers Refuse a Truce', in G. Mungham and G. Pearson, (eds.) Working Class Youth Culture, Routledge and Kegan Paul, London

Reynolds, D. (1976) 'The Delinquent School', in
    P. Woods (ed.) The Process of Schooling,
    Routledge and Kegan Paul, London
Reynolds, D. and Sullivan, M. (1979) 'Bringing
    Schools Back In', in L. Barton (ed.) Schools,
    Pupils and Deviance, Nafferton, Driffield
Reynolds, D. and Sullivan, M. (1980) 'Towards a New
    Socialist Sociology of Education', in L. Barton
    (ed.) Schooling, Ideology and the Curriculum,
    Falmer Press, Lewes
Reynolds, D. and Sullivan M. (1982) 'The Comprehensive
    Experience', in L. Barton (ed.) Schools, Teachers
    and Teaching, Falmer Press, Lewes
Simon, B. (1975) Education and the Labour Movement,
    Lawrence and Wishart, London
Whitty, G. (1982) Ideology, Politics and Curriculum,
    (Open University Course E353, Unit 8), The
    Open University, Milton Keynes
Wiener, M.J. (1982) English Culture and the Decline
    of the Industrial Spirit, Cambridge University
    Press
Williams, R. (1976) 'Base and Superstructure in
    Marxist Cultural Theory', in New Left Review, 82
Willis, P. (1977) Learning to Labour, Saxon House,
    Farnborough
Young, M. and Whitty, G. (1977) Society, State and
    Schooling, Falmer Press, Lewes
Zeitlin, I.M. (1981) 'Karl Marx: Aspects of this
    Social Thought and their Contemporary Relevance',
    in B. Rhea (ed.) The Future of the Sociological
    Classics, George Allen and Unwin, London

IDEOLOGY, AGENCY AND THE PROCESS OF SCHOOLING

Henry A. Giroux

INTRODUCTION

My own work has developed in a socio-historical
context in the United States in which the notion of
theory as a mode of understanding and critical mediation has been subsumed within a rationality that
emphasises the practical and pragmatic.   That is,
tied to the literal and the immediacy of experience,
traditional educational theory has been locked into
a paradigm seemingly incapable of interrogating
either the principles that structure its own discourse
or the principles that underlie the configuration of
meaning and power that constitute the dominant society and the place of schools within it.
     What we are presented with and victimised by in
this paradigm is an epistemology, a mode of thinking,
that has been flattened out and reduced to the celebration of methodological refinement, that is, a
preoccupation with control, prediction, and observation.   Lost in this theoretical calculus are the
basic rudiments of critical thought-in other words,
behind traditional theory's insistence on a definition of truth that appears to be synonymous with
objective methodological inquiry and empirical verification there is a structured silence regarding how
normative interests provide the grounding for theory
and social inquiry.
     What informs my own perspective is the assumptic
that theory is a central mediating category that needs
to be recovered and redefined in relation to the
notions of empirical work and transformative praxis.
More specifically, this means that theory must be
seen as a distinct analytical moment, which while
connected to empirical work and practice, cannot be
collapsed into the latter.   Theory must be seen as
abstract and anticipatory in character.   It is

rooted in a dialectical logic that makes the concepts of understanding and possibility its central moments. Put another way, theory and practice never stand in an immediate unity, for theory must be informed by an oppositional discourse that preserves its alienation or critical distance from the facts and experiences of the given society. The tension, indeed, the conflict with practice belongs to the essence of theory and is grounded in its very structure.

Theory, in my view, is linked not merely to the pursuit of knowledge and understanding, but also to a comprehension that knowledge is produced in a social and historical context in which there is a constant battle over relations of meaning, one which points to a more fundamental conflict over relations of power. Every theoretical framework stands in a particular relation to a society that defines what counts as knowledge, that constructs social relations according to specific interest, and which, in the advanced industrial countries of the West, upholds specific structures of inequality.

Theory is always partisan with regard to its relationship to dominant ideologies and relations of power. I make no claim to objectivity; on the contrary, I want to argue that any theory of schooling that matters should embrace partisan goals that point to what should be the basis of learning and action, i.e., the struggle for a qualitatively better life for all. In this case, the truth of theory is incompatible with the present, with the existing society.

In short, I believe that within a radical problematic one finds questions and relations that highlight a central tension that should inform any critical notion of schooling and educational research, a tension that moves methods of inquiry beyond the claims of objectivity and value-free research. Instead, questions emerge that point to the antagonistic nature of social reality, and how such a reality might be changed so as to release its unactualised potentialities. Thus, theory in this sense proceeds from the theorist's awareness of his or her own partiality. It is neither neutral nor objective. Such a partiality consists in its goals: the reconstruction of society based on non-exploitative relations and the restoration of human beings as the self-conscious, self-managing subjects of human society.

Educational theory and practice stand at an impasse. Despite the important outpouring of work in the last decade on such topics as the hidden

curriculum, class and gender reproduction, ideology
and culture, and theories of the state and schooling,
educational theorising remains trapped in a dualism
that separates issues of human agency from structural
analyses.   Both traditional and radical perspectives
on schooling are caught in a theoretical straitjacket
that either suppresses the significance of human
agency and subjectivity, or ignores those structural
determinants that lie outside of the immediate experiences of teachers, administrators, students, and
other human actors.   The absence of a full consideration of the dialectic between consciousness and
structure in the work of radical educational theorists
is at the root of their failure to develop a more
critical theory of schooling.   This becomes particularly clear in those modes of discourse that presuppose that schools are merely agencies of social
and cultural reproduction.   In these all too familiar
accounts, power and agency are attributes almost
exclusively of the dominant classes and the institutions they control.   Even where resistance, agency
and mediation appear in accounts of the 'excluded
majorities' in the schools, such constructs are
situated within the context of a paralysing pessimism
that often consigns them to the logic of defeat and
domination rather than to the imperatives of struggle
and emancipation (Giroux, 1981).
     Central to the development of a radical pedagogy
is a reformulation of this dualism between agency and
structure, a reformulation that can make possible a
critical interrogation of how human beings come
together within historically specific social sites
such as schools in order both to make and reproduce
the conditions of their existence.   Essential to
this project is a fundamental concern with the question
of how we can make schooling meaningful in order to
make it critical, and how we can make it critical in
order to make it emancipatory.   I will argue in this
essay that the precondition for the development of a
critical theory of schooling is a reworking of the
notion of ideology;   it is through a fuller understanding of ideology that a theory can be developed which
takes seriously the issues of agency, struggle and
critique.   It is to an exploration of this issue
that I will now turn.

IDEOLOGY AND EDUCATIONAL THEORY AND PRACTICE

The relationship between ideology and schooling is
problematic.   In part, this results from the powerful influence that technocratic rationality has

exercised historically on the development of educational theory and practice. Within this tradition, the fact that schools are both ideological and instructional sites has been ignored. Wedded to the celebration of facts and the management of the 'visible', positivist rationality excludes from its perspective those categories and questions that point to the terrain of ideology. Fixated on the logic of immediacy, such theorists found refuge in the world of appearances and thus refused to interrogate the internal logic of the curriculum in order to reveal its hidden meanings, structured silences, or unintended truths. Notions such as 'essence', false consciousness, and immanent critique were safely tucked away in favour of the discourse of administration, management and efficiency. Consequently, there has been little room within the logic of dominant educational theory and practice to deconstruct the established meanings and received practices that characterise the day to day workings of schools.

From a radically different perspective, Marxism has had a long and extensive tradition in which ideology has played a significant role as a critical concept in the ongoing critique of capitalism and its institutions. However, within that tradition the meaning and applicability of the notion of ideology has remained elusive and equivocal (Sumner, 1979; Larrain, 1979). The result has been that Marxist thought, with few exceptions, has failed to develop a systematic treatment of the concept; consequently, the concept of ideology as a heuristic and critical theoretical tool has not played a role consistent with its potential in radical theory and practice.

The Marxist tradition is not informed by a unitary concept of ideology; one finds instead a plethora of interpretations and analyses of the meaning and value of the concept. Among these wide ranging interpretations there are hints and fleeting images of what the theoretical terrain of ideology might look like; needless to say, if the relation between schooling and ideology is to be understood, the most important of these theoretical insights need to be identified and integrated into a more comprehensive theoretical framework. Thus it is important to interrogate the dominant Marxist versions of ideology in order to see what is missing from them. This in turn demands a brief critical analysis of some of the assumptions that underlie the often contradictory and complex treatment of ideology in current Marxist social theory.

I think it is accurate and fitting to begin by

arguing that ideology in the most traditional and orthodox Marxist sense has been primarily concerned with relations of domination rather than with the relations of struggle and resistance. One consequence has been a host of interpretations that define ideology in largely pejorative terms: as false consciousness (Marx, 1972), as nonscientific beliefs (Althusser, 1969), or as a set of beliefs that functic so as to legitimise domination (Habermas, 1975). In these interpretations, ideology has operated at such a high level of abstraction that it provides few clues as to how subjectivities are constituted in schools; by denying the complex and contradictory nature of human consciousness and behaviour, these accounts suppress the possibilities of mediation and resistance. Ideology has also been treated by a smaller number of Marxist theorists in the positive sense as a set of beliefs and modes of discourse constructed to satisfy the needs and interests of specific groups. For example, Lenin (1971) viewed ideology as a positive force to the degree that it provided the working class with the attitudes and skills necessary for self-determination. Similarly, Gouldner (1976) has made one of the most compelling attempts to rescue ideology from its pejorative status by arguing that all ideologies contain the possibility for developing a critical view of the world. However, in addition to the question of whether ideology is to be viewed in a positive or pejorative light there is a related question as to whether ideology should be viewed primarily in objective or subjective terms. For instance, both Althusser (1969, 1971) and Volosinov (1973) view ideology as having a materiality rooted, respectively, either in practices produced in Ideological State Apparatuses such as schools, or in the materiality of language, representations and 'signs'. For both Althusser and Volosinov, ideologies address and constitute the human subject. But the human subject is the missing referent here, as are relations of struggle waged outside the 'text', among real human beings who bleed, cry, despair and think. On the other hand, the subjective and psychological character of ideology can be found in the work of critical theorists such as Marcuse (1964) or in the work of culturalists such as Williams (1977) and Thompson (1966). In these perspectives, either ideology is situated within the psychic structure of the oppressed or it is the central, active force constituted through shared experiences and common interests.

310

In the Marxist tradition, then, there is a central tension between a view of ideology as an all-encompassing mode of domination and a view of ideology as an active force in the construction of human agency and critique. Similarly, there is a tension between the notion of ideology as a material force and ideology as a mode of meaning. Each of these positions is by itself theoretically flawed, and each alone is only partially useful in providing a critical theory of ideology for radical educators. In order to constitute a theory of ideology as the basis for a critical theory of schooling, it will be necessary to situate it within a theoretical perspective that takes seriously the notion of human agency, struggle and critique.

IDEOLOGY: DEFINITION, LOCATIONS AND FEATURES

Any definition of ideology has to wrestle not only with the question of what it is but also with the question of what it is not. I want to begin with the latter point. One view of ideology in particular that must be abandoned before the concept can be rescued from its own history is the Althusserian notion that ideology exists in material apparatuses and has a material existence. As Johnson (1979a) points out, Althusser's argument transforms a "genuine insight" into a "reckless hyperbole" (p. 59). To argue that ideologies are located in concrete social practices and have specific effects on such practices is an important insight, but to stretch the meaning of ideology to make it synonymous with the material world so generalises the concept as to render it meaningless as an analytical tool. Moreover, this definition of ideology falsely collapses the distinction between ideological struggle and material struggle. That is, it confuses struggles over meanings, discourse, and representation with struggles over the concrete appropriation and control of capital, territory and other such resources. Of course, both forms of struggle are related, but they cannot be collapsed into each other. For example, schools are cultural apparatuses involved in the production and transmission of ideologies. It is one thing to talk about the school as a site where conflicting ideologies are fought over, a site where a conflict is waged over relations of meaning; it is another thing altogether to view schools as political and economic institutions - material embodiments of lived experience and historically sedimented antagonistic relations - that need to be seized and controlled by subordinate groups so they can be used in the interests of such groups.

The distinction between ideology and the materiality of culture is an important one; it cannot be reduced to a simple dualism of ideas counterposed to material reality. The relation is more complex than this. On the one hand, ideology can be viewed as a set of representations produced and inscribed in human consciousness and behaviour, in discourse and in lived experiences. On the other hand, ideology is concretised in various 'texts', material practices and material forms. Hence, the character of ideology is mental, but its effects are both psychological and behavioural; they are not only felt in human action but are also inscribed in material culture. Thus, ideology as a construct includes a notion of mediation that does not limit it to an ideal form (Aronowitz, 1981). I want to argue that ideology has an active quality, the character of which is defined by those processes "by which meaning is produced, challenged, reproduced and transformed' (Barrett, 1980, p. 97). Within this perspective, ideology refers to the pro- duction, consumption and representation of ideas and behaviour, all of which can either distort or illu- minate the nature of reality. As a set of meanings and ideas, ideologies can be either coherent or con- tradictory; they can function within the spheres of both consciousness and unconsciousness; and, finally, they can exist at the level of critical discourse as well as within the sphere of taken-for-granted lived experience and practical behaviour (Bourdieu, 1977; Bourdieu and Passeron, 1977; Giddens, 1979; Marcuse, 1955). The complexity of the concept is captured in the notion that while ideology is an active process involving the production, consumption, and represen- tation of meaning and behaviour, it cannot be reduced to either consciousness or a system of practices on the one hand or to either a mode of intelligibility or a mode of mystification on the other. Its character is dialectical, and its theoretical strength stems both from the way it shuns reductionism, and from the way it bridges the seemingly contradictory moments mentioned above.

But a number of qualifications must be made if the definition of ideology developed thus far is to be prevented from collapsing into the kind of sociol- ogy of knowledge that, as Adorno (1967) remarks, suffers from the weakness of calling "everything into question and criticising nothing" (p. 37). While the characteristic feature of ideology is its location in the category of meaning and thought production, its critical potential only becomes fully clear when it is linked to the concepts of struggle and critique. When linked to the notion of struggle, ideology illuminates the important relationships among power, meaning and interest. This suggests at one level the important insight provided by Marx in his claim that ideologies constitute the medium of struggle among classes at the level of ideas (Marx, 1969b), as well as the corollary insight provided by Gramsci's (1971) comment that ideologies "organise masses, and create the terrain on which men move, acquire consciousness of their position, struggle, etc." (p. 377).

Both Marx and Gramsci suggest that any theory of ideology has to include a theory of power, one that takes as its central concern social antagonisms and class struggle. The linkage of ideology and struggle points to the inseparability of knowledge and power; it emphasises that ideology refers not only to specific forms of discourses and the social relations they structure but also to the interests they further (Gouldner, 1976). Thus, when Marx (1969a) linked ideology to the sectional interests of dominant groups in society he pointed to a form of ideology critique whose function is, in part, to uncover class-specific mystification and to point to concrete struggles aimed at the overcoming of class domination.

This form of ideology critique indicates the need to penetrate beyond the discourse and consciousness of human actors to the conditions and foundation of their day to day experiences. Critique in this sense functions to uncover falsifications and to identify the conditions and practices that generate them. Ideology critique in this instance centres around a critical analysis of the subjective and objective forces of domination, and at the same time reveals the transformative potential of alternative modes of discourse and social relations rooted in emancipatory interests. It is also important to argue that ideology critique involves more than critically analysing modes of knowledge and social practices in order to determine whose interests they serve. It is important to recognise that in addition to its functional role in the construction and maintenance of the power of dominant social formations, ideology operates as a relatively autonomous set of ideas and practices, whose logic cannot be reduced merely to class interests. Again, its meaning and specificity cannot be exhausted by defining its functional relation to class interests and struggle. In this case, ideology critique not only focusses on whether a specific ideology functions so as to serve or resist class or other forms of domination; on the contrary, it also identi-

fies the contents of the ideologies in question and
judges the "truth or falsity of the contents themselves" (Adorno, 1973, p. 131). That is, if the
notions of ideology and ideology critique are really
to serve emancipatory class interests, ultimately they
cannot be separated from the question of truth claims.
It is important to maintain this understanding of the
transformative and active quality of ideology when we
consider the link between ideology and human agency.
As both the medium and the outcome of lived experience,
ideology functions not only to limit human action but
also to enable it. That is, ideology both promotes
human agency and at the same time exercises force over
individuals and groups through the 'weight' it assumes
in dominant discourses, selected forms of socio-
historical knowledge, specific social relations, and
concrete material practices. Ideology is something
we all participate in, and yet we rarely understand
either the historical constraints that produce and
limit the nature of that participation, or what the
possibilities are for going beyond existing parameters
of action in order to think and act in terms that
speak to a qualitatively better existence. The
nature of ideology and its usefulness as a critical
construct for radical pedagogy can be further illumi-
nated by focussing on its location and functions
within what I choose to call its operational field.
In the most general sense, ideology operates at the
level of lived experience, at the level of representations embedded in various cultural artifacts, and
at the level of messages signified in material practices produced within certain historical, existential
and class traditions. I want to examine briefly the
relations between ideology and each of these respective
locations while concentrating primarily on how ideology functions at the level of lived experience. In
doing so, I will further delineate a notion of ideology critique and its relevance to radical pedagogy.

IDEOLOGY, HUMAN EXPERIENCE AND SCHOOLING

Central to understanding how ideology functions in the
interest of social reproduction is the issue of how
ideology works on and through individuals to secure
their consent to the basic ethos and practices of the
dominant society. Equally important for an understanding of how ideology functions in the interest of
social transformation is the issue of how ideology
creates the terrain for reflection and transformative
action. I do not believe that the concept of ideology can be located either in the sphere of conscious-

ness, as in traditional Marxism, or exclusively within the realm of the unconscious, as Althusser (1969, 1971) and his followers argue. Following Gramsci (1971), I want to argue that human behaviour is rooted in a complex nexus of structured needs, common sense and critical consciousness, and that ideology is located in all of these aspects of human behaviour and thought so as to produce multiple subjectivities and perceptions of the world and everyday life. The interface of ideology and individual experience can be located within three specific areas: the sphere of the unconscious and the structure of needs; the realm of common sense; and the sphere of critical consciousness. Needless to say, these areas cannot be neatly defined nor do they exist in isolation. But by using them we can move from an analysis focussing on whether consciousness is true or false, to the more fundamental issue of what consciousness is and how it is constituted. Moreover, the argument that ideology exists as part of the unconscious, common sense and critical consciousness points to an ideological universe in which contradictions exist both in and outside of the individual. This is similar to Williams's (1977) argument that the ideological field in any given society includes contradictions within and between what he calls emerging, residual and dominant ideologies. Meaning as it is produced and received within this complex of ideologies and material forces is clearly not reducible to the individual but has to be understood in its articulation with ideological and material forces as they circulate and constitute the wider society. In other words, ideology has to be conceived as both the source and effect of social and institutional practices as they operate within a society that is characterised primarily by relations of domination, a society in which men and women are basically unfree in both objective and subjective terms. This becomes clearer if we examine the relations between ideology and these three spheres of meaning and behaviour separately.

IDEOLOGY AND THE UNCONSCIOUS

Traditional Marxism limited the parameters of ideology almost exclusively to the realm of consciousness and the notion of domination. Lost from these approaches was any attempt to analyse the effects of ideology on the body and the structure of personality. In other words, there were very few attempts to examine how ideology produced effects at not only the level of knowledge but also at the level of needs and desires. Locked within a theoretical straitjacket that defined ideology as 'merely' oppressive, orthodox Marxism failed to explore either how people acted against their own interests, thereby sharing in their own oppression, or what compelled them to stand up and resist oppression in the face of intolerable odds. Foucault (1980) raises this point poignantly in his comment: "What enables people ... to resist the Gulag ... what can give (them) the courage to stand up and die in order to utter a word or a poem?" (p. 136).

Within the last few decades, Marcuse (1955), Althusser (1969) and others have attempted to reconstruct the meaning of ideology and to demarcate its location and effects so as to include the sphere of the unconsciousness and the structure of needs. Althusser's (1969, 1971) insistence that ideology is grounded unconsciously represents a major contribution in redefining the meaning and workings of the concept. It points to the limits of consciousness in explaining the nature of domination while simultaneously pointing to the power of the material practices and social relations through which people live their experiences and generate meanings. But although Althusser provides a service in linking ideology to the unconscious, he is still trapped within a notion of domination that leaves little room for resistance, or, for that matter, for a dialectical notion of ideology.

The work of the Frankfurt School, especially Marcuse's (1955) analysis of how ideology becomes sedimented as second nature in the structure of needs represents a much more productive starting point for investigating the link between ideology and its unconscious grounding. Marcuse claims that domination is rooted historically not only in the socioeconomic conditions of society, but also in the sedimented history or structure of needs that constitute each person's disposition and personality. For Marcuse, ideology as repression is a historical construct rooted in the reified relations of everyday life, relations characterised by "the submission of social reality to forms of calculability and control" (Feenberg, 1981, pp. 62-63). Lukacs (1968) points to the social character of repressive ideology in his notion of reification, in which concrete relations between human beings are made to appear as objectified relations between things. Adorno (1967-1968) and Marcuse (1955) capture the subjective dynamic of reification in the concept of second nature. For them ideology as reification implies a mode of uncon-

sciousness in which the historically contingent nature
of social relations under capitalism has been 'for-
gotten' and takes on the appearance of mythic perman-
ence and unchanging reality. Ideology as second
nature is history congealed into habit, rooted in the
very structure of needs. Thus, ideology not only
shapes consciousness but also reaches into the depths
of personality and reinforces through the patterns
and routines of everyday life needs that limit "the
free self activity of social individuals and ... their
qualitatively many sided system of needs" (Heller,
1974, p. 104).

Unlike Althusser (1971) and Bourdieu (1977) who
cast the connection between ideology and the unconscious in modes of ironclad domination from which
there appears no escape, Marcuse (1955) and Heller
(1974) treat the linkage dialectically and posit its
emancipatory as well as dominating possibilities.
For instance, both theorists argue that since needs
are historically conditioned they can be changed.
Moreover, the unconscious grounding of ideology is
rooted not only in needs that are repressive but also
in needs that are emancipatory in nature, i.e. needs
based on meaningful social relations, community,
freedom, creative work and a fully developed aesthetic
sensibility. This emphasis on the contradictory
nature of needs reveals the tensions within the personality structure as well as the corresponding
tensions in the larger society. Inherent in these
contradictory tensions is the possibility of the full
and many-sided development of 'radical' needs and the
elimination of the conditions that repress them.
Thus, ideology as located in the unconscious is both
a moment of self-creation and a force for domination.

A number of important questions emerge from this
analysis, two of which will be explored below. First,
what elements of ideology critique can be developed
from the analysis provided by the Frankfurt School
theorists and Heller? Second, what is the relevance
of this type of ideology critique for a theory of
schooling?

The critique of ideology as grounded in the
unconscious provides the basis for an analysis of
those aspects of everyday life that structure human
relations in order to reveal their historical genesis
and the interests they embody. What appears as
'natural' must be demystified and revealed as a
historical production both in its content, with its
unrealised claims or distorting messages, and in the
elements that structure its form. Ideology critique
becomes historical in a double sense: on the one

hand, it reaches into the history of social relations and reveals the truth or falsity of the underlying logic that structures such relations; on the other hand, it probes into the sedimented history of the personality and attempts to illuminate the sources and influences at work at the very core of the need and personality structure. In addition, it points to the importance of identifying, analysing and transforming those social practices that sustain the gap between economic and cultural wealth and the reality of human impoverishment. Furthermore, ideology critique within this perspective suggests the importance of educating people to recognise the interest structure that limits human freedom, while simultaneously calling for the abolition of those social practices that are its material embodiment. Heller (1974) is quite correct in arguing that for radical needs to be developed, individuals and groups have to nurture an ongoing self-critical awareness of their existence while at the same time developing qualitatively different social relations to sustain them.

What is crucial to recognise is the role that needs play in structuring our behaviour, whether it be in the interest of social and cultural reproduction or in the interest of self-determination. If we are to take human agency seriously, we must acknowledge the degree to which historical and objective societal forces leave their ideological imprint upon the psyche itself. To do so is to set the groundwork for a critical encounter between oneself and the dominant society and to acknowledge what this society has made of us and what it is we no longer want to be. Finally, ideology critique as it is applied to the unconscious grounding of human behaviour becomes meaningful only if it is ultimately explored in relation to consciousness and the possibility of a critical monitoring of the relationship between consciousness and the structures and ideologies that make up the dominant society.

The implications of this form of ideology critique for educational theory and practice centre primarily around the development of a depth psychology that can unravel the way in which historically specific experiences and traditions get produced, reproduced and resisted at the level of daily school life. This approach points to two major concerns. First, it points to the need to identify the tacit messages embodied in the day to day routines that structure all aspects of the school experience and to uncover the emancipatory or repressive interests they serve.

It also suggests developing a mode of critique that comprehends the forces at work that mediate between the structural relations of schooling and their lived effects. Students bring different histories with them to school; these histories are embedded in class-, gender- and race-specific interests that shape their needs and behaviour, often in ways they do not understand and often in ways that work against their own interests. To work with working-class students, for instance, under the purported impetus of a radical pedagogy would mean not only changing their consciousness, but simultaneously developing social relations that sustain and are compatible with the radical needs in which such a consciousness would have to be grounded in order to be meaningful. A case in point would be developing a pedagogy that made working-class sexism an object of analysis and change. It would be essential that such a pedagogy not only interrogate the language, ideas and relations that are informed by the logic of sexism, but that it be developed within classroom social relations based on nonsexist principles and concerns. Second, this approach to radical pedagogy points to the need for an understanding by teachers of the relation between cultural capital and ideology as a basis for confirming the experiences that students bring with them to the school. Students must first view their own ideologies and cultural capital as meaningful before they can critically probe them. The point here may be obvious. Students cannot learn about ideology simply by being taught how meanings get socially constructed in the media, and other aspects of daily life. Working-class students also have to understand how they participate in ideology through their own experiences and needs. It is their own experiences and needs that have to be made problematic to provide the basis for exploring the interface between their own lives and the constraints and possibilities of the wider society. Thus, a radical pedagogy must take seriously the task of providing the conditions for changing subjectivity as it is constituted in the individual's needs, drives, passions and intelligence as well as changing the political, economic, and social foundation of the wider society.

In short, an essential aspect of radical pedagogy centres around the need for students to interrogate critically their inner histories and experiences. It is crucial for them to be able to understand how their own experiences are reinforced, contradicted and suppressed as a result of the ideol-

ogies mediated in the material and intellectual
practices that characterise daily classroom life.
Clearly, this form of analysis is not meant to reduce
ideology and its effects to the sphere of the unconscious; rather it is to argue for its importance as
a major component of educational theory and radical
praxis. For it is in the dialectical relations
between consciousness and unconsciousness on the one
hand and experience and objective reality on the
other that the basis for critical thought and action
has to be grounded and developed. The prevailing
system of needs in capitalist society, or any repressive society, must be understood in terms of its
historical genesis and the interests it embodies and
serves. For radical educators, this is the first
step in breaking with the logic and institutions of
domination. This must be followed by a radicalisa-
tion of consciousness and the reconstruction of
social relations that materially reinforce the logic
of emancipatory interests.

IDEOLOGY AND COMMON SENSE

One of the major contributions of Marx was his insight
that consciousness has to be explained as part of the
historical mode of one's existence. That is, thought
and its production cannot be separated from one's
world; more specifically, forms of consciousness
must be recognised as forms of life that are social
and historical in nature. At the same time Marx
(1969b) was equally insistent that while consciousness
is an essential component of any activity, a critical
analysis of society has to look beyond the level of
lived beliefs and examine the social relations in which
these beliefs are embedded. For Marx (1969a), Gramsci
(1971) and other Western Marxists, ideology was not
exhausted through its representations in the unconscious. While the latter is an important ideological
sphere it is not the only one. To reduce ideology
exclusively to the realm of the unconscious is to
leave human agents without the benefit of critical or
any other consciousness. Gramsci (1971), in particular, provides insight into the location and effects
of ideology in the sphere of common sense he called
contradictory consciousness. He begins with the
important assumption that human consciousness cannot
be equated with, or exhausted in, the logic of domination. On the contrary, he views consciousness as
a complex combination of good and bad sense, a contradictory realm of ideas and behaviour in which elements
of accommodation and resistance exist in an unsteady

state of tension. More specifically, common sense in the Gramscian view points to a mode of subjectivity characterised by forms of discursive consciousness imbued with authentic insights into social reality as well as distorting beliefs that serve to mystify and legitimate that reality. In addition, common sense effects and manifests itself in nondiscursive behaviour marked by the same combination of accommodation and resistance. However, both discursive and non-discursive common sense function without the benefit of critical interrogation. It is the grounding of common sense in an uncritical mode of mediation, a mode of mediation which is unconscious of its relation to the larger social totality, that is its singular characteristic.

Common sense represents a limited mode of self-consciousness, one that is contradictory in nature and ill-equipped to grasp either the force that constitutes it or its effects on the social totality. However, Gramsci's notion of common sense must be distinguished from views of ideology that exist solely in the unconscious or from notions of false conscious-ness. Common sense represents a realm of conscious-ness informed by a complex of contrasting subjectivi-ties. Disorder rather than harmony characterises common sense; it contains a dialectical interplay of hegemonic and insightful beliefs and practices. While agency does not disappear in this account, it lacks the self-consciousness needed to resolve its contradictions and tensions or extend its partial insights into a coherent critical perspective through which it can engage its own principles. Gramsci (1971) points to this issue in his comment on contra-dictory consciousness:

> The active man-in-the-mass has a practical activity, but has no clear theoretical consciousness of his practical activity, which nonetheless involves understanding the world in so far as it transforms it. His theoretical consciousness can indeed be historically in opposition to his activity. One might almost say that he has two theoretical consciousnesses (or one contradictory consciousness): one which is implicit in his activity and which in reality unites him with all his fellow workers in practical transformation of the real world; and one, superficially explicit or verbal which he has inherited from the past and uncritically absorbed (p. 333)

321

Underlying Gramsci's discussion of the relationship between ideology and common sense are a number
of assumptions and implications that have relevance
for educational theory and practice. First, Gramsci
rescues the human subject by positing a notion of
ideology that does not obliterate the mediating facul-
ties of ordinary people. At the same time he recognises that while domination pre-exists, its effects
and outcomes are open-ended. Thus, contradictory
consciousness does not point <u>primarily</u> to domination
or confusion, but to a sphere of contradictions and
tensions that is pregnant with possibilities for
radical change. In my view, ideology becomes a
critical construct to the degree to which it reveals
the truths as well as the concealing function of
common sense as outlined by Gramsci. Second,
Gramsci's notion of ideology and common sense
addresses an important dialectical relation between
discourse and practical activity. In this view,
ideology exists not only on the level of speech and
language, but also as lived experience, as practical
conduct in everyday life. What Gramsci argues for
is a mode of analysis that uncovers the contradictory
moments in discourse so that they not only can be
used to reveal their own underlying interests but
also can be restructured into a form of critical
consciousness that can "make coherent the problems
raised by the masses in their practical activity"
(Karabel, 1976, p. 169). In this way, common sense
becomes subjected to a critical interrogation via its
own thought processes and practical activity as these
constitute and reproduce the conduct of everyday life.
In pedagogical terms, this suggests taking the typi-
fications of educational discourse and their attendant social relations and stripping them of their
objective or so-called natural character. Instead
of being treated as a given, they must be viewed
within historical and social relations that are
produced and socially constructed. This leads to a
final insight about common sense, one that is drawn
directly from the work of such Frankfurt School
members as Adorno, Horkheimer, and Marcuse.
    For the Frankfurt School, the notion of common
sense could only be understood by analysing its
dialectical relation to the wider social totality.
Inherent in the form and substance of common sense
was the logic of commodity structure: that is,
common sense was constituted by taken-for-granted
categories and practical activity divorced from the
agents and conditions that produced them. Social
practices and categories appeared objectified, as

unquestioned givens cut off from the socio-historical processes and interests through which they had evolved. Within this perspective, ideology critique functioned both to unmask the messages revealed in common sense and to interrogate the truth claims and the societal functions of the interests that structure common sense. There is an important dimension of ideology critique in this formulation, one that is indispensable for a radical pedagogy. Radical practice begins, in this case, with a break from the positivist emphasis on immediacy, an immediacy which, as Schmidt (1981) comments, "daily deludes individuals with a nature-like invariance of their life relationships" (p. 104). Ideology critique assumes an added dimension in this case. In other words, it posits the need for a historical consciousness, one that begins with an analysis of the reifications of daily life and takes the rigidified, congealed relations that reduce teachers and students to 'bearers' of history as the basis for probing into history and discovering the conditions that generated such conditions in the first place. Historical consciousness as a moment of ideology critique and radical pedagogy, within this perspective. functions "so as to perceive the past in a way that (makes) the present visible as a revolutionary moment" (Buck-Morss, 1981, p. 61). This leads us to the relationship between ideology and reflective consciousness, the most potentially radical of the three spheres in which ideology is located.

IDEOLOGY AND CRITICAL CONSCIOUSNESS

The notion that ideology has as one of its important features a critical 'moment' that situates it in the realm of critical thinking presents a direct challenge to those theories of ideology which either reduce ideology to false consciousness or disparage it by contrasting it to what is termed science. I want to argue here that ideology can act as a critical moment in the production of meaning by illuminating the rules, assumptions and interests that structure not only the thinking process but also the material such processes take as an object of analysis. The ideol-ogical dimension that underlies all critical reflec-tion is that it lays bare the historically and soci-ally sedimented values at work in the construction of knowledge, social relations and material practices. In other words, it grounds the production of knowledge, including science, in a normative framework linked to specific interests. As Aronowitz (1980) makes clear, those who argue for the science/ideology division reproduce the very notion of ideology they critique, i.e., ideology as mystification. He writes, "The concept of the science/ideology antinomy is itself ideological because it fails to comprehend that all knowledge is a product of social relations" (p. 97).

To locate a theory of ideology in the sphere of critical consciousness highlights the normative basis of all knowledge and points to the active nature of human agents in its construction. The underlying grammar of ideology finds its highest expression in the ability of human beings to think dialectically. To view both the object of analysis and the processes involved in such analysis as part of a complex mode of producing meaning represents not simply the active side of ideology but its most critical dimension. Thus, ideology implies a process whereby meaning is produced, represented and consumed. The critical aspect of that process represents a reflexive understanding of the interests embodied in the process itself and how these interests might be transformed, challenged, or sustained so as to promote rather than repress the dynamics of criti- cal thought and action. Ideology in this sense suggests that all aspects of everyday life that have a semiotic value are open to reflection and critique just as it points to the need for a critical atten- tiveness to all aspects of self-expression.

Through ideology critique, critical thinking is made more than an interpretative tool; it is situ- ated within a radical notion of interest and social transformation. Critical analysis, in this case, becomes the distinct but important precondition for radical praxis, with a twofold purpose. On the one hand, it follows Adorno's (1973) insistence that the task of ideology critique is the explosion of reifi- cation, a breaking through of mystifications and a recognition of how certain forms of ideology serve the logic of domination. This means not only analysing the hidden ideological elements in any object of analysis, whether it be a school curriculum or a set of social relations, and revealing their social function; it also means releasing their unintentional truths, the suppressed utopian elements contained in what they include as well as what they leave out. This involves breaking apart or decon- structing the ideas and structuring principles in a cultural artifact and then placing them in a different framework that allows one to see the limits of specific ideas and formal properties, while simul- taneously discovering the new and vital elements in them that could be appropriated for radical purposes. For instance, in looking at most literacy models, a radical educator would have to first identify the ideology that informs their content and methodology. It might then be possible to appropriate certain fundamental aspects of the models but within a theoretical framework in which literacy is treated not merely as a technique but as a constitutive process of constructing meaning and critically interrogating the forces that shape one's lived experiences. This points to the second aspect of ideology critique that I alluded to earlier, that such a critique must be informed by a spirit of relentless negativity, one that promotes the critical independence of the subject as well as the restructuring and transformation of an oppressive social reality. Ideology critique as a form of critical consciousness opposes the knowledge of technocratic rationality, and implies instead a dialectical knowledge that illuminates contradictions and informs the critical judgments needed for individual and social action.

The link between ideology and the notion of truth is not to be found in the peddling of prescriptions or in a deluge of endless recipes; instead, it is located in what Benjamin (1969) has called the distance between the interpreter and the material, on the one hand, and the gap between the present and the possibility of a radically different future on the other. The value of viewing ideology as a complex process in the production and critique of meaning becomes more concrete through an examination of how meaning functions as a constitutive force in the structuring and mediation of representations in school artifacts and in classroom social relations.

IDEOLOGY, REPRESENTATIONS AND CLASSROOM MATERIAL PRACTICES

In order to grasp fully the relationship between agency and structure as part of a radical pedagogy, a theory of ideology must be capable of comprehending the way in which meaning is constructed and materialised within 'texts', that is, within cultural forms such as films, books, curriculum packages, fashion styles and so on. Thus, ideology critique is not limited to the hidden or visible processes in the realm of subjectivity and behaviour but is extended to the "study of observable material processes - the manipulation of signs in specific ways and specific contexts" (Bennett, 1981, p. 28). The work of Volosinov (1973), Eco (1976), Coward and Ellis (1977)

325

and Kress and Hodge (1979) has been invaluable in this regard in emphasising the relative autonomy of the representations that construct the limits and parameters within which meaning is produced, negotiated and received by individuals. Of course, in this 'structuralist' approach, 'signs' constitute consciousness and the notion that signs could be both the medium and the product of consciousness is denied. In other words, ideology as representations of expressed ways of thought, experience and feeling is not given very much theoretical weight. This is clearly captured in Volosinov's claim that "Individual consciousness is not the architect of the ideological superstructure, but only a tenant lodging in the edifice of ideological signs" (Volosinov, 1973, p. 6). But while it is true that representations and signs address (interpolate) and situate individuals, the human beings they address are more than just a reflex of the texts in question. Human agents always mediate the representations and material practices that constitute their lived experiences through their own histories and their class- and gender-related subjectivities. This is true within the parameters defined by the school, the family, the workplace or any other social site. What is needed to offset the one-sided theory of ideology provided by many structuralists is a more fully developed theory of mediation and reception (Barrett, 1981). Such an approach would link agency and structure in a theory of ideology so as to treat dialectically the roles of the individual and group as producers of meaning within already existing fields of representations and practices. As Johnson (1979b) suggests, failure to address this question means that we run the risk of getting trapped in modes of structuralist analysis that overlook "the moment of self creation, of the affirmation of belief, or the giving of consent" (p. 234).

The starting point for developing a more dialectical theory of ideology and schooling rests with the acknowledgment that individuals and social classes are both the medium and the outcome of ideological discourses and practices. Meaning is located both in the various dimensions of subjectivity and behaviour and in 'texts' and classroom practices that structure, limit and enable human action. The theory of ideological processes that follows draws on the concepts of reproduction, production and reconstruction, all of which will be delineated within the context of the analysis presented below.

Ideology, Agency and the Process of Schooling

Reproduction as used below refers to texts and social practices whose messages, inscribed within specific historical settings and social contexts, function primarily to legitimate the interests of the dominant social order. I want to argue that these can be characterised as texts and social practices <u>about</u> pedagogy (Lundgren, in press) and refer primarily to categories of meaning constructed so as to legitimise and reproduce interests expressed in dominant ideologies. The acts of conception, construction and production that characterise texts <u>about</u> pedagogy usually have little to do with the contexts in which such texts are applied, and the principles that structure them almost never lend themselves to methods of inquiry that encourage dialogue or debate. Such texts and practices objectively represent the selection, fixation and legitimation of dominant traditions. For instance, both the form and the content of such texts tend to treat teachers and students as reified elements in the pedagogical process. Even in the more sophisticated versions of such texts such as the Humanities units Buswell (1980) examined, the logic of powerlessness prevailed, albeit in recycled forms. She writes:

> The texts directed pupils to books and information kept elsewhere which was part of the aim of teaching them to 'learn'. But a 'particular' answer was still required and finding it became a complicated orienteering exercise conducted through the printed word whereby acquiring any content was made more difficult. The emphasis in all the units was on following the precise instructions and replicating what someone else had produced, very little creativity was required. (pp. 302-303)

This reified view of knowledge is a classic example of Freire's (1973) 'banking model' of schooling and is found not only in the structuring principles that inform such texts but also in their content as well. Brown (1981) in an extensive examination of recent children's history books attempted to find texts that did the following: (a) recognise human agency, (b) relate past experiences to the present so as to stimulate intellectual curiosity, (c) link material conditions to social relations, (d) present history as more than 'dressed up' figures and facts, and, finally, (e) treat history

as open-ended and subject to interpretation. What
he actually found were books that contained an anti-
urban bias, promoted their content in "commercial
studio aesthetics", celebrated technology outside
the human relations in which it functioned and
collapsed history into great moments, while simultaneously using a language that suppressed conflict.

There is a growing amount of research that
points to the increased use of prepackaged curriculum
materials that accentuate delivering instruction while
at the same time removing conception and critique from
the pedagogical act. Apple (1982) argues that such
curriculum materials represent a new form of control
over both teachers and students, one that indicates
a process of deskilling and the emergence of more
powerful forms of rationality that embody changing
modes of control within the nature of capitalist
relations of production. Control in this case is
removed from face-to-face contact and is now situated in the impersonal processes and logic of highly
rationalised managerial relations. The effects of
these prepackaged materials on schooling represent
a new dimension in the reproduction of texts and
material practices about pedagogy. This is evident
in Apple's (1982) claim that

> Skills that teachers used to need, that
> were deemed essential to the craft of
> working with children - such as curriculum
> deliberation and planning, designing
> teaching and curricular strategies for
> specific groups and individuals based on
> intimate knowledge of these people - are
> no longer as necessary. With the large-
> scale influx of prepackaged material,
> planning is separated from execution.
> The planning is done at the level of
> production of both the rules for use of
> the material and the material itself.
> The execution is carried out by the teacher.
> In the process, what were previously con-
> sidered valuable skills atrophy because
> they are less often required (p. 146).

Each of these examples provides a mode of ideology critique that reveals how reproductive ideologies
work. Buswell illustrates how specific principles
structure the text and classroom social relations so
as to legitimate modes of learning that promote pass-
ivity and rule following rather than critical engagement on the part of teachers and students. Brown

(1981) both points to the structural silences in a
text, those ideas and values that are left out and
thus rendered illegitimate, and at the same time
analyses the social function of the existing text.
Apple, on the other hand, shows how the principles
that structure the production and use of curriculum
materials are rooted in specific interests that
reinforce a division of labour that separates conception from execution at the level of teaching
itself. In all of these cases texts about pedagogy
function so as to suppress human agency while at the
same time legitimating the power and control of the
dominant classes. However, what is missing from
these analyses and what is needed to complement them
is a historical critique that moves beyond simply
registering the ideologies embedded in the form and
content of curriculum materials and practices. It
is imperative to link such ideological representations to historically constituted social relations
as they appear in schools. For example, Barrett
(1980) illuminates this issue when she argues that
female models are more persuasive to male customers
than male models in similar roles are to female customers because the female stereotype bears the weight
of social relations that have a long history. Clearly,
the only way to understand such stereotypes is to
situate them in the social relations that have constituted them historically.
    But as important as this mode of ideology
critique is, it has failed to develop a theory of
production. That is, it has failed to analyse how
reproductive ideologies as they exist in texts and
social practices get mediated. It is particularly
important to acknowledge that texts are always mediated in some fashion by human subjects. Meanings are
always produced by human agents when they confront
and engage cultural forms such as curriculum texts,
films and so forth. As Arnot and Whitty (1982) and
Jameson (1979) have stressed, educational meanings
and practices are "read" by teachers and students
through interpretative and selective principles that
bear the weight of pre-existing situations and constituted ideologies. The relation between inscribed
messages and lived effects is a tenuous one indeed
and cannot be viewed through a reductionist logic
that collapses one into the other. The way in which
a teacher or student engages a text or specific social
relation is, in fact, a "function of his or her place
in society" (Barrett, 1980, p. 87). This form of
ideology critique must locate the various ideological
discourses and multiple subjectivities that construct

and constitute meaning for students from different
class-, gender- and race-specific backgrounds
(Therborn, 1981). This demands being attentive to
the cultural capital that characterises different
student experiences and to the ways in which students
actually produce meanings via their historical, positional, family and class backgrounds. By penetrat-
ing these ideologies and cultural forms it becomes
possible for teachers to unravel the mediations that
give meaning to school experience and to understand
how they might function in the interest of accommodation, resistance or active change.

This leads to my final point regarding the relations among ideology, texts and social practices.
The principle of reconstruction shifts the theoretical
terrain from the issues of reproduction and mediation
to a concern for critical appropriation and transformation. This suggests a mode of ideology critique
in which the interests that underlie texts, representations and social practices would be not only identified but also deconstructed and refashioned with
the aim of developing social relations and modes of
knowledge that serve radical needs. The task of
reconstruction is not simply to analyse knowledge and
social relations for either their dominating ideologies or their subversive unintentional truths, but
to appropriate their material elements, skills and
critical knowledge in order to restructure them as
part of the production of new ideologies and collective experiences. Thus, knowledge production is
linked to transformative activities and is situated
within a problematic that takes as its ultimate aim
the development of forms of radical praxis both within
and outside of schools. Brenkman (1979) captures a
critical aspect of this issue in his call for the
development of a Marxist cultural hermeneutics:

> Its project is twofold. Interpretations
> which read cultural texts in relation to
> their historical situations and effects
> must conserve or subvert meanings accord-
> ing to their validity not for an already
> constituted tradition but for a community
> in process. And, secondly, interpretation
> must be connected to the project of re-
> claiming language practices that unfold the
> horizon of this community. Such a her-
> meneutics becomes valid only as it serves
> to construct oppositional cultural exper-
> iences, an oppositional public sphere. It
> has a political task. The dominant tendency

of our cultural institutions and
practices - from the organisation of the
learning process in the schools and the
academic modes of knowledge which support
them to the mass mediated forms of communication which pre-empt speaking itself - is
to undermine the very possibility for
human beings to interpret the discourses
that found their identities, shape their
interactions and regulate their activities.
Only a process of interpretation which
counters this tendency, actively and practically, can preserve the possibilities of
a historical consciousness founded on collective experience. (p. 109)

A reconstructive perspective would promote the
conditions necessary for the development of what
Lundgren (in press) calls texts _for_ pedagogy. These
would be curriculum materials and school practices
appropriated and/or produced by the teachers and
educators who use them. Such texts refer to both a
process and a product. As a process, such texts
embody and demonstrate principles that link conception and execution while simultaneously promoting a
critical attentiveness to forms of knowledge and
social practices informed by principles that promote
enlightenment and understanding. Such texts would
be attentive to procedures that locate knowledge in
specific historical contexts and would attempt to
uncover the human interests in which it is grounded.
As products, such texts become the medium for a
critical pedagogy aimed at providing students with
the knowledge, skills and critical sensibility they
need to be able to think dialectically. That is,
students need to be able to grasp the ways in which
the concrete world opposes the possibilities inherent
in its own conditions; they need to be able to reach
into history so as to transform historical into critical thought; and finally, they need to be able to
penetrate critically the categories of common sense
and begin to move beyond a world constituted through
such categories. In short, whereas texts about
pedagogy, along with the social relations engendered
by them, are rooted in the logic of authoritarianism
and control, texts _for_ pedagogy contain interests
that may promote modes of schooling based on the
critical dimensions of an emancipatory ideology.
Ideology is a crucial construct for understanding how meaning is produced, transformed and consumed
by individuals and social groups. As a tool of

331

critical analysis, it digs beneath the phenomenal forms of classroom knowledge and social practices and helps to locate the structuring principles and ideas that mediate between the dominant society and the everyday experiences of teachers and students. As a political construct, it makes meaning problematic and poses the question as to why human beings have unequal access to the intellectual and material resources that constitute the conditions for the production, consumption and distribution of meaning. Similarly, it raises the question of why certain ideologies come to prevail at certain times and whose interests they serve. Hence, ideology 'speaks' to the notion of power by accentuating the complex ways in which relations of meaning are produced and fought over.

REFERENCES

Adorno, T. (1967) 'The Actuality of Philosophy', Telos, 31, pp. 120-133

Adorno, T. (1967-1968) 'Sociology and Psychology, I and II', New Left Review, 46 and 47, pp. 67-68, 79-96

Adorno, T. (1973) Negative Dialectics, The Seabury Press, New York

Apple, M. (1982) Education and Power, Routledge and Kegan Paul, Boston

Althusser, L. (1969) For Marx, Vintage Books, New York

Althusser, L. (1971) 'Ideology and the Ideological State Apparatuses', in L. Althusser (ed.), Lenin and Philosophy and Other Essays, Monthly Review Press, New York

Arnot, M. and Whitty, G. (1982) 'From Reproduction to Transformation: Recent Radical Perspectives on the Curriculum from the USA', British Journal of Sociology of Education, 3, pp. 93-103

Aronowitz, S. (1980) 'Science and Ideology', Current Perspectives in Social Theory, 1, pp. 75-101

Aronowitz, S. (1981) Crisis in Historical Materialism: Class Politics and Culture in Marxist Theory, J.F. Bergin Publishers, New York

Barrett, M. (1980) Women's Oppression Today, Verso Press, London

Barrett, M. (1981) 'Materialist Aesthetics', New Left Review, 126, pp. 86-93

Benjamin, W. (1969) Illuminations, Schocken Books, New York

Bennett, T. (1981) Popular Culture: History and Theory

Open University Press, London

Bourdieu, P. (1977) Outline of Theory and Practice, Cambridge University Press

Bourdieu, P. and Passeron, J.C. (1977) Reproduction in Education, Society and Culture, Sage Publications, London and Beverly Hills

Brenkman, J. (1979) 'Mass media: From collective experience to the culture of privatization', Social Text, 1, pp. 14-109

Brown, J. (1981) 'Into the minds of babes: A journey through recent children's books', Radical History, 25, pp. 127-145

Buck-Morss, S. (1981) 'Walter Benjamin - Revolutionary Writer, I', New Left Review, 128, pp. 50-75

Buswell, C. (1980) 'Pedagogic Change and Social Change', British Journal of Sociology of Education, 1, 3, pp. 293-306

Coward, R. and Ellis, J. (1977) Language and Materialism, Routledge and Kegan Paul, London

Eco, U. (1976) A Theory of Semiotics, Indiana University Press, Bloomington, Indiana

Feenberg, A. (1981) Lukacs, Marx and the Sources of Critical Theory, Rowman and Littlefield, Totowa, N.J.

Foucault, M. (1980) Power/Knowledge: Selected Interviews and Other Writings, (C. Gordon, ed.), Pantheon Books, New York

Freire, P. (1973) Pedagogy of the Oppressed, The Seabury Press, New York

Giddens, A. (1979) Central Problems in Social Theory, University of California Press, Berkeley

Giroux, H. (1981) Ideology, Culture and the Process of Schooling, Temple University Press, Philadelphia

Gouldner, A. (1976) The Dialectic of Ideology and Technology: The origins, grammar and future of ideology, The Seabury Press, New York

Gramsci, A. (1971) (Selections from prison notebooks) (Q. Hoare and G. Smith, eds. and trans.), International Publishers, New York

Habermas, J. (1975) Legitimation Crisis, Beacon Press, Boston

Heller, A. (1974) The Theory of Need in Marx, Allison and Busby, London

Jameson, F. (1979) 'Reification and Utopia in Mass Culture', Social Text, 1, pp. 130-148

Johnson, R. (1979(a)) 'Histories of Culture/Theories of Ideology: Notes on an impasse', in M. Barrett et al. (eds.), Ideology and Cultural Production, St. Martin's Press, New York

Johnson, R. (1979(b)) 'Three Problematics: Elements of a Theory of Working Class Culture', in J. Clarke et al. (eds.), Studies in History and Theory, Hutchinson, London

Karabel, J. (1976) 'Revolutionary Contradictions: Antonio Gramsci and the problem of intellectuals' Politics and Society, 6, pp. 123-172

Kress, G. and Hodge, R. (1979) Language as Ideology, Routledge and Kegan Paul, London

Larrain, J. (1979) The Concept of Ideology, Hutchinson London

Lenin, V.I. (1971) What Is To Be Done? International Publishers, New York

Lukacs, G. (1968) History and Class Consciousness, MIT Press, Cambridge, Mass.

Lundgren, U. (In press) Between the Scholared and the School, Deakin University Press, Geelong, Australia

Marcuse, H. (1955) Eros and Civilization, Beacon Press, Boston

Marcuse, H. (1964) One Dimensional Man, Beacon Press, Boston

Marx, K. (1969(a)) The Eighteenth Brumaire of Louis Bonaparte, International Publishers, New York

Marx, K. (1969(b)) Preface to the Critique of Political Economy, International Publishers, New York

Marx, K. (1972) The German Ideology, International Publishers, New York

Schmidt, A. (1981) (History and Structure)(J. Herf, trans.), MIT Press, Cambridge, Mass.

Sumner, C. (1979) Reading Ideologies, Academic Press, London

Therborn, G. (1981) The Ideology of Power and the Power of Ideology, New Left Books, London

Thompson, E.P. (1966) The Making of the English Working Class, Vintage Press, New York

Volosinov, V.V. (1973) Marxism and the Philosophy of Language, Seminar Press, New York

Williams, R. (1977) Marxism and Literature, Oxford University Press, London

ACKNOWLEDGMENT

Substantial parts of this paper have been previously published in the Journal of Education, Boston University. We are grateful for permission to republish it.

AUTHOR INDEX

Author Index

Subject Index